EXPERIENTIA, VOLUME 1

Society of Biblical Literature

Symposium Series

Victor H. Matthews
Series Editor

Number 40

EXPERIENTIA, VOLUME 1

EXPERIENTIA, VOLUME 1

INQUIRY INTO RELIGIOUS EXPERIENCE
IN EARLY JUDAISM AND CHRISTIANITY

Edited by

Frances Flannery

Colleen Shantz

Rodney A. Werline

Society of Biblical Literature

Atlanta

EXPERIENTIA, VOLUME 1

Library of Congress Cataloging-in-Publication Data

Experientia, volume 1 : inquiry into religious experience in early Judaism and Christianity / edited by Frances Flannery, Colleen Shantz, and Rodney A. Werline.
    p. cm. — (Society of Biblical Literature symposium series ; no. 40)
    Includes bibliographical references and indexes.
    ISBN 978-1-58983-368-5 (paper binding : alk. paper) — ISBN 978-1-58983-369-2 (electronic library copy)
    1. Experience (Religion)—History—Congresses. 2. Church history—Primitive and early church, ca. 30-600—Congresses. 3. Judaism—History—Post-exilic period, 586 B.C-210 A.D.—Congresses. 4. Bible—Criticism, interpretation, etc.—Congresses. I. Werline, Rodney Alan, 1961- II. Flannery, Frances. III. Shantz, Colleen.
    BS2410.E97 2008b
    248.2—dc22

2008030156

15 14 13 12 11 10 09 08 07   5 4 3 2 1
Printed in the United States of America on acid-free, recycled paper conforming to ANSI/NISO Z39.48-1992 (R1997) and ISO 9706:1994 standards for paper permanence.

CONTENTS

Part 3. Paul and Religious Experience

Abbreviations

AB	Anchor Bible
ALGHJ	Arbeiten zur Literatur und Geschichte des hellenistischen Judentums
AnBib	Analecta biblica
ANF	*Ante-Nicene Fathers*
ANRW	*Aufsteig und Niedergang der römischen Welt: Geshichte und Kultur Roms im Spiegel der neueren Forschung. Edited by H. Temporini and W. Haase. Berlin, 1972-*
ANTC	Abingdon New Testament Commentaries
AOAT	Alter Orient und Altes Testament
BETL	Bibliotheca ephemeridum theologicarum lovaniensium
BGBE	Beiträge zur Geschichte der biblischen Exegese
BJS	*British Journal of Sociology*
BTB	*Biblical Theology Bulletin*
BZ	*Biblische Zeitschrift*
BZAW	Beihefte zur Zeitschrift für die alttestamentliche Wissenschaft
CBET	Contributions to Biblical Exegesis and Theology
CBQ	*Catholic Biblical Quarterly*
CBQMS	Catholic Biblical Quarterly Monograph Series
CRINT	Compendia rerum iudaicarum ad Novum Testamentum
ErJb	*Eranos-Jahrbuch*
FRLANT	Forschungen zur Religion und Literatur des Alten und Neuen Testaments
FZPhTh	*Freiburger Zeitschrift für Philosophie und Theologie*
HDB	*Harvard Divinity Bulletin*
HR	*History of Religions*
HSS	Harvard Semitic Studies
HTR	*Harvard Theological Review*
HUCA	*Hebrew Union College Annual*
ICC	International Critical Commentary
IDB	*The Interpreter's Dictionary of the Bible. Edited by G. A. Buttrick. 4 vols. Nashville, 1962*

JAAR	*Journal of the American Academy of Religion*
JBL	*Journal of Biblical Literature*
JECS	*Journal of Early Christian Studies*
JJS	*Journal of Jewish Studies*
JNES	*Journal of Near Eastern Studies*
JRS	*Journal of Roman Studies*
JSJ	*Journal for the Study of Judaism in the Persian, Hellenistic, and Roman Periods*
JSJSup	Journal for the Study of Judaism in the Persian, Hellenistic, and Roman Periods: Supplement Series
JSNT	*Journal for the Study of the New Testament*
JSNTSup	Journal for the Study of the New Testament: Supplement Series
JSOT	*Journal for the Study of the Old Testament*
JSOTSup	Journal for the Study of the Old Testament: Supplement Series
JSP	*Journal for the Study of the Pseudepigrapha*
JSPSup	Journal for the Study of Pseudepigrapha: Supplement Series
JSSSup	Journal of Semitic Studies. Supplement Series
JTS	*Journal of Theological Studies*
LCL	Loeb Classical Library
LSJ	Liddell, H. G., R. Scott, H. S. Jones. *A Greek-English Lexicon.* 9th ed. with revised supplement. Oxford, 1996
NovT	*Novum Testamentum*
NTS	*New Testament Studies*
Numen	*Numen: International Review for the History of Religions*
OBT	Overtures to Biblical Theology
OTP	*Old Testament Pseudepigrapha.* Edited by James H. Charlesworth. 2 vols. New York, 1983, 1985
PDM	*Papyri demoticae magicae.* Demotic texts in PGM corpus as collated in H. D. Betz, ed. *The Greek Magical Papyri in Translation, including the Demotic Spells.* Chicago, 1996
PGM	*Papyri graecae magicae: Die griechische Zauberpapyri.* Edited by K. Preisendanz. Berlin, 1928
PVTG	Pseudepigrapha Veteris Testamenti Graece
RHPR	*Revue d'histoire et de philosophie religieuses*
SBLDS	Society of Biblical Literature Dissertation Series
SBLEJL	Society of Biblical Literature Early Judaism and Its Literature
SBLMS	Society of Biblical Literature Monograph Series
SBLSP	*Society of Biblical Literature Seminar Papers*
SBLSymS	Society of Biblical Literature Symposium Series

SBLWGRW	Society of Biblical Literature Writings from the Greco-Roman World
SCHNT	Studia ad corpus hellenisticum Novi Testamenti
SHR	Studies in the History of Religions (Supplement to *Numen*)
SNTSMS	Society for New Testament Studies Monograph Series
SP	Sacra pagina
SPhilo	*Studia philonica*
StPatr	Studia patristica
STDJ	*Studies on the Texts of the Desert of Judah*
SUNT	Studien zur Umwelt des Neuen Testaments
SVTP	Studia in Veteris Testamenti Pseudepigraphica
TANZ	Texte und Arbeiten zum neutestamentlichen Zeitalter
TDNT	*Theological Dictionary of the New Testament*. Edited by G. Kittel and G. Friedrich. Translated by G. W. Bromiley. 10 vols. Grand Rapids, 1964–1976
TSAJ	Texte und Studien zum antiken Judentum
VC	*Vigiliae christianae*
VCSup	Vigiliae Christianae Supplement Series
WBC	World Biblical Commentary
WUNT	Wissenschaftliche Untersuchungen zum Neuen Testament
ZNW	*Zeitschrift für die neutestamentliche Wissenschaft und die Kunde der älteren Kirche*
ZTK	*Zeitschrift für Theologie und Kirche*

INTRODUCTION: RELIGIOUS EXPERIENCE, PAST AND PRESENT

Frances Flannery
with Nicolae Roddy, Colleen Shantz, and Rodney A. Werline

This volume represents the efforts of the first sustained, collective scholarly inquiry into the topic of "religious experience" in the field of early Jewish and early Christian studies. Most of the articles gathered here were presented at annual meetings of the Society of Biblical Literature in a new program unit entitled "Religious Experience in Early Judaism and Early Christianity Consultation" (now a "Section"), the members of which are colloquially referred to as "the Experientia Group."[1] This international effort includes scholars researching a wide variety of topics in biblical studies, using disparate methods drawn not only from biblical studies but from other disciplines as well, including anthropology, archaeology, sociology, neuro-biology, and neuro-psychology. All of these scholarly investigations, some of which are included here, are held together by one endeavor: to take seriously the articulation (whether explicit or indirect) of ancient authors' experiences of the divine.

While inquiry into "religious experience" has never been investigated collectively in biblical studies, it did once hold a central place in the generalized academic study of religion, although for some forty years the endeavor has met serious resistance. There have been appropriate and cogent cautions, arising as lessons from past scholarship, against loose definitions of "religious experience" and against reckless assumptions about *Verstehen,* or the extent to which we as modern interpreters could claim to understand the experience of an ancient person. Indeed, there have been warnings against claiming an understanding of

---

1. The founders of the consultation, inaugurated in 2005, are Frances Flannery (James Madison University) and Rodney Werline (Barton College). Members of the Steering Committee include Christopher Rowland (Oxford University), Alan Segal (Barnard College, Columbia University), Nicolae Roddy (Creighton University), Daphna Arbel (University of British Columbia), and Dietmar Neufeld (University of British Columbia). Other active participants have made contributions to this and future volumes.

any other person's subjective experience—the beneficial yet dead-ended insight of deconstructionism and post-structuralism.[2] Such a cautionary tone is still echoed in many of the contributions to this volume. Yet, while recognizing the limits on what we can do—that is, somehow accessing and/or replicating the personal experiences of the ancients—the Experientia Group pursues the details that *can* be probed. This commitment is fuelled by the recognition that the texts that are the sources of scholarship on early Judaism and early Christianity often have as their *raison d'être* some religious experience of author and/or of community that should be the focus of scholarly attention. What we *can* do is to take seriously the textual *articulation* of religious experience in antiquity.

No scholarship comes about in a vacuum, and this present endeavor arises from a long, but discontinuous, history of the study of religious experience. In his work *Religion after Religion,* Steven M. Wasserstrom locates an early trajectory of this approach to the study of "experience" as a core element of "religion" in nineteenth century German Romantics, particularly Schelling (1775–1854).[3] As Wasserstrom puts it, the Romantics transformed "theosophy" into "myth as tautegory," placing central emphasis on symbol as a carrier of meaning in and of itself rather than as a rationalistic allegory in reference to a system outside of the symbol.[4] By thus taking symbol to be a communicative expression of reality, they paved the way for later philosophers and scholars of religion who sought to locate the center of religion in the non-rational. Also important in this period are the philosophical arguments of Kant (1724–1804), who maintained that God is not perceivable through understanding or reason, but only through moral experience,[5] and Schleiermacher (1768–1834), who spoke of God-consciousness as a "feeling of absolute dependence" of the finite on the infinite.[6]

---

2. See Michel Foucault, *Archeology of Knowledge and the Discourse on Language* (New York: Pantheon Books, 1979); Jacques Derrida, *On Grammatology* (corrected edition; trans. G. C. Spivak; Baltimore: Johns Hopkins University Press, 1998); cf. Clifford Geertz, *The Interpretation of Cultures* (New York: Basic Books, 1973 [1966]).

3. Steven M. Wasserstrom, *Religion after Religion: Gershom Scholem, Mircea Eliade, and Henry Corbin at Eranos* (Princeton, N.J.: Princeton University Press, 1999), 39, 49, 54, 56. See idem, "Medium of the Divine," in the present volume as a response to Part 2: Text and Religious Experience.

4. Wasserstrom, *Religion after Religion,* 35–36, 54–55.

5. See Immanuel Kant, *Critique of Pure Reason* (trans. N. K. Smith; 1781; repr., New York: Palgrave Macmillan, 2003), *Foundations of the Metaphysics of Morals* (2nd ed.; trans. L. W. Beck; 1785; repr., Upper Saddle River, N.J.: Prentice Hall, 1989), and *Critique of Practical Reason* (trans. H. W. Cassirer; 1787; repr., Milwaukee, Wisc.: Marquette University Press, 1998).

6. See Friedrich Schleiermacher, *On Religion: Speeches to Its Cultured Despisers* (trans. R. Crouter; 1799; repr., Cambridge: Cambridge University Press, 1996).

At the turn of the twentieth century, William James highlighted the issue further in *The Varieties of Religious Experience*.[7] Approaching religious experience from a psychological perspective, James argued that "religious sentiment" resembled other human sentiments, but it was simply directed toward a "religious object."[8] The proposition allowed James to explain the wide variety present in accounts of religious experience—they were as idiosyncratic as the people reporting them.[9] At the same time, he hoped to remove a recent damning critique of religion, primarily from Freud,[10] that viewed religious experience simply as a manifestation of psychological pathologies and neuroses, a thesis that Carl Jung was similarly engaged in refuting.[11] James's primary paradigm for religious experience was mysticism, which he claimed was the essential nature of all religious experience, though the level of intensity of the experience differed from person to person. He identified two primary features of mystical experiences: they are ineffable, yet also noetic, conveying knowledge.[12] To a lesser extent, he also considered such experiences to be transient (confidently averring that these generally last less than a half hour!) and characterized by passivity on the part of the mystic.[13] For James, the key to a wider reality is our non-rational consciousness:

> Our normal waking consciousness, rational consciousness as we call it, is but one special type of consciousness, whilst all about it, parted from it by the flimsiest of screens, there lie potential forms of consciousness entirely different. . . . No account of the universe in its totality can be final which leaves these other forms of consciousness quite disregarded.[14]

Though James's classic work stimulated the thoughts of some humanists, it had little influence on biblical studies.[15]

---

7. William James, *The Varieties of Religious Experience: A Study in Human Nature* (New York: The Modern Library, 1994). The book preserves his Gifford Lectures on Natural Religion, given in Edinburgh in 1901–1902. For an analysis of the nuances of the work, see Wayne Proudfoot, *Religious Experience* (Berkeley and Los Angeles: University of California Press, 1985).

8. James, *Varieties of Religious Experience*, 32–33.

9. Ibid., 32–33, 445.

10. See above all Sigmund Freud, *The Future of an Illusion* (1927; repr. in vol. 21 of *The Standard Edition of the Complete Psychological Works of Sigmund Freud*; ed. J. Strachey with A. Freud; London: Hogarth, 1961), 43.

11. See, e.g., Carl Jung, *Memories, Dreams, Reflections* (ed. A. Jaffé; trans. R. and C. Winston; New York: Vintage, 1963); and idem, "Response to Job," in *The Portable Jung* (ed. J. Campbell; New York: Viking 1975), 519–650.

12. James, *Varieties of Religious Experience*, 414–15.

13. Ibid.

14. This quote is found in ibid., 298.

15. An exception is A. D. Nock's famous work on conversion, *Conversion: The Old and the New in Religion from Alexander the Great to Augustine of Hippo* (Oxford: Clarendon, 1933), which discusses James in the opening chapter.

By contrast, Rudolf Otto's *The Idea of the Holy* (1869–1937) had a more direct and lasting impact on biblical scholarship.[16] Otto gave a language to religious experience, without wading into the mire of the burgeoning psychological sciences, by deliberations on what he dubbed the "*mysterium tremendum*," an encounter with the numinous.[17] His compact but complex phrase describes the awe-filled, intense, non-rational attraction and repulsion that characterizes so many subjective accounts of encounters with the divine, even if his analysis of the "wholly other" (*ganz Andere*) can easily be labeled as limited and Christian-centric.

Whatever influences one might posit in these early stages, the most identifiable moment in the serious contemplation of experience as a, or even the, core element of religion came with the History of Religions School, which reached its zenith in the mid-twentieth century. Gershom Scholem (1898–1982), Henry Corbin (1907–1978), and various members of the Chicago School, best represented by Joachim Wach (1989–1955), Joseph Kitagawa (1915–1992), and of course Mircea Eliade (1907–1986), responded with a surprisingly unified tidal wave against those who had reduced the phenomenon of "religion" to another discipline, whether it be economics (Marx, Weber), psychology (Freud), or sociology (Durkheim). Rather, by locating mysticism in the center of the study of religion and displacing reason as the central focus, the History of Religions scholars responded with an empathetic analysis of the history of particular religions, as well as of transhistorical "religion." They privileged myth, symbol, and the imaginal, and above all, they posited that *subjective experiences of the divine*, which some of them apparently held to be universally human, constitute the core of religion as a phenomenon.[18]

Clearly, the outstanding figure of the History of Religions School is Mircea Eliade. Nearly twenty years after his death, the value of his contribution to the study of religion still provokes intense, if not always well-informed discussion, attracting a level of critical attention commensurate with the degree of his intellectual stature. There is enough autobiographical evidence[19] to suggest that it was

---

16. Rudolf Otto, *The Idea of the Holy: An Inquiry into the Non-Rational Factor in the Idea of the Divine and Its Relation to the Rational* (trans. J. W. Harvey; London: Oxford University Press, 1928; revised edition).

17. Otto, *The Idea of the Holy*, 25.

18. Along different lines, see also Gerardus van der Leeuw (1890–1950), who described the phenomenological "essences" of various facets of religion "as they present themselves," such as sacred time, love, compassion, and mysticism. Above all, see Gerardus van der Leeuw (1890–1950), *Religion as Essence and Manifestation: A Study in Phenomenology* (1933; repr., Princeton, N.J.: Princeton University Press, 1986).

19. And now there is even a semi-autobiographical novella, Mircea Eliade, *Youth without Youth* (ed. M. Calinescu; trans. M. L. Ricketts; Chicago: University of Chicago Press, 2007), and the film adaptation by Francis Ford Coppola, *Youth without Youth* (Sony Pictures, 2007).

this Romanian-American esoterist's personal, mystical orientation to the world that led him to posit an external reality of the numinous intruding into the mundane world, one that produces an intense personal encounter mediated through sensory experience. It cannot be ignored that the personal lives of Eliade, Corbin, Scholem, and others in *Eranos* circle, helped shape the emergence of the field of the History of Religions and its presuppositions.[20]

Building upon Otto's description of *mysterium tremendum* and rejecting more empiricist approaches, Eliade's facile acknowledgment of transcendent, metaphysical realities remains the weakest and most misunderstood pillar in his phenomenological approach to the history of religions, and thus the obvious target for critics. At the risk of oversimplification, the Achilles' heel of the History of Religions School seems to be that Eliade (and Corbin, and others) implicitly presumed a way in which universal reality is *really* configured: "Perhaps the most important function of religious symbolism . . . is its capacity for expressing . . . certain patterns of ultimate reality that can be expressed in no other way."[21]

Private, unobservable experience as the primary basis for critical claims is of course suspect.[22] However, whether or not one should describe the landscape of extraordinary experience in terms psychological or phenomenological, we can— as scholars of early Judaism and Christianity—attempt to *describe, identify, and locate* the transformative personal response to an extraordinary encounter taking place in a religious context—whether conceived of as exploding into mundane reality and flooding the human senses, or as bubbling up from the depths of the unconscious. We can also recall that such experiences are inseparable from the cultural matrices in which they are perceived,[23] and that they may therefore be experienced communally as well as individually.

---

20. This is the subject investigated in Wasserstrom, *Religion after Religion.*

21. Mircea Eliade, *Two and the One* (New York: Harper & Row, 1969), 205; repr. of *Two and the One* (trans. J. M. Cohen; London: Harvill, 1965). Similarly, although Eliade purports to give the point of view of "religious man," his assertions about sacred reality often sound positivist, e.g.: ". . . where the sacred manifests itself in space, *the real unveils itself,* the world comes into existence" (Mircea Eliade, *The Sacred and the Profane: The Nature of Religion* [trans. W. R. Trask; San Diego: Harcourt Brace, 1959], 63; italics his).

22. This is particularly the case in Corbin's writings, since he assumes the point of view of esoteric knower, even stating: "The true meaning is derived not from conclusions reached through deductions or inference but can be unveiled and transmitted only by 'the one who knows'"; in Wasserstrom's opinion, Corbin placed himself, "the individual Gnostic, the individual modern esoterist" in this privileged position (Henry Corbin, *"The Meaning of the Imam,"* in *Shi'ism* [ed. S. H. Nasr; Albany, N.Y.: State University of New York Press, 1988], 177; Wasserstrom, *Religion after Religion,* 64–65).

23. It can no longer easily be maintained that a prior "experience" is later followed by a cultural "interpretation"; rather, both occur simultaneously and inseparably in the processing of human consciousness. See Troels Engberg-Pedersen, "The Construction of Religious Experience in Paul," in this volume. On the neuro-physiological mechanisms of Religiously Interpreted

Thus, while acknowledging the profound debt we owe to the History of Religions School for its focus on experience, the collective effort represented in this volume may be distinguished from that approach, as well as from previous ones, in several ways.

First, the scholars represented in this volume seek to redress a criticism leveled at the "History" of Religions School, namely, the ironic charge that their results are ahistorical.[24] The articles in this volume contextualize their investigations in *texts* arising in particular *contexts* and communities. Also, by concentrating our efforts in terms of early Jewish and early Christian cultures, which have an obvious and close relationship, we also are free of the accusation that the study of comparative religions makes one comparatively religious. That is, the articles in this volume remain situated historically and culturally.

In this way, we collectively build on the work of several individual scholars who have emphasized the role of religious experience in specific investigations of early Judaism and early Christianity. Although an exhaustive list is not possible here, a few pre-eminent examples must be mentioned. Michael E. Stone often gives sustained and careful attention to the topic of experience in his analyses of Second Temple Judaism. Christopher Rowland consistently argues that the key to the apocalyptic worldview is direct communication of heavenly mysteries that results in an experience of reality from a divine-like perspective. And Daniel Merkur anticipated the multi-disciplinary model of our current investigation in proposing psychological bases for the experiences of the visionaries of the Jewish apocalypses.[25]

Second, since the majority of earlier scholars of religious experience located mysticism at the center of religion, their understandings of the former were necessarily limited by prevailing definitions of mysticism. Although variously construed, scholarly understandings of "mysticism" have conventionally emphasized "the discipline required of a mystic path" (John E. Collins), "non-sensual

---

States of Consciousness, or RISCs, see especially Alan F. Segal, "Religious Experience and the Construction of the Transcendent Self," in *Paradise Now: Essays on Early Jewish and Christian Mysticism* (Atlanta: Society of Biblical Literature, 2006), 27–40 and Colleen Shantz, *Paul in Ecstasy* (New York: Cambridge University Press, forthcoming).

24. Obviously, if Scholem is counted amongst the members of this "school," he is an clear exception to the accusation.

25. See, e.g., Michael E. Stone, "Apocalyptic: Vision or Hallucination?" *Milla wa-Milla* 14 (1974): 47–56; idem, *Fourth Ezra: A Commentary on the Book of Fourth Ezra* (Hermeneia; ed. F. M. Cross; Minneapolis: Fortress, 1990); Christopher Rowland, *The Open Heaven: A Study in Apocalypticism in Judaism and Early Christianity* (New York: Crossroad, 1982), 11, 14; Daniel Merkur, "The Visionary Practices of Jewish Apocalypticists," in *Essays in Honor of Paul Parin* (vol. 14 of *The Psychoanalytic Study of Society*; ed. L. B. Boyer and S. A. Grolnick; Hillsdale, Mass.: Analytic, 1989), 119–48. Other examples exist, but until this volume and its comprehensive bibliography, one would generally only run into them by happenstance.

and supralogical means" (Joseph Dan), and expressions of private concerns rather than public religion (Dan Merkur).[26] However, prevailing boundaries placed on "mysticism" have recently been challenged in the academy, as is evident most of all in the work of the Early Jewish and Early Christian Mysticism Group.[27] Scholars such as Daphna Arbel have placed renewed emphasis on the role of experience, or "gaining direct experience of God and the divine reality," as the very goal of *merkabah* and *Hekhalot* mysticisms.[28]

Third, even with new understandings of "mysticism" that are emerging, mystical experiences were typically—and are often still—distinguished from reason and sustained reflection.[29] Yet in this volume Celia Deutsch convincingly examines Philo and Clement's self-professed authorial experiences to dispel this notion, showing that the rational–irrational dichotomy is specious with respect to considerations of religious experience.[30] As Rodney Werline argues, we can and should expand the types of experiences that we label as "religious experience."[31] His arguments support Deutsch's position that, under the right circumstances and informed by the right institutional and cultural medium of interpretation, scribal activity, exegesis, and rational study and reflection may all constitute "religious experiences."

Fourth, unlike some in the Chicago School, we are not necessarily bound to an understanding of myth and symbol as the paramount expressions of the ineffable experience with the divine, although some of our authors might well choose to explore these emphases. For example, many of the articles in this volume treat

---

26. John E. Collins, *Mysticism and New Paradigm Psychology* (Savage, Md.: Rowman & Littlefield, 1991), xix–xx; Dan Merkur, *Gnosis: An Esoteric Tradition of Mystical Visions and Unions* (Albany, N.Y.: State University of New York Press, 1993), 11; Joseph Dan, "In Quest of a Historical Definition of Mysticism," *Studies in Spirituality* 3 (1993): 58–90, quote from p. 66. For these typical stances and more, see Daphna Arbel, *Beholders of Divine Secrets: Mysticism and Myth in the Hekhalot and Merkavah Literature* (Albany, N.Y.: State University of New York Press, 2003), 14–17.

27. On communal identities and practices in redefining mysticism, see especially April D. DeConick, "What is Early Jewish and Christian Mysticism?" in *Paradise Now: Essays on Early Jewish and Christian Mysticism* (ed. April D. DeConick; Atlanta: Society of Biblical Literature, 2006), 1–24.

28. Arbel, *Beholders of Divine Secrets*, 23; for a somewhat similar view see Christopher Rowland, "Visionary Experience in Ancient Judaism and Christianity," in DeConick, ed., *Paradise Now*, 41–56.

29. Eliade's view is illustrative. In discussing how "religious man" apprehends "the transcendental category of height," he states, "all this is not arrived at by a logical, rational operation . . . [but it is] revealed to the whole man, to his intelligence and his soul. It is a total awareness of man's part." Eliade, *Sacred and the Profane*, 119.

30. Celia Deutsch, "Visions, Mysteries, and the Interpretive Task: Text Work and Religious Experience in Philo and Clement," in this volume.

31. See Rodney Werline, "Prayer and Demon Possession in Mark," in this volume.

ritual, either as a mimesis of experience or a reexperiencing of original experience, as Eliade had it,[32] or as the constituent, enacted experience itself.[33]

Part 1 of this volume, "Body and Self in Religious Experience," situates experience in the body itself, as a way of balancing earlier investigations that almost always locate religious experience somewhere in the mind, spirit, or psyche.[34] Frances Flannery introduces the methodological implications of the section by explaining the ways in which past scholarship has considered the body with respect to ritual and experience, and by gesturing toward future directions of study. Alan Segal challenges the very notion of the soul/body dichotomy that is often presupposed for Paul, arguing that this earliest written articulation of Christian religious experience is informed by a notion of self-identity that involves the process of angelification. Richard Horsley examines the narratives of demon possession recorded in the Gospel of Mark, describing how these texts reflect the interplay of experience and cultural construction through several interpretive moments. Using insights from ethnographic accounts of possession in other cultures, he argues that possession is a culturally mediated expression of imperial and colonial oppression, manifested as spirits invading the body. Finally, Rodney Werline draws on Bourdieu, Good, and Rappaport to outline a method for understanding prayer as *religious* experience, in that prayer is communally and authoritatively constructed as religious. His approach has implications for widening our understanding of "religious experience" beyond extraordinary encounters with the divine. Also, since prayer is a ritual enacted by the body and actually performed in the early Christian community, his argument takes us beyond "mere text."

Part 2, "Text and Religious Experience" draws careful attention to the many levels of textual analysis possible in the study of religious experience. Reprising his original response in the Religious Experience in Early Judaism and Early Christianity Consultation of the Annual Meeting of the Society of Biblical Literature in 2005, Steven M. Wasserstrom provides cautionary tales from the American Academy of Religion that speak to this collective endeavor to study textual articulations of religious experience in early Jewish and early Christian literature. Next, Celia Deutsch investigates the authorial/scribal processes of Philo and Clement in terms of rational, even philosophical religious experience. Robin Griffith-Jones then draws attention to audiences' receptions of text in his investigation of the Gospel of John as a communal, transformative *Lesemysterium*. One

---

32. Mircea Eliade, *Patterns in Comparative Religion* (New York: Sheed & Ward, 1958).

33. For the methodological basis of this approach see Roy A. Rappaport, "Enactments of Meaning," in *Ritual and Religion in the Making of Humanity* (Cambridge: Cambridge University Press, 1999), 104–38.

34. In so doing, we draw on the insights of Catherine Bell (*Ritual Theory, Ritual Practice* [New York: Oxford University Press, 1992]), who argues that scholars of ritual have tended to privilege mental over bodily understandings.

implication of Griffith-Jones's work is that earlier assumptions that limit "religious experience" to something like Paul's experience on the road to Emmaus—i.e., individual, "mystical" and non-liturgical—are unnecessarily narrow. Crispin Fletcher-Louis goes beyond the levels of author and audience to suggest that the experiences of scholars themselves are a fruitful object of scrutiny, particularly in terms of their treatment of religious experience. Furthermore, somewhat like Segal, he highlights the role of self- and communal-identity in the construction of a theological anthropology in the apocalypses.

The circumstances of Paul pose a complex case for those interested in religious experience. For that reason, part 3 is dedicated to the question of "Paul and Religious Experience" and the four essays included here touch on some of the many challenges of the topic. The Pauline corpus seems to offer both the most tantalizing access to religious experience and some quite complex problems regarding our access to that experience (e.g., the role of Acts, the varieties of first person speech that appear in the letters, and the various temptations to anachronistic readings). Appropriately, Troels Engberg-Pedersen introduces part 3 through an examination of the contested history of interpretation of Paul's religious experience and the relative neglect that has since resulted. Engberg-Pedersen describes the important objections (based on rhetorical analysis, awareness of cultural difference, and insights from anthropology) that have been raised against studying Paul's experiences, proposing a more theoretically nuanced way to take up the conversation again, balancing the awareness that Paul's experiences "always came in interpreted form" with the understanding nonetheless "that something *happened*" that warranted interpretation. Next, Bert Jan Lietaert-Peerbolte examines Paul's ascent text in 2 Cor 12:1–4. On the one hand, Lietaert Peerbolte argues that Paul's description of ascent to the "Paradise" is decisively influenced by the cultural construct and practices of apocalypticism. On the other hand, he understands the description of the ascent—and perhaps apocalypticism itself—to be dependent on religious experience, in this case an altered state of consciousness. John Miller steps away from the difficulties of first-person accounts in order to concentrate his attention on the problem of Luke's narrative depiction of the apostle Paul. Miller illustrates how the literary features of Luke-Acts demonstrate the importance attributed to the "interior" nature of dreams/visions as an experience of God. Finally, Colleen Shantz takes a different kind of "interiorized" view of Paul's experiences by exploring the neuro-biological processes that facilitate such religious experiences. Her study has implications not only for understanding features of the texts, but like Merkur's earlier work,[35] for extending the scope of inquiry beyond texts to "real" persons, or at least to bodies. The section closes with Rollin Ramsaran's response to the four articles represented in this focused case study on religious experience in early Judaism and early Christianity.

---

35. Merkur, "Visionary Practices of Jewish Apocalyptists."

In conclusion, unlike the scholars of the History of Religions School, who generally possessed an anti-modernist stance,[36] our new phase of the endeavor to investigate religious experience in early Judaism early Christianity benefits from a crucial insight of the approach called postmodernism, in particular, the difficulties of "letting the sub-altern speak."[37] To adapt this for biblical studies, we suggest that when scholars in the twenty-first century begin the arduous task of interpreting ancient texts, it is all too easy to dismantle the ancient authorial voice into a speechless subaltern defined only through the hermeneutics of the scholar, whatever they may be. We contend that the decades-long shift away from an emphasis on experience in the study of religion has made precisely this error, given that the sacred texts we study often seem to arise precisely as a result of some transformative moment in the life of an ancient author or community. Although our tools for recovering this voice may not ever be wholly adequate to the task, this volume aims to re-privilege and respect that ancient experience. Much work remains to be done, but we are pleased to inaugurate this exciting stream of collective scholarship in biblical studies.

March 19, 2008

---

36. This certainly makes sense given that these sensitive persons wrote in post-World War II circumstances; see Wasserstrom, *Religion after Religion*, 127–44.

37. Gayatri Chakravorty Spivak, "Can the Subaltern Speak?" in *Marxism and the Interpretation of Culture* (ed. Cary Nelson and Larry Grossberg; Chicago: University of Illinois Press, 1988), 271–313. Also see "Subaltern Studies: Deconstructing Historiography," from *Selected Subaltern Studies* (ed. Ranajit Guha and Gayatri Spivak; Oxford: Oxford University Press, 1988).

Part 1
Body and Self in Religious Experience

The Body and Ritual Reconsidered, Imagined, and Experienced

Frances Flannery

In her classic work on ritual, Catherine Bell persuasively argues that those who have theorized ritual are themselves informed by a dichotomized privileging of abstract Mind over material Body.[1] In a subtle but important way, such mind-body, spirit-body, or ideal-real dualism is also discernable in past scholarship on religious experience that privileged myth and symbol over ritual. This could hardly be clearer than in Eliade's essay on "Symbolism of the 'Centre'," in which he reduces ritual to a representation of myths and symbols:

> . . . myths *and rites* [italics mine] always disclose a *boundary situation* [italics his] of man {*sic!*}—not only a historical situation. A boundary situation is one which man discovers in becoming conscious of his place in the universe. It is primarily by throwing light upon these boundary situations that the historian of religions fulfils his task. . . . By directing attention to the survival of *symbols and mythical themes* [italics mine] in the psyche of modern man, by showing that the spontaneous re-discovery of *the archetypes of archaic symbolism* [italics mine] is a common occurrence in all human beings, irrespective of race and historical surroundings, depth-psychology has freed the historian of religions from his last hesitations.[2]

Having thusly construed the real import of rites as a survival of myths and symbols, it is only a small step for Eliade to reduce bodily experience to symbolism as well: "Still with the aid of the history of religions, man might recover the symbol-

---

1. Catherine Bell, *Ritual Theory, Ritual Practice* (New York: Oxford University Press, 1992).

2. Mircea Eliade, *Images and Symbols: Studies in Religious Symbolism* (New York: Sheed & Ward, 1961), 34–35.

ism of his body, which is an anthropocosmos."[3] Typically, this was the manner in which the history of religions school tended to examine bodily experience.[4]

It is noteworthy that many other scholars, with very different interests than Eliade, have also viewed the significance of ritual in terms of its "symbolic" nature. Theodor Gaster understands ritual as mimesis of eternal myth,[5] and other studies of varied nature consider ritual in terms of symbolic action, whether it is symbolic of liminality and communal identity (Van Gennep and Turner), pollution (Douglas), or communal violence (Girard).[6] Despite having differing foci, each of these studies construes ritual as a referent for something else that is more important. For instance, even when Victor Turner examines the extremely potent experiences that ritual affords, he views ritual structurally, as a symbol of a larger communal reality, whether status transition or liminality.[7] Thus, drawing from Van Gennep, Turner analyzes ritual as a kind of story, even speaking of "ritual plot."[8] The significance of this tendency is that, although seemingly varied in their approaches to ritual, many theorists locate the significance of ritual only in its *symbolic import,* its informational aspect.

A few scholars have approached ritual quite differently by arguing that the experience of *enacting ritual* is itself meaningful. Roy Rappaport has stressed that the significance of ritual results from the form of the ritual itself, which effectively enacts its meaning within a certain authoritative communal matrix.[9] For example, a wedding is not symbolic of marriage, rather the action and social matrix surrounding that action produces the new status of the couple. Simply put, the significance of ritual does not lie in its symbolism:

---

3. Even further, he claims that for "modern man," "regaining awareness of his own anthropocosmic symbolism . . . is an authentic and major mode of being." Eliade, *Images and Symbols,* 36–37.

4. Certainly, not all studies that examine the symbolism of the body ignore bodily *experience* to the extent that Eliade does. For an excellent study of body and religious experience, as well as symbol, see Gananath Obeyesekere, *Medusa's Hair: An Essay on Personal Symbols and Religious Experience* (Chicago: University of Chicago Press, 1981).

5. Gaster explains: "The purpose of *ritual* is to present a situation formally and dramatically in its immediate punctual aspect—as an *event* or *occurrence . . . myth,* on the other hand, present[s] it in its ideal, transcendental aspect" (Theodor Gaster, "Myth and Story," *Numen* 1 [1954]: 187). See also idem., "Myth, Mythology," *IDB* 3:481–87; *Myth, Legend, and Custom in the Old Testament* (New York: Harper and Row, 1969).

6. Arnold Van Gennep, *The Rites of Passage* (trans. M. B. Vizedom and G. L. Caffee; 1908; repr., Chicago: University of Chicago Press, 1960); Victor Turner, *The Ritual Process: Structure and Anti-Structure* (Chicago: Aldine, 1969); Mary Douglas, *Purity and Danger* (1966; repr., London: Routledge, 2002); René Girard, *Violence and the Sacred* (trans. P. Gregory; Baltimore: Johns Hopkins University Press, 1977).

7. Victor Turner, *The Ritual Process,* 10, 42, 58–60, 127, 167–69, 189.

8. Turner, *The Ritual Process,* 50–52.

9. Roy A. Rappaport, "Enactments of Meaning," in *Ritual and Religion in the Making of Humanity* (Cambridge: Cambridge University Press, 1999), 104–38.

Ritual is not merely another way to "say things" or "do things" that can be said or done as well or better in other ways. The form that is ritual is surely without communicational equivalents and thus, possibly, without functional or metafunctional equivalents. That ritual's abilities are intrinsic to its form and in indissoluble association only with its form, goes far to account for its ubiquity.[10]

Similarly, Grimes has recognized the efficaciousness of ritual in his study on reinvented ritual,[11] specifically bringing attention to the bodily dimensions:

> The human body is not an inert object. It is carried, "worn," decorated, ignored, *experienced*. Not only is our exterior – our skin, hair, eyes, teeth, and so on – enculturated, but so is our interior. How deeply we breathe, how we habitually feel about ourselves, where we sense our center to be, how we imagine, feed, and care for a fetus in the uterus . . . all these are shaped by the histories behind us and the societies around us.[12]

Pierre Bourdieu has likewise examined practice in a way that understands the body as more than simply the mechanism for expressing a *symbolic* action. Rather, the body is the site of actual practice and ritual, and the linguistic *habitus* is inscribed *in the body*.[13]

If these theorists are correct, and if "religious experience" is a category that exceeds but includes ritual, then it seems that *the body* is quite often a significant site of religious experience. Perhaps such an observation is obvious to real practitioners of religion around the globe who express profound and transformative bodily experiences of the divine, but it has not been the focus of much past scholarship on religious experience. In examinations of early Judaism and early Christianity, scholarly categories such as "ascent to heaven," "otherworldly journey," and "ecstasy" often assume out-of-body experiences (OBE) to be normative "mystical" experiences, and discussion of "visionary" materials may be informed by this bias, only occasionally considering bodily symptoms of the visionary experience.[14]

---

10. Rappaport, "Enactments of Meaning," 138.

11. Ronald L. Grimes, *Deeply into the Bone: Re-Inventing Rites of Passage* (Berkeley and Los Angeles: University of California Press, 2000).

12. Grimes, *Deeply into the Bone*, 17 (italics mine). A different entrance into thinking about ritual and the body is to consider ritual *behavior* as performative, communicative, and transformative. Driver argues that ritualizing is basic to human, and indeed to animal behavior. See Tom F. Driver, "Ritualizing: The Animals Do It and So Do We," in *Liberating Rites: Understanding the Transformative Power of Ritual* (Boulder, Colo.: Westview, 1998), 12–31.

13. Pierre Bourdieu, *Outline of a Theory of Practice* (Cambridge: Cambridge University Press, 1977); idem, *Language and Symbolic Power* (Cambridge: Cambridge University Press, 1991), 17.

14. For exceptions to this generalization, see especially Michael E. Stone, "Apocalyptic: Vision or Hallucination?" *Milla wa-Milla* 14 (1974): 47–56; and Dan Merkur, "The Visionary

In addition to a reconfiguring of scholarly understandings of the importance of the body in ritual, a final methodological consideration compels us to move bodies from the periphery to the center of studies on *ancient* religious experience. It has been pointed out exhaustively that we cannot really "know" the experience of ancient peoples, since all we have is texts, and, except in the case of Paul, these are normally anonymous or pseudepigraphic texts at that. Thus, it may be objected, any textual description of ancient religious experience, or even of rituals or experiential effects on the body, may be fictional, with no ties to "real" religious experience.

However, many articulations of religious experience in early Jewish and Christian texts relate bodily experiences that parallel similar descriptions from vastly different traditions. For example, trembling is known from the descriptions of ancient apocalyptic seers encountering divine beings (e.g., 4 Ezra 5:14; Dan 7:15, 10:17),[15] and is also experienced by Sudanese women possessed with *zar* spirits;[16] apocalyptic seers like Daniel write down their revelatory dreams (Dan 7:1; cf. 4 Ezra 14:42), and male devotees possessed by Dodo spirits in Niger write what they are taught in dreams or claim an invisible force moves their hand and writes for them.[17] The list may be multiplied.

This is not to fall into the same comparative-religions-trap of the Chicago School—certainly the *meaning* of the bodily experience should absolutely be studied within each discrete cultural context. Rather, this is to say that although we live in a completely different environment than the authors of the sacred texts of early Judaism and early Christianity, we share one thing, namely, a basic biological make-up. We share embodiment as humans. Thus, though minimal, there is in fact *something* we can know about religious experience in antiquity. When articulations of bodily experience are provided that cohere with bodily experiences from other cultures, it is likely they are not merely "textual," as in "fictional." Although such articulations of bodily experience are certainly *culturally mediated* and *literarily refracted* to varying degrees, anyone interested in "real" religious experience in antiquity has a possible inroad here to a level of experience beyond the text.[18]

Practices of Jewish Apocalypticists," in *The Psychoanalytic Study of Society 14: Essays in Honor of Paul Parin* (ed. L. B. Boyer and S. A. Grolnick; Hillsdale, Mass.: Analytic, 1989), 119–48.

15. See Michael E. Stone, *Fourth Ezra: A Commentary on the Book of Fourth Ezra* (Hermeneia; Minneapolis: Fortress, 1990), 115; idem, "Apocalyptic: Vision or Hallucination?"

16. See, e.g., the case of Amna (Susan M. Kenyon, "The Case of the Butcher's Wife: Illness, Possession and Power in Central Sudan," in *Spirit Possession: Modernity and Power in Africa* [ed. H. Behrend and U. Luig; Madison, Wisc.: University of Wisconsin Press, 1999], 89–108, esp. 96).

17. Adeline Masquelier, "The Invention of Anti-Tradition: Dodo Spirits in Southern Niger," in Behrend and Luig, *Spirit Possession*, 34–50, esp. 41.

18. See also Jonathan Boyarin ed., "Introduction," in *The Ethnography of Reading* (Berkeley and Los Angeles: University of California Press, 1993), 1–9, esp. 2–3.

The essays in "Part 1: The Body and Self in Religious Experience," move us in the right direction by focusing on the real persons behind texts, through attending to the body as a site of experience. Alan Segal questions the entire presupposition of a body-soul dichotomy in Paul's thinking. He makes the eminently persuasive case that Paul's disclaimer of "whether in the body or out of the body, I do not know" (2 Cor 12:2) indicates that Paul's notion of ascent to heaven was not *de facto* informed by a Platonic idea of the soul, separable from the body. Segal argues that Paul's own account—the only first-century Jewish or Christian autobiographical account of a visionary ascent—posits his self-identity not in terms of a soul and a body, but of "an angelic alter-ego." Resurrection, according to Paul, will entail full transformation into a spiritual, that is, an angelic body, which is bodily but not fleshy (Segal). What Segal has done is to illuminate more sharply the central importance of bodily experience and bodily identity not only in 2 Corinthians, but throughout Paul's writings: for example, ". . . the Lord Jesus Christ . . . will change our lowly body to be conformed in shape to his glorious body" (Phil 3:20–21). Furthermore, if Segal is correct in his assertion that Paul's notion stands in harmony with other early Christians' self-identity as well, we should reappraise the semantic range of a number of terms in early Jewish and Christian writings, including "spirit," "soul," "body," "resurrection," and "ascent."

Next, arguing that religious experience cannot be separated from socio-economic and political experience, Richard Horsley examines demon possession in the Gospel of Mark as an expression of Roman imperial oppression of Judea. Avoiding the simple "parallelomania" of the history of religions school by attending carefully to cultural setting, Horsley draws on case studies of possession in Sudan, ancient Greek cities, and Jewish scribal circles to demonstrate one *function* of the experience of possession by spirits. Since numerous studies show that possession often occurs in cultural contexts of foreign invasion and oppression,[19] Horsley notes that in certain contexts, spirit possession is subordinated peoples' experience on the bodily level of the "invasion of alien forces" that they also experience on the communal level. His perception leads to a reading of the plot of the Gospel of Mark that emphasizes the anti-imperial message of the whole narrative. And, in my reading, he is not simply treating the body as an "anthropocosmic" symbol of imperial oppression; rather, he is saying that the experience of a spirit invading the body is the personal and communal expression of imperial oppression.

Finally, Rodney Werline has significantly sharpened a methodological move that has bearing on many studies of religious experience in antiquity. Werline

---

19. E.g., Fritz W. Kramer, *The Red Fez: Art and Spirit Possession in Africa* (1987; trans. Malcolm R. Green; repr., New York: Verso, 1993); Janice Boddy, *Wombs and Alien Spirits: Women, Men, and the Zar Cult in Northern Sudan* (Madison, Wisc.: University of Wisconsin Press, 1989).

wishes to highlight what makes prayer—or any ritual or practice—a religious experience. Drawing on Bourdieu's theory of practice, Good's insights from medical anthropology, and Rappaport on ritual, Werline argues for an answer that depends on cultural context. A practice becomes a *religious* practice, he explains, when an authoritative person, text or institution says so, such that those enacting the practice experience it as a *religious* experience. Here, Werline is also implicitly drawing on Geertz' definition of religion as culture, I think, but he is perhaps going farther than Geertz in recognizing the practice of religion by real, embodied people, instead of privileging the pattern of religion.[20]

Werline also moves carefully between the levels of literary and social analysis. On the level of narrative, Jesus uses the practice of prayer to expel demons (Mark 9:29) and to conquer the ancient foe Yamm (Mark 6:45–52). On the level of the audience reception of the Gospel of Mark, early Christians viewed these episodes as models for the effects of their own practice of praying. For this society, the bodily practice of prayer enacts participation in the cosmic struggle against evil forces, in imitation of Christ. What Werline leaves us with, then, is a way into the inner experience of early Christians, that is, through practice experienced religiously in a specific cultural context.

Although these three authors employ different approaches regarding distinct topics of religious experience, it seems to me that they make a similar move with respect to taking the bodily experiences and identities of Paul and/or early Christians seriously. Where there is transformation, such as from a human into an angel (Segal), it is *experienced bodily*, as a new kind of existence. Where there are symbols, such as of invasive imperial oppression (Horsley), they are *somatized* in the way they are experienced. Where there is ritual, such as prayer (Werline), it is *enacted by the body* and thereby made effective in the cosmic realm. To the extent that scholars attend to religious experience, I suggest that we should also attune our ear to the "bodily sincerity"[21] that emerges through articulations of religious experience and rituals in antiquity.

---

20. Jonathan L. Jackson pointed me to the excellent example of how Geertz handles ritual and individual experience in Clifford Geertz, "Ritual and Social Change: A Javanese Example," in *The Interpretation of Cultures* (New York: Basic Books, 1973; reprint 2000), 142–69, see esp. 153–69; cf. 15–16.

21. The phrase is used in the work of Jerzy Grotowski, innovative director of ritual theater. See Jerzy Grotowski, *Towards a Poor Theater* (New York: Simon & Schuster, 1968); idem, "Holiday: The Day that is Holy," in *The Drama Review* 17.2 (1973): 113–19. For an excellent account of Grotowski's significance from the point of view of ritual studies, see Ronald L. Grimes, *Beginnings in Ritual Studies* (1982; repr., Columbia, S.C.: University of South Carolina Press, 1995), 164–88.

THE AFTERLIFE AS MIRROR OF THE SELF

Alan F. Segal

The concept of the self is one of the most difficult and interesting topics in intellectual history, Eastern or Western. The self is, of course, partly just the physical feeling of being in our bodies—our consciousness. But that feeling is also theorized multiply in any society, giving meaning to our physical feelings. We might call this combination of intellectual explanation and the feeling of being conscious, *self-consciousness*, partly a physical experience and partly a culturally mediated idea. If it is explicitly and philosophically theorized, we might call it *critical self-consciousness*. In this paper I want to explore how the experience of the resurrected body in the writings of Paul gives rise to a conception of the self, which underlies Christian self-understanding. Mystical experiences, apocalypses and visions, as well as heavenly journeys and near-death experiences (NDEs), all of which are characteristic of Paul's religious life, have reinforced notions of the afterlife—including, among others, the immortality of the soul and resurrection in numerous cultures. Paul's canonical writings testify to these same experiences and views.

Especially in Christianity of late antiquity, attempts were made to synthesize the notion of resurrection with the Platonic notion of the soul. This was because it was the dominant intellectual conception of the day, and as Christianity began to appeal to intellectuals, it was necessary to theorize the relationship. That it became a massive theological enterprise is clear to all readers of early church thought. But there were exceptions. The New Testament and especially Paul, but also Justin, Athenagoras, and Tertullian, all eschew the Platonic self in favor of an apocalyptic resurrection body. It is that conception that I wish to explore in this paper, especially in Paul.

PAUL'S OWN MYSTICISM

Paul gives us a totally different and at once conceivable notion of a bodily transformation. I will try to show that the notion of resurrection belief comes with its own experience of the self—*not a soul but an angelic alter-ego*. In 2 Cor 12:2, Paul says that he himself, like the biblical and mythical Enoch, has also traveled (ἁρπαγέντα, "seize") to the heavens looking for the answer to cosmological problems. This is one of the highest spiritual gifts that Paul can imagine, and it is meant to establish his credentials as a receiver of spiritual gifts (πνευματικά, 1 Cor 9:11; 14:1; 2 Cor 2:13). Paul's references to apocalypses and visions, as well as heavenly ascent, put him squarely within apocalyptic tradition. Although the account of Paul's ecstatic conversion in Acts is a product of Luke's literary genius, Paul gives his own evidence for ecstatic experience in 2 Cor 12:1–10:

> I must boast; there is nothing to be gained by it, but I will go on to visions and revelations of the Lord. I know a man in Christ who fourteen years ago was caught up (ἁρπαγέντα) to the third heaven—whether in the body or out of the body I do not know, God knows. And I know that this man was caught up into Paradise—whether in the body or out of the body I do not know, God knows— and he heard things that cannot be told, which man may not utter. On behalf of this man I will boast, but on my own behalf I will not boast, except of my weaknesses. (2 Cor 12:1–5)

As in Gal 1, Paul calls this experience an ἀποκαλύψεις, an "apocalypse," a "revelation" (2 Cor 12:1). Just as in Acts and Gal 1, the actual vision is not described. Unlike Luke's general description of Paul's conversion and Gal 1, however, this passage contains hints of a heavenly vision or possibly two different ones, depending on whether the paradise visited in the ascension can be located in the third heaven.[1] The vision is both mystical and apocalyptic.[2] The Pauline passage is also deeply rooted in Jewish ascension traditions, which imposed a certain structure of ascent on all reports of this period.[3] Similar ascensions can be seen in apocalyptic

---

1. Paradise, or the Garden of Eden, was often conceived as lying in one of the heavens, though the exact location differs from one apocalyptic work to another. See Martha Himmelfarb, *Tours of Hell: The Development and Transmission of an Apocalyptic Form in Jewish and Christian Literature* (Philadelphia: University of Pennsylvania Press, 1984). *2 Enoch*, for example, locates them in the third heaven; however, it may have been influenced by Paul's writings, even though the shorter version mentions worship in the Temple in a way that suggests it is still in existence, thus antedating 70 C.E.

2. In different ways, the close relationship between mysticism and apocalypticism has been touched upon by several scholars of the last decade, myself included. See Alan F. Segal, *Two Powers in Heaven: Early Rabbinic Reports about Christianity and Gnosticism* (Leiden: Brill, 1977); Ithamar Gruenwald, *Apocalyptic and Merkabah Mysticism* (Leiden: Brill, 1979); and now especially Christopher Rowland, *The Open Heaven: A Study of Apocalyptic in Judaism and Early Christianity* (New York: Crossroads, 1982) and Jarl Fossum, *The Name of God and the Angel of the Lord: Samaritan and Jewish Concepts of Intermediation and the Origin of Gnosticism* (WUNT 1.36; Tübingen: Mohr Siebeck, 1985).

3. See also Alan F. Segal, "Heavenly Ascent in Hellenistic Judaism, Early Christianity and their Environment," *ANRW* 23.2:1333–94; Mary Dean-Otting, *Heavenly Journeys: A Study of the Motif in Hellenistic Jewish Literature* (Frankfurt: Peter Lang, 1984); Ioan Petru Culianu, *Psychanodia I: A Survey of the Evidence of the Ascension of the Soul and its Relevance* (Leiden:

literature—for instance, *1 En.* 39:3; 52:1, and 71:1–5 as well as *2 En.* 3, 7, 8, 11 and *3 Bar.* 2.

Most people understand 2 Cor 12 as referring to Paul himself, with the rhetoric demanding that he stress his modesty.[4] To identify himself as the heavenly traveler would be boasting, and it would have conceded the point that special revelatory experience grants special privileges, which is what he is fighting against in the passage. This would contradict his statement that charismatic gifts cannot themselves prove faith (1 Cor 12–13). Yet, if the dominant interpretation is correct, Paul is actually tactfully revealing some information about his own religious experience in this passage.

Christopher Morray-Jones has very persuasively argued that Paul's experience in 2 Corinthians corresponds to the Temple vision of Acts 22:17.[5] He has also recently published a brilliant analysis of the famous "transparent illusion" in the Hekhalot texts.[6] The conclusions seem reasonable. Even if Morray-Jones's conclusion is not accepted, the evidence of 2 Corinthians is undoubtedly a first-century report of a heavenly ascent, which Paul says is important for Christian experience.

We should not think of 2 Cor 12 as the *verbatim* recording of Paul's actual experience. Rather we should think of it as his mature reflections on the experience after years of thinking about it and Christian learning. Converts learn the meanings of their experience in their new community. This is true of Paul's

---

Brill, 1983). Culianu has also published a more general work, *Expériences de l'Extase: Extase, ascension et récit visionnaire de l'hellénisme au moyen âge* (Paris: Payot, 1984), introduction by Mircea Eliade. The verb ἁρπάζω in Greek and its Latin equivalent *rapto* is sometimes shared with pagan ascensions (*sol me rapuit*, etc.), but also probably initially denotes both the rapture of vision and the specific heavenly journeys of Enoch (Hebrew: לקח = Greek: μετέθεκεν).

4. See William Baird, "Visions, Revelation, and Ministry: Reflections on 2 Cor 12:1–5 and Gal 1:11–17," *JBL* 104 (1985): 651–62. See also Christopher Forbes, "Comparison, Self Praise, and Irony: Paul's Boasting and the Conventions of Hellenistic Rhetoric," *NTS* 32 (1986): 1–30. Paul does not say that the man saw nothing; he only mentions what the man heard. While we are on the subject of difficulties, a significant exception to the identification of Paul with the mystic in 2 Cor 12 is Morton Smith, *Clement of Alexandria and a Secret Gospel of Mark* (Cambridge: Harvard University Press, 1975); idem, *Jesus the Magician* (New York: Harper and Row, 1978). Smith believed that the passage refers to Jesus, although Paul never met the man Jesus. Shortly before Smith's death, he reconsidered this opinion and told me one day at lunch that he now agreed that Paul was speaking of himself and that he had an argument to demonstrate it. Unfortunately, Smith was unable to write up these perceptions before his death. As we shall see, the passage is probably another record of the kind of experience Paul has in meeting the risen Christ, this time in heaven.

5. C. R. A. Morray Jones, "Paradise Revisited (2 Cor 12:1–12): The Jewish Mystical Background of Paul's Apostolate," *HTR* 86 (1993): 177–217, 265–92.

6. See C. R. A. Morray-Jones, *A Transparent Illusion: The Dangerous Vision of Water in Hekhalot Mysticism: A Source-Critical and Tradition-Historical Inquiry* (JSJSup 59; Leiden: Brill, 2002).

mysticism as well; even though he is our first Christian writer, he is not the first Christian. He learned his Christianity from the community in Damascus and, in turn, became a spokesperson for it. His subsequent Christian experience cannot have failed to have affected his memories of these events, as that is a quite common and widely verified aspect of conversions even today.[7] This implies a significant growth of his maturity of Christian thought in the years between his conversion and his writings that we cannot clearly delineate.

Paul's Christian interpretation of these apocalyptic mystical visions is also a mark of his long association with the Christian community.[8] The Christian nature of his vision is due to the experience itself as he interprets it. We need not suppose that the divine nature of Paul's revelation precludes influence from his supporting Christian community as well. All converts naturally find the meaning of their conversions in the community that values them and that meaning is revealed to them progressively after the conversion.

We should note that Paul does not utilize the concept of a soul (ψυχή) to effect this heavenly travel. Not being sure of whether the ascent took place in the body or out of the body is the same as saying that one is not taking account of the Platonic concept of the soul. Had Paul been using the Platonic version, he certainly would have known quite well that the only way to go to heaven, to ascend beyond the sublunar sphere, is by leaving the body behind. Indeed, we shall see several important places, especially 1 Cor 15, where Paul's concept of "soul" is quite limited, unschooled by Platonic ideas of the soul's immortality.

Rather, Paul uses the term *spirit* (πνεῦμα) more frequently. Paul's *pneumatology* derives from the traditional language of biblical prophecy and it is also the way Paul understands resurrection to arrive. This suggests that Paul may have understood being *in Christ* as a literal exchange of earthly body for a new *pneumatic*, spiritual one to be shared with the resurrected Jesus at the *eschaton*, since *spirit* is the source of all Paul's knowledge gained in visions. For him it is not yet concrete reality because it is not fully present. On the other hand, the spiritual vision is not hallucination either. It is prophecy in process of becoming concrete.

Even if Paul is not sure of how a visionary journey could be taken, *we* are. The question of whether a heavenly journey could take place in or out of the body may be settled for us only by assuming that this was an ecstatic journey, a religiously interpreted state of consciousness (RISC). Modern science balks at the notion of physical transport to heaven, except in space ships, whereas a heavenly journey in vision or trance is credible and understandable. This only underlines

---

7. Brian Taylor, "Recollection and Membership: Converts Talk and the Ratiocination of Commonality," *Sociology* 12 (1978): 316–23. See also James A Beckford, "Accounting for Conversion," *British Journal of Sociology* 29.2 (1978): 249–62; David Snow and Richard Machalek, "The Sociology of Conversion," *Annual Review of Sociology* 10 (1984): 167–90.

8. Martin Hengel, *The Pre-Christian Paul* (Philadelphia: Trinity Press International, 1991).

Paul's interesting conflation of what to us seems to be two different categories. So we are not free to ignore that fact when we try to establish what actually happened. When a heavenly journey is described literally, the cause may be literary convention or the belief of the voyager; but when reconstructing the actual experience, only one type can pass modern standards of credibility.

Paul's confusion as to whether his ecstatic journey to heaven took place in the body is a rare insight into first-century thinking, since it demonstrates either a disagreement in the community or more likely a first-century mystic's inability to distinguish between bodily and spiritual journeys to heaven. In effect, then, Paul is merely saying that the ascender was experiencing a religiously altered state of consciousness (RASC). But our world no longer supports his quandary; nor did the ancient world shortly after Paul's time. They adopted the Platonic notion of the soul, which answered the question sufficiently for them. Indeed, the answer still informs religious life today. It seems likely, however, that the presence of a heavenly journey is itself a signifier that ecstatic experience is taking place.

THE SPIRITUAL BODY AND ITS PRESENCE IN ASCENT MYSTICISM

We must ask how Paul conceived such a journey to take place without a developed concept of the soul. The first answer may just be that he thought it took place in a body. As we will see, the best descriptor of this body would be a *spiritual body*. He has already told us that he is not sure whether the ascender was "in the body" or not. He is quite sure that resurrection will not be fleshly, though it may be bodily (1 Cor 15:40). Since it already seems clear that Christ's body, as it appeared to him in visions, and the body of the resurrected believer are parallel, it must be that the ascender's body and the body of the resurrection are analogous as well. The demonstration appears to be 1 Cor 15:44 where Paul describes a mystical notion of a spiritual body (σῶμα πνευματικόν) that is received by the Christ and finds residence in it in the same way that God can inspire the prophets or Enoch can become part of the son of man.

Paul uses a prophetic anthropology to explain this spiritual body. God gives the prophet his spirit and the spiritual body participates in the resurrection. This puts Paul in the same category as the apocalypticists who first recorded the notion of bodily resurrection. It also puts him rather far from those classes of people who championed the notion of the immortality of the soul, though Paul, being an apostle to the gentiles, may know of the doctrine. He certainly seems familiar with Stoic and Cynic doctrines and methods of argumentation.[9]

---

9. Abraham J. Malherbe, *The Cynic Epistles* (Atlanta: Scholars Press, 1977); idem, *Moral Exhortation, A Greco-Roman Sourcebook* (Philadelphia: Westminster, 1986); Troels Engberg-Pedersen, *Paul and the Stoics* (Edinburgh: T&T Clark, 2000). See now the interesting article

As long as the date of *1 En.* 70–71 cannot be fixed exactly and as long as evidence of the Dead Sea Scrolls remains provocative and debatable, Paul himself remains the earliest author explicitly expressing this kind of angelic transformation in Judaism. The transformation that Paul achieves is coterminous with achieving resurrection in the afterlife. If his discussion of transformation can be related to apocalyptic mysticism in Judaism, he also becomes the only Jewish mystic of this period to relate this personal experience confessionally. The difference between this experience and the other ancient Near Eastern journeys to heaven—Adapa, Etana, Enoch, and so on—is that from this period onward, the journey is most often being made through RISC. In Paul's case, we have an anomalous case where he is not sure whether it is made in the body or in the spirit. But it seems clear that spiritual bodies and angelic bodies must now be considered analogous. They are bodily but they are not flesh. Paul believes that they are bodies like the heavenly bodies, but there are also distinctions to be made between heavenly bodies (1 Cor 15:41). This suggests that Paul would rank Christ higher than an ordinary angel but that they all exist in the same class of heavenly body.

There is adequate evidence, then, that many Jewish mystics and apocalypticists sensed a relationship between the angels and important figures in the life of their community. The roots of this tradition are pre-Christian, though the tradition is massively developed by Christianity. Furthermore, Jewish scholars have overlooked Christianity as evidence for the existence of these traditions in first-century Judaism. Paul did not have to be a religious innovator to posit an identification between a vindicated hero and the image of the *kavod*, the manlike figure in heaven, although the identification of the figure with the risen Christ is obviously a uniquely Christian development.[10] If so, along with the mysterious,

---

by Peter Lampe, "Paul's Concept of a Spiritual Body," in *Resurrection: Theological and Scientific Assessments* (ed. T. Peters, R, J. Russell, M. Welker; Grand Rapids: Eerdmans, 2002), 103–14.

10. Whether Paul identifies the figure purely on the basis of his vision or because of previous instruction in mystical and apocalyptic Judaism is a question that admits of no practical solution. The question does not demand a specific solution since we know how closely individual mystical experience adheres to communal rules. Paul's visions make most sense as a new Christian development within an established Jewish apocalyptic and mystical tradition. Paul or his close contemporary no doubt learned some of it and likely had experiences in a Christian community that confirmed, and indeed educated, his visionary experience that Christ was the figure on the throne. This is altogether natural. It is impossible to isolate what parts are traditional and which parts are his own revelation, for the elements of apocalyptic and mystical revelation, as we have already seen, are traditional in many respects. Only the identification of the Christ as the figure on the throne was novel by most Jewish standards, yet that would have been normative in Christian community. Each Jewish sect had its distinctive beliefs and Christianity is no exception is this respect. Paul's experiences are, when seen in this light, not unique in, so much as characteristic of, Jewish mystical thought. Indeed, they give us good evidence that the mystical ascent of adepts to heaven was already known in the first century.

anonymous psalmist from Qumran (1QH), Paul is a rare Jewish mystic to report his own personal, identifiably confessional mystical experiences in the fifteen hundred years that separate Ezekiel from the rise of Kabbalah.

TRANSFORMATION INTO THE CHRIST

When Paul is not faced with a direct declaration of personal mystical experience, he reveals much about mystical religion as it was experienced in the first century. Paul himself designates Christ as the image of the Lord in a few places (2 Cor 4:4; Col 1:15 [if it is Pauline]; and he mentions the μορφῇ [form, shape] of God in Phil 2:6).[11] More often he talks of transforming believers into "the image of His son" in various ways (Rom 8:29; 2 Cor 3:18; Phil 3:21; 1 Cor 15:49; also Col 3:9), as we have already seen. These passages are critical to understanding what Paul's experience of conversion was. They must be seen in closer detail to understand the relationship to Jewish apocalypticism and mysticism, from which they derive their most complete significance for Paul. Paul's longest discussion of these themes occurs in 2 Cor 3:18–4:6. Here he assumes the context rather than explaining it completely:

> Now the Lord is the Spirit, and where the Spirit of the Lord is, there is freedom. And we all, with unveiled face, beholding the glory of the Lord, are being changed into his likeness from one degree of glory to another; for this comes from the Lord who is the Spirit. Therefore, having this ministry by the mercy of God, we do not lose heart. We have renounced disgraceful, underhanded ways; we refuse to practice cunning or to tamper with God's word, but by the open statement of the truth we would commend ourselves to every man's conscience in the sight of God. And even if our gospel is veiled, it is veiled only to those who are perishing. In their case the god of this world has blinded the minds of the unbelievers, to keep them from seeing the light of the gospel of the glory of Christ, who is the likeness of God. For what we preach is not ourselves, but Jesus Christ as Lord, with ourselves as your servants for Jesus' sake. For it is the God who said, "Let light shine out of darkness," who has shone in our hearts to give the light of the knowledge of the Glory of God in the face of Christ. (2 Cor 3:18–4:6)

Paul begins this passage by reference to the spiritual nature of the Christ, calling him both *Lord* and *Spirit*. He ends this passage by identifying *the Glory of God* with Christ. The Glory of the Lord is angelic in form, an avatar of the principal angelic manifestation of God, as described in Exodus. The question is how literally does he mean it? There is no reason to think that he is not being fully literal

---

11. In this section, I am particularly indebted to Gilles Quispel, "Hermetism and the New Testament, Especially Paul," *ANRW* 2, 1998.

and candid, since transformation was a sensible expectation of apocalyptic Jews in the first century. Paul is using these terms in their biblical technical sense to identify the Christ with the human manifestation of God and then suggest that this is the same as his spiritual visions of Christ.

In 2 Cor 3:18, Paul says that believers will be changed into Christ's likeness from one degree of glory to another. He refers to Exod 33 and 34, where Moses's encounter with the angel of the Lord is narrated. Earlier in that passage, the angel of the Lord is described as carrying the name of God (Exod 23:21). Moses sees the *Glory of the Lord*, makes a covenant, receives the commandments upon the two tables of the law and, when he comes down from the mount, the skin of his face shines with light, as the Bible states (Exod 34:29–35). Moses thereafter must wear a veil except when he is in the presence of the Lord. Paul assumes that Moses made an ascension to the presence of the Lord, was transformed by that encounter and that his shining face is a reflection of the encounter, perhaps even as a foretaste of his angelic destiny.

Paul's term the *Glory of the Lord* must be taken both as a reference to Christ and as a technical term for the *kavod*, the human form of God appearing in biblical visions. In 2 Cor 3:18, Paul says that Christians behold the Glory of the Lord as in a mirror and are transformed into his image.[12] For Paul, as for the earliest Jewish mystics, to be privileged enough to see the *kavod* or Glory (δόξα) of God is a prologue to transformation into His image (εἰκών). Paul does not say that all Christians have made the journey literally, but compares the experience of knowing Christ to being allowed into the intimate presence of the Lord, to be given

---

12. The use of the mirror here is also a magico-mystical theme, which can be traced to the word עין occuring in Ezek 1. Although it is sometimes translated otherwise, עין probably refers to a mirror even there, and possibly refers to some unexplained technique for achieving ecstasy. The mystic bowls of the magical papyri and Talmudic times were filled with water and oil to reflect light and stimulate trance. The magical papyri describe spells that use a small bowl that serves as the medium for the appearance of a god for divination: e.g., PGM IV, 154–285; PDM 14.1–92, 295–308, 395–427, 528–53, 627–635, 805–840, 841–850, 851–855; Hans Dieter Betz, *The Greek Magical Papyri in Translation: Including the Demotic Spells* (2nd ed.; Chicago: University of Chicago Press, 1996), 40–43, 195–200, 213, 218–19, 225–26, 229, 236–39. The participant concentrates on the reflection in the water's surface, often with oil added to the mixture, sometimes with the light of a lamp nearby. Lamps and charms are also used to produce divinations, presumably because they can stimulate a trance under the proper conditions. For example, the Reuyoth Yehezkel mention that Ezekiel's mystical vision was stimulated by looking into the waters of the River Chebar. It seems to me that Philo appropriates the mystic imagery of the mirror to discuss the allegorical exposition of scripture. See his *The Contemplative Life*, 78 and Dieter Georgi, *Die Gegner des Paulus im 2. Korintherbrief* (Neukirchen-Vluyn: Neukirchener Verlag, 1964), 272–73. Also, Paul's opponents look into the mirror and see only the text, but because Paul and those truly in Christ actually behold the glory of the Lord, they have clearer vision.

entrance to God's court (see Dan 7:9–12; Exod 24:10–12; Ezek 1; 1 Kgs 22:19–23). And he himself has made that journey.

The result of the journey (over several years of proselytizing) is to identify Christ as the *Glory of the Lord*. When Paul says that he preaches that Jesus is *Lord* and that God "has let this light shine out of darkness into our hearts to give the light of knowledge of the Glory of God in the face of Christ" (4:6), he seems clearly to be describing his own conversion and ministry, just as he described it in Gal 1, and just as he is explaining the experience to new converts for the purpose of furthering and strengthening their conversion.[13] His apostolate, which he expresses as a prophetic calling, is to proclaim that the face of *Christ* is the "Glory of God." It is very difficult not to read this passage in terms of Paul's description of the ascension of the man to the third heaven and conclude that Paul's conversion experience also involved his identification of Jesus as the "Image" and "Glory of God," as the human figure in heaven, and thereafter as Lord, Spirit, Christ, Son, and Savior.

This is an explicit working out of the prophecy of Dan 12. In fact, one could say it is the experience of feeling Dan 12 coming to fruition in one's own experience. Daniel 12 suggests that those who lead others to wisdom (or "the enlighteners;" המשבלים) will shine as the brightness of the heavens, like the stars and that they will be among those resurrected for eternal reward. We know that the reference to "stars" is merely another way of suggesting angels (e.g., Job 38:7; Judg 5:20; see also Josh 10:11; see also Cicero, *Resp.* 6.26.28–29 [i.e., *Dream of Scipio*]; *1 En.* 108; *T. Mos.* 9–10). The connection between stars and divinity is in fact centuries older than Judaism, as it is part of Canaanite myth (e.g., CTA 2, 7, 11). The "Parables of Enoch" (*1 En.* 37–71) contains the interesting narration of the transformation of Enoch into the son of man, but no one can be sure that this is not itself a Christian addition to the text, since it agrees so completely with the transformation that Paul outlines.[14] Without Paul we could not suppose that this

---

13. See Beverly Gaventa, *From Darkness to Light: Aspects of Conversion in the New Testament* (Philadelphia: Fortress, 1986), 45–48. Paul again is including his experience of transformation into his ministry, as he is here answering a communal question. He uses the imagery of darkness and light, which Gaventa notes is key to his conversion vocabulary. It is equally important to note how important the social aspect of this mysticism/apocalypticism is to Paul. In calling him a mystical Jew, we discover a whole social and ethical side to first-century mystical writings that we normally miss, because we tend to separate ethics, apocalypticism, and mysticism in a way that Paul never does. Paul's writings are quintessentially social and ethical; yet behind them lies a mystical experience that he calls ineffable and that is always confirmed in community.

14. The romance of exaltation to immortality was hardly a unique Jewish motif; rather it was characteristic of all higher spirituality of later Hellenism—witness the Hermetic literature. Even in a relatively unsophisticated text like the magical Recipe for Immortality (the so-called Mithras Liturgy) of third-century C.E. Egypt, the adept gains a measure of immortality by

experience is evidenced in the first century because the date of *1 En.* 37–71 and the meaning of some of the Qumran material is uncertain. Nor would we know that the mystical experience was even possible within Judaism.

The identification of Christ with the Glory of the Lord brings a transformation and sharing of the believer with the image as well. This is the same as regaining the image of God that Adam lost. This transformation is accomplished through the death and rebirth in Christ, which can be experienced in direct visions as Paul apparently did, or by anyone through baptism. But the important thing is to note how completely the theophanic language from Greek and Jewish mystical piety has been appropriated for discussing what we today call conversion. It is Paul's primary language for describing the experience of conversion because it gives a sense of the transformation and divinization (or angelification) that he feels is inherent in his encounter with the risen Christ. This transformation and angelification is authenticated in communal life, in social transactions (for instance, 1 Cor 12–14, also 1 Cor 5:1–5).

The purpose of the analogy is clear: whenever anybody turns to the Lord through Christianity, the veil of Moses is removed. Upon the faces of the new Christians is the reflection of Christ, since they bear the same image as Christ. I. M. Lewis again has outlined the effect of such a claim of "spirit possession" in society.[15] The Christians were a peripheral group in Jewish society, whose claim to have direct access to the truth through the spirit rendered pharisaic claims of authoritative exegesis irrelevant. As with the Qumran community, to claim angelomorphism while on earth is essentially to say that they are a new and very privileged kind of person.

Concomitant with Paul's worship of the divine Christ is transformation. Paul says in Phil 3:10 "that I may know him and the power of his resurrection and may share his sufferings, becoming like him in his death" (συμμορφιζόμενος τῷ θανάτῳ αὐτοῦ). Later, in Phil 3:20–21, he says: "But our commonwealth is in heaven, and from it we await a Savior, the Lord Jesus Christ, who will change (μετασχηματίσει) our lowly body to be conformed in shape (σύμμορφον) to his glorious body (τῷ σώματι τῆς δόξης αὐτοῦ) by the power which enables him even to subject all things to himself."

Paul exhorts his followers to imitate him as he has imitated Christ: "Brethren, join in imitating me, and mark those who so live as you have an example in us." The followers are told to imitate Paul as he himself imitates Jesus. All of this suggests that the body of believers will be literally refashioned into the glorious body of Christ, a process that starts with conversion and faith but ends in the Parousia,

---

gazing directly on the god and breathing in some of his essence or requesting him to dwell inside (PGM IV, 710).

15. I. M. Lewis, *Ecstatic Religion: An Anthropological Study of Spirit Possession and Shamanism* (Baltimore: Penguin, 1971).

the shortly-expected culmination of history. It will all depend on a notion of body that is a new spiritualized substance, a new body that is not flesh and blood, that cannot inherit the kingdom (1 Cor 15:30).

Paul's depiction of salvation and the transformation of the believer are based on his understanding of Christ's glorification, partaking of early Jewish apocalyptic mysticism for its expression.[16] The basic notion of transformation into an angelic or astral form may even have survived from a pre-Christian setting because Paul does not mention resurrection here at all. Clearly glorification is doing the work of resurrection in this passage. Likewise, in Rom 12:2 Paul's listeners are exhorted to "be transformed (μεταμορφοῦσθε) by renewing of your minds." In Gal 4:19 Paul expresses another, very similar transformation: "My little children, with whom I am again in travail until Christ be formed (*morphed*, μορφωθῇ) in you!"

This transformation, surprisingly, is to be effected by being morphed into Christ in his death (συμμορφιζόμενος τῷ θανάτῳ αὐτοῦ, Phil 3:10). This identification with the death of Jesus is a crucial issue for understanding Paul's religious experience. Paul predicts that the believer will be transformed into the glorious body of Christ, through dying and being reborn in Christ. Paul's central proclamation is: Jesus is Lord and all who have faith have already undergone a death like his and so will share in his resurrection by being transformed into his form, spirit, and shape. This proclamation reflects a baptismal liturgy, implying that baptism provides the moment whereby the believer comes to be "in Christ." Christianity may have been a unique Jewish sect in making baptism a central rather than a preparatory ritual, but some of the mystical imagery comes from its Jewish past, probably through the teachings of John the Baptist.[17] In any case, Paul seems to be connecting this with the martyrdom of Jesus and John, as we shall see.

---

16. Scholars like Seyoon Kim who want to ground all of Paul's thought in a single ecstatic conversion experience, which they identify with Luke's accounts of Paul's conversion, are reticent to accept this passage as a fragment from Christian liturgy, because to do so would destroy its value as Paul's personal revelatory experience. But there is no need to decide whether the passage is originally Paul's (hence received directly through the "Damascus revelation"), since ecstatic language normally is derived from traditions current within the religious group. Christian mystics use Christian language, Muslim mystics use the languages developed for mysticism in Islam and no mystic is ever confused by another religion's mysticism unless it is the conscious and explicit intent of the mystic's vision to do so. See R. C. Zaehner's *Hinduism and Muslim Mysticism* (New York: Schocken, 1969); Steven Katz, "Language, Epistemology, and Mysticism," in *Mysticism and Philosophical Analysis* (ed. S. Katz; New York: Oxford University Press, 1978), 22–74. In this case the language is not even primarily Christian. The basic language is from Jewish mysticism, though the subsequent exegesis about the identification of the Christ with the figure on the throne is Christian; the vision of God enthroned is the goal of Jewish mystical speculation.

17. Nils A. Dahl, *The Crucified Messiah* (Minneapolis: Augsburg, 1974); James D. G. Dunn, *Baptism in the Holy Spirit: A Re-Examination of The New Testament Teaching on the Gift of the Spirit in Relation to Pentecostalism Today* (Philadelphia: Westminster, 1977).

Alternatively, Paul can say, as he does in Gal 1:16, that "God was pleased to reveal His Son in me (ἐν ἐμοί)." This is not a simple dative but refers to his having received in him the Spirit, in his case through his conversion. Being *in Christ* appears to mean being united with or transformed into his heavenly image. The same, however, is available to all Christians through baptism.

Paul's conception of the risen body of Christ as the spiritual body (1 Cor 15:43–44) at the end of time and as the body of Glory (Phil 3:21) thus originates in Jewish apocalypticism and mysticism, modified by the unique events of early Christianity. Spirit is a synonym for the "glory" and "form" that Christ has already received. The meaning of Rom 8:29 can be clarified likewise by Jewish esoteric tradition. There, as we have seen, Paul speaks of God as having "foreordained his elect to be conformed (σύμμόρφους, again) to the image of his Son." Paul uses the genitive here rather than the dative as in Phil 3:21, softening the identification between believer and savior. But when Paul states that believers conform to the image of his Son, he is not speaking of an agreement of mind or ideas between Jesus and the believers. The word behind the English word "conformed" is σύμμορφον again. Appearing in an oblique case, the word σύμμόρφους itself still suggests a spiritual reformation of the believer's body into the form of the divine image. Paul's language for conversion—being transformed in Christ—develops out of mystical Judaism.

1 CORINTHIANS 15

Paul's main discussion of resurrection comes in 1 Cor 15. In that letter, he begins by showing that those who understand real wisdom are truly initiated into the revelations of the Holy Spirit. The language sounds something like what may be imagined to have taken place in mystery cults, as many scholars have pointed out. But why guess as to its possible relationship to a hypothetical piety in this period when it is demonstrably close to the language of Jewish apocalyptic mysticism that we find at Qumran. For instance, 1 Cor 2:6–10:[18]

> Yet among the mature we do impart wisdom, although it is not a wisdom of this age or of the rulers of this age, who are doomed to pass away. But we impart a secret and hidden wisdom of God, which God decreed before the ages for our glorification. None of the rulers of this age understood this; for if they had, they would not have crucified the Lord of glory.
>
> But, as it is written, "What no eye has seen, nor ear heard, nor the heart of man conceived, what God has prepared for those who love him," God has

---

18. See Marcus Bockmuehl, *Revelation and Mystery in Ancient Judaism and Pauline Christianity* (WUNT 36; Tübingen: Mohr Siebeck, 1990; repr., Grand Rapids: Eerdmans, 1997), 167–77.

revealed to us through the Spirit. For the Spirit searches everything, even the depths of God. (1 Cor 2:6–10)

Paul writes in the context of considerable communal argumentation and factional dispute. His interpretation of the gospel has been called into question by his opponents. He avers that his only source is the risen Christ; his only proof (1 Cor 2:6) is his success, which is supplied by the Spirit.[19]

In this context, Paul speaks of those who are qualified (2:6), the mature ones who evidently share his perspective and, perhaps, to some extent his experience. This is a plausible extrapolation when the term refers so often to the initiated in the mystery religions. But quite close to home, at Qumran, knowledge and *perfection* were expected of the membership and only *the perfected ones* had access to the full secrets of the sect (1QS 1:8; 2:2; 3:3, 9; 5:24; 8:20; 9:2, 8–19).[20]

Mystery is one of the central tenets of Qumran. Paul also describes the revelation of the crucified messiah as a mystery (1 Cor 2:8). Even so, it also contrasts with mystery at Qumran. Paul's mystery is not secret in the way that mystery at Qumran was. Although it needs to be taught and it is not evidently universally accepted, it does not itself need to be secret. It finds its particular adherents. Paul evidently thinks all Christians will be transformed, whereas at Qumran it looks like the transformation is restricted only to the priests officiating in the heavenly Sabbath service.

In 1 Corinthians, Paul discusses the issue of the final disposition the body before he discusses the issue of resurrection and transformation itself. In this passage he may also be responding to the Greek notion that the body decays while the soul lives on. A. J. Wedderburn has astutely observed that the issue in 1 Cor 6 is the normal conception of the afterlife in a Greek environment.[21] It is in this context that Paul takes up the issue of the body:

"All things are lawful for me," but not all things are beneficial. "All things are lawful for me," but I will not be dominated by anything. "Food is meant for the stomach and the stomach for food,"[22] and God will destroy both one and the other. The body is meant not for fornication but for the Lord, and the Lord for the body. And God raised the Lord and will also raise us by his power. (1 Cor 6:12–14)

---

19. Bockmuehl, *Revelation and Mystery*, 158.

20. Ibid., 159.

21. A. J. M. Wedderburn, "The Problem of the Denial of the Resurrection in 1 Corinthians XV," *NovT* 23 (1981): 229–41.

22. The quotation may extend to "both one and the other."

The Greeks believe that the body is destined for destruction. But Paul does not follow through with a Platonic analysis of the immortality of the soul.[23] Instead, he stays in the apocalyptic-mystical world of Judaism, defending and sharpening that notion in view of the Greek assumptions about the continuity of life after death. Paul immediately suggests that the body will survive death, for it belongs to the Lord. God will raise it in glory and perfection by means of the spirit, just as he raised up the body of Jesus, who is even now in his spiritual state.

This kind of talk will demand a clarification in a Greco-Roman context. But, as Paul is still discussing various moral issues within the community, he postpones his discussion until later in the letter, to 1 Cor 15. In 1 Cor 15, Paul sums up his entire religious experience in an apocalyptic vision of the resurrection of believers. Paul begins with a description of his previous preaching and suggests that if his listeners give up belief in the resurrection then they believe in Christ in vain:

> Now if Christ is proclaimed as raised from the dead, how can some of you say there is no resurrection of the dead? If there is no resurrection of the dead, then Christ has not been raised; and if Christ has not been raised, then our proclamation has been in vain and your faith has been in vain. We are even found to be misrepresenting God, because we testified of God that he raised Christ—whom he did not raise if it is true that the dead are not raised. For if the dead are not raised, then Christ has not been raised. If Christ has not been raised, your faith is futile and you are still in your sins. Then those also who have died[24] in Christ have perished. If for this life only we have hoped in Christ, we are of all people most to be pitied. (1 Cor 15:12–19)

Paul claims to have given them, indeed emphasized as the first importance, the true teaching, as he had himself received it. And that teaching is simply that Christ died for sins in accordance to scripture, that he was entombed and rose three days later, all in accordance with scripture. There is no doubt that this is earliest Christian teaching with regard to the resurrection: it is part of the primitive *kerygma* or proclamation of the church.

MARTYRDOM AND TRANSFORMATION

For him the identification with Jesus mystically makes everyone a martyr and, logically, makes everyone qualified for the resurrection rewards of a martyr. Those who believe in Christ are worthy of the same rewards as the martyrs, who can expect not just a bodily existence at the final end of history, but who can also

---

23. Like me, Peter Lampe suggests that Paul is arguing against Greek notions of immortality and replacing them with his own. See Lampe, "Paul's Concept of a Spiritual Body," 103–14.

24. Greek: "fallen asleep."

expect the further reward of the martyred few ("those who lead many to knowledge") as heavenly angels (stars) for having enlightened the world:

> We are afflicted in every way, but not crushed; perplexed, but not driven to despair; persecuted, but not forsaken; struck down, but not destroyed; always carrying in the body the death of Jesus, so that the life of Jesus may also be manifested in our bodies. (2 Cor 4:8–10)

Even more so for those who actually suffer for their faith. These spiritual experiences of transformation into the Christ form analogies to the life and death of Jesus. Those who suffer as the Christ suffered can expect some identification with the exalted Christ (σύμμορφος). And more concretely it means that the believer must be ready to accept suffering as part of Christian discipleship.[25]

For Paul there is not much recognition that a resurrection without the end time is very strange. Paul apparently feels that the time is peculiarly out of joint because the first resurrection has happened but the end has not yet come about. Clearly, he thinks that the end will shortly arrive. And, as we know, the demonstration that the age has begun is the actual appearance of Jesus *to him* (Gal 1:12; 2 Cor 3:12–18).

As we have seen, Paul—in contradistinction to some later gnostic traditions—begins from the supposition that the death and burial was real and hence the resurrection was actual and in accordance with scripture (1 Cor 15:3). Paul then lists those to whom the post-resurrection Jesus appeared. In Paul's understanding, the post-resurrection appearances rather than the physical presence of Jesus are primary. He includes himself modestly in the list of those to whom Jesus had appeared. But if the list had been made up of those who knew Jesus in the flesh, Paul would have been left out. The corruptible flesh of the earthly Jesus is not the point for Paul. He is deliberately widening the concept of apostleship to include persons like himself who have a spiritual relationship with the Christ. For him, it is Jesus the heavenly redeemer who reveals himself to his chosen, who is the proof of faith, not merely those who may have heard Jesus's preaching.

Paul then asserts that all these people saw the same thing and preach the same thing and believe the same thing. And indeed, Paul asserts that the Corinthians had believed exactly that when he was there with them. In vv. 12–19 Paul claims that the deniers of the resurrection of the dead are denying the gospel that they had received and initially believed. He begins a series of arguments that ends in the *reductio ad absurdum* that "if Christ has not been raised, then our proclamation has been in vain and your faith has been in vain." This argument only makes sense to believers; no one else would see the absurdity of the conclusion that he reaches.

---

25. Thorwald Lorenzen, *Resurrection and Discipleship: Interpretive Models, Biblical Reflections, Theological Consequences* (Maryknoll, N.Y.: Orbis Books, 1995), 158.

But, in fact, they need not have been either; they could merely have been following ordinary Greek popular thought in a Platonic vein, thinking that the soul is immortal but that the body cannot be raised from the dead (nor would anyone want to be embodied, given the choice). That is to say, they may only have been ordinary Greeks for whom the Christian message of the resurrection of Jesus might naturally have been interpreted in a different context than the apocalyptic one out of which Paul originally spoke. A person might survive death through the immortality of the soul in Greek thought, but a bodily resurrection was never any significant part in Greek thinking.[26]

It is not necessarily true, as Paul argues, that all those who died in Christ would have been thought by his listeners to have perished. The deceased believers could have been viewed as merely receiving their divine reward on the basis of their deeds, or knowledge, or the soul's natural inclination.[27] However, as Paul suggests, such notions deny the salvific nature of Christ's death in totality. It is the bodily resurrection of Jesus that guarantees that God's plan for the final destruction of the evil ones of the world is already set in place. For if the soul is immortal by nature and that is the highest form of immortality to be achieved, then the sacrifice of Christ is unnecessary.

In 1 Cor 15:20–28 Paul stops arguing against enemies and begins articulating his own notions. He shows that the resurrection of Christ entails the future resurrection of all the righteous dead as Christ is the "first fruit of them who have fallen asleep" (v. 20), yet again using the term that is clearly dependent upon Dan 12 and, in turn, Isa 26 (see also, e.g., LXX Ps 87:6). Probably then, the scriptural passage that Paul had in mind earlier (1 Cor 15:3) is none other than Dan 12:2: "And many of those who sleep in the dust of the earth shall awake, some to everlasting life, and some to shame and everlasting contempt. And those who are wise shall shine like the brightness of the firmament; and those who turn many to righteousness, like the stars forever and ever" (Dan 12:2–3).

The Christian innovation is to have identified the angelic figure or divine figure who brought judgment, the son of man of Dan 7:13 and which could also be called "the Lord," with Jesus the Messiah, or Χριστός. No other movement so

---

26. This has recently been reaffirmed by N. T. Wright, *The Resurrection of the Son of God* (Minneapolis: Fortress, 2003).

27. This is, in fact, the position of Birger Pearson, *The Pneumatikos-Psychikos Terminology in 1 Corinthians* (SBLDS 12; Missoula, Mont.: Scholars Press, 1973) and Richard Horsley in "Pneumatikos vs. Psychikos: Distinctions of Spiritual Status among the Corinthians," *HTR* 69 (1976): 269–88. They maintain that Philonic exegesis in fact defines the background of the opponents of Paul at Corinth, people who knew Philo's exegesis of the two creation stories in Genesis as talking about two *anthropoi*, the spiritual man (the idea of man) and earthly man (the mortal, embodied human). Paul defeats this exegesis with his own; see Martinus de Boer, *The Defeat of Death: Apocalyptic Eschatology in 1 Corinthians 15 and Romans 5* (JSNTSup 22; Sheffield: JSOT Press, 1988), 101.

far has shown any interest in conflating "Lord" with "the Messiah," though the Qumran community had already identified divine terms like 'El, with the principal angels of God (11QMelch). On the basis of Dan 7:9–13 and Dan 12, together with Pss 8 and 110, the Christian community found the scriptural support that clarified what God had in mind for the end of history.

We can now see this in better detail. Since Jesus died as a martyr, expectations of his resurrection would have been normal in some Jewish sects.[28] But the idea of a crucified messiah was unique. In such a situation, the Christians only did what other believing Jews did in similar circumstances: they turned to biblical prophecy for elucidation. No messianic text suggested itself as appropriate to the situation. But Ps 110:1 was exactly apposite: The LORD says to my lord: "Sit at my right hand until I make your enemies your footstool."[29]

Here was a description of the enthronement of a Davidic descendant, now understood as a heavenly enthronement after death and resurrection. Yet nothing in the Psalm makes death or resurrection an inevitable part of the narrative. It must have come from the historical experience of the events of Jesus's life, not the other way around. The early Christian community, after they experienced these events, found the scripture that explained the meaning of the events. Thereafter, Ps 110:1 could be combined easily with Dan 7:9–13, the description of the enthronement of the "son of man." Dan 7:9–13 seemed to prophesy Christ's exaltation and ascension because Jesus could be identified with the son of man, angelic figure, who is, in turn, identified with the second "Lord" in the quotation from Ps 110. Daniel 12:2 had promised astral, angelic immortality to those who taught wisdom, confirming the entire set of expectations. The combination of Ps 110 with Dan 7:13 (possibly together with Ps 8) give us a good explanation for the difficult *spiritual body* phrase in Paul's writing, as we shall soon see. In short, the combination of these two passages, seen together with Jesus's martyrdom as the messiah of Israel, produced the *kerygma* of the early church. It was this as well that allowed Paul to come to the conclusions that he did, though he also received revelations and visions which confirmed the teaching.

---

28. See Alan F. Segal, *Rebecca's Children: Judaism and Christianity in the Roman World* (Cambridge, Mass.: Harvard University Press, 1986), 60–67, 78–95 for a thumbnail sketch of this development.

29. The Hebrew makes clear that the two Lords refer to different personages, one God and the second the King. But the Greek uses κύριος to refer to both Lords. Thus, it is easy to make both Lords into divine designations. Wilhelm Bousset, *Kyrios Christos: A History of Belief in Christ from the Beginnings of Christianity to Irenaeus* (trans. J. E. Steely; Nashville, Tenn.: Abingdon Press, 1970).

1 Corinthians 15:37–57

First Corinthians 15:35–57 is one of the most systematic expositions of the Jewish mystical and apocalyptic tradition, which seems so central to Paul's message of the meaning of Christ's resurrection. The coming end means transformation and resurrection for all who believe in him:

> But someone will ask, "How are the dead raised? With what kind of body do they come?" Fool! What you sow does not come to life unless it dies. And as for what you sow, you do not sow the body that is to be, but a bare seed, perhaps of wheat or of some other grain. But God gives it a body as he has chosen, and to each kind of seed its own body. Not all flesh is alike, but there is one flesh for human beings, another for animals, another for birds, and another for fish. There are both heavenly bodies and earthly bodies, but the glory of the heavenly is one thing, and that of the earthly is another. There is one glory of the sun, and another glory of the moon, and another glory of the stars; indeed, star differs from star in glory. So it is with the resurrection of the dead. What is sown is perishable, what is raised is imperishable. It is sown in dishonor, it is raised in glory. It is sown in weakness, it is raised in power. It is sown a physical body, it is raised a spiritual body. If there is a physical body, there is also a spiritual body. Thus it is written, "The first man, Adam, became a living being"; the last Adam became a life-giving spirit. But it is not the spiritual that is first, but the physical, and then the spiritual. The first man was from the earth, a man of dust; the second man is[30] from heaven. As was the man of dust, so are those who are of the dust; and as is the man of heaven, so are those who are of heaven. Just as we have borne the image of the man of dust, we will[31] also bear the image of the man of heaven. What I am saying, brothers and sisters,[32] is this: flesh and blood cannot inherit the kingdom of God, nor does the perishable inherit the imperishable. (1 Cor 15:37–50)

In 1 Cor 15:35 Paul begins a brief exposition of the nature of the resurrection body. He is, in this passage, outlining a notion of afterlife that has nothing to do with immortality of the soul; it is an offshoot of Jewish apocalypticism, out of which the Christian *kerygma* grows. But he is also cognizant of the beliefs of the audience so he merely ignores and does not argue against the immortality of the soul. Instead, he fastens again on the notion of spirit to explicate how the physical body of believers will be transformed by the resurrection. His argument has nothing to do with what happened to Christ during the passion nor does he mention any empty tomb. His argument is made by analogy with his own experience and,

---

30. Other ancient authorities add "the Lord."
31. Other ancient authorities read "let us."
32. Greek: "brothers."

by expressing it this way he is trying to keep faith with his own experience of the Spirit of God. His use of language of the body is entirely unique.

The term for "physical body" is not exactly what one might expect, but this is due to an unfortunate English translation. Neither the term σῶμα σαρκικόν (fleshly body) nor the term σῶμα φυσικόν (physical body) occurs; rather the term that occurs is σῶμα ψυχικόν, "ensouled body" (1 Cor 15:44), a word that can mean *natural body* but is not the most obvious term for it. Since it combines the word for soul with the term for body, it is in a sense the totality of the Platonic ensouled-body as the Hellenistic world understood it. In a Platonic system, this would only mean human bodies as we know them, with matter and soul both, i.e., corruptible bodies. Because *psyche* could be taken to mean life in the physical sense in a non-Platonic setting, it is not necessarily a problem, strange though it may look; σῶμα ψυχικόν does occur in Hellenistic literature with that meaning.[33]

However, the contrasting term, σῶμα πνευματικόν, is a complete contradiction in terms for anyone in a Platonic system, especially when contrasted with the psychic body just mentioned: "It is sown a physical body, it is raised a spiritual body. If there is a physical body, there is also a spiritual body" (1 Cor 15:44).[34]

There is no easy way to subsume this pair of statements into Platonism. What Paul is doing, however, is contrasting the Platonic view of humanity (the unredeemed, body composed of soul and flesh) with his own view of the redeemed body, one that now has been transformed by the *spirit* of God. One might say that Paul is trying to characterize his apocalyptic vision in a Hellenistic context, something like Josephus did for the speech of Eleazar ben Yair. But Paul's message only really makes sense within its Jewish, apocalyptic context. For Paul life in its most basic sense, *psychic* life is also bodily life. *Pneumatic*, spiritual life is bodily as well, though he will immediately reiterate that flesh and blood cannot inherit the kingdom of God (1 Cor 15:50). The *psychic body* is thus the ordinary body (flesh and soul); the σῶμα πνευματικόν is the ordinary body subsumed and transformed by the spirit. In short, Paul is sermonizing with an eye toward mission: he is contrasting Greek views with the new view he is promulgating.

---

33. See, e. g, Albert Dihle, ψυχικός, *TDNT* 9: 661.

34. It may be that, in this place, Paul is representing something like a very sophisticated minority opinion in Greek culture, thinking that everything, even the soul, is a kind of body—albeit a refined and indestructible one. After all, he distinguishes between the earthly body and the resurrection body. Indeed, this is a kind of *interpretatio Graeca* of Paul's analysis here. If so, he is likewise, and I think primarily, speaking out of his apocalyptic Judaism. He is entirely consistent with his Hebrew past at the same time. In any event, he acknowledges the bodily aspect of the resurrection but uses the term spirit to preserve the previous identity of those resurrected in their new perfected state. This is also the predominant view of the New Testament, except Hebrews, John, and 1 and 2 Peter, where psyche evidently refers to the physical life of persons and animals.

Even though flesh and blood cannot inherit the kingdom of God, the risen Christ is a "body of glory" (1 Cor 15:30). This new, spiritual, glorious body, which is the redeemed, resurrected body, is equivalent to Christ's body. And so the new body that God gives His faithful in the resurrection will be a *pneumatic* or *spiritual body* augmented by the *Spirit* of God. Indeed, Paul has been given a foretaste of the redeemed body because the Spirit of God already lives in him. As the end approaches, the working of the spirit will grow stronger and stronger until the final transformation.

This completely coheres with Paul's notion that the fleshly way to salvation is not through observances of times and rituals, not through Jewish rituals or gentile rituals, for that matter. Fleshly rituals are not a spiritual, transforming way to salvation. He argues that the nature of the resurrection body is different from anything we know, just as the nature of various flesh is different. Paul, in fact, leaves the issue of the nature of immortality in a peculiarly intermediate position. He affirms that those who believe will have an imperishable bodily nature but he suggests that the faithful will receive it by bodily resurrection. The body of the resurrection will not be flesh and blood. It will be a body created in a sudden change, by σύμμορφος. He knows from his visions that the process of transformation into a glorified, spiritual body has already begun. The process will be completed at the last trumpet.

The eschaton and destiny of all believers will entail a transformation that does not necessarily do away with the body but *transforms* it to a spiritual substance. Paul makes an explicit analogy with the stars, which are both spiritual and bodies at the same time. And that analogy is not merely adventitious. It links the transformation process with the passage in Dan 12:3 yet again, since Dan 12:3 describes the wise as transformed into stars. The transformed in Christ will have, in short, the same substance as the stars, which are luminous and spiritual in nature. This is, for Paul, the very fulfillment of the end of time, as promised by Dan 12:3.

As Paul connects his own conversion with his resurrection in Christ, so it is resurrection that brings the salvation of God and a return to the pristine state of humanity's glory before Adam's fall. He says this explicitly in 1 Cor 15:21: "For as by a man came death; so by a man has also come resurrection of the dead." Paul makes Adam and Christ into contrasting images of fall and salvation respectively. But Paul seems to have more than Jesus's earthly existence in mind, since he uses the term ἄνθρωπος, which can also refer to his resurrected nature: "Just as we have borne the image of the man of dust, we shall also bear the image of the man of heaven."[35] The agent that begins and is responsible for this change on earth is the Spirit. The Spirit brings the Christ that is within believers; the Spirit itself is the agent of Christ. The risen Jesus is to be experienced as a life-giving spirit

---

35. Robin Scroggs, *The Last Adam: A Study in Pauline Anthropology* (Philadelphia: Fortress, 1966), 75–114.

now, which explains how the transformation of the believer starts, and which also implies that it culminates in the apocalyptic end.[36]

In 1 Cor 15:45, Paul turns his attention to the relationship between transformation within the believer and the coming end. When speaking of the resurrection, Paul describes a reciprocal relationship between Adam and Christ: just as Adam brought death into the world so Christ, the second Adam, will bring resurrection. This depends upon interpreting Adam's divine likeness as identical to the *Glory* that the Christ had or received. Because of the first human, all humanity is brought to death; but because of Christ's divine image all will be brought to life (1 Cor 15:21–22). The first person, Adam, became only a living *soul* (ψυχὴν), whereas the last Adam, the Christ, became a life-giving *spirit* (πνεῦμα) (1 Cor 15:45). The first was of the earth and therefore earthly; the last is from heaven, therefore divine. Just as humanity has borne the outward image of the old Adam, those who inherit the kingdom will also bear the inward spiritual εἰκών of the heavenly man (1 Cor 15:47–49). Paul, however, is not so much talking about the man Jesus as he is talking about Christ's exalted nature as ἄνθρωπος. Since the imagery is so dependent upon the contrast between fallen and raised states, this passage may also imply a baptismal setting. It is also interesting that the alternation is conceived in bodily terms, not as a transmigration of souls.

The image of man is also part of the process of inward transformation for Paul. A great many of his uses of ἄνθρωπος (man) suggest that a transformation of *all* believers is his objective. For instance, Rom 6:6 says: "We know that our old self (literally our old "humanness," ἄνθρωπος=human being) was crucified with him so that the sinful body might be destroyed, and we might no longer be enslaved to sin." Or in another, equally provocative place, Paul says (2 Cor 4:16): "So we do not lose heart. Though our outer nature (ἄνθρωπος=human being) is wasting away, our inner nature is being renewed every day." In both cases, the translation has obscured that the underlying Pauline word is ἄνθρωπος, "human," used to designate the internal state of transformation within us. But this is the very term that Paul uses to designate the "son of man" in Dan 7:13.

What is so striking about Paul's vocabulary is that it eschews the Platonic self, the eternal self that returns to heaven, for a more Jewish mystical notion of resurrected body, which is a body in transformation through faith, and culminates at the end of time with an angelic body for those who are justified and lead others to wisdom. It is the first Christian attempt to make sense of Jesus's resurrection. It starts from the fact of Jesus's martyrdom and emphasizes that the self willing to undergo martyrdom is victorious over the tyrannical forces of this world. The canonical Gospels go even further in that they stress the fleshly nature of Jesus's

---

36. See James D. G. Dunn, *Jesus and the Spirit: A Study of the Religious and Charismatic Experience of Jesus and the First Christians as Reflected in the New Testament* (Philadelphia: Westminster, 1975).

resurrection body. It is their position, rather than Paul's really, that becomes standard for Christianity.

But the Gospels' literalness eventually causes a converse problem when Christianity encounters Platonism later on. Many church fathers try to make Christianity compatible with the much more understandable immortality of the soul. Immortality of the soul is a propaedeutic for everyone. Proper care and education of the soul yields immortality. That was not the lesson of Jesus's martyrdom.

These are early reactions to the good news of Jesus's resurrection. Later Christian thinkers, especially those who were at home in the intellectual milieu of Platonism, try to synthesize Paul's new vocabulary of inwardness, a new mysticism, built on the apocalyptic vision of the end of time with the notion of the immortal soul.[37] Other than Paul himself, the exceptions to this new enterprise are few—mainly Justin, Athenagoras, and Tertullian. With the exception of these three church fathers, the dominant intellectual history of the West tries to combine the triumph with Christ with the immortality of the soul, suggesting that we leave our outward state behind to reclaim our soul's natural state of immortality. But Paul, being an apocalypticist with a readiness to follow Christ's martyrdom, knows the necessity of martyrdom and its transformative nature. Paul connects the inward state with the outward state and says they are both transformed by God. The inward state is not necessarily causing the outward condition of the world, nor is the outward condition of the world causing the inward state. Rather, both are being transformed by God's plan and they make us as "selves" the best that we can be: by being made angels by our trials on earth.[38]

---

37. See Walter Wink, *The Human Being: Jesus and the Enigma of the Son of Man* (Minneapolis: Fortress, 2002), 207–11.

38. A version of this essay will appear in a forthcoming issue of *Studia Theological*.

"My Name is Legion": Spirit Possession and Exorcism in Roman Palestine

Richard A. Horsley

Introduction: Problematic Previous Approaches to Possession

Demon possession and Jesus's exorcisms prove especially difficult when attempting to understand ancient people's religious experiences. Modern western interpreters of Jesus, particularly those of a more liberal orientation, have been skittish about demon possession and exorcism, for such bizarre phenomena did not appear to be comprehensible in modern scientific terms. Biblical scholars therefore classified Jesus's actions in Gospel stories that did not conform with modern rational and natural criteria as miracles or magic, concepts foreign to the Gospel sources.

In order to "explain" (or "explain away") spirit-possession among ancient Galileans and Judeans, modern interpreters have most often used *psychological* explanations. They diagnosed cases of possession by an "unclean spirit" as hysteria, neurosis, or schizophrenia.[1] More recently, ancient spirit possession has been diagnosed in more sophisticated terms as multiple personality disorder.[2] Following that lead, recent interpreters of Jesus's exorcisms explain demon-possession in terms of the possessed person's projection of repressed emotions and inner conflicts onto an outside "unclean spirit."[3] This approach, however, projects the assumption of a modern western concept of the self as (normally) an inte-

---

1. But one must ask Gospel interpreters, as medical anthropologists finally asked themselves, "what, besides a protective shield, do we gain from calling . . . an individual possessed by a spirit a paranoid, a neurotic, or an hysteric?" See Vincent Crapanzano, "Introduction," in *Case Studies in Spirit* Possession (New York: Wiley and Sons, 1977), 14.

2. Felicitas D. Goodman, *How About Demons? Possession and Exorcism in the Modern World* (Bloomington: Indiana University Press, 1988), 15–23.

3. Stephan L. Davies, *Jesus the Healer: Possession, Trance, and the Origins of Christianity* (New York: Continuum, 1995), 86–93; John Dominic Crossan, *Jesus: A Revolutionary Biography* (San Francisco: Harper-San Francisco, 1994).

grated person, for whom multiple forces and their conflicts reside internally. The ancients' belief that a person was possessed, in contrast, assumed the opposite of an integrated person: it assumes that a person is possessed by an outside force. Instead of "projection," therefore, the Gospel sources portray not an "introjection" but an invasion of alien forces into certain persons, who become the "hosts" of the "unclean spirits."

A modern western psychological approach simply does not take indigenous cultural beliefs and representations seriously. The result is that interpreters of Gospel episodes not only anachronistically isolate the person experiencing an invasion by outside forces but also pathologize the experience of possession. Even the explanation of spirit-possession as an "altered state of consciousness" comes close to the modern presumption of the separate and normally "integrated" self.[4] Just as people's consciousness depends on their culture, so presumably would an "altered state of consciousness" depend on the same culture. In short, it is highly unlikely that the culture in which Jesus operated shared the modern western assumption of an independent integrated self.

Finally, while modern interpreters tend to understand religious experience as individual and personal, for ancient Judeans and Galileans, including those who were involved in the various Jesus movements, religious experience was inseparable from political-economic experiences. Personal religious experience, moreover, was embedded in collective or corporate experience as well. At the very least, the strength of our interpretations depends on our recognition that such views imbue the texts that we are reading. Even more, by setting aside our cultural biases, we may actually gain fuller insight into the historical experiences of possession in ancient Palestine. The working assumptions for this paper are therefore that religious experience is not separate from political-economic experience and that personal experience is embedded in collective or corporate experience as well. On the basis of these two assumptions, we can attempt to appreciate other people's personal and collective social-religious experience as it is expressed in and shaped by texts and other media, in contrast to what is often done in biblical studies, which is to translate other people's experience into our own terms.

MEDICAL ANTHROPOLOGY: THE SOCIAL AND POLITICAL MEANING OF ILLNESS AND HEALING

The recent development of critical medical anthropology may offer a far more appropriate approach to spirit possession and exorcism as portrayed in the Gospels. Medical anthropology developed in response to the spread of western medicine to other, "undeveloped" countries, especially after World War II. From

---

4. Goodman, *How About Demons?* 5–6; Crossan, *Jesus*, 87–88; John J. Pilch, "Altered States of Consciousness: A 'Kitbashed' Model," *BTB* 26 (1996): 33–38.

the outset it was critical of the ethnocentrism and reductionism of western bio-medicine. This emphasis in the discipline may also then supply a corrective to the field of New Testament studies, which has been relatively uncritical of its own ethnocentrism.

"Meaning-centered" medical anthropology recognizes that illness is culturally constructed. This recognition requires some conceptual clarification vis-à-vis a relatively narrow, reductionist western medicine. The latter uses the term "*disease* [to] refer to a malfunctioning of biological and/or psychological processes," which it then attempts to diagnose and *cure*.[5] Medical anthropologists think more broadly in terms of *illness*, as the psychosocial experience of and cultural meaning attributed to a particular disease. As Arthur Kleinman explains:

> Illness includes secondary personal and social responses to a primary malfunctioning . . . , processes of attention, perception, affective response, cognition, and valuation, . . . communication and interpersonal interaction, particularly within the context of the family and social network.[6]

While "disease" requires a "cure," the response that corresponds to *illness* is *healing*. Both the diagnosis of illness and the healing appropriate to it are culturally constructed.

"Critical" medical anthropologists expand the scope of their investigation of influences on illness and healing to include historical, social structural, political, and economic forces. Realizing that these factors generally go unattended, they have begun to examine the lasting effects of colonialism, expanding capitalist enterprises, and a globalizing economic system. They attempt to understand "health issues in light of the larger political and economic forces that pattern interpersonal relationships, shape social behavior, generate social meanings, and condition collective experience."[7] Cultures are not simply systems of meaning that orient humans to one another and their world. They are also "webs of mystification" that disguise political and economic realities, particularly the power-relations that determine sickness and the possibility of healing.[8] Certain representations of illness may well be "misrepresentations" that serve the interests of the elites who control cultural production. Many of these "critical" anthropologists also point out, with Foucault, that "where there is power, there is [also] resistance," and with

5. Arthur Kleinman, *Patients and Healers in the Context of Culture* (Berkeley and Los Angeles: University of California Press, 1980), 72.

6. Ibid.

7. Merrill Singer, "Reinventing Medical Anthropology: Toward a Critical Realignment," *Social Science and Medicine* 30 (1990): 179–87, 181.

8. Roger M. Keesing, "Models, 'Folk' and 'Cultural,'" in *Cultural Models in Language and Thought* (ed. Dorothy Holland and Naomi Quinn; Cambridge: Cambridge University Press, 1987): 369–95.

James C. Scott, that subordinated people such as peasants have traditionally honed certain "arts of resistance" that may operate in culturally disguised forms.[9]

This critical perspective and agenda offer a more adequate approach to the spirit possession that Jesus encountered. Many episodes in the Gospel sources implicitly if not explicitly indicate that political-economic forces have decisively impacted the illnesses among the people. If we want to understand spirit-possession and exorcism in a given society, therefore, then far from reducing the portrayal from the society itself into the concepts of modern bio-medicine or psychology, we must investigate the portrayal of spirit possession and exorcism in its own cultural context.

FRANTZ FANON, SPIRIT POSSESSION, AND EXORCISM AMONG AFRICAN PEOPLES

Well before the emergence of critical medical anthropology, Frantz Fanon, Paris-trained psychiatrist and director of a mental hospital in Algeria during the anti-colonial struggle against French rule in the 1960s, had recognized and critically analyzed the effects of colonial domination on spirit possession. From his clinical practice he found spirit possession rampant in Algeria in the early 1960s. He recognized not only that "where there is power there is resistance," but also that overwhelming power generated efforts among the dominated that were both self-defensively creative and debilitatingly mystifying.[10]

Fanon's observations are relevant to the period of Roman conquest and the pressures of Roman rule that seriously impacted Galilean and Judean society at the time of Jesus. On the basis of his work, one can suggest that this domination may well have produced a "web of mystification" that disguised the concrete power relations and determined the possibility and manner of healing. In addition, I will draw on comparisons with more accessible information from other cultures in order to assist in partially overcoming the fragmentary nature of the information on spirit possession in ancient Palestine.[11]

---

9. Michel Foucault, *The History of Sexuality, Vol. 1: An Introduction* (trans. Robert Hurley; New York: Vintage 1978): 95–96; and earlier, Frantz Fanon, *The Wretched of the Earth* (New York: Grove Press, 1968 [1963]); James C. Scott, *Domination and the Arts of Resistance* (New Haven, Conn.: Yale University Press, 1990).

10. Fanon, *The Wretched of the Earth*. Among New Testament scholars, Paul Hollenbach ("Jesus, Demoniacs, and Public Authorities: A Socio-Historical Study," *JAAR* 99 [1981]: 567–88) boldly pioneered the exploration of the social-psychological and ideological pertinence of Fanon's analysis. It remains to explore the political-historical relevance of Fanon; see some first steps in Richard A. Horsley, *Hearing the Whole Story: The Politics of Plot in Mark's Gospel* [Louisville, Ky.: Westminster John Knox, 2001], chapter 6.

11. Davies, *Jesus the Healer*. And perhaps such information from other peoples in other times will help our colleagues who previously have simply scoffed at the suggestion that the demon possession addressed by Jesus could have been related to Roman domination of Palestine.

This comparative material derives from studies of a number of African peoples who, before and after European incursions, represented strangers as indigenous aspects of their own culture in various rites in which the strangers' spirits play a role.[12] Swahili peoples, for example, took grief and illness as indications that spirits of strangers or *pepo* wished to embody themselves in the ill people and to demand sacrifices and worship.[13] They named the *pepo* with the Arabic word *sheitani*, "Satan." Possessed persons were understood as hosting, variously, the spirits of the Arabs or the spirits of the people of Kilimanjaro (*Kilima*) or those of Europeans (*Kizungu*).[14] Because these spirits were not necessarily understood as threatening, it would be inappropriate to interpret such possession by alien spirits in western psychological terms simply as "identification with the aggressor."[15]

However, where the alien spirits are experienced as threatening, the possession appears to be more defensive or self-protective. In the early-twentieth century, many of the Kamba people were possessed by *Kijesu*, as a consequence of the Christian mission. Kramer offers this description of the scene:

> No sooner did these people catch a glimpse of a red fez, or a European, than they fell to the ground, groaning and moaning and writhing convulsively, or they felt an irresistible desire to shake everyone by the hand. They sang of *vwana jesu*, the Lord Jesus, and God who comes to earth to save humanity, slashed themselves with knives without bleeding, and burned themselves with torches without suffering any harm ... or tried to protect themselves from such attacks by huddling under blankets and avoiding the sight of anything that triggered them.[16]

The alternative to conversion was possession by Jesus. *Kijesu*, it seems, was not so much the spirit of Jesus as of the broader Christian mission, the whole alien culture that threatened the traditional way of life. This massive invasion by strangers was not easily manageable in a regular exorcism cult.

The *zar* cult in Sudan offers an example of how a people embedded in local village communities dealt with the cumulative effect of domination by outside forces. The indigenous African people in the Sudan were dealing with the enduring results first of the conversion of its males to Islam and of influence by Arabic culture, then with the successive foreign influences from Ethiopia, the incursion of the British military, and the more recent influence of American medical and development initiatives. The women continued to cultivate traditional African culture after the men became Muslim, while they also developed the *zar* cult in

---

12. Fritz W. Kramer, *The Red Fez: Art and Spirit Possession in Africa* (trans. Malcom Green; New York: Verso, 1993), chapters 1–2, esp. pp. 71–72.

13. Ibid., 97.

14. Ibid., 99.

15. Cf.. John Domic Crossan, *The Historical Jesus: The Life of a Mediterranean Jewish Peasant* (San Francisco: HarperCollins, 1991), 316–18.

16. Kramer, *The Red Fez*, 100.

which they entertained possession by alien spirits in order then to exorcise them. The various names of the *zayran* reflect the successive outside forces that came to dominate their lives as they were met by the women's resistance in village society, in the guise of accommodation, negotiation, and mollification.[17]

The list of the many hostile *zayran* included the *Bashawat*, the spirits of the Pashas and Turkish conquerors, and European spirits such as "Lord Cromer," who led the British military expedition through Sudan.[18] The *Khawajat* were light-skinned spirits of the Europeans and other Westerners, alternatively referred to as *nasarin*, Nazarenes (Christians). These spirits demanded "clean" Western foods, such as bottled beverages, white bread, and tinned meats, that represented the power of the Western conquerors. Another aspect of the power of these spirits was their immeasurable wealth. One standard ritual dealing with these spirits was that of *mayz*, "mess." A long banquet table with a tablecloth and European style metal cutlery was decked out with foods such as tea biscuits, Danish cheese, olives, tinned sausages and fish, cherries, oranges, bananas, jam, "towst" (French bread), bottled beer, sherry, Pepsi, and single shot vials of whisky, brandy or other liquor. Participants in the ritual danced around the table, swaggering, speaking "English" and pretending to drink from the bottles and otherwise acting out their impressions of Europeans. A typical exchange, in Arabic, between two "Europeans" swaggering around arm in arm: "C'mon, let's go to Church." "Naa, let's go to the bar." Particularly striking among the Western spirits was "Dona Bey," an American doctor and big game hunter who put away quantities of whisky and beer and toted a huge elephant gun. Fairly clearly he embodied Western technological overkill, destroying what he hunted, and the new dominion of medical science, all framed in licentious indulgence.[19]

The peoples who had already established cults of possession could deal with the impact of European colonialism by expanding their range of alien spirits and adapting their already-existing ceremonies of diagnosis, negotiation, and exorcism.[20] For other, largely homogenous peoples less acquainted with possession by alien spirits, however, the sudden European invasion and colonization was far more traumatic. Their possession by spirits that represented Western influences was more complete. In Tonga, for example, possessed women danced while washing compulsively with scented soaps and "drank soapy water in order to make the insides of their bodies clean and sweet-smelling."[21]

European invasion and colonization also made a sudden impact on homogenous peoples with centralized political authority, such as the Zulu. The rapid

17. Janice Boddy, *Wombs and Alien Spirits: Women, Men, and the Zar Cult in Northern Sudan* (Madison, Wisc.: University of Wisconsin Press, 1989), 269–70.

18. Ibid., 291–94.

19. Ibid., 289–90.

20. Kramer, *Red Fez*, 116–17.

21. Ibid., 118–22.

spread of the impact of mining operations, combined with the mixture of migrant workers from different peoples, all placed under the control of overwhelming European power, accelerated the disintegration of traditional social forms. A bewildering array of previously unknown alien spirits under the control of sorcerers suddenly attacked people who would become possessed, by (spirits of) Sothos, Indians, and Europeans. The possessed would sob and rage uncontrollably, run back and forth in a daze, tear clothes off their bodies, or try to kill themselves. "There was no appeasing these raving hordes of spirits, let alone domesticating them as helpful spirits."[22] The possession of these people displayed the combination of their estrangement from their own culture and their vulnerability to the foreign powers.

In desperate attempts to marshal their traditional cultural resources against the invasive spirits, traditional Zulu healers, especially the *izangoma*, the possessed mediums of their ancestors, attempted exorcism.[23] To reinforce the exorcism of alien spirits the *izangoma* "inoculated" their subjects with "soldiers," *amabutho*, to defend them against further attack.[24] The "soldiers" spoke through their hosts in foreign languages, such as English or railroad sounds. The hosts of the "soldiers" used alien objects such as machine oil or white men's hair to symbolize their protective new identity.[25] In these fascinating cases the healers made positive use of less threatening alien powers in order to resist and ward off the greater alien powers that were destroying their traditional culture and identity.

In many of the traditional possession cults that expanded their inventory of alien spirits to negotiate with the newly invasive European forces, the primary participants were women and those who had little direct political influence. However, as the invasive European colonization intensified, men began organizing possession dances as well. One of the most prominent of these was the *beni ngoma* ("band-dance") that began in the 1890s, spread widely, and continued through the 1920s. Such dances emphasized colonial attire—at first British and German military uniforms, and later the civilian dress and fancy accoutrements of colonial officials, with their hair neatly groomed and parted. Possessed participants in the *hauka* cult that spread in West Africa in the 1920s imitated Islamic authority figures, French and British colonial officers, and the flag, uniforms, and drill formations of the British army.[26]

More political in their implications and eventual effects were the charismatic possession cults led by prophets. These cults created a wider community of peoples struggling against the effects of colonial invasion and repression. They moved

22. Ibid., 125.
23. Ibid., 125.
24. Bengt G. M. Sundkler, *Bantu Prophets in South Africa* (London: Oxford University Press, 1961), 248–49.
25. Kramer, *The Red Fez*, 126.
26. Ibid., 134–35.

from local focus and diverging interests to more common interests over against the colonizing forces. In an unprecedented move, these charismatic movements claimed exclusive and unlimited authority, an idea they appropriated from and used against the colonizing power and/or Christian mission. Like the latter, these African prophetic movements demanded selfless devotion to a broader cause and unity. Not by accident many of these prophetic movements prepared the way for and were the precursors of more politically oriented anti-colonial movements.

ROMAN EMPEROR CULT IN GREEK CITIES

African peoples were not the only ones to deal with the impact of alien forces, particularly imperial domination, by incorporating spiritual powers into their culture. Further, one should not imagine, in colonialist fashion, that supposedly "uncivilized" peoples were the only ones to experience spirit possession, while "advanced" civilizations were more fully "rational." The ancient Greek cities subjected by the Roman Empire dealt with Roman power by incorporating the divinized emperor into their traditional temples, festivals, and pantheons.[27] The incorporation of alien forces is parallel and similar in significant ways to the African cases, and even the forms were somewhat parallel.

In contrast to the relatively egalitarian African peoples with limited division of labor, the ancient Greek cities were sharply divided, with the vast majority of peasants and urban poor dominated by a tiny proportion of wealthy elite who controlled the land and headed the centralized political-economic structures and central cultural-religious institutions. Like other ancient imperial regimes, the Romans made alliances with the elites of subjected cities. Starting within a decade of the victory of "Augustus" at the battle of Actium, the elites of Greek cities took the initiative in adding the emperor to the pantheon of their respective religious institutions. In traditional temples they erected statues of Caesar alongside the statues of the gods to whom the temples were dedicated. They installed shrines of the emperor in between the temples of the city gods that surrounded the public space of the city centers (*agora*), and they dedicated traditional festivals and games to the emperor and renamed them in his honor. As a result of all these steps, the presence of the emperor came to pervade public space—although the emperor never set foot in any of those cities. The magnates of the Greek cities also restructured the annual cultural calendar and set up inscriptions and monuments honoring Caesar as the savior of who had established peace and security for the world.

---

27. For recent studies delineating how Roman imperial power took religious-political form, see the selections from the work of Paul Zanker and Simon Price in Richard A. Horsley, ed., *Paul and Empire: Religion and Power in Roman Imperial Society* (Harrisburg, Pa.: Trinity Press International, 1997), chapters 3 and 4.

The visible and ritual presence of imperial power thus became prominent in public space and even structured the annual rhythm of public life. Not only was imperial power incorporated into the traditional religion of Greek cities, but, indeed, it became the most important among the many powers that impacted or determined their common life and it grew to be the focus of the cities' religions. However, since we have virtually no sources for ordinary people in antiquity, we have no idea of what they thought about the incorporation of imperial power into the traditional city religion. We have no idea if they, like their superiors, were possessed by the presence of the emperor.

RESPONSES TO IMPERIAL POWER IN ROMAN JUDEA

Judeans and Galileans also incorporated alien imperial powers into their culture. This was done in very different ways, though, by the ruling priestly aristocracy who controlled the Temple, on the one hand, and the scribal circles who served as their retainers, on the other. The high priests, who owed their position of power and privilege to their imperial overlords, honored the emperor and the imperial city, Roma, in their Temple sacrifices and other representations. Under Herod the Great, for example, an imperial Roman eagle was erected over the main gate of the Temple in Jerusalem.

In contrast, scribal circles that produced Judean literature in the late Second Temple period responded in two ways: on the one hand, they appropriated imperial schemes into their representation of the ultimate sovereignty of the God of Israel, while, on the other, they represented Hellenistic and Roman imperial power as hostile to and destructive of their common life. The appropriation of imperial views is not unexpected given that the scribes served as retainers to the priestly aristocracy and, therefore, represented the interests of their patrons to a considerable degree. Yet as those responsible for cultivation of Israelite cultural tradition, they had also developed a sense of their own authority directly under the God of Israel, and not derivative from the high priesthood. Thus, in the Judean literature that we know as biblical, scribes represented God as an ancient Near Eastern king in the heavens attended by the "sons of God." These *bene-'elohim* appear to have been the gods of the surrounding foreign kingdoms and empires incorporated into the Israelite culture, similar to the spirits of foreigners among African peoples, but more systematically and transcendently conceptualized. At the same time, YHWH himself held exclusive power and authority over Israel and wielded his transcendent spiritual power in a fairly direct way for the deliverance and protection of Israel. "Angels" were just that, messengers, and there was no Satan.

However, in apocalyptic literature and Qumran texts of the later Second Temple period under the rule of the Hellenistic and Roman empires, representation of God and the heavenly forces that rule earthly affairs changed significantly. "The Book of Watchers," the earliest text of Enoch literature (*1 En.* 1–36), for example, represented God as an imperial king far removed from the day-to-day workings of life, dealing with his subjects only through an elaborate imperial court with multiple ranks and layers of (divine) imperial officers, some of whom rebelled against the divine order. In the myth of "the Watchers," the heavenly Watchers, having been attracted by the beautiful daughters of men, descend to earth and conceive great giants with them (*1 En.* 6–11). It is clear from the imagery in the ensuing lines that this was an explanation for, as well as a representation of, the devastating effect of the Hellenistic imperial conquests and demand for tribute from subject peoples:

> They were devouring the labor of all the sons of men, and men were not able to supply them. And the giants conspired to kill men and to devour them (*1 En.* 7:3). 'Asael [a chieftan of the Watchers] taught men to make swords of iron and weapons and shields and breastplates and every instrument of war (8:1).[28]

The most striking Judean scribal-priestly attempt to come to grips with the impact of imperial domination was the elaborate dualism of spirits in the Qumran *Community Rule* and the *War Rule*. In contrast to the manifold and particularistic spirits and demons among African peoples, the *Community Rule* articulated a generalized grand scheme of two dominant divine spirits that control human affairs. Spiritual dualism was their explanation as well as symbolization of how historical developments could seem so utterly "out of control" of God, enabling them to believe that God was still ultimately in charge and would (imminently) act against the Angel of Darkness. The members of the priestly and scribal community at Qumran understood themselves as individually and collectively possessed and guided by the Spirit of Truth/Light, while attacked and tempted by the Spirit of Darkness (1QS 3–5). Thanks to the strict discipline and solidarity of their covenant community, including ritual curses against the forces of Darkness, they warded off potential possession by the spirits of Darkness, and thus had no need for exorcism. Living under the guidance of the Angel of Truth, they anticipated that the God of Israel would soon act to resolve the extreme crisis of historical life by terminating the rule/power of the Angel of Darkness.

When such texts are read with a historical sensitivity to the way in which religious life was embedded in ancient politics, the political implications of dualism become clearer. The domination of life by the Spirit of Darkness and the Spirit of Light included the struggle of the Qumran community against Roman imperial forces. The *War Rule* (1QM) explicitly articulates one example of this struggle. The powerful operation of the spiritual army of Belial (the Spirit of Darkness) is the explanation for how the *Kittim*, the code name for the Romans, could wield such overwhelming domination.

---

28. Translation from George W. E. Nickelsburg and James C. VanderKam, *1 Enoch: A New Translation Based on the Hermeneia Commentary* (Minneapolis: Fortress, 2004).

In anticipation of God's action to deliver a people under attack by defeating the Angel of Darkness and its spirits, the Qumranites were actively preparing to engage in battle against the *Kittim*, when the time came for the final war between the Spirit of Darkness and the Spirit of Light. They rehearsed ritual warfare against the *Kittim*, ostensibly drawing on Israelite holy-war ideology, marching in designated companies with trumpets and banners, clearly as a counterpart of the threatening imperial armies of the Romans (1QM 1:3–4, 13–14; 17:5–8; 18:4– 5). In their ritual military drills, the Qumran community resembled some of the possession cults among African peoples in the early-twentieth century. In their possession by the Spirit of Light, which protected them from the Prince of Darkness, they resembled in particular the Zulu people whose alien spirits had been exorcized and replaced by "soldiers." Possession by protective spirits enabled both the Zulus and the Qumranites to hold their own against imperial domination that threatened destruction of their traditional way of life—a threat that was also experienced in the form of spirits, that is, spirits that were invasively destructive.

The above survey of African peoples, ancient Greek cities, and Judean scribal circles suggests that possession by spirits is intertwined with invasion of alien forces, particularly imperial conquest and domination. Belief in and possession by foreign spirits is a principal way that subordinated peoples deal with the invasive effects that outside forces far beyond their own control and comprehension have on their lives.

Spirit Possession and Exorcism in the Gospel of Mark

Finally, this essay turns to an analysis of demon possession in Mark, with a special consideration of the Beelzebul controversy. Adapting a critical medical anthropological approach to the spirit possession among Galileans, Judeans, and others in ancient Palestine portrayed in the Gospels means that we can no longer focus narrowly on individual stories isolated from their broader socio-literary context. Episodes of spirit possession and exorcism were integral components of Mark's overall story. As components of Mark's Gospel, episodes about spirit possession give us access not to particular cases of spirit possession, but to how spirit possession was constructed in Galilean and Judean culture.[29]

Markan accounts of Jesus's mission display remarkable "historical verisimilitude" in their portrayal of life in Roman Palestine as it is portrayed in contemporary Judean texts.[30] Both depict the same basic conflict between the Roman, Herodian, and high priestly rulers, on the one hand, and the Judean and

---

29. See further Horsley, *Hearing the Whole Story*, 136–48.

30. For more detail, see Richard A. Horsley, *Galilee: History, Politics, People* (Valley Forge, Pa.: Trinity Press International, 1995); and idem, *Archaeology, History, and Society in Galilee: The Social Context of Jesus and the Rabbis* (Valley Forge, Pa.: Trinity Press International, 1996).

Galilean peasants on the other. In Judean and Galilean society, the fundamental social forms were family and village community. The village "assemblies" (i.e., *synagogai* in Greek, *knesset* in Aramaic) were forms of self-governance and the expression of local cooperation of the semi-independent local communities. Under the economic pressures of taxation by multiple layers of rulers (Roman, Herodian, and high priestly), these village communities were beginning to disintegrate, their constituent families falling into debt, with varying degrees of hunger and malnutrition. Given this context, it is surely significant that in the Lord's Prayer the appeal for the Kingdom of God is made concrete in the petitions for "daily bread" and "cancellation of debts."

In connection with the prominence of illnesses and spirit possession among the people with whom Jesus interacts, one should pay more attention to the collective social trauma that Galileans in particular may have undergone in the repeated Roman conquest and reconquest of the area than has been the case in much of earlier scholarship on these phenomena. The Romans had carried out major massacres in Magdala in 53–52 B.C.E. and in the villages such as Nazareth, around Sepphoris, in 4 B.C.E. (*A.J.*, 14.119–120; 17.288–289). Galileans would have been especially familiar with the scorched-earth tactics of the Roman legions, as they devastated villages, slaughtered and enslaved the inhabitants, and crucified ostensible rebel leaders in order to terrorize the populace.[31]

A few key aspects of Galilean and Judean culture in the first century also stand out in ancient Judean texts. The cultural ideal, particularly in popular Israelite tradition, was that the people be independent of foreign rule, free to live directly under the rule of their God, who had liberated them from slavery under Pharaoh in Egypt and given them the Mosaic covenantal as a guide for their independent political-economic life. Realization of the ideal remained quite elusive as Israelite peoples had been subject to one empire after another for centuries, and longed for the time in the future when the debilitating effects of oppressive rule would be overcome and the people would be personally and collectively whole. Not surprisingly they remembered the stories of Moses, the original prophet of liberation, through whom God had wrought acts of power for the people, and stories of Elijah, whose program of renewal of Israel had included healings and multiplication of food for a suffering people (1 Kgs 17).

Galilean and Judean culture also had explanations for any personal and collective malaise, the debilitating effects of their situation. Perhaps the most prominent was that illness and misfortune were divine punishment for not having kept the covenantal commandments—the result of themselves or their ancestors having "sinned." This explanation was rooted in the sanctioning mechanism of the Deuteronomic covenant, in which the people called down curses on

---

31. Susan P. Mattern, *Rome and the Enemy: Imperial Strategy in the Principate* (Berkeley and Los Angeles: University of California Press, 1999).

themselves and their children if they failed to keep the provisions of the covenant (Deut 27–28).

The overall plot of Mark's Gospel story presents the renewal of Israel over against the Roman and Jerusalem rulers. The first public action Jesus takes, after his general announcement that the kingdom of God is at hand and calling of four disciples, is an exorcism in the midst of the village assembly in Capernaum.[32] In contrast to the Zar cult in northern Sudan, the setting of Jesus's action is not a gathering set up for the explicit purpose of exorcism, but the regular assembly of villagers for matters of self-governance and prayers. If ancient Galileans and nearby peoples had a standard procedure or special "cult" for exorcizing demons, we have no evidence for it, although there were evidently other exorcists about. Comparable to the gatherings specifically for purposes of exorcism in the Zar cult, it is the presence of the exorcist, Jesus, in the midst of the village gathering that seems to have provoked the "unclean spirit" to burst forward and cry out, "What have you to do with us, Jesus of Nazareth? Have you come to destroy us? I know who you are, the Holy One of God" (Mark 1:24). The demon recognizes Jesus as the agent with divine power to destroy himself and other "unclean spirits."

With the presence of the exorcist and the reaction of the "unclean spirit," a decisive, violent battle has been engaged for the control of the possessed person. This episode does not use the usual term for exorcism ("cast out," ἐκβάλλειν). The key term ἐπιτιμᾶν—distinctive among Mark's exorcism episodes and never used in other Hellenistic exorcism stories—is the Greek equivalent of the Hebrew term גער used in Psalms and late Hebrew prophecy.[33] The term signifies something far stronger than a "rebuke" (NRSV), something more like "vanquish" or "destroy." Certain psalms appealed to God as a divine Warrior coming in judgment to "destroy," "root out," or "vanquish" foreign nations or imperial regimes who conquer and take spoil from Israel (e.g., Pss 9:6; 68:31; 78:6; 80:16). A late prophetic text even uses the term with reference to Satan: "The LORD subject you (גער/ἐπιτιμᾶν) O Satan!" (Zech 3:2). In Dead Sea Scroll literature, גער is used for Abram's or God's subjection of evil spirits (1QGA) and more ominously with reference to the struggle between God and Belial (i.e., Prince of Darkness, Satan). Most pertinent to the exorcism in Mark's story is a passage in the War Scroll (supplemented from 4Q491):

> During all the mysteries of his [Belial's] malevolence he has not made us stray from Thy covenant; Thou has driven his spirits [of destruction] far from [us] (גער). Thou hast preserved the soul of Thy redeemed [when the men] of his dominion [acted wickedly].

---

32. Horsley, *Hearing the Whole Story*, 137–38.
33. See further, Howard Clark Kee, "The Terminology of Mark's Exorcism Stories," *NTS* 14 (1968): 232–46.

Judging from this use of language, therefore, we must conclude that in this Markan episode the "unclean spirit," who is plural or one among many, is understood as a demonic force that has invaded and taken possession of a villager in a way that has been destructive of the common life. That threat to communal good is why Jesus is portrayed as a figure endowed with the "power/authority" to aid the people by subjecting the spirit; in the process, the kingdom of God is established and God's people delivered and renewed.

The Beelzebul discourses, with parallel yet different versions in Mark and Q (Mark 3:22–27; Luke 11:14–23; Matt 12:22–30), offer a programmatic statement of what is happening in Jesus's exorcisms. The pattern of the story indicates that both the scribes from Jerusalem and Jesus the rustic Galilean prophet understand demon possession and Jesus's exorcism not as isolated ad hoc cases, but as related battles in a wider war that has been engaged between spiritual forces. The Jerusalem scribes accuse Jesus of casting out demons by the Beelzebul, the prince of demons. Beelzebul, which means something like "Baal, the Prince," is clearly a carryover from the ancient Canaanite Baal, Lord Storm, which had long been vilified by the Hebrew prophets and then demonized by representatives of the Jerusalem temple. As in the European witch hunts, representatives of the ruling political-religious institutions charge that popular healers are themselves possessed and drawing on powers that, since not officially sanctioned, are therefore demonic (not just pagan).[34] It seems unlikely that scribal retainers experienced spirit possession. Yet they not only recognized the reality of demons, but also believed in a leader or ruler of the demonic forces—at least enough to charge Jesus with being possessed by him.

Jesus's response to the charge indicates that Galileans and others at the popular level, at least in the Jesus-movement associated with Mark's Gospel, also understood spirit-possession as more than isolated ad hoc cases. It is not difficult to unpack the culturally coded aspects implicit in Jesus's response. That he had been performing a number of exorcisms indicates that demon possession was widespread. The demons that possessed people were not freelance operators, but wide-ranging forces that were invading and controlling people's lives, and whose ruler was Satan. The struggle between Satan's forces and the divine power operative through Jesus, moreover, was understood in a way similar to the opposition of Spirits at Qumran, although in a more popular and less intellectually systematic way. Satan's forces were locked into a struggle apparently with the power/Spirit of God. This struggle was so intense that it was absurd to imagine that Satan's "kingdom" or "house"—two fundamental metaphors of political control—could be divided against itself. This coded story suggests that prior to Jesus's

---

34. See Richard A. Horsley, "Who Were the Witches? The Social Role of the Accused in the European Witch Trials," *Journal of Interdisciplinary History* 9 (1979): 689–715; idem, "Further Reflections on Witchcraft and European Folk Religion," *HR* 19 (1979): 71–95.

mission, the struggle against the demons had evidently not been going well. The "Strong Man" had been too powerful, able to resist efforts to "take back" what he had taken over, that is people and/or people's lives. However, the exorcisms through which Jesus reclaimed the goods seized by Satan constituted evidence that the Strong Man had been tied up and his power taken away, evidently by God (or by Jesus). That reversal provided the basis for the climactic statement in the parallel Beelzebul discourse in Q: "If by the finger of God I cast out demons, the kingdom of God has come upon you." (Q/Luke 11:20). As in the Qumran community, so in the Beelzebul discourse, what is happening in people's "earthly" (personal-social) lives is closely interrelated with, indeed determined by, a decisive struggle between spiritual powers at a transcendent "heavenly" level.

In the Q version of the Beelzebul discourse, Jesus declares that his exorcisms are effected "by the finger of God," thus indicating that they constitute a new exodus from foreign rule.[35] Such an understanding suggests that Jesus's exorcisms as manifestations of the kingdom of God entail the end of Roman rule. In an analogous image in the Markan version, Jesus's exorcisms indicate that the Strong Man has been bound and also imply the end of any political rule dependent on the demonic forces. The next exorcism episode in Mark's Gospel story dramatizes this connection—the encounter with the Gadarene demoniac (Mark 5:1–20).

Socially and politically, the most revealing episode of spirit-possession in Mark is that of Gadarene (or Gerasene) demoniac.[36] The man possessed by an unclean spirit had become extremely violent, attacking others and even injuring himself. Accordingly, the village community in which he lived had tried every conceivable means to control his violent outbursts.

No one could restrain him anymore, even with a chain; for he had often been restrained with shackles and chains, but he wrenched apart the chains and broke the shackles in pieces; and no one had the strength to subdue him. Night and day among the tombs and on the mountains he was always howling and bruising himself with stones. (5:3–5).

As in the Zar cult in the Sudan, a key step in the exorcism by which the spirit is separated from the host is the identification of the spirit by the intervention of the exorcist. Correspondingly, Mark's Jesus asks, "What is your name?"; a reply follows, "My name is Legion" (v. 9). In the standard, older interpretation and translation of this Latin loan word as merely meaning "many," the implications of the name are obscured. However, the ancient hearers of the Gospel, painfully aware of how they had been subjected by Roman military forces, would have recognized the identity of the demon immediately as "Roman Legion," i.e., a "battalion" of Roman troops who were known to have wrought extreme violence

---

35. See Exod 8:19 and the Egyptian magicians declaration that Moses's miracles are the work of the "finger of God."

36. The following discussion is based on Horsley, *Hearing the Whole Story*, 140–41.

against subjected peoples such as themselves. Other language in the episode confirms that the identity of the demon is Roman troops: the "company" "charges" down the slope into the Sea (suggesting Mediterranean Sea, not Galilean lake). In that "charge" down the bank, moreover, "Legion" also self-destructs in the Sea from whence it came into the country; the "Roman army" implodes, as it were, reminiscent of the destruction in the Sea of the Egyptian armies pursuing the escaping Israelites. Further, the texts echoes Daniel's mythic vision in which a succession of empires described as demonic sea monsters—like those in ancient Near Eastern mythology—rise up from the waters and wreak violence and suffering upon God's people. Mark's Jesus sends these demonic powers back into the chaos from which they mythologically originated.

The identity of the demon that causes such violence by a village member against the rest of the community has been revealed. But the story is not over, and the next step reveals yet another important dimension of demon possession in Roman Palestine. The other people in the village, far from celebrating what has happened, cannot get Jesus out of their area quickly enough; they cannot face what has just been revealed. The complexity of this episode forces us to recognize that belief in and possession by spirits/demons is a self-protective mechanism. This self-protection, however, comes at the price of mystifying the concrete power relations. The belief that their misfortunes and malaise were caused by demons, and not the Romans or their own sins, enabled the people not to blame themselves and not to blame their God. Yet focusing on demons was mystifying insofar as it diverted attention from brutal Roman conquest and imperial rule as the cause of their malaise. Belief in and possession by demons had a self-preservative effect in that it prevented them from engaging in what would have been suicidal action against their conquerors in that passion for liberty that was so deeply rooted in Israelite cultural tradition. This self-protective spirit possession, combined with the confidence that their God was ultimately in control and would resolve the struggle with demonic forces at some point in the future, enabled the people to continue their traditional way of life, however debilitated by demon possession and the imperial domination that demon beliefs obscured. In the Legion episode, however, Jesus offered a "diagnosis" of the diagnosis of misfortunes as due to demon possession. The force that was bringing such violence upon the people, once the demon could be identified, was Legion, i.e., Roman military forces.[37]

CONCLUSION

In all of the cases examined, spirit possession and exorcism of spirits were ways of accommodating, adjusting to, and resisting the domination of foreign

---

37. See also Christian Strecker, "Jesus and the Demoniacs," in Wolfgang Stegemann et al., eds., *The Social Setting of Jesus and the Gospels* (Minneapolis: Fortress, 2002), 117–32.

powers, often imperial invasion and domination. The cases of African peoples, the elites of ancient Greek cities subjected to Rome, and scribal texts struggling with Hellenistic and Roman imperial rule, all provide analogous experiences of subject peoples that help us discern the same dynamics in popular spirit possession at the time of Jesus and his practice of exorcism. Like the prophetic movements in Africa that led up to anti-colonial movements, Jesus's exorcisms as portrayed in Mark and Q led toward more conscious direct opposition to the foreign imperial rule, which was represented in the phenomenon of spirit possession.

THE EXPERIENCE OF PRAYER AND RESISTANCE TO DEMONIC POWERS IN THE GOSPEL OF MARK[1]

Rodney A. Werline

Though many adherents of various religions may find it odd, prayer as a religious *experience* requires some justification, for critical scholars typically understand prayer as a religious *practice*, but probably would not think of it as experience. While many factors may contribute to this inclination to overlook prayer as experience, one particular cause stands prominent: the tendency to isolate and identify what one might consider extraordinary religious experiences as the standard of experience, such as intense "conversion" experiences, speaking in tongues, or mystical ascensions into the heavens. This tendency results in part from the pioneering work by the Harvard psychologist William James in his *The Varieties of Religious Experience*, in which he focuses primarily on the more intensely personal claimed encounters with the divine, with emphasis on the individual and the mystical.[2] James's work led early inquirers of religious experience to Paul, who claims mystical experiences (2 Cor 12:1-4) and is reported to have experienced dramatic "conversion," as well as speaking in tongues more than any of the Corinthians (1 Cor 14:18).[3] Of course, interest in the extraordinary phe-

---

1. This essay in many ways follows in the wake of Richard Horsley's contribution on the experience of demon possession in this volume. Horsley applies socio-political and medical anthropological methods in order to explore the experience of demon possession in Roman Galilee and Judea. I also greatly benefited from conversations with Colleen Shantz about anthropological theory. Certainly, though, I accept all responsibility for any inaccuracies in this essay.

2. William James, *The Varieties of Religious Experience: A Study in Human Nature* (New York: The Modern Library, 1994). The book is the result of his Gifford Lectures on Natural Religion, in Edinburgh in 1901–1902. James defined religion and religious experience almost exclusively in individualist terms: "Religion, therefore, as I now ask you arbitrarily to take it, shall mean for us *the feelings, acts, and experiences of individual men in their solitude, so far as they apprehend themselves to stand in relation to whatever they may consider divine*" (37; emphasis his).

3. See, e.g., Arthur Darby Nock, *Conversion: The Old and the New in Religion from Alexander the Great to Augustine of Hippo* (London: Oxford University Press, 1933); Alan F. Segal, *Paul*

nomena behind these reports is legitimate and useful. However, early Jews and early Christians did not confine their encounters with the divine, the spiritual, the holy, or God to extraordinary encounters; they also believed that the practice of various religious rituals, including prayer, functioned as religious experience.

Expansion of the category religious experience to include these other practices or phenomena may be open to the criticism that virtually all of life has consequently become religious experience, which therefore leaves the designation "religious experience" ineffectual and imprecise because of its all-encompassing scope. However, two preliminary observations mitigate such a criticism. First, people living in first-century C.E. Roman Judea, Galilee, or Syria would not have distinguished between the secular and the religious as the modern western academicians. Actually, observations of the American religious setting may suggest that many twenty-first century Jews and Christians would not distinguish between the secular and the sacred in the same manner as many members of the religious studies academy. Thus, western scholars need to continue to adjust their assumptions and assessments of the way that religious adherents view and live in their worlds.

Second, one can and should expand the category of religious experience to include phenomena outside of the extraordinary while still setting boundaries for what may rightfully be called religious experience. If an authoritative figure, an authoritative text, or an institution declares or prescribes a practice as a *religious practice*, those who perform it would most likely perceive the experience of the action as a *religious* experience.[4] Further, societies may have long-established practices and rituals that everyone simply culturally "knows" are connected to, or lead to, religious experience.[5] In either above case, practice is and/or leads to a religious experience because an authority outside of the individual has defined

---

the Convert: The Apostolate and Apostasy of Saul the Pharisee (New Haven, Conn.: Yale University Press, 1990); Luke Timothy Johnson, *Religious Experience in Earliest Christianity: A Missing Dimension in New Testament Studies* (Minneapolis: Fortress, 1998).

4. Cf. Roy A. Rappaport, *Ritual and Religion in the Making of Humanity* (Cambridge Studies in Cultural Anthropology 110; Cambridge: Cambridge University Press, 1999), 118–26. In his definition and explanation of ritual, Rappaport stresses that ritual action is "*encoded by someone other than the performer* himself (sic)" and requires a person "*necessarily to conform to it*" (118, italics his).

5. Cf. Pierre Bourdieu, *The Logic of Practice* (trans. Richard Nice; Stanford, Calif.: Stanford University Press, 1990), 55–58. Here I especially apply Bourdieu's idea of *habitus*. He defines *habitus* as "systems of durable, transposable dispositions, structured structures predisposed to function as structuring structures, that is, as principles which generate and organize practices and representations that can be objectively adapted to their outcomes without presupposing a conscious aiming at ends or an express mastery of the operations necessary in order to attain them" (53). *Habitus* possesses "an infinite capacity for generating products—thoughts, perceptions, expressions and actions—whose limits are set by the historically and socially situated conditions of its production..." (55).

the action in this way; people believe that they are having or moving toward a religious experience because they are told that they are.[6] This can be true as long as a member of the culture submits to the interpretation, or at least plays along to a certain degree, and can individually appropriate the action as an experience.[7]

These methodological distinctions become quite significant for clarifying what can be examined as and about religious experience, at least as I discuss it in this essay. First, they recognize the often-stated problem that the actual experience is inaccessible, all the more so when the only evidence in possession is ancient texts and not ancient persons. Second, they focus first on what is observable—the external, in this case communal authority and practice. Thus, one can explore experience from the "outside" and move toward some suggestions about the "inside," rather than beginning on the "inside" of the individual. Surely, whatever the internal experience might be, external forces acting on and regulating the individual shape the person's experience of the world. These forces can be analyzed and one can then propose how these are part of an individual's experience. Especially valuable in this enterprise are Pierre Bourdieu's theories about symbolic power, practice and experience. His theory, complemented by features of Byron Good's medical anthropology and Roy Rappaport's understanding of ritual, forms the methodological and theoretical foundation for this present inquiry into prayer as a prophylactic against demonic forces in the Gospel of Mark.

Approaching Mark

Based on the perspective briefly described above, an examination of the role of prayer within the matrix of demonic powers in the Gospel of Mark calls for special attention to issues of symbolic power and practice. The prominent powers in Mark lie with the symbol of the kingdom of God, which is present in the ministry and person of Jesus, over against Beelzebul—Satan, the prince of demons (Mark 3:22–27). Jesus has come to bind this "strong man" and establish a new community of brothers and sisters who "do the will of God" (vv. 21, 31–35). [8]

---

6. This distinction between a practice that "leads to a religious experience" and a practice that "is a religious experience" may be rather slight and is somewhat cautious. However, a group may not consider some ritual activity as the experience, but rather only what leads to the desired experience. For example, from an emic perspective, a group may not understand rituals related to dream incubation as the religious experience, but only the dream. An anthropologist analyzing such activity from an etic perspective, however, may understand both the rituals and the dream as religious experience.

7. Rappaport (*Ritual and Religion*, 119–21, 124–26) explains that practice does not always mean belief in the practice, but perhaps simply public acceptance.

8. For more detailed discussion of this particular interpretation of Mark, see Ched Myers, *Binding the Strong Man: A Political Reading of Mark's Story of Jesus* (Maryknoll, N.Y.: Orbis, 1988), 134–68.

The author establishes prayer as essential in this encounter with demonic powers through the actions and teachings of Jesus, which have become the authority in general for this early Christian community. While the gospel does not include the content of these prayers, I assume that Markan Christians did sometimes practice prayer for this reason; prayer as a prophylactic is not simply a literary trope. Prayer was already a socially established action that possessed special functions in the Jewish culture of these particular early Christians, and it has become part of the collective cultural knowledge of this group. However, more than simply depicting prayer as a one-to-one remedy for withstanding demonic forces, in Mark the act becomes a means through which the believer participates in and experiences the cosmic struggle between the kingdom of God and Satan.

PRAYER AND CONFRONTATION WITH DEMONIC POWERS:[9]
THE TEMPTATION IN THE WILDERNESS

The threat from demonic forces appears early in the gospel. After Jesus's baptism, at which the heavenly voice identifies Jesus as the "Son, the Beloved" (Mark 1:11), the Spirit casts Jesus into the wilderness where he encounters Satan and wild beasts:

> And the Spirit immediately drove him out into the wilderness. He was in the wilderness forty days, tempted (πειραζόμενος) by Satan; and he was with wild beasts and angels waited on him (1:12–13).[10]

As the "Son" Jesus is thus placed in confrontation with the demonic world, which provides a basic opposition throughout the gospel. With a reference to "beasts," Mark seems to suggest that Jesus has now entered into an ancient mythic struggle between God and the demonic monsters of chaos.[11] These beasts appear in Dan 7 as the forces behind a series of empires. The reference to the angels attending to Jesus also evokes the apocalyptic worlds of *1 Enoch* and Daniel in which angels strive against demonic powers and sometimes attempt to intervene for humans who suffer from these malevolent spirits.[12] With this tersely described scene, a hostile cosmos filled with menacing forces has sprung into existence.

---

9. For a popular presentation of this role of prayer in Mark, see Rodney A. Werline, *Pray Like This: Understanding Prayer in the Bible* (London: T&T Clark, 2007), 101–12.

10. All biblical quotations are from the NRSV.

11. See Myers, *Binding the Strong Man*, 130. His emphasis on the cosmic struggle as part of Mark's worldview significantly informs my essay.

12. See, e.g., Dan 10:10–14, a text in which an angelic figure has been prevented from coming to Daniel by the "prince of the kingdom of Persia," the demonic angel who is empowering the Persian Empire. George W. E. Nickelsburg (*Jewish Literature between the Bible and Mishnah* [2nd ed.; Minneapolis: Fortress, 2005], 77–79) recognizes the language of struggle

Jesus begins his preaching and ministry when he emerges from the wilderness: "The time is fulfilled, and the kingdom of God has come near; repent and believe the good news" (1:15). The announcement of the nearness of the kingdom of God may be another allusion to Dan 7, where the kingdom is given over to the "holy ones" (i.e. angels),[13] after the demonic beasts have met their destruction. The nearness of the kingdom establishes the possibility that the confrontation between Jesus and the demonic might continue. Accordingly, Jesus encounters a man with an "unclean spirit" in a synagogue (vv. 21–28). Seeming to know that Jesus's appearance signals an assault on demonic powers, the unclean spirit within the man cries out: "What have you to do with us? Have you come to destroy us? I know who you are, the Holy One of God" (v. 24).

The first scene that depicts Jesus at prayer follows the story of the healing of Peter's mother-in-law (vv. 29–31) and healings and exorcisms at sundown (1:32–34): "In the morning, while it was still very dark, he got up and went out to a deserted place, and there he prayed" (v. 35). This journey into a "deserted place" (ἔρημον τόπον) sounds eerily like the beginning of the temptation scene. In this instance, however, Jesus remains alone in the wilderness, no powers of darkness appear. Far from being a simple "retreat" or "rest period" after hard work, or a mere transitional scene, the practice of prayer appears to have prepared Jesus for another surge of work in the kingdom of God, which includes exorcisms, for when the disciples, who have been searching for him, find him, Jesus responds:

> "Let us go on to the neighboring towns, so that I may proclaim the message there also; for that is what I came out to do." And he went throughout Galilee, proclaiming the message in their synagogues and casting out demons (vv. 38–39).[14]

This connection between Jesus's work of the kingdom of God in opposition to demonic forces and the practice of prayer continues through the gospel.

---

between angelic powers and demonic forces in Dan 7, which in this case has real implications in history. Similarly, in 1 En. 9, the four archangels intercede on behalf of humans because they suffer from the evil deeds of the fallen watchers—angelic powers. In the following chapter (10:4–15), three archangels are commissioned to aid humanity by binding the watchers and destroying their offspring, the Giants. Cf. also what appears to be a struggle between the Angel of Light and the Angel of Darkness in the 1QS 3:13–26.

13. See John J. Collins, A Commentary on the Book of Daniel (Hermeneia; Minneapolis: Fortress, 1993), 302, 312–18.

14. Adela Yarbro Collins (Mark: A Commentary [Hermeneia; Minneapolis: Fortress, 2007], 177) makes no connection between the prayer and the struggle against demonic forces. She rather states that this prayer at the beginning of Jesus's ministry corresponds to the prayer in Gethsemane at the conclusion of Jesus's ministry. According to Collins, the prayers are simply for "divine guidance and support" in Jesus's activities.

Confrontations with the Sea

Twice Mark pits Jesus against the sea. In the first scene, Jesus and the disciples are crossing the Sea of Galilee on their way to the region of the Gadarenes (Gerasenes) (4:35–41), where Jesus will face a "Legion" of demons in a man. Jesus has fallen asleep in the stern when the winds and waves mount against the boat. The disciples having awakened him to the crisis of their boat about to be swamped, Jesus acts:

> [A]nd they woke him up and said to him, "Teacher, do you not care that we are perishing?" He woke up and rebuked (ἐπετίμησεν) the wind, and said to the sea, "Peace! Be still (πεφίμωσο)!" Then the wind ceased and there was a dead calm. He said to them, "Why are you afraid? Have you still no faith?" (4:38b–39)

The earlier allusions to the "beasts" of Dan 7 in Mark 1 invites the interpretation that Mark here thinks of the sea in terms of God's ancient foe, Yamm, the source of the demonic imperial powers in the world (cf. Dan 7:2).[15] Interestingly, Daniel sees the beasts in a "night" "dream-vision," in which he also witnesses the "four winds of heaven stirring up the great sea" (vv. 1–2). In Mark, Jesus, asleep in the boat at night, wakes to encounter the wind and the sea, which he rebukes and silences. The combination of "rebuke" (ἐπιτιμᾶν) and "be still" (φιμοῦν) appeared in the first exorcism scene in Mark as Jesus rebukes and silences the demon: "And Jesus rebuked (ἐπετίμησεν) him, saying, "Be silent (φιμώθητι) and come out of him!" (1:25).[16] In the calming of the sea, Jesus is exorcizing the ancient foe Yamm

---

15. Daniel Harrington (*The Gospel of Matthew* [Collegeville, Minn: Liturgical, 1991], 122–23) makes this same argument for the story as it appears in Matt 8:23–27. Many commentators also note the similarities between the calming of the sea and Ps 107:23–30:

Some went down into the sea in ships . . .
they saw the deeds of the Lord,
   his wondrous deeds in the deep.
For he commanded and raised the stormy wind,
   which lifted up the waves of the sea.
They mounted to the heaven, they went down to the depths;
   their courage melted away in their calamity . . .
Then the cried to the Lord in their trouble,
   and he brought them out from their distress;
he made the storm still,
   and the waves of the sea were hushed . . .

16. For ἐπιτιμάω, see also 3:12. John Ashton (*The Religion of Paul the Apostle* [New Haven, Conn.: Yale University Press, 2000], 63–69) in an excursus also notes the use of these terms in exorcism scenes and the calming of the sea. However, Ashton's primary interest lies in a claim that both Jesus and Paul exhibited shaman-like characteristics, an argument containing significant problems. Adela Yarbro Collins (*Mark: A Commentary*, 259–60) argues that the story resembles the story of Jonah. She notes the vocabulary shared between this story and Jesus's

by the same means that he casts out demons from humans! Again, Mark imagines Jesus as acting within this grand, mythic cosmos in which great forces do battle.

The sea returns in Mark 6:45–52, and this time prayer precedes Jesus's encounter with the waters. After Jesus feeds the five thousand, he sends the disciples back across the sea toward Bethsaida while he dismisses the crowd. After the crowd has dispersed, Jesus ascends a mountain to pray (v. 46). The disciples struggle to cross the sea because of an adverse wind. Seeing their predicament, early in the morning Jesus walks on the water toward them. Since Jesus "rebuked" and "silenced" the sea in chapter 4, he now seems to be victoriously treading on the back of YHWH's ancient, evil foe, which offers no resistance to him.[17] Meanwhile, the disciples continue to strain against the wind. However, when Jesus gets into the boat, the wind ceases without a word from him (v. 51). At this point in the narrative these mythic forces appear to be completely submissive to Jesus. He can rightly offer the words of a salvation oracle to the disciples: "Do not be afraid" (v. 50), reminiscent of Isa 41:10. The disciples struggle to understand Jesus's identity and power and to have faith in him, a pattern that continues throughout the gospel; just as they "strain" against the "wind," they will also struggle against powerful forces and with what is revealed to them. Nevertheless, for the purposes of the argument in this essay, Mark has again connected prayer and Jesus's encounters with a traditional demonic cosmic force, the sea. As do the demons in the instances of Jesus's exorcisms, so too the sea bows to his power.

The Disciples' Struggles

The disciples do not receive instructions about prayer in Mark's narrative until chapter 9. The passage stands within a transitional section in Mark in which the narrative moves Jesus toward Jerusalem. The journey becomes an expression of discipleship as the disciples follow Jesus and he teaches them in private along the way (ὁδός) to Jerusalem.[18] Through this section Jesus continues to inform the disciples of his impending suffering and death in Jerusalem, a teaching that sets the serious tone for all else that Jesus tells them. In this section, therefore, appear instructions that are vital for the community. Mark's placement of Jesus's teaching about prayer in this section is not an afterthought; it is strategic. The

---

first exorcism (261). However, she claims that "the reason why the sea is treated like demons is that demons or evil spirits were thought to be responsible for inclement weather" (261). For an explanation of the term ἐπιτιμᾶν, see Richard A. Horsley, *Hearing the Whole Story: The Politics of Plot in Mark's Gospel* (Louisville/London/Leiden: Westminster John Knox, 2000), 137–38.

17. While Adela Yarbro Collins lists YHWH's ability to control the sea among her examples of a deity controlling the sea (*Mark: A Commentary*, 328), she places more emphasis on the theophanic aspects of the scene and compares them to the theophanies to Moses and Elijah (333–38).

18. See ibid., 397–98.

way to Jerusalem leads toward the seat of demonic forces embodied in the empire and those who conduct its business—Rome and the Jerusalem priestly elite. The author marks the practice as crucial, and the disciples must learn its importance in the struggle against evil.

The instructions about prayer and demonic forces come at the conclusion of another exorcism scene. Descending from the mountain on which Jesus has been transfigured (9:2–13), Jesus and three disciples who accompanied him find the remaining disciples in an intense argument with some scribes (9:14–29). The argument centers on a boy who has an evil spirit that the disciples are unable to expel. The boy's father informs Jesus about the problem:

> Teacher, I brought you my son; he has a spirit that makes him unable to speak; and whenever it seizes him, it dashes him down; and he foams and grinds his teeth and becomes rigid; and I asked your disciples to cast it out, but they could not do so. (vv. 17–18)

When the boy appears before Jesus, the demon seemingly recognizes Jesus and seizes the boy. Looking upon the sight, the father implores Jesus to do something if he is able. There follows a brief confrontation between Jesus and the father over the importance of faith, and the father begs Jesus to help his "unbelief" (vv. 22–24). Jesus then "rebukes" (ἐπετίμησεν) the spirit and adjures (ἐπιτάσσω) it to come out of the boy. The exorcism concluded, the disciples inquire of Jesus in private concerning why they could not expel the demon (vv. 28–29). Jesus instructs them: "This kind can come out only through prayer" (v. 29).

Just as the blind man, Bartimaeus, will represent the disciples' struggle "to see" (11:46–52), and they struggled to row against an "adverse wind," Mark brings into correspondence the disciples' lack of faith (v. 19) with the father's struggle to believe (v. 22). If the disciples want to confront demonic powers as Jesus does, they must engage in the practice of prayer as he has done throughout the gospel. In Mark, the confrontation with demonic forces will only intensify from this point on in the narrative, and prayer will continue to be required.[19]

CONFRONTATION WITH EMPIRE

The final confrontation with demonic power in Mark arrives when Jesus is arrested, the trial takes place, and the execution is carried out. Mark has closely aligned the Romans, their Jerusalem priestly clients, and the scribal retainers with demonic power throughout the gospel.[20] Now Jesus will meet this power face to

---

19. Cf., Myers, *Binding the Strong Man*, 255.

20. A key piece of evidence is the argument with the scribes who have come from Jerusalem to challenge the power behind Jesus's exorcisms (Mark 3:19b–27). Since the Jerusalem scribes apparently "blaspheme" the work of the Holy Spirit (vv. 28–30), they line up on the side

face. In preparation for this conflict, Jesus again withdraws from the crowds in order to pray, this time to the Garden of Gethsemane. As on the mountain, he takes Peter, James, and John with him a little farther away from the other disciples (14:32–42). When Jesus returns to them, he finds them asleep. Again, he exhorts them, this time urging them to understand that the "time of trial" (πειρασμόν) has come and that they must pray in order not to fall (v. 38). The appearance of the word "trial" (πειρασμός) recalls Jesus's "testing" (πειράζειν) in the wilderness with the beasts and Satan at the beginning of the gospel (1:13). The test has resumed. Because the disciples have slept and not engaged in prayer, their courage vanishes in the presence of imperial evil, and they are not able to endure the time of trial, forsaking Jesus to face the empire alone.

The Temple

In the narrative of Mark's world, the practice of prayer can bring down institutions that have come under imperial and demonic influence. The temple has become such an institution for Mark because the priestly elite have assisted in administering Roman rule in Judea. In chapter 11, Jesus, referring to the temple mount as "this mountain," tells the disciples that if they unite faith and prayer then amazing changes might occur:

> Jesus answered them, "Have faith in God. Truly, I tell you, if you say to this mountain, 'Be taken up and thrown into the sea,' and if you do not doubt in your heart, but believe that what you say will come to pass, it will be done for you. So I tell you, whatever you ask for in prayer, believe that you have received it, and it will be yours. (11:22–24)

Taken within the context of Mark's understanding of the kingdom of God in opposition to demonic powers and the practice of prayer, Jesus's words do not suggest that the disciples will have all their wishes fulfilled if they simply pray and have enough faith. Rather, Jesus indicates that in the coming of the kingdom of God even the agent of imperial power in Judea may be brought down through the practice of prayer.

Habitus[21]: Apotropaic Prayers in other Second Temple Texts

Mark is not the first author from this era to represent prayer as a means of resistance to demonic forces; the idea and the practice were already part of

---

of the "strong man," Satan. See Ched Myers, *Binding the Strong Man*, 164–66. Note also that Jesus's first exorcism takes place in a synagogue (1:21–28), perhaps another repudiation of the ruling establishment (ibid., 139–52).

21. See Bourdieu, *The Logic of Practice*, 53–58.

Second Temple cultural knowledge and Mark's habitus. For example, the Dead
Sea Scrolls contain a number of apotropaic prayers. Esther Eshel divides these
prayers into two groups: 1) prayers of non-sectarian origin, which include *Aramaic Levi Document*, two prayers in the apocryphal psalms 11QPs[a], and two in
the book of *Jubilees*; and 2) prayers of sectarian origin, which include 4Q510–
4Q511, 4Q444, 6Q18, and 1QH[a] Frg. 4. Along with these Eshel examines several
incantations against demons (4Q560, 8Q5, 11Q11).[22] Among the fascinating features that Eshel examines are the following. 11QPs[a] and *Jub.* 6:1–7 and 12:19–20
ask for protection in the form of knowledge and health, and petition that the
demons not "have control over" the person's mind and body.[23] In this way the
people will not sin and they will not suffer illnesses from the demons' presence.
Similar themes appear in the sectarian prayers, only with more emphasis on the
community's ideology and theology.[24] Psalm 91 figures prominently in 11Q11, an
incantation text, as it also does in Jesus's temptation scene in Q (Matt 4:6//Luke
4:10).[25] Incantations are addressed directly to the demon.[26] In many of these
prayer texts the myth of the origin of evil spirits from the "Book of the Watchers"
in *1 Enoch* 1–36 proves foundational.

The book of Tobit contains two prayers used as part of a "spell" to drive away
a demon named Asmodeus, who has killed seven husbands of Sarah on their wedding nights (Tob 3:7–9). Sarah offers her prayer as a complaint about her situation
(3:11–15), to which Raphael is immediately dispatched, along with the commission of assisting Tobit, in order to "heal" (ἰάσασθαι) both Tobit and Sarah (v. 17).
This healing takes the form of "setting her free" (λῦσαι) from the demon (v. 17).
Tobias offers another prayer (8:5–7), which takes place on the wedding night after
he has burned fish liver on the embers, chasing the demon to the remote parts of
Egypt (vv. 1–3). There Raphael catches up with him and binds him.[27]

---

22. See Esther Eshel, "Apotropaic Prayers in the Second Temple Period," in *Liturgical Perspectives: Prayer and Poetry in Light of the Dead Sea Scrolls, Proceedings of the Fifth International Symposium of the Orion Center for the Study of the Dead Sea Scrolls and Associated Literature, 19-23 January, 2000* (ed. Esther G. Chazon; STDJ 48; Leiden: Brill, 2003), 69.

23. Ibid., 76–78. For more characteristics, see David Flusser, "Psalms, Hymns, and Prayers," in *Jewish Writings of the Second Temple Period* (CRINT Section 2; ed. Michael Stone; Philadelphia: Fortress, 1984), 560–61.

24. Eshel, "Apotropaic Prayers," 79–84.

25. Ibid., 84–85.

26. Ibid., 87.

27. Cf. the binding of the Watchers in *1 Enoch*. This portion of the story may also be influenced by the Watchers tradition. For more, see George W. E. Nickelsburg, "Tobit and Enoch: Distant Cousins with Recognizable Resemblance," *SBLSP* 27 (1988): 54–68.

THE PRACTICE OF PRAYER AND RELIGIOUS EXPERIENCE

For Mark prayer is a ritual practice that resists demonic forces in the world, in whatever form one might encounter them, and the text does this in ways that have often been recognized in cultural anthropology. Apotropaic prayers stood within the *habitus* of the author—as seen in the examples from Second Temple Judaism above—who then appropriated them to this unique and particular setting. Prayer as a prophylactic against demonic forces, therefore, as part of the *habitus* of the culture, already possessed cultural currency and stood among the range of available predispositions of the Markan community. The writer defines its role for this particular community by depicting Jesus as a model of this ritual and as a teacher about the practice. The disciples' failure to pray and their ensuing capitulation to the powers provides a cautionary example for those who encountered this gospel. Further, the placement of the ritual within a worldview of a grand cosmic struggle also intensifies prayer's importance. This means that those who practice these prayers as an "obvious" and "given" way to act—to them—have located themselves within the cosmos and social structure, and are religiously situated.[28]

Thus far, then, I have indicated the way in which apotropaic prayers became "routinized" behavior for this segment of the early church. I can now explore the way in which this practice becomes experience, and more specifically religious experience. Key to understanding the experience is recognition that prayer is a real practice done in the body; people actually *enact* it. For Bourdieu, prayer as a ritual action is a very "this-worldly" practice that addresses real concerns in this world.[29] In real, concrete action, the believer understands that she or he experiences a transcendent religious reality. From the anthropological point of view, this experience has become religious experience not because it inherently contains or participates in the holy, but because the community has identified it as such. Rappaport has made this point quite clearly;[30] a particular act may have numinous qualities because the community understands and treats it as possessing such powers.[31] That religious practice becomes a religious experience that takes

---

28. Cf. Rappaport's idea of ritual as self-referential (*Ritual and Religion*, 104), which means those who perform a ritual do not simply convey information about themselves to others, but also transmit information about themselves to themselves: "Participation in a ritual ... is not only informative but self-informative."

29. Cf. Bourdieu, *The Logic of Practice*, 95: "Magical and religious actions are fundamentally 'this-worldly' ... being entirely dominated by the concern to ensure the success of production and reproduction, in a word, survival, they are oriented towards the most dramatically practical, vital and urgent ends."

30. Rappaport, *Ritual and Religion*, 277–304. In this conclusion, Rappaport is quite close to Durkheim's understanding that the experience of the holy or religion is actually the community experiencing itself.

31. This is the assessment of Rappaport, *Ritual and Religion*, 380.

place in the body becomes quite significant when one revisits demon possession and demonic power in Mark. The body is the most basic place in which a person experiences power, as Bourdieu asserts: "Symbolic power works partly through the control of other people's bodies ..."[32]

Not surprisingly, the experience of socio-political tension might easily be cast as a spiritual struggle, for both are powers seemingly beyond human control. In an occupation, people lose control over their bodies and the way that they interact in and experience culture; control is imposed on them. Severe disruptions in life that result from perceived physical issues will be experienced, talked about, and seen in relationship to the social structures and pressures present in the culture. As Byron Good notes, and with which Bourdieu would surely agree:

> Disease occurs, of course, not in the body, but in life. Localization of a disorder, at very best, tells little about why it occurs when or how it does. Disease occurs not only in the body—in the sense of an ontological order in the great chain of being—but in time, in place, in history, and in the context of lived experience and the social world. Its effect is on the body in the world![33]

As Horsley has shown, this is the case in Mark in the text's association of demon possession with imperial rule.

Prayer is enacted in the body, and as an act prescribed by God through Jesus through the Markan community, it locates the petitioner within a grand cosmic struggle that encompasses the kingdom of God, and imperial and local politics. In the performance the believer is experiencing God's rule, for as Bourdieu states: "The body believes what it plays at. . . ."[34] "It does not represent what it performs," it *enacts* it, and in enacting it, it is experienced.[35] Thus, prayer is not simply symbolic action. In the act the believer also brings the "past" of Jesus's work and world and makes it become part of the "present,"[36] as Bourdieu continues: "it [i.e., the body] does not memorize the past, it *enacts* the past, bringing it back to life. What is 'learned in the body' is not something that one has, like knowledge that can be brandished, but something that one is. This is particularly clear in non-literate societies, where inherited knowledge can only survive in the incorporated state."[37] The Markan community's cosmos presented real threats. In the practice

---

32. Bourdieu, *The Logic of Practice*, 69.

33. Byron Good, *Medicine, Rationality, and Experience: An Anthropological Perspective* (Cambridge: Cambridge University Press, 1994), 133.

34. Bourdieu, *The Logic of Practice*, 73.

35. Ibid. For Bourdieu, the *habitus* at every moment "structures new experiences in accordance with the structures produced by past experiences within the limits defined by their power of selection, brings about a unique integration, dominated by the earliest experiences, of the experiences statistically common to members of the same class" (60).

36. Ritual theorists would designate this action as a type of *mimesis*.

37. Bourdieu, *The Logic of Practice*, 73.

of prayer—a religiously prescribed practice given by Jesus through the authority of the community—the believers lived the experience of that world.

PART 2
TEXT AND RELIGIOUS EXPERIENCE

THE MEDIUM OF THE DIVINE

Steven M. Wasserstrom

Arnaldo Momigliano took me out for pancakes.[1] He had read a graduate school paper I had written and he wished to discuss it. Over syrup, as I rhapsodized on religious experience of the holy man in the Islamic eighth century in my application of Peter Brown's "The Rise and Function of the Holy Man in Late Antiquity,"[2] Professor Momigliano was, as they say, underwhelmed.[3] There are two things that I recall the great historian said in response. Peter Brown was *his* student, and—here he leaned in a bit—*everyone* has religious experiences!

As interloper from the American Academy of Religion,[4] I accepted Frances Flannery's kind invitation to visit the inauguration of this SBL program unit, the Religious Experience in Early Judaism and Early Christianity Consultation.[5] I take it that I've been called on to represent what used to be called comparative religion. Let me hasten to reassure you that this is not to make you comparatively religious, as the old line has it. My charge, rather, concerns the means by which scholars in Religious Studies may or may not understand "religious experience."

Let me advocate first on behalf of an old devil. The "experience" of others is by definition inaccessible. Even as it drives, say, the dream of transfiguration

---

1. This presentation was originally given as a response at the annual meeting of the National AAR and SBL, Philadelphia, November 19, 2005. Thus, I retain the informal voice and lack of extensive apparatus appropriate for brief, oral presentation. Even to the slight extent that I have some acquaintance with psychology of experience and philosophy of experience, I leave those aside on this occasion.

2. Peter Brown, "The Rise and Function of the Holy Man in Late Antiquity," *JRS* 61 (1971): 80–101.

3. The paper appeared as "The Moving Finger Writes: Mughīra ibn Saʿīd's Islamic Gnosis and the Myths of its Rejection," *HR* 25 (1985): 1–29.

4. The American Academy of Religion (AAR) is a professional organization that convenes meetings alongside the Society of Biblical Literature (SBL).

5. The Consultation has since been renewed as the Religious Experience in Early Judaism and Early Christianity Section.

through love.[6] Even if in antiquity aspirations to merge with others flourished in the name of religion.[7] Even so, erasure of distinctions is troublesome, to say the least, for those of us tasked with analysis. In addition to their diminution of differences, claims for a "deep" understanding of "religious experience" are, in any case, simply circular. They appoint a psychic event familiar to the scholar to serve as exalted object of inquiry; this object is recognizable when encountered because it looks like what the scholar already recognizes: his own original "experience."[8]

Now this is, granted, not a very sophisticated example, but it makes the point. For the hardheaded among us, there can be no empirical purchase on the experiential past, period. We guess, project, speculate, imagine, but we cannot *know* the inner life of our forebears. Understanding experience from ancient texts cannot be empirical, at least not in the sense recognized by our sciences of society—it is neither sociological, nor historical, nor economic, etc. My concern in this regard rests with what we can and should say to our students through our teaching; that is to say, how we will conduct our academic understanding of the "inner life" of religion.

The first question, perhaps, is whether the very term "experience" opens or closes such understanding. I agree with Crispin Fletcher-Louis's position that the very jargon of "religious experience" itself often closes understanding.[9] Let us take a pertinent example: construing "vision mysticism" in terms of (extreme) experience. Alas, even the most vivid phantom flies beyond textual barricades, never to be grasped. Hermeneuts committed to such "phantasmics," tend, on my observation, to be seduced by this very flight of symbols, symbols especially of ascent, which carry us away. To be carried away, however, is hardly identical with understanding. I suspect an infinite regress, and the inescapable circularity, of such "phantasmics."

Is there no way out of this frustration? It depends on what one means by "out." Insofar as any report of visions comes couched in symbols, accessing experience of the ancients falls into the category of the aesthetic. The model here is poetry, its paradigm is inspiration—being carried away—but the larger problem is political. By political, I mean neither party politics nor the politics of identity. I

---

6. For a more thorough analysis of these issues for religious studies, see Steven M. Wasserstrom, *Religion after Religion: Gershom Scholem, Mircea Eliade, and Henry Corbin at Eranos* (Princeton, N.J.: Princeton University Press, 1999), 191–93.

7. Franz Rosenthal, "I Am You," in *Individual Piety and Society in Islam* (Individualism and Conformity in Classical Islam; ed. A. Banani and S. Vryonis, Jr.; Malibu, Calif.: Undena, 1977), honoring Shelomo Dov Goitein.

8. In putting it this way, I run the risk of reinventing a wheel, or, at least, a circle: this may or may not be the (in)famous hermeneutical circle.

9. See Crispin Fletcher-Louis, "Religious Experience and the Apocalypses," in the present volume.

mean the legitimization, the collective empowerment, of the rights of the herme-neut; in other words, the politics pertinent to a reading community.

What the AAR and SBL reading communities share is, if not full-blown frustration, at least an inescapable ambivalence: we know that "professional understanding" of what is by definition incomprehensible is the oxymoron that consoles with its inescapability, because we are let off the hook of demonstrability. Let me be as clear as I can. To take ancient texts of religious experience seriously as writing we must take the medium of writing seriously. Beyond their semantic content, that is, we must engage our texts as texts. And I mean something more than the requisite form, content, function, and context. There are fundamental challenges, after all, concerning the very dating of our sources The dating of the texts of merkabah mysticism is a case in point, one germane to several of the papers in the present volume. Peter Schäfer's Berlin team proved that the texts available for understanding Hekhalot literature and Jewish magic do not date to antiquity. They are all medieval.[10]

Lateness of so many sources is only one of several reasons why we will still be frustrated in a quest for antiquity's "original" experiences. Or, consider the ini-tiatory novel, a genre classically designed, so it seems, to introduce a person to such original experiences. When one has finished *The Golden Ass* of Apuleius one has passed a level of initiation in mysteries; that is, if nothing else, one has watched the narrator Lucius shift from the asinine body to the ethereal soul. This trajectory of seeming spiritualization, however, is misrepresented by Festugière and Nock as being a species of "redemption."[11] I am not saying that we should not take *The Golden Ass* for what it purports to be, as a sort of mystery. But I accept the argument that it is a *Lesemysterium*, a Reading Mystery, an initiation by means of a book. Book XI of *The Golden Ass* might represent the best-surviv-ing description of the ancient mysteries, and so has been exploited perennially by scholars to describe the inner workings of ancient mystery initiations. But having taught it for many years I conclude that it does not initiate by giving glimpse of mystery ritual, with a historicity that we cannot judge, but rather through reading the novel itself, which we can indeed judge.[12]

---

10. Peter Schäfer, ed., Zusammenarbeit mit Margarete Schlüter und Hans Georg von Mutius, *Synopse zur Hekhalot-Literatur* (TSAJ 2; Tübingen: Mohr Siebeck, 1981); idem, ed., *Geniza-Fragmente zur Hekhalot-Literatur* (TSAJ 6; Tübingen: Mohr Siebeck, 1984); Peter Schäfer and Shaul Shaked, eds., *Magische Texte aus der Kairoer Geniza* (3 vols.; TSAJ 42: Tübin-gen: Mohr Siebeck, 1994–1999).

11. A. J. Festugière, *La Révélation d'Hermès Trismégiste* (4 vols., Paris, 1949–54) or *Personal Religion among the Greeks* (Berkeley and Los Angeles: University California Press, 1960); A. D. Nock, *Conversion: The Old and the New in Religion from Alexander the Great in Augustine of Hippo* (Oxford: Oxford University Press, 1933).

12. Similarly, see Robin Griffith-Jones, "Transformation by a Text: The Gospel of John," in this volume.

No one "relives" the experiences of the pagan Lucius in *The Golden Ass* any more than those of Brown's Christian Holy Man or his Jewish visionary counterpart among the merkabah mystics. Even if we could do so, I tend now to agree with Momigliano's postprandial wisdom, that such "reliving" would be trivial in any event. To my students I safely offer no hope of replication. As teacher of religious studies I can guide them to no replicable experience. Any such enticement carries with it the danger of mystagogery, and they pay too much tuition to receive phantasmic flights of wish fulfillment in return.

As consolation for how demystifying this hard-nosed approach may be, one might remember that demystification is a friend of understanding. The art historian Edgar Wind concluded *Pagan Mysteries in the Renaissance* by inverting E. M. Forster's *bon mot* that a symbol is "a Sphinx who dies as soon as her riddles are answered." In contrast, Wind suggested that "a great symbol is the reverse of a sphinx; it is more alive when its riddle is answered."[13]

Let me take another example. While now largely forgotten, at one time the name Joachim Wach (1898–1955) would have been known to all students of religion. Wach founded the school of religious studies at the University of Chicago.[14] His work, however, is today not much more than an historical curiosity to many in the field, who presently can tell you only that he was responsible for importing *Verstehen* as a professional ideal. As we all know, for a generation of students of religious studies, *Verstehen*, "Understanding," the lynchpin of Wach's system, seemed the ideal compromise between disenchantment and "going native." "Understanding" was ideal for a religious studies that had its experience and ate it too.[15] However, while we find Wach's program properly outmoded, that does not require us to abandon the work of understanding.

Let us accept, for the moment, scientific promises that we can understand the religious experience of others. Let us speculate with them that current and near future alternatives of empiricism and naturalism provide sufficient analytic oomph for understanding experience. I worry about the perils of such naturalistic explanation—especially of what Alan Segal calls Religiously Interpreted States of

---

13. Edgar Wind, *Pagan Mysteries in the Renaissance* (New York: W. W. Norton, 1968), 235.

14. See my "The Master-Interpreter: Notes on the German Career of Joachim Wach (1922–1935)," in *Hermeneutics in History: Joachim Wach, Mircea Eliade, and the Science of Religions* (ed. Christian Wedemayer and Wendy Doniger: Oxford: Oxford University Press, forthcoming).

15. The only full-scale study of sustained value is that of Rainer Flasche, *Die Religionswissenschaft Joachim Wachs* (New York: de Gruyter, 1978). A reasonable discussion of Wach's foundational 1924 *Religionswissenschaft* monograph can be found in Jeppe Sinding Jensen, *The Study of Religion in a New Key: Theoretical and Philosophical Soundings in the Comparative and General Study of Religion* (Aarhus: Aarhus University Press, 2003), 162–65. Jensen believes that this monograph "was the first book-length presentation of methodological and theoretical issues from the study of religion related, in a systematic manner, to questions from the philosophy of science," *Study of Religion*, 162, n. 2.

Consciousness (RISC).[16] Segal's neurological futurism promises entré into mysteries of the brain and the visions inherent in the nervous system. Of course, for insiders, a shift from experience to consciousness, as posited by RISC theories arising from cognitive science or neurophysiology, still dissipates native delight in belonging to a community that shares certain experiences. Furthermore, as "experience studies" penetrates nervous systems and "consciousness," dangers of exploitation increase considerably. Designer pharmaceuticals, for instance, may "reproduce" ancient ecstasies.[17] In other words, "religious experiences" could be reduced to mere "technique."

But enough science fiction.

I agree with Celia Deutsch[18] that we humanists have no choice but to privilege Logos. As a teacher of religious studies, when called upon to elucidate scriptures or canonical reports of transpersonal experience, I look to the religious past not for the holy book as guide for my life, but rather to ancient life as guide for understanding a holy book. A *book*. In a sense we have not yet taken the media character of the holy book seriously enough, especially if we treat it condescendingly only as a semantic channel for transportation into an "experience." In other words, I see the common hope in the papers presented here not in "experience," not in visionary flight, but in the mediation of what Deutsch calls Logos. That is to say, we cannot reproduce original *stigmata*, but we do still have available to us *aenigmata*, by which I mean signs. Deutsch nicely identifies text work as mystery rite and reminds us that the language of sanctuary and Temple locates these enigmas spatially. Textual experience itself, then, performs the Mishna's locative "what is above/what is beneath/what is before/what is after." Reading this way, the text does not transcend time and space but rather locates the student in properly imaginable dimensions of time and space.

But does merely imaginative reading achieve interpretive meta-leverage? Does it allow us to stand aside the self-reporting discourse of "experience"? Can we find Archimedean meaning in experience by operating outside of it? Can we, in short, leverage it into understanding?

---

16. See Alan F. Segal, "Religious Experience and the Construction of the Transcendent Self," in *Paradise Now: Essays on Early Jewish and Christian Mysticism* (ed. A. DeConick; Atlanta: SBL Press, 2006); also see idem, "The Afterlife and Mirror of the Self," in this volume. I take RISC as a double circumlocution. It withdraws the stinger from RASC (Religiously Altered States of Consciousness), which in turn de-fanged ASC, Altered States of Consciousness. This dilution of the terminology tracks along the trajectory taken when NRM, New Religious Movements, replaced "cult."

17. See the mischievous imagining of such world in Stanislaw Lem, *Peace on Earth* (San Diego: Harcourt, 1994).

18. Celia Deutsch, "Visions, Mysteries and the Interpretive Task: Text Work and Religious Experience in Philo and Clement," in this volume.

Perhaps, but only if we steer clear of those dangers. On the one hand, we must avoid the Scylla of the emerging cognitive science of religion (the dream of a new cognitivist elite, virtually all of whom are scientists or are at least scientific in orientation); on the other hand, the Charybdis of ever-more-attenuated modes of close reading alone (the dream of such old cognitivist elites as those emulating Leo Strauss[19]).

With a growing number of colleagues, I turn to a Third Force, media theory of religion.[20] On this rather more modest proposal, which neither replicates ecstasies nor promises salvation, we turn to the media of communication as such. What we can know of texts about religious experience, in other words, is not that they are experiences but that they are texts. And as texts, they operate like any other text. We read not just the semantic surface of an ancient text—what it seems to say, what is usually called its "meaning"—but also its transmission, replication, commodification, reception, its full function, the "Book As Symbolic Universe." We are studying episodes in the "history of writing," but only if by "writing" a trembling respect intervenes to deter just another pseudo-clarity. For our interpretive challenge is not to be absorbed back into the semantic controls of a soothing home-faith-community, who construe the text as Scripture or apocalypse, or vision, or whatever. Rather, we mere teachers stick with human communication, and stay painfully with interpretations that end in death only and not life after death.

On the old model of *Verstehen*, a few readers understand, but most do not—and cannot. Of course it is unpleasant to lose privileges. But unless we divest ourselves of our self-flattering claims to be privileged readers, readers who are confident when they teach about religious experience, we can't effectively join the new universe of knowledge. For better or worse, a googled wikipedic library ain't in Kansas anymore. The majority of religious believers who have ever lived are alive today. Digitalization and instantaneity transform human culture. But by cooperating with the inevitable, incorporating the future's modes of knowledge, which are already well with us, into our work of understanding, we might quit the tiny club of pretend understanders, and join the swelling ranks of those unrepresented by a cognitivist elite.

Such a proposal I take to be pragmatic. It is certainly not anti-religious. Gershom Scholem gave the inaugural address for a conference on Types of Redemption, in which he affirmed, with Kant, the necessity of religious experience in a study of religion: "I am not orthodox, but it is evident to me that without the restoration of such a 'fruitful bathos of experience' (*fruchtbaren Bathos der*

---

19. Perhaps the most sophisticated defense is now that of Heinrich Meier, *Leo Strauss and the Theological-Political Problem* (trans. M. Brainard; Cambridge: Cambridge University Press, 2006).

20. For orientation, see Samuel Weber and Hent de Vries, eds., *Religion and Media* (Palo Alto, Calif.: Stanford University Press, 2001).

Erfahrung), which arises out of the reflection and transformation of human words in the medium of the divine, nothing of your project can be realized."[21] Of course, Scholem does not tell us what he means by "the medium of the divine"—but that is a story for another day.

For us humanists the crux of understanding, in the meantime, lies not with what we can know but what we cannot know. If we replace "transcending the human condition" as ideal of study, I offer nothing other than a very old alternative, that of the limits of human knowledge. One of the original Humanists began his autobiography this way: "I always wanted to know whatever is knowable in the world . . . But it was not within my power to satisfy the desire as I wished."[22] Montaigne likewise laments, but accepts, what we cannot know: "The frontiers of our research are lost in dazzling light. Plutarch, writing of the fountainheads of history, says that when we push our investigations to extremes, they all fall into vagueness, rather like maps where the margins of known lands are filled in with marshes, deep forests, deserts, and uninhabitable places."[23]

We push temporally in a new age like the *terra incognita* that Montaigne evokes in spatial terms. We are in uncharted territory. Montaigne's valedictory essay "On Experience" uses our term in a different sense, that is, in the sense of being an "experienced" mechanic or gigolo. Experience in this sense is synonymous with understanding. What it is that experience teaches us is something, one hopes, that we have understood. Experienced teachers know that there is no pure pedagogy. With Montaigne, the "feebleness of our condition means that we can make habitual use of nothing in its natural unsophisticated purity."[24]

Just as the word experience has two meanings, so does the word medium. On my desk's cupboard I have taped a chart of scale, ranging from one nanometer, "the diameter of a Carbon-60 Buckyball" to 100,000 light years, "the diameter of the Milky Way's disk." We are located at a point on the scale that Emerson calls the "mid-world." In the universe of human experience, for Emerson, "the middle region of our being is the temperate zone."[25] I want to suggest that it is not for us scholars and teachers to get too close to religious experience—mid-range is about right. Neither close up nor long distance lenses should work for us, but rather an acuity that is about average, that is, medium-range.

---

21. From Scholem's 1932 "open letter" to Hans Joachim Schoeps, as cited in David Biale, *Gershom Scholem: Kabbalah and Counter-History* (2nd ed; Cambridge Mass.: Harvard University Press, 1982), 130.

22. Nepiachus, as cited by Wayne Shumaker, *Renaissance Curiosa* (Binghamton, N.Y.: Center for Medieval and Early Renaissance Studies, 1982), 92.

23. Michel de Montaigne, *The Complete Essays* (trans. M. A. Screech; Hammondsworth: Penguin, 1995), 611.

24. Montaigne, "We can savour nothing pure" in *The Complete Essays*, 764.

25. Ralph Waldo Emerson, *Essays & Lectures* (ed. Joel Porte; New York: Library of America, 1983), 480.

One thing is clear and that is the increasing rate of acceleration of digitalized complexity. For all the obvious advantages wrought by the information revolution, hyper-lucidity, I submit, is a dangerous seduction. Ultra-high-definition viewing of all points along the scale is now routinized and made universally, instantly, accessible. Do we want to stare at religious experience with such clarity? Instead of an answer, I return to Montaigne one last time.

> ... [it is] true that for the usages of the life and service of the common weal there can be an excess of purity and discernment in our wits; such penetrating clarity has too much subtleness and inquisitiveness. We must weigh down our wits and blunt their edge to render them more obedient to precedent and practice; we must coarsen them and darken them to give them the proportions of this earthy darksome life.[26]

Or, at least, we can take them out for pancakes.

---

26. Montaigne, "We can savour nothing pure," 766.

Visions, Mysteries, and the Interpretive Task: Text Work and Religious Experience in Philo and Clement

Celia Deutsch

Ancient Jewish and Christian authors made claims about religious experience in relation to text work in a variety of ways.[1] In this article, I examine two Alexandrian authors, the one, Philo, a Jew, and the other, Clement, a Christian much influenced by Philo. I focus on two texts, Philo's *Spec.* 3.1–6 and Clement's *Strom.* V.4.19.1–20.1, showing ways in which both authors use the language of mystery religions available in the dominant culture to describe text work as related directly to contemplation of the divine. The authors are separated by approximately a century and a half; Philo died sometime after his diplomatic mission to Rome in 39–40 C.E., and Clement flourished at the end of the second century.[2] The texts themselves are very different. The passage from *Special Laws* begins the third book of a commentary on the Ten Commandments, part of the larger "*Exposition of the Laws*," and is an autobiographical interjection.[3] The passage from the *Stromata* occurs in an extended discussion of allegorical interpretation in a work that is a gathering of Clement's teaching, presented for the most advanced of his learners.

---

1. This article is based on a paper given for the Religious Experience in Early Judaism and Early Christianity group at the Annual Meeting of the American Academy of Religion/Society of Biblical Literature, Philadelphia, November 19, 2005.

2. For Philo's dates, see John M. G. Barclay, *Jews in the Mediterranean Diaspora: From Alexander to Trajan (323 BC–117 CE)* (Berkeley and Los Angeles: University of California Press, 1996), 58–59. For Clement's dates, see André Méhat, *Étude sur les 'Stromates' de Clément d'Alexandrie* (Patristica Sorbonensia 7; Paris: Édition du Seuil, 1966), 46.

3. *The Special Laws* is part of a larger body of commentaries that scholars often call *Exposition of the Laws of Moses*; cf. Peder Borgen, "Philo of Alexandria: Reviewing and Rewriting Biblical Material," *Studia Philonica Annual* 9 (1997): 52.

Philo, *Spec.* 3.1–6
There was a time when I had the leisure for
philosophy (φιλοσοφία) and contemplation of the universe
(θεωρία τοῦ κοσμοῦ) and everything in it . . . . I did not
have lowly or base thoughts (ταπεινὸν φρονῶν ἢ χαμαίζηλον)
nor did I grovel about in search of reputation or
wealth or bodily comfort, but I seemed (ἐδόκουν) to be
carried up high in the air by some divinely given inspiration of the
soul (κατά τινα τῆς ψυχῆς ἐπιθειασμὸν) and to travel together
with sun and moon and the heaven and indeed the whole universe . . . .
But . . . Envy, the hater of the good, suddenly fell upon me and
plunged me into the sea of civic cares . . . . All the same, I hold out,
suffering, I have the yearning for Instruction(Παιδείας) established
in my soul from the earliest time of my life, which always has mercy
and pity on me, taking me and raising and lifting me up . . . . And if
unexpectedly there happens to me a brief spell of good weather
and calm from civil turmoil, soaring with wings I ride on the waves not
only borne by the air but breathed on by the breezes of Knowledge
(Ἐπιστήμης) who often persuades me to run away to spend my days
with her . . . . Yet it is fitting for me to bring thanksgiving to God . . .
that I . . . can also open the soul's eyes . . . and am illumined by the
light of Sophia, not being consigned to life in the darkness. So
consequently, here I am not only daring to read in the sacred
messages of Moses, but loving Knowledge, stooping to peep into
each one and to unfold and make manifest those that are not familiar
to the multitude.[4]

Clement, *Strom.* V.4.19.1–20.1
But since they have not wished to believe either
justly in the good nor in knowledge unto salvation,
we ourselves claim as our own what belongs to
them for all things are God's, and most of all
since the good things have come through us to the
Greeks, let us handle these things as they naturally
hear them. For certainly this great crowd does not
estimate the intelligent or the just by truth
but by whatever is pleasing to it. Surely they
will be pleased not more by what is different from
them, but more by what resembles them, so much they are

---

4. The translation is my own. Unless otherwise noted, I have used the translations of Philo in the Loeb Classical Library edition.

blind and dumb, not having intelligence or the
courageous and quick-sighted vision of a soul that
loves contemplation (φιλοθεάμονος) which only the Savior
bestows, so that they are like the uninitiated into
the mysteries (ὥ σπερ ἐν τελεταῖς ἀμύητον) and un-musical
at the choral dances who are neither purified (καθαρὸν)
nor worthy of the pure truth, dissonant and
undisciplined and material (ἐκμελὲς δὲ καὶ ἄτακτον καὶ ὑλικόν),
they must yet be made to stand outside the divine choir.
For indeed we compare spiritual (πνευμάτικοι) things to
the spiritual. For this reason indeed, the method
of concealment being truly divine and absolutely
for us placed in the innermost sanctuary (ἀδύτῳ) of
truth, the absolutely sacred Word, called by the
Egyptians, the inner sanctuary (ἀδύτων), and
the veil (παραπετάσματος) by the Hebrews,
speaking in riddles. Only those had access who were
consecrated, those who were dedicated to God, those
circumcised from the desire of the passions, through
love of God alone. It is not allowed for the unpurified
to have access to what is pure, to which Plato also
agrees. Hence, the prophecies and oracles are spoken
through enigmas and the mysteries are not manifest
unrestrainedly to all who approach, but with certain
purification and previous instruction.[5]

Philo is an Alexandrian Jew and Clement a Christian, born in Athens but living
in Alexandria.[6] However, both Philo and Clement lived and worked in the
broader context of the culture of Roman Egypt, where intellectual elites such as
our authors were profoundly marked by the Platonic heritage, were at the very
least aware and often participated in the mysteries, and honored the function of

---

5. The translation is my own. I have given the references for Clement according to *Clemens Alexandrinus* (ed. Otto Stählin; 4 vols.; Griechischen christlichen Schriftsteller der ersten drei Jahrhunderte; Leipzig: Hinrichs, 1905–36). When I have used the English translation of the *Ante-Nicene Fathers* series, I have given the reference immediately following the GCS, according to volume and page numbers. Otherwise the translations are my own.

6. On Philo and his social context, see Barclay, *Jews in the Mediterranean*, 158–80. For Clement, see Eric Francis Osborn, *Clement of Alexandria* (Cambridge: Cambridge University Press, 2005), 1–27.

the sacred scribe.[7] And that context gives us a framework in which to understand
the two passages under discussion in the present article.

It may be nothing short of folly to bring together two such magisterial figures
in the confines of a brief essay. However, I believe it worth the attempt because of
the place of these two thinkers in subsequent tradition, especially Christian tradition.[8] Philo and Clement alike suggest that they believe that text work is a site
for religious experience, and that they do their interpretive work in the context
of what they deem to be an experience of divine impulsion and revelation. In our
passages that process is associated with the language of the mysteries.

There are other texts where parallels between our two authors are more read-
ily apparent, places where Clement quotes his predecessor verbatim, for example.[9]
However, I have chosen these two passages because they illustrate something of
the way both writers considered the relation of text work to religious experience
and used mystery language to articulate that reflection.

---

7. On mystery and other cults in late-antique Alexandria, see Christopher Haas, *Alexandria in Late Antiquity: Topography and Social Conflict* (Baltimore: Johns Hopkins University
Press, 1997), 128–72. For examples of Philo's use, in other contexts, of language drawn from
the mysteries, see Burton L. Mack, *Logos und Sophia: Untersuchungen zur Weisheitstheologie
im hellenistischen Judentum* (SUNT 10; Göttingen: Vandenhoeck & Ruprecht, 1973), 144–47,
158–61, 167–71, 186–89. The classic statement is by Erwin Goodenough, *By Light, Light: the
Mystic Gospel of Hellenistic Judaism* (New Haven, Conn.: Yale University Press, 1935). On the
function of the sacred scribe, see David Frankfurter, *Religion in Roman Egypt: Assimilation and
Resistance* (Princeton, N.J.: Princeton University Press, 1998), 238–64.

8. Philo's lasting influence was on Christian rather than Jewish tradition; see David Runia,
Philo in Early Christian Literature: A Survey (CRINT 3; Minneapolis: Fortress, 1993); David
Winston, "Philo's *Nachleben* in Judaism," *Studia Philonica Annual* 6 (1994): 103–10. Adopted by
Clement, Origen, and Gregory of Nyssa, Philo's work provided the categories for eastern Chris-
tian analysis of the person's relation to the divine, as well as methodology for the interpretation
of Scripture. On Clement's place in Christian thought, see Bernard McGinn, *The Foundations
of Mysticism: Origins to the Fifth Century* (vol. 1 of *The Presence of God: A History of Western
Christian Mysticism*; New York: Crossroad, 1991), 101.

9. See Annewies van den Hoek, *Clement of Alexandria and His Use of Philo in the Stromateis: An Early Christian Reshaping of a Jewish Model* (VCSup 3; Leiden: Brill, 1988). For an
extended example of such parallels see the interpretation of the high priest and the tabernacle, in Philo, *Leg.* 2.56; *Somn.* 1.216; *Mos.* 2.71–135; Clement, *Strom.* 5.6.32–40. Van den Hoek
comments on these parallels; see *Clement of Alexandria*, 116–47; see also Judith L. Kovacs,
"Concealment and Gnostic Exegesis: Clement of Alexandria's Interpretation of the Tabernacle,"
*Studia Patristica: Papers Presented at the Twelfth International Conference on Patristic Studies
Held in Oxford, 1995* (StPatr 31; ed. Elizabeth A. Livingstone; Leuven: Peeters, 1997), 415–37;
van den Hoek, *Clement of Alexandria*, 116–47.

PHILO

Φιλοσοφία, Θεωρία AND THE BIBLE

Philo begins Book III of *Special Laws*, that part dealing with the commandments against adultery, murder, and related offenses, with a statement filled with nostalgia for a quieter time, saying, "when I had the leisure for φιλοσοφία, and contemplation of the universe . . . ." Contemplation is explicitly associated with φιλοσοφία elsewhere in the Philonic corpus.[10] Θεωρέω and its cognate θεωρία often signify the gazing, beholding, the vision that represents the mature activity of the sage in the Platonic tradition.

The object of philosophical contemplation varies, whether or not it is explicitly related to philosophy. Θεωρέω and its cognate θεωρία frequently have the universe or the heavenly bodies as object, evoking *Spec.* 3.1–6.11. Elsewhere, the object of the vision may be τὸ ὄντα, God,[12] or the divine realities (τοῖς θείοις).[13] In other cases, one sees, apprehends, that God is, even when God's essence is beyond human apprehension.[14]

"Philosophy" includes logic, physics, and ethics in the Greek curriculum, which Philo has followed.[15] But the immediate context of our passage, as well as usage elsewhere, suggests that "philosophy" here refers to study of Bible.[16]

---

10. E.g., *Opif.* 77; *Leg.* 1.57–58; *Abr.* 162–164; *Mos.* 2.66; *Decal.* 98.

11. E.g., θεωρέω: *Somn.* 2.26; *Abr.* 161; θεωρία: *Opif.* 77–78; *Mut.* 76; *Abr.* 164; *Decal.* 98; *Spec.* 1.176, 269; 2:52; *Prob.* 63; *Contempl.* 64, 90.

12. *Mut.* 82; *Leg.* 3.172–173. The verbs in the latter passage are ὁράω and βλέπω.

13. *Praem.* 26.

14. E.g., *Praem.* 40; *Mut.* 10; cf. Ellen Birnbaum, *The Place of Judaism in Philo's Thought: Israel, Jews and Proselytes* (BJS 290; Atlanta: Scholars Press, 1996), 61–127; Gerhard Delling, "The 'One Who Sees God' in Philo," in *Nourished with Peace; Studies in Hellenistic Judaism in Memory of Samuel Sandmel* (ed. F. E. Greenspahn, E. Hilgert, and B. L. Mack; Chico, Calif.: Scholars Press, 1984), 28–42; C. T. R. Hayward, "Philo, the Septuagint of Genesis 32:24–32 and the Name 'Israel': Fighting the Passions, Inspiration and the Vision of God," *JJS* 51(2000): 209–26; Francesca Calabi, "La luce che abbaglia: una metafora sulla inconoscibilità di Dio in Filone de Alessandria," in *Origeniana Octava; I, Origen and the Alexandrian Tradition; Origene e la tradizione alessandrina* (ed. L. Perrone, P. Bernardino and D. Marchini; papers of the 8th International Origen Congress Pisa, 27–31 August 2001; Leuven: Leuven University Press, 2003), 223–32; Chadwick, "Philo," 148. On the inadequacy of speech in face of the contemplative experience, see *Her.* 71; *Fug.* 92; *Migr.* 12; cf. David Winston, "Philo and the Contemplative Life," in *From the Bible through the Middle Ages* (ed. Arthur Green; vol. 1 of *Jewish Spirituality*; New York: Crossroad, 1986), 219.

15. *Leg.* 1.57; *Spec.* 1.336; cf. John Dillon, *The Middle Platonists, 80 B.C. to A.D. 220* (rev. ed.; Ithaca, N.Y.: Cornell University Press, 1996), 145.

16. E.g., *Spec.* 2.61–62; *Mos.* 2. 215–216; *Contempl.* 28, 67, 69, 89; possibly *Migr.* 34–35; see my article, "Text Work, Ritual and Mystical Experience: Philo's *De Vita Contemplativa*," in *Paradise Now: Essays on Early Jewish and Christian Mysticism*, SBLSymS 11 (ed. April DeConick;

I believe that Philo refers to the study of the Bible as "philosophy" because he understands its contents to be those of the Greco-Roman philosophical curriculum. In Greek philosophy, physics attends to the universe, cosmology. The Bible contains "physics," the cosmogony of the opening chapters of Genesis[17] and it includes ethics, as illustrated in Exodus through Deuteronomy, and in Philo's commentary *Special Laws*.[18]

Although he does not do so in *Spec.* 3.1–6, Philo occasionally associates the Λόγος with the Bible, perhaps even identifies the two.[19] Physics, which implies contemplation of the universe, also implies contemplation of the Λόγος, for the Λόγος contains the ἰδέας (Ideas, Forms) that are the models for that which the universe encompasses.[20] The Λόγος, repository of the ἰδέας, can be known through the sacred text, which itself is λόγος—word, speech, discourse, rationale. Philo tells us that the patterns of creation of the universe, or Ideas, are to be identified with "the laws set before us in these books" (*Mos.* 2.11). Later he says that Moses, the sage par excellence, "saw with his soul the immaterial forms of the material objects about to be made" (τῶν μελλόντων ἀποτελεῖσθαι σωμάτων ἀσωμάτους ἰδέας τῇ ψυχῇ θεωρῶν, *Mos.* 2.74).[21] The Middle Platonic understanding of the Logos, repository of Ideas, as that through which the world is made, converges with a certain reading of the opening chapter of Genesis where God creates the world, the firmament, and humankind through speech.[22]

The Λόγος mediates creation (*Somn.* 1.69). The Λόγος is also the mediator of revelation; it is the Λόγος, for example, that appears to Moses in the burning bush.[23] The Λόγος is also known in the study of the sacred text that contains the narrative of creation and revelation.

Atlanta: Society of Biblical Literature, 2006), 287–311. V. Nikiprowetzky (*Le commentaire de l'Écriture chez Philon d'Alexandrie* [ALGHJ 11; Leiden: Brill, 1977], 26) believes *Migr.* 34–35 to refer to allegorical interpretation of Scripture. Sze-Kar Wan ("Charismatic Exegesis: Philo and Paul Compared," *Studia Philonica Annual* 6 [1994]: 58) acknowledges the possibility, but believes that φιλοσοφίαν δογμάτων γραφὴν more likely refers "only generally to literary composition.".

17. Cf. *Opif.* 8; *Fug.* 68.

18. Cf. also *Mos.* 2.11, 216.

19. E.g., *Leg.* 1.93; 2.105; 3.8, 11, 36, 106, 110; *Det.* 66, 68. See Winston, "Philo and the Contemplative Life," 202.

20. For a discussion of Philo's understanding of the Logos, see Winston, "Philo and the Contemplative Life," 201–11; John Dillon, "Reclaiming the Heritage of Moses: Philo's Confrontation with Greek Philosophy," *Studia Philonica Annual* 7 (1995):108–23 (116–20); H. Chadwick, "Philo," in *The Cambridge History of Later Greek and Early Medieval Philosophy* (ed. A.H. Armstrong; Cambridge, UK: Cambridge University Press, 1967), 142–45.

21. The translation is mine.

22. E.g., *Leg.* 1.19, 21; 3.96.

23. *Somn.* 1. 231–32; *Mos.* 1.66; cf. Chadwick, "Philo," 144.

Ascent and the Mysteries

So here, in *Special Laws*, Philo begins a new section of his commentary, not simply with a statement of personal religious experience, but with a comment about text work—φιλοσοφία—and contemplation of the universe (θεωρίᾳ τοῦ κόσμου) in the process of study of the Bible. By extension, that study will include the ethical matters that he will subsequently consider as Philo continues his exegesis of the "ten words" in the rest of *Special Laws*. This opening statement frames our passage, and signals to us that Philo will have something to tell us about the ways in which he understands text work and religious experience to be interrelated.

Philo describes his experience using two additional categories. The first is the vocabulary of ascent. He tells us that, in earlier times he soared, seemingly carried aloft by God-given inspiration, and traveled with the heavenly bodies. Even yet, when there is a moment's respite from burdensome civic responsibilities, Philo soars again, borne aloft by the "breezes of Knowledge." Flight and ascent are favorite images of Philo.[24] He uses them to speak about the ultimate stage in the philosophical process. The imagery is drawn from Plato,[25] who uses it with language reflecting the Eleusinian mysteries in Phaedrus 250BC.[26]

---

24. See *Opif.* 70–71; *Spec.* 1.37, 207; 2.45; *Leg.* 1.38; 3.71, 84; *Det.* 27–28, 86-90; *Deus* 151; *Plant.* 23–25; *Migr.* 184; *Fug.* 62–63; *Mut.* 66–67, 179–180; *Somn* 1.139; *Praem.* 30, 121–22; *QE* 2.40; cf. Winston, *Philo of Alexandria: The Contemplative Life, the Giants, and Selections*, with preface by John Dillon (New York: Paulist, 1981), 329, n. 6. John R. Levison includes *Dec.* 175 and *Gig.* 53–54 in his discussion of "the ascent of the mind and allegorical interpretation;" "Inspiration and the Divine Spirit in the Writings of Philo Judaeus," *JSJ* 26 (1995): 271–323 (294–98). However, while both texts concern inspired interpretation, neither speaks of the ascent. As far as I am aware, the association of ascent with text work occurs only in our passage, in *Spec.* 1.37 and *Plant.* 23-26. On the theme of ascent in Philo, see Peder Borgen, "Heavenly Ascent in Philo: An Examination of Selected Passages," in *Pseudepigrapha and Early Biblical Interpretation* (ed. James H. Charlesworth and Craig A. Evans; Sheffield: JSOT, 1993), 246–68; Alan F. Segal, "Heavenly Ascent in Hellenistic Judaism, Early Christianity and Their Environment," *ANRW* 23.2:1354–58; idem, *Life After Death: a History of the Afterlife in Western Religion* (New York: Doubleday, 2004), 345–46; Winston, "Philo and the Contemplative Life," 211–15.

25. See *Phaedo* 109E; *Phaedr.* 246A–256B; *Rep.* 7.514A–518B; *Theatetus* 176; Winston ("Philo and the Contemplative Life," 215) notes that Philo quotes *Theatetus* 176A at *Fug.* 62–63; McGinn, *The Foundations of Mysticism*, 26-30; cf. Alan F. Segal, *Life after Death*, 235.

26. Walter Burkert, *Ancient Mystery Cults* (Cambridge, Mass.: Harvard University Press, 1987), 92–93. The *Phaedrus* (250BC) uses *mystai* and *epoptai*, terms used of initiates to the mysteries, for those who have made the ascent prior to bodily existence. For use of these terms in relation to the Eleusinian mysteries and their occurrence in Plato's *Phaedrus*, see Kevin Clinton, "Stages of Initiation in the Eleusinian and Samothracian Mysteries," in *Greek Mysteries: the Archaeology and Ritual of Ancient Greek Secret Cults* (ed. Michael B. Cosmopoulos London: Routledge, 2003), 50–78; on *Phaedr.* 250BC, see especially 56.

The ascent is also a journey through the heavens.[27] In that earlier, more lei-
sured time, Philo tells us, he "seemed to be carried up high in the air by some
divinely given inspiration of the soul and to travel together with the sun and moon
and the heaven and indeed, the whole universe . . ." (Spec. 3.1). The imagery, as
well as the use of συμπεριπολεῖν, evokes other texts in which Philo describes the
heavenly journey.[28] In Opif. 69–71, for instance, he describes at length the stages
of the ascent-journey. In Opif. 70, he uses the word to name the visionary's join-
ing in the dance of the planets.[29] He is "seized by a sober intoxication, like those
filled with Corybantic frenzy" (Opif. 71). Finally, in Praem. 121, Philo says that
the mind of the "initiate into the divine mysteries is called the fellow traveler of
the heavenly bodies as they revolved in ordered march." In Praem. 121 as well as
Opif. 69–71, Philo joins the imagery of ascent and heavenly journey with vocabulary of dance and ecstasy, echoing the mysteries.[30]

Παιδεία AND ASCENT

Now, however, in Spec. 3.1–6, Philo tells us that he is beset by the tension
caused by the demands of civic responsibility on the one hand and his longing
for study and contemplation on the other. Nonetheless, in moments of respite,
Instruction, personified Παιδεία, rescues Philo, serving as the medium of ascent
and flight.

Philo's use of παιδεία here is interesting. In his work the word has several
meanings. It can mean "discipline."[31] It is thus related to virtue. Alternatively,
it can signify "instruction" in the general sense.[32] Often, however, Philo uses it
in reference to the school subjects, the ἐγγύκλια. The term represents the curriculum astronomy, rhetoric, music, "and all the other branches of intellectual
study" (Congr. 11).[33] One must pursue these subjects before one can progress to
philosophy; indeed, Philo describes his own engagement with the curriculum of

---

27. Cf. Borgen, "Heavenly Ascent in Philo," 253–54; David Winston, "Sage and Super-Sage
in Philo of Alexandria," in The Ancestral Philosophy; Hellenistic Philosophy in Second Temple
Judaism; Essays of David Winston (ed. Gregory E. Sterling; BJS 331; SPhilo 4; Providence: Brown
Judaic Studies, 2001), 173.

28. Use of this verb also evokes Plato's Phaedrus; cf. John Levison, "Inspiration and the
Divine Spirit," 289. Συμπεριπολέω also occurs with φιλοσοφία in Spec. 1.37.

29. Cf. Borgen, "Heavenly Ascent in Philo," 253–54.

30. On dance as part of the mysteries, see Christiane Sourvinou-Inwood, "Festival and
Mysteries: Aspects of the Eleusinian Cult," in Cosmopoulos, Greek Mysteries, 33; Walter Burkert,
Greek Religion: Archaic and Classical (trans. John Raffan; Oxford: Basil Blackwell and Harvard
University Press), 286–87.

31. E.g., Leg. 2.89, 90, 92; Agr. 42, 44; Plant. 126; Ebr. 80–81; Congr. 88, 94.

32. E.g., Sacr. 122; Det. 66; Ebr. 95.

33. Philo also lists the specific subjects in Agr. 18 and Ebr. 48–49. Philo associates παιδεία
and the ἐγγύκλια in Cher. 3, 6; Agr. 18, 158; Ebr. 33, 48–49; Congr. 12, 14, 20, 22, 23, 72, 73, 121,

preliminary studies (*Congr.* 72–76). Nonetheless, Philo insists that these pursuits are preliminary and must be set aside with the illumination that accompanies the gift of Σοφία.[34]

Σοφία's ILLUMINATION AND THE MYSTERIES OF THE TEXT

Philo breaks into thanksgiving that he can open the soul's eyes, and that he is "illumined by the light of Sophia, not being consigned to life in the darkness . . . ." This illumination is related to Philo's speaking earlier of Παιδεία as lifting him up (3.4). There Παιδεία signifies not only a general reference to "Instruction," but the ongoing use of the skills, such as grammar, that Philo would necessarily bring to the task of allegorical interpretation of the biblical text, "philosophy." The reference may also allude to astronomy, which would prepare him for the experience of heavenly journey.[35] Because Instruction is associated with ἀρετή, Philo's usage also implies that he himself is engaged in the practice of the virtue that can be understood as encompassing the "ten words," which is the object of Philo's attention in Special Laws.[36]

With the signaling of illumination by Σοφία, we again encounter the language of the mysteries. Mysteries were often celebrated at night.[37] In many instances, darkness prevailed in the hall of mysteries at the beginning of some rituals. The first stage was characterized by ritual blindness.[38] Initiation brought sight; the *mystes* saw the *dromena*, the *deiknymena* displayed in the sanctuary.[39] Indeed, light and darkness formed part of the pattern of antithesis characterizing the mysteries.[40] Philo tells us here that he is illumined by Σοφία, who is, in the broader context of his work as well as the intellectual world of Second Temple

---

127, 154. He sometimes calls the ἐγκύκλια the μέσην παιδείαν ("lower instruction"); e.g., *Cher.* 3, 6; *Ebr.* 48–49; *Congr.* 12, 14, 20, 22, 145.

34. *Sacr.* 79.

35. See especially *Abr.* 69–71; also *Migr.* 178; *Her.* 98; *Congr.* 49–51.

36. On the relation of the curriculum, of παιδεία, to virtue, see Bruce W. Winter, *Philo and Paul among the Sophists: Alexandrian and Corinthian Responses to a Julio-Claudian Movement* (2nd ed.; Grand Rapids: Eerdmans, 2002), 80–94.

37. E.g., the initiation into the Isis mysteries; see Apuleius, *Metamorphoses*, 11.23.

38. Cf. Clinton, "Stages of Initiation," 50, 65–66.

39. Cf. Burkert, *Greek Religion*, 288; Marvin Meyer, ed., *The Ancient Mysteries: A Sourcebook: Sacred Texts of the Mystery Religions of the Ancient Mediterranean World* (San Francisco Calif.: Harper, 1987), 11.

40. Burkert, *Ancient Mysteries*, 93.

Judaism, divine Wisdom, agent of creation and revelation.[41] Philo associates her, even equates her in places, with the Logos.[42]

Illumining Philo as *mystis*, Sophia is associated with light, a characteristic assigned to Isis in Egyptian sources.[43] Moreover, in his use of mystery language, he tells us that he is not left "in the dark," in a state of un-initiation, but that he has been brought to the final stages of religious experience, of contemplation (θεωρία). Sophia is the mystagogue who has led Philo to illumination.[44] Philo continues to have access to the experience of contemplation, of vision, even in the tumultuous years of distracting civic responsibilities.

Just as Instruction, Παιδεία, takes him on the ascent, so flight, ascent, illumination brings continued study of the "sacred messages of Moses (ἱεροῖς Μωυσέως)."[45] Philo not only reads, but he stoops to peer into those messages in order to disclose meanings hidden from the multitude. Philo is speaking here of his allegorical interpretation of the text, most immediately his work in the *Special Laws*. He lays out the text, disclosing the invisible hidden in the visible, the soul of the letter concealed in the body of the text as he says elsewhere.[46] He unfolds its meanings for the multitude. These meanings, he tells us elsewhere, are accessible only to those who see (ὁρατικοῖς, *Plant.* 36), or to the initiated (μύσται, *Cher.* 48).[47]

At this point Philo uses another metaphor drawn from the mysteries. He stoops to peer into the messages of Moses—words that suggest peering through

41. Cf. my *Lady Wisdom, Jesus, and the Sages: Metaphor and Social Context in Matthew's Gospel* (Valley Forge, Pa: Trinity, 1996), 9–23; Winston, "Philo and the Contemplative Life," 202–8.

42. On the relationship of Λόγος and Σοφία in Philo's thought, see Burton Mack, *Logos und Sophia*, 108–79. The Λόγος is the source of Σοφία (*Fug.* 137–138); Salvatore R. C. Lilla, *Clement of Alexandria: A Study in Christian Platonism and Gnosticism* (Oxford: Oxford University Press), 208–09. However, in *Leg.* 1.65, Σοφία is the source of Λόγος.

43. On the association of Isis with light, see James M. Reese, *Hellenistic Influence on the Book of Wisdom and Its Consequences* (AnBib 41; Rome: Pontifical Biblical Institute, 1970), 47. Philo's reference to illumination by the light of Σοφία recalls *Contempl.* 68, where he speaks of the Therapeutrides who contemplate Σοφία's teachings under the power of divine illumination. The Wisdom of Solomon, likely another Alexandrian Jewish source, also associates Sophia with light (Wis 7:26, 29).

44. On the mystagogue, see Clinton, "Stages of Initiation," 65–66.

45. Philo associates inspired interpretation with light elsewhere, e.g., *Migr.* 34–35; cf. Levison, "Inspiration and the Divine Spirit," 282–84.

46. See *Contempl.* 78; *Migr.* 93; on the "body of the text" in Philo, see David Dawson, "Plato's Soul and the Body of the Text in Philo and Origen," in *Interpretation and Allegory; Antiquity to the Modern Period* (ed. John Whitman; Leiden: Brill, 2000), 89–107.

47. Philo does not use the word ἀλληγορία in *Cher.* 48. However, he is speaking about the reception of the allegorical interpretation of Gen 4:1–2 (*Cher.* 40). Cf. Barclay, *Jews in the Mediterranean*, 67.

a low door into a sanctuary chamber. Perhaps the sanctuary is a cave.[48] The language suggests closeness to the earth, bending, and stooping and it evokes the reference in the beginning of the passage. Philo tells us in the opening lines of *Spec.* 3.1–6 that he did not entertain base thoughts, slime-like thoughts (ταπεινὸν φρονῶν ἢ χαμαίζηλον). Rather, in the pursuit of philosophy and contemplation he made the ascent, took flight, and enjoyed the fullness of initiation. From on high, Philo peered down (διακύπτων) and saw earthly things as they truly are (3.2). Now, at the end of *Spec.* 3.1–6, Philo uses the same verb (διακύπτειν, 3.6) to refer explicitly to the interpretation of the text. We again see vocabulary that suggests closeness to the earth. However, usage at the end of the passage is different. This time it is a correlative of flight: ascent. In the convergence of imagery there is a paradox: stooping to peer as into a chamber—the ritual chamber of the "sacred messages of Moses"—becomes a correlative of flight.

Παιδεία, Ἄσκησις AND THE INTERPRETATIVE TASK

In *Spec.* 3.1–6 Philo suggests that his ascent has been prepared by a certain ascetical discipline, as well as by the preliminary studies of Παιδεία.[49] He does not use the word ἄσκησις, but he tells us that he did not seek "reputation or wealth or bodily comfort," which he contrasts directly with the quest to make the ascent. Later Philo associates concerns for honor, wealth, and comfort with the earth. He did not, he says, have "lowly or base thoughts"—χαμαίζηλον thoughts—literally "low-growing thoughts," "ground-seeking thoughts." In *Spec.* 3:1–6, moderation of physical satisfaction and eschewing of social honor is part of the practice implied by the references to Παιδεία and Σοφία.

There is a certain irony here: Philo, as a member of a family that was both wealthy and prominent, did not need to concern himself with such matters. Wealth, honor, and comfort were his by birthright. Nonetheless, his remark suggests a certain detachment deemed necessary for the philosophical quest.[50] Such

---

48. On the cave in the Eleusinian mysteries, see Clinton, "Stages of Initiation," 67.

49. See Thomas E. Phillips, "Revisiting Philo: Discussions of Wealth and Poverty in Philo's Ethical Discourse," *JSNT* 83 (2001): 111–21; T. Ewald Schmidt, "Hostility to Wealth in Philo of Alexandria," *JSNT* 19 (1983): 85–97. In *Leg.* 3.156–57, Philo speaks of his own difficulty in moderating his indulgence at the banquet table. On moderation, see *Ebr.* 56–62; *Spec.* 4.102; *QG* 2.67. On disregarding the opinion of others, see *Ebr.* 56–62. On discipline, withdrawal, ἀπάθεια, see *Leg.* 3. 71, 129–34; *Plant.* 98; *QG* 4.178); cf. Chadwick, "Philo," 147–48; Winston, "Was Philo a Mystic?" in *The Ancestral Philosophy*, 162–65; David C. Aune, "Mastery of the Passions: Philo, 4 Maccabees and Earliest Christianity," in *Hellenization Revisited: Shaping a Christian Response within the Greco-Roman World* (ed. Wendy E. Helleman; Lanham, Md.: University Press of America, 1994), 126–34.

50. On Philo's social status, see Barclay, *Jews in the Mediterranean*, 158–63. David Mealand saw this discrepancy between Philo's espousal of moderation and his personal affluence as an

language inverts the values of Mediterranean societies of antiquity with their focus on honor, status and wealth, and finds its most vivid embodiment in the community of Therapeutae and Therapeutrides at Lake Mareotis, described in Philo's *De Vita Contemplativa*.

CLEMENT

Γνῶσις AND ALLEGORICAL INTERPRETATION

One hundred and fifty years later, the Athenian-born Clement, teaching in Alexandria, adopted Philo's understanding of the sacred text as bearing multiple levels of meaning. Here, as in other matters, Clement's usage finds parallels in Justin's work.[51] But Philo's impact is even more evident in this regard.[52] Although Clement does not use the metaphors of ascent and flight in our specific passage—those occur elsewhere in its broader context[53]—he, like Philo, joins language of vision and cult in relation to the allegorical interpretation of the biblical text in ways that evoke the mysteries.

The passage we consider here represents the beginning of a long section on γνῶσις and the allegorical meaning of Scripture (*Strom.* V.4.19.1–9.58.6). It occurs in the context of a summary of the basic argument of *Strom.* V. In V.4.21.4, he says:

> All then, in a word, who have spoken of divine things,
> both Barbarians and Greeks, have veiled the first
> principles of things, and delivered the truth in
> enigmas, and symbols and allegories, and metaphors, and
> such like tropes (τὴν δὲ ἀλήθειαν αἰνίγμασι καὶ συμβόλοις
> ἀλληγορίαις τε αὖ καὶ μεταφοραῖς καὶ τοιούτοις τισὶ
> τρόποις παραδεδώκασιν, ANF 2: 449).

---

inconsistency in his thought; "Philo of Alexandria's Attitude to Riches," *ZNW* 69 (1978): 258–64. Others have resolved the difficulty; cf. T. Ewald Schmidt, "Hostility to Wealth," 85–97; Thomas E. Phillips, "Revisiting Philo," 111–21.

51. Dawson (*Allegorical Readers: Cultural Revision in Ancient Alexandria* [Berkeley and Los Angeles: University of California Press, 1992], 187) says, "Although Clement does not refer to Justin by name, it is virtually certain that he was familiar with Justin's writings." See also Chadwick, "Clement of Alexandria," in *Cambridge History*, 170; Lilla, *Clement of Alexandria*, 18.

52. Cf. van den Hoek, *Clement of Alexandria*; Runia, *Philo in Early Christian Literature*, 132–56.

53. The motif occurs in the context of our passage in V.6.32.1–40.4; V.12.78.2; and V.13.83.1. Elsewhere, see, e.g., *Strom.* IV.25.155.1–5; IV.26.165.1–172.3; VII.3.13.1–2; 10.55.1–57.5. See also *Exc.* 27; *Ecl.* 56–57. Cf. Judith L. Kovacs, "Concealment and Gnostic Exegesis," 420, 432.

In this section, Clement turns to the example of Greeks and Egyptians, as well as the Hebrew Bible and New Testament, for justification of the use of allegorical exegesis.[54] He presents allegorical interpretation as a universal phenomenon.[55] The passage assumes that the reader knows something about the mysteries. Our discussion of Philo suggested that in those cults the initiated who have undergone various kinds of purification are admitted into the chamber where they are allowed to see the sacred objects and/or ritual drama. Concealment and disclosure, purification and instruction, and vision are all part of the vocabulary of the mysteries.[56]

"Greeks," Allegory, and the Mysteries

Clement introduces the passage by telling us that he wants to use language that "Greeks" (Ἕλλησιν)—that is, pagans—will understand. This is appropriate, after all, since everything good has come to the Greeks "through us" (παρ' ἡμῶν).[57] Thus, he implies the reason not only for the use of allegory but also his use of the categories of the mysteries. But who are the "Greeks?" After all, Clement is Greek, at the very least by culture, and most likely of Athenian birth.[58] For Clement, human beings are classified into three groups: Greeks, Jews and Christians. *Stromata* 6.5.41.6 suggests that, for him, religious practice constitutes "the most salient marker of peoplehood."[59] Christians are a "people composed of other peoples."[60] They are a τρίτῳ γένει σεβόμενοι Χριστιανοί, a third race. In our passage, then, Clement suggests that he is using imagery that will be comprehensible to his pagan audience, to those not of his "people." This connection implies that allegorical interpretation thus functions in the rhetoric of identity formation.

---

54. Kovacs, "Concealment and Gnostic Exegesis," 414.

55. *Strom.* V.4.19.1–9.58.6 presents numerous examples from a wide variety of cultures known to Clement. Cf. Jean Pépin, *Mythe et allégorie; les origins grecques et les contestations judéo-chrétiennes* (2nd ed.; Paris: Études augustiniennes, 1976), 266.

56. Cf. Marvin W. Meyer, *Ancient Mysteries*, 4–5, 10; Burkert, *Greek Religion*, 276–304.

57. Cf. also *Strom.* VI.3.28.1–34.3. On Clement's views of Greek philosophy, see Lilla, *Clement of Alexandria*, 9–59; André Méhat, *Étude sur les 'Stromates'*, 346–94; Daniel Ridings, "Clement of Alexandria and the Intended Audience of the *Stromateis*," *Studia Patristica: Papers Presented at the Twelfth International Conference on Patristic Studies Held in Oxford, 1995* (StPatr 31; ed. Elizabeth A. Livingstone; Leuven: Peeters, 1997), 517–21.

58. Cf. Méhat, *Étude sur les 'Stromates'*, 42–44.

59. Denise K. Buell, "Rethinking the Relevance of Race for Early Christian Self-Definition," *HTR* 94 (2001): 449–76 (461); for further discussion on the function of discourse about ethnicity, see idem, *Why This New Race? Ethnic Reasoning in Early Christianity* (New York: Columbia University Press, 2005).

60. Buell, *Why This New Race?*, 122. See *Strom.* 3.9.70.1–2; 6.5.39.4–42.3; 6.13.106.4–107.1; Judith M. Lieu, *Christian Identity in the Jewish and Graeco-Roman World* (Oxford: Oxford University Press, 2004), 238–68.

Clement tells us that those who do not have understanding or the proper kind of vision cannot be admitted to the choir. This evokes *Protr.* 1.5–30, in which the Logos, the new song, "sings" through Greek poetry and Hebrew Scriptures as well as in the words of Jesus, who is Word and Teacher. It also evokes the tropes of the mystery rituals in which singing and dancing exercise an important role in setting the mood.[61] The language suggests that allegorical interpretation of the text is analogous to participation in a mystery ritual. Those who can see, who have the proper kind of vision, join in the chorus. "Vision" and "choir" function as boundary language, indicating those who are within and who without.

VISION AND TEXT

In *Strom.* V.4.19.1–20.1, it is the gift of vision that allows the interpreter to penetrate the enigmas concealing the "secret truths" (τῆς ἀληθείας ἀποκείμενον) of the text. The adjective φιλοθεάμονος (contemplative), is related to θεωρία and its cognates, and therefore is important in Clement's vocabulary.[62] For Clement, as for his predecessor Plato, θεωρία is a kind of vision that is referred to truth or the Word of God.[63] It has God as its ultimate object,[64] and is a correlative of γνῶσις.[65] Clement understands the sacred text as guiding the "eye" to contemplation.[66]

This perspective is more evident in the broader context of our passage. Later in Book V, in 6.32.1–40.4, the exegesis of the priestly vestments and the tabernacle, Clement tells us that the gnostic, "having become son and friend, is filled quite full with unsated contemplation face to face" (υἱὸς καὶ φίλος γενόμενος, πρόσωπον ἤδη πρὸς πρόσωπον ἐμπίπλαται τῆς ἀκορέστου θεωρίας, 40.1). This vision is the goal of the various revelations described in chapter 6.67. By allegorically explaining the parts of the tabernacle, the section displays the "progressive initiation into the knowledge of God, from pagan disbelief through a faith that relies on sense-perception to a direct vision of the invisible and inexpressible

---

61. Burkert, *Greek Religion*, 286–87.

62. On θεωρία in Clement's writing, see McGinn, *The Foundations of Mysticism*, 104–7; Kovacs, "Concealment and Gnostic Exegesis," 421; Chadwick, "Clement of Alexandria," 179; Edward Baert, "Le thème de la vision de Dieu chez s. Justin, Clément d'Alexandrie et S. Grégoire de Nysse," *FZPhTh* 12 (1965): 439–97 (456–80).

63. E.g., *Strom.* V.3.16.1–2; cf. Claude Mondésert, *Clément d'Alexandrie: introduction à partir de l'Écriture* (Paris: Aubier, 1944), 111, n. 4.

64. E.g., *Strom.* I.19.94.5; V.1.7.7; see McGinn, *The Foundations of Mysticism*, 106.

65. E.g., *Strom.* VII.10.56.1–5; cf. Mondésert, *Clément*, 111, n. 4. In this passage, θεωρία is associated with ascent and γνῶσις. See also VII.10.57.1–2, where the verb is the correlative ἐποπτεύω νοτ θεωρέω; in VII.10.58.1–6 Clement speaks of the ascent without using θεωρία or θεωρέω.

66. *Strom.* I.1.10.4.

67. Cf. Kovacs, "Concealment and Gnostic Exegesis," 421.

One."[68] This vision is the culmination of the experience of the divine in relation to the study and interpretation of the biblical text.

In chapter 6, contemplation has to do with ascent to the world of the ideas, putting off the things of the senses (V.6.39.3–40.4). It is only thus that the gnostic is able to come into the presence of God and experience θεωρία (40.1).[69] In V.4.19.1–20.1, the passage under examination in this article, vision is a correlative of initiation into the mysteries, as it is in the usage of the mysteries themselves.[70] The initiate sees the mysteries, sees the interior of the closed chamber, sees that which is hidden by the ἄδυτον or veil, sees that which is enacted or performed, and joins the chorus.

Clement usually uses μυστήριον or μυστήρια to signify doctrines accessible to those who have made the "initiation" that leads to γνῶσις.[71] Μυστήριον is part of Clement's esoteric vocabulary, marking the boundaries between the ordinary faithful and the gnostics on the one hand, and, on the other, between the "true" gnostics who are within the community and the false Gnostics who follow teachers like Basilides and Valentinus.[72]

Γνῶσις, Sanctuary, and Text

Our immediate passage does not use the term γνῶσις. However, in the context of Clement's work, γνῶσις is implied by the references to those who have the right kind of vision, to the πνευμάτικοι, to those who are "circumcised in the desire of the passions" (τοῖς περιτετμημένοις τὰς τῶν παθῶν ἐπιθυμίας). This is part of the vocabulary of the Valentinian Gnostics that Clement appropriates to

---

68. Ibid, 422–23; Kovacs notes that the parts of the tabernacle parallel the "sequence of Clement's work," with the *Protr.* directed to unbelievers, the *Paid.* to simple believers (I.1.,1.1–3.3), and the *Strom.* to the Christian seeking perfection (I.1,11.1–18.1); "Concealment and Gnostic Exegesis," 422. For a summary of the discussion of Clement's writings and their relationship to one another, see Eric Osborn, *Clement of Alexandria*, 5–15.

69. Cf. van den Hoek, *Clement of Alexandria*, 143.

70. Cf. Meyer, *Ancient Mysteries*, 5; Burkert, *Greek Religion*, 283, 287.

71. E.g., *Strom.* I.1.13.1, 4; I.1.15.3; V.10.61.1; V.14.90.3; VI.11.95.1; VII.1.4.3; VII.1.6.1; cf. Lilla, *Clement of Alexandria*, 146–48.

72. E.g., *Strom.* V.1.3.2–3; on Clement's esotericism, see Guy Stroumsa, "Clement, Origen, and Jewish Esoteric Traditions," in *Origeniana sexta* (ed. Giles Dorval and Alain Le Boulluec with Monique Alexandre; Leuven: Peeters, 1995), 54–59. Lilla demonstrates ways in which Clement appropriates and transforms Gnostic categories; *Clement of Alexandria*, especially 144–63. Kovacs demonstrates that Book V of the *Stromata* is largely a response to Valentinians; "Concealment and Gnostic Exegesis," 418–20. Here and elsewhere, I use the lower case for "gnostic" to designate Clement's Christian elite, and the upper case to designate the heretical Gnostics whom he opposes.

formulate his own understanding of faith and γνῶσις.[73] Γνῶσις is "the knowl-edge of the thing in itself, or the knowledge which harmonizes with what takes place" (*Strom.* II.17.76.3; *ANF* 2:364). This kind of knowledge is "the strong and sure demonstration (ἀπόδειξις) of what is received by faith, built upon faith by the Lord's teaching conveying [the soul] on to infallibility, science and comprehen-sion" (*Strom.* VII.10.57.3; *ANF* 2:539). The spiritual interpretation of Scripture is a dimension of γνῶσις.[74]

It is significant that the text speaks of those who are "outside the divine choir" (ἔξω θείου χοροῦ) because they lack the necessary understanding and vision. They are not "spiritual," and spiritual things can only be disclosed to the πνευμάτικοι. For this reason, Clement says, the sacred Word (ἱερὸν ἀτεχνῶς λόγον) is hidden in the shrine or inmost sanctuary (ἄδυτον)) according to the Egyptians), or by the veil (παραπετάσματος according to the Hebrews). The latter is an allusion to the veil that divided the Holy of Holies from the Sanctuary; here Clement brings together imagery from the mysteries with that from the Septuagint regarding the Temple.[75]

But what are the sanctuary, the veil? And just what is actually concealed? The sanctuary and the veil—that which contains and hides—as well as the content—what is contained and hidden—represent the sacred Word who is the Instructor[76] and calls people to faith. The Λόγος is hidden in the sanctuary, the text of Scrip-ture—also called the Λόγος—that is almost entirely given in riddles (αἴνιγματων, *Strom.* V.6.32.1). The Λόγος who is Lord and Christ gives Himself to those who can enter into "mystic contemplation" (ἐποπτικὴ θεωρία, *Strom.* V.10.66.2).[77] By combining ἐποπτικὴ with θεωρία, Clement evokes the highest level of participa-tion in the mysteries, in which there were

> two classes of celebrants, . . . the mystai who
> took part for the first time, and the epoptai, watchers,
> who were present for at least the second time. They saw
> what the mystai did not yet see; perhaps the latter
> had to veil themselves at certain phases of the
> celebration.[78]

---

73. Lilla, *Clement of Alexandria*, 118–19; Kovacs, "Concealment and Gnostic Exegesis," 427–28, n. 66.

74. *Strom.* VI.15.115.4–116.2; see McGinn, *The Foundations of Mysticism*, 104; Lilla, *Clement of Alexandria*, 56, 136–42.

75. See Exod 26:31–35; the LXX uses καταπέτασμα instead of παραπέτασμα to translate פרכת.

76. *Strom.* II.4.16.2; cf. *Paed.* 1.1.4.

77. On this passage, see McGinn, *The Foundations of Mysticism*, 372–73, n. 84. On the Logos in Clement, see Lilla, *Clement of Alexandria*, 199–212; Chadwick, "Clement," 177; Mark J. Edwards, "Clement of Alexandria and His Doctrine of the Logos," *VC* 54 (2000): 159–77.

78. Burkert, *Greek Religion*, 287; also 283 and 324; italics in Burkert's text.

Λόγος, THE BIBLICAL TEXT, AND THE INEXPRESSIBLE GOD

The Logos is hidden in the text of Scripture, in a manner analogous to the Incarnation through which the Son puts on the "tunic" (χιτών), which represents the flesh (σάρξ) and the world of sense (αἴσθησις, Strom. V.6.39.2–4). In Strom. V.3.16.1 (ANF 2:448), Clement cites John 14:6: "Now the Word of God says: 'I am the truth.'" Thus he makes explicit the identification of Logos as Christ the Son with the Logos of the text. That which is hidden is the Λόγος, God's Son, concealed in the text of Scripture. That text is both shrine and veil. This is where Clement's use of ritual language in relation to text work most radically departs from that of Philo.[79] While Philo associates the biblical text and thus the interpreter's work with the Λόγος, a divine emanation or intermediary, Clement identifies the Λόγος with Christ, God's Son. The biblical text is another "body" or "incarnation" of the Λόγος, and the relation of Λόγος to text a much more prominent theme in Clement's work than in Philo's.

For Clement, that which is hidden is also the Λόγος, understood as the deeper meaning of the literal text—"Prophets and Law" (τὰ προφητικὰ καὶ τὰ νομικά; V.6.32.1) as well as Gospels. This reality, he says, has its analogue in the practice of Egyptian priests who use the symbols of hieroglyphics to convey meaning and in the Greek poets and philosophers who conceal their teaching in riddles, symbols, allegories (Strom. V.7.41.1–9.58.6). But why should the deeper meaning of the sacred text, a Word meant for the whole community, be hidden? Such concealment is necessary, for one thing, in order to entice the reader to penetrate the significance of the text (Strom. VI.15.115.1). Furthermore, Clement tells us that the gnostic "is impressed with the closest likeness, that is with the mind of the Master" (Strom. VI.15.115.1; ANF 2:506). That identification requires preparation on all levels—moral, intellectual, and ascetical (Strom. VII.10.55.1–13.83.5).[80] In other words, not everyone is capable of receiving the "mysteries," the hidden meaning. As does Philo, Clement believes that full knowledge of the text is disclosed only to the elite.[81]

Ultimately, it is necessary for the sacred text to bear its deeper meaning in a hidden fashion, as a riddle or enigma, because God is transcendent. Clement comments on Plato, saying, "For the God of the universe, who is above all speech, all conception, all thought, can never be committed to writing, being inexpressible even by His own power (ἄρρητος ὢν δυνάμει τῇ αὑτοῦ, Strom. V.10.65.2; ANF 2:460).[82] Clement adduces further evidence from biblical texts, both Hebrew Bible

---

79. Cf. Osborn, Clement of Alexandria, 82.

80. On the relation of the various aspects of the gnostic's life, see McGinn, The Foundations of Mysticism, 103–7.

81. See also Strom. I.12.55.1–56.3; cf. Lilla, Clement of Alexandria, 56–59.

82. Clement is quoting Plato's Epistle II.312D; 314B–C.

and New Testament (V.11.71.5–82.4). The divine is unutterable, and the deeper meaning of Scripture must be concealed because the divine self is hidden.[83]

ACCESS TO THE SANCTUARY OF THE TEXT

The divine self is ultimately unknowable, hidden, yet the Logos is subject to demonstration and description since it is identified with the Jesus Christ revealed in the sacred text.[84] Allegories, riddles, hidden things can be penetrated and the deeper meaning of the text accessed through the guidance of a teacher who serves as interpreter and guide (ἐξηγητοῦ τινος καὶ καθηγητοῦ, *Strom.* V.9.56.4). One is reminded that the mystes needs a mystagogus.[85] So the reader needs a guide to lead her/him in the ritual of the mystery of the text and its meaning. This is the gnostic's role. The primary Instructor is, of course, the one who is Wisdom and Word,[86] but there is also the gnostic who, because of his contemplation and learning, mediates "contact and fellowship with the Divinity" (πρὸς τὸ θεῖον συνάφειάν τε καὶ κοινωνίαν ἐμμεσιτεύει, VII.9.52.1; *ANF* 2:538).[87]

Access to the meaning of the text requires preparation. In *Strom.* V.4.19.4, Clement cites Plato as stating that it is "not lawful for the 'impure to touch the pure'" (οὐ καθαρῷ γὰρ καθαροῦ ἐφάπτεσθαι οὐ θεμιτὸν εἶναι συνεδόκει καὶ Πλάτωνι).[88] The language suggests that the mystai must undertake ritual purity observances in order to offer sacrifice and participate in the mystery.[89] This

---

83. On the apophatic quality of Clement's mysticism, see Dawson, *Allegorical Readers*, 32–234; Deirdre Carabine, "A Dark Cloud: Hellenistic Influences on the Scriptural Exegesis of Clement of Alexandria and the Pseudo-Dionysius," in *Scriptural Interpretation in the Fathers* (ed. Thomas Finan and Vincent Twomey; Dublin: Four Courts, 1995), 65–68; Riemer Roukema, "La transcendence et la proximité de Dieu dans le christianisme ancient," *RHPR* 82 (2002): 15–31 (22-23); for a discussion of this aspect of Clement's thought in the context of the Platonic heritage, see Osborn, *Clement of Alexandria*, 111–31.

84. Cf. Manlio Simonetti, "Theologia e cristologia nell' Egitto cristiano," in Alberto Campani (ed.), *Egitto cristiano: aspetti e problemi in età tardo-antica* (Roma: Institutum Patristicum Augustinianum, 1977), 23.

85. Burkert, *Greek Religion*, 287, in reference to the Eleusinian mysteries.

86. *Strom.* VII.2.7.4; cf. the *Paid.* I.1.1.96–13.103.5. The latter is a description of Christ as the Instructor in virtue.

87. Cf. Judith L. Kovacs, "Divine Pedagogy and the Gnostic Teacher," *JECS* 9 (2001): 3–25. On the figure of the teacher in Alexandria, see Karen Jo Torjesen, "The Alexandrian Tradition of the Inspired Interpreter," in Perrone, Bernardino and Marchini, *Origeniana Octava I*, 287–99; Runia, *Philo in Early Christian Tradition*, 123; Simonetti, "Teologia e cristologia," 18.

88. Cf. *Phaedo* 67b.

89. For an example of ritual purification and the mysteries, see Apuleius, *Metamorphoses*, 11.23; in Meyer, *Ancient Mysteries*, 188–89. Also Pausanius IX.20.4; Burkert, *Greek Religion*, 78. Burkert notes that a "bath followed by dressing in new robes forms part of . . . initiations into mysteries. . . ."

observance is a correlative of instruction (προρρήσεων, V.4.20.1). Clement does not speak at length here about purification. Later he does say that purification is by confession (ὁμολογία) and contemplation by analysis (ἀνάλυσει, V.11.71.2). Purification appears to be one step in a three-fold process on the path to wisdom or γνῶσις, the first of which is illumination through instruction (V.10.60.2).[90] Clement tells us that those who are purified can respond to the call of the Λόγος who cries out in the sacred text (*Strom.* II.6.26.3). He says again, in Book V, that the gnostic Word purifies and that the Λόγος "by means of the Scripture inspires fuller intelligence" (πλείονα τὸν νοῦν διὰ τῆς γραφῆς ἐνδιδόντος, *Strom.* V.6.40.1; ANF 2:454).

The purified, then, have access to the shrine of the text. They are purified by the Λόγος embodied in the text, and that purification as propaedeutic is correlative with sacrifice. The sacrifice necessary for γνῶσις, for θεωρία, is "unswerving separation from the body and its passions" (θυσία δὲ ἡ τῷ θεῷ δεκτὴ σώματός τε καὶ τῶν τούτου παθῶν ἀμετανόητως χωρισμός, V.11.67.1).

<h2>ASCETICAL PRACTICE, ENCYCLICALS, AND THE TEXT</h2>

All of this suggests that γνῶσις, as it is related to access to the "deeper" meaning of the text, implies an ascetical practice. That extends beyond moderation of eating, drinking, sleep, and the use of material goods to include meditative separation from sense perception itself.[91] This extension is displayed in Strom. V.6.37.1–40.4, where Clement comments on the high priest's robe.[92] He tells us that the gnostic Levite is purified through the Logos and enters the world of the ideas where he reaches the fullness of the contemplative experience (V.6.40.1).

Later, in chapter 11, Clement will speak at greater length about the process of "separation from the body and its passions" (σώματός τε καὶ τῶν τούτου παθῶν ἀμετανόητος χωρισμός, V.11.67.1). There he describes the example and teaching of Socrates and Pythagoras. Pythagoras, Clement says, enjoined his disciples to a five-year silence "that, separating themselves from the objects of sense, they might with the mind alone contemplate the Deity" (V.11.67.2–3). Would-be Christian gnostics should separate themselves from "all that belongs to bodies and things called incorporeal," and cast themselves "into the greatness of Christ, and thence advance into immensity by holiness, we may reach somehow to the conception of the Almighty, knowing not what He is, but what He is not" (V.11.71.3; ANF 2:461).

---

90. Cf. Carabine, "A Dark Cloud," 67.

91. On the relation of text work, meditation and transformation in the context of Greco-Roman philosophy, see Pierre Hadot, *Philosophy as a Way of Life: Spiritual Exercises from Socrates to Foucault* (ed. Arnold I. Davidson; transl. Michael Case; Oxford: Blackwell, 1995), 81–125.

92. Cf. Exod 28:1–43; Lev 16:23–24. Clement's comments echo Philo here. See *Mos.* 2.117–35; *Spec.* 1.85–95; *QE* 2.114.

Γνῶσις in relation to the deeper meaning of the text implies not only the preparation of ascetical practice. It also requires the preparation afforded by the ἐγκύκλια. These prepare the soul for contemplation of the Ideas (τὰ νοητά) by the very nature of their various functions (*Strom.* I.19.93.5). Dialectics allows the person to perceive the reality of things and to separate from the passions (I.28.176.1–179.2).[93] Astronomy trains the person to contemplate the heavens (IV.26.169.1). Contemplation of the movement of the heavens and the order of the universe allows the person to disengage from the earthly realm and to go "to the intelligible realm from that of sense perception" (ἐπὶ τὰ νοητὰ μετατίθησιν ἀπὸ τῶν αἰσθητῶν, VI.11.90.4). A similar task is allotted to geometry (VI.9.80.2).[94]

Conclusions

Philo and Clement describe text work as mystery rite and the sacred text as sanctuary. Such language suggests intense religious experience, which encompasses affective as well as intellectual encounter with the divine. It serves other purposes as well. Mystery language is not only about intense religious emotion and the articulation of meaning about fundamental human questions of birth and death, and ongoing survival. It is also about community. It is about boundaries that mark off who is "inside" and who is "outside." In this, the metaphor of the sanctuary is particularly appropriate, with its suggestion of spatial boundaries.

Philo and Clement use this cultic language in relation to their own community as well as to those outside. Internally, claims to privileged experience in relation to the hermeneutical task may serve to legitimate their interpretations of the text. Their interpretations are authoritative because they are among the initiated who have direct contact with the divine. They do their work in the context of ascent and sanctuary, and can thus guide others in their own initiation. In their own contexts, Philo and Clement use the language of the mysteries to engage in internal debates. Philo may have in mind those who would jettison the letter of the law while focusing on its inner meaning (*Migr.* 89–93).[95] Philo's interpretation of the "10 words" will maintain the letter all the while probing its deeper, hidden meanings. His interpretation is authorized by his experience of heavenly ascent and access to the sanctuary of Moses's sacred messages. The reference to Παιδεία as preparation for the heavenly journey may relativize the place of the ἐγγύκλια as preparation for illumination. Thus, it could serve Philo's ongoing struggle with the seductive attractions of the Sophists whom he accuses of using the preliminary studies for their own ends rather than as means in the philosophical quest.[96]

---

93. See also *Strom.* VI.10.80.4.

94. Cf. Lilla, *Clement of Alexandria*, 169–73.

95. Cf. *Migr.* 89–93; cf. Barclay, *Jews in the Mediterranean*, 169; Dawson, *Allegorical Readers*, 118–19.

96. Cf. Winter, *Philo and Paul among the Sophists*, 80–94.

Finally, claiming the mystery language first used by Plato in relation to philosophy, Philo makes an implicit claim about his own interpretive work. The biblical text is the "true" philosophy and the inspired exegete stands in the place of Plato and his other successors.

Clement mounts his polemic against those Gnostics outside the community, who make a travesty of the sacred text by presenting the Christian gnostic as the initiate who has access to the sanctuary of the text. To those within his community who might be tempted by Gnostic teaching he presents the community's interpretation of biblical texts, the access to the hidden meanings of the text, and the way to make the ascent to true γνῶσις. Clement's "true" gnostics are set off from those false "Gnostics" who distort the text of Scripture and misinterpret its meanings (*Strom.* VII.16.93.1–105.6).[97]

Both Philo and Clement legitimate, respectively, Judaism and Christianity as "philosophies" that can compete with the best of the Greek philosophical tradition and the Egyptian traditions represented by the priestly scribes.[98] In the specific context of *Spec.* 3.1–6, this refers to the proper interpretation of the laws summarized under the "ten words" (δέκα λόγοι, *Spec.* 1.1), and begins a section in which he will address the commandment against adultery (3.7–8). The context of Clement's *Stromateis* legitimates his treatment of and practice of allegory. Associating text work with religious experience positions the speaker as being in a superior position in relation to those "outside" the sanctuary of the comprehension of the hidden meaning, both within and outside the communities. Use of mystery language with its implied and explicit allusions to initiation and admission to the sanctuary, suggests that the hermeneutical task is one of intimacy with the divine and thus valorizes the interpreter's work. Philo and Clement both interpret their own hermeneutical work in the categories of the dominant culture of Alexandria. In that process both valorize their own religions as "philosophy," and they interpret Greco-Roman philosophy through the lens of their own sacred texts, positioning themselves in a relation of superiority to their competitors both within the community and outside.

---

97. Dawson, *Allegorical Readers*, 230–32.

98. See the Chaeremon fragments, particularly fragment 10; Pieter Willem van der Horst, *Chaeremon: Egyptian Priest and Stoic Philosopher: The Fragments Collected and Translated with Explanatory Notes* (Études preliminaries aux religions orientales dans l'empire romain 101; Leiden: Brill, 1984), 17; see also *P.Oxy.* 11.1381.32–52; David Frankfurter, *Religion in Roman Egypt*, 238–64; for parallels between Philo and Chaeremon, see my "The Therapeutae, Text Work, Ritual, and Mystical Experience," 304.

Transformation by a Text: The Gospel of John

Robin Griffith-Jones

What Jesus Did, the Gospel Does

In his classic article on the stranger from heaven, Wayne Meeks observed that the Gospel of John *"functions for its readers in precisely the same way that the epiphany of its hero functions within its narratives and dialogues."*[1] Meeks then elaborates: "The book defines and vindicates the existence of the community that evidently sees itself as unique, alien from its world, under attack, misunderstood, but living in unity with Christ and through him with God . . . ." But this focus does not yet do justice to the Jesus of John's gospel. Within the story Jesus riddles, teases, warns, and promises; he also heals, gives sight, and brings to new life. And what Jesus does among the actors in the gospel, so—as Meeks observed—the gospel does among its recipients. How? By taking, I suggest, the individual readers through the riddles and warnings and healings of Jesus that the gospel records— and so, by bringing the readers to that new life of which John writes.

The gospel is written not merely to describe and vindicate the setting of its recipients, but rather to give those recipients, in and through its reception, what John regards as new health, new sight and new life. The gospel was a tool of mystagogy, cast as a narrative.[2] How, then, was "birth again from above" prepared for and brought about? What was its effect?[3] How are we to catch a glimpse of that process, at our vast distance from the communal and catechetical structure within

---

1. Wayne Meeks, "The Stranger from Heaven in Johannine Sectarianism," reprinted in *The Interpretation of John* (ed. John Ashton; Edinburgh: T&T Clark, 1986), 162.

2. Rudolf Bultmann, *The Gospel of John: A Commentary* (trans. G. R. Beasley Murray; Oxford: Blackwell, 1971), 605–6, warned: "The Revealer is the access to God . . . and what is more . . . the only access. Not, however, in the sense that he mediated the access and then became superfluous; i.e., not in the sense of a mystagogue, who brings doctrines and celebrations that are the means to the vision of God." This does nothing to weaken the present proposal. The gospel no more becomes superfluous after its apparent mastery by the reader than does the Jesus of whom it speaks.

3. Let us speak at this stage of the author-editor who would have accepted responsibility for the text in its present form, as "John," and of those people as the "readers" of whom this John

which it was probably undergone? We must survey the intellectual, cognitive and emotional responses to which hearing or reading the gospel might be expected to have given rise.[4]

A drama is played out within the readers, as they envisage and define themselves successively as the cripple, the blind man and Lazarus, brought from incomprehension through healing to new birth from above.[5] They are to see themselves as reborn (at chapter 11) and so as members of the innermost circle of Jesus's disciples, admitted to the final and private discourses (chapters 13–17); they are to share the ascent of Jesus at chapter 17, and so, with the understanding of initiates, are to watch the new creation's completion at the death of Jesus, and are finally (at chapter 20) to see themselves, in the garden of the resurrection, as inhabitants of a newly recreated Eden. Hereby the gospel could reassure readers attracted—or, as John would think, distracted—by the claims of other Christian groups to experience and to offer journeys to a more exclusive paradise, the heavenly Holy of Holies. Such journeys were redundant since Jesus himself was the new Temple; the sights and knowledge that had seemed to belong exclusively in heaven were offered to John's readers in their growing insight into Jesus, as they read or heard the gospel itself. John's gospel is in many ways an apocalypse, upside-down. In many ways, but not in all; for the gospel was performed and encountered in liturgy—in precisely that setting that could offer its participants some participation (which we will have to define with care) in the life and worship of heaven.

John is advancing a vast schema of replacement and renewal in which the Word has tabernacled among us. Sacred places have been displaced by the sacred person (1:51): the Temple itself by Jesus (2:13–23), its worship by worship in spirit and truth (4:23), the rituals of its rededication by the role of Jesus (chapters 7–9), the Passover sacrifices in its courts by the death of Jesus on the cross, its Edenic sanctuary by the sight of the risen Jesus. This replacement is poignant. Twenty years after the destruction of Jerusalem, Judaism must find substitutes for the sanctity and roles of the Temple. In John's gospel a chiefly Jewish community was proclaiming, as a new Temple, the Jesus whom the Temple's own authorities had helped to kill. Readers who reached the Paradise of John 20 were, in their imagination, in the Temple's Edenic Holy of Holies, and so had by their journey through the gospel reached the goal, in a new form, of a seer's journey to heaven.

---

would say, if asked, that he had hoped and expected they would read or hear his text. We return below to these readers.

4. A general reading of the gospel in these terms is given by the present author, *The Four Witnesses* (San Francisco: Harper, 2000), 281–377.

5. It is clearly important for this argument that John expected his gospel to be encountered as a sequential whole; the order of events *matters*. Thus, regardless of any sources used in the creation of the Gospel, I will be treating the final canonical product as a literary whole.

Two sequences matter in John's mystagogic schema: the events in the story of Jesus, and the revelatory events within the readers. John actively reminds the readers that they can now see in the events of Jesus's life what those around Jesus could not; and the readers are of course to bring that insight to their reading of the gospel. But they are not for that reason simply to ignore the viewpoint of those around Jesus; for without some adoption of that viewpoint the readers cannot undergo the gospel's sequential, cumulative story for themselves. So John, from the start, sets two viewpoints side by side. After Jesus's first "sign," the disciples trust in him (2:11) as the readers might; after his second the disciples remember what is written (2:17); and then and there we are told that after his resurrection, they will remember Jesus's explanation (2:22)—and at last those around Jesus before the resurrection catch up with those reading the gospel after it.[6] John's readers have got to learn how to "read" Jesus's enigmatic speech and actions from both these vantage-points, and it is the gospel itself that will teach the readers how to do so. Here is the first of the gospel's many lessons in reading well.

The intercalation of the two viewpoints has a startling effect. In the gospel's first half the readers are offered, as a function of their imaginative self-definition, rebirth from the death they share with Lazarus *before* they read in the gospel's second half of the dying, risen or ascended Jesus. Why? To understand Jesus's death, the readers must first undergo the transformation that only that death had made possible.[7]

This transformation could not be effected by mere argument alone, but by two closely interconnected uses of the readers' imagination: by the imaginative experience *both* of the health, sight, and life that John's Jesus had brought in his life to those he met *and thereby* of the health, sight, and life that this Jesus now offered in the gospel to John's readers. These readers were not intended as observers to appraise the miracles, but as those who themselves were encountering Jesus to undergo the miracles; John was stirring—and steering—their imagination not to acknowledge the symbolism of various past healings but to experience present healing themselves. The order and details of John 1–11 are vital to the experience to be undergone by its readers. Therefore, at the risk of approaching too closely the style of a commentary, we will watch the sequences of events unfold before and within the reader. Hereby I hope to establish (rather than simply assert) the

---

6. Raymond Brown describes 1:35–2:11 as "the conspectus of Christian vocation," *The Gospel according to John (i–xii)* (2 vols.; AB 29–29A; Garden City, N.Y.: Doubleday, 1966–70), 1:77. John exploits, as well as the readers' retrospect, their overview of the whole story. At 6:27–28 the crowd connects true nourishment with doing the works of God: a connection that should indeed be made by those who have encountered 4:14 and 4:34—as the readers have but the crowd had not.

7. There are important implications to be drawn from these claims for any modern preaching that seeks to be loyal to the practices, within the early churches, to which scripture bears witness.

basis on which I will finally build this paper's claims for the (notoriously obscure) function of John's Easter stories.

John 1–11: The Rebirth of the Readers from Above

John is working to effect a cumulative and transformative experience in his readers as they adopt, with a self-conscious but sympathetic imagination, the varying points of view of successive characters. The Prologue lays out the understanding of Jesus to which John plans to bring his readers: they are to be given the power to become children of God (1:13).[8] The gospel is written by an initiate, working in the name of initiates, for the benefit of those who are imagined not to be initiates at the gospel's start. John and his fellow leaders can say, as such readers cannot, "We *have seen* his glory" (1:14); "What we know, we speak, and *what we have seen*, we bear witness to" (3:11). Sight and insight are paired throughout the gospel until John himself draws at its close the distinction, which the gospel itself has been eliding, between past presence and present imagination: "Blessed are those who have not seen and have believed" (20:29). The readers are encouraged at the gospel's close to acknowledge the devices to which John has subjected them throughout; they will come to acknowledge what can—and must—really be "seen" and how, and what forms of sight must (by contrast) be transcended or foregone.

In the following paragraphs we survey just some of the critical moments in John's execution of his design. In this sketch we will attend to the first disciples, Nicodemus, the Samaritan Woman, the cripple, the blind man, and Lazarus.

On the advice of the Baptist, Andrew and his companion follow Jesus. "What are you looking for?" "To see where you are staying." "Come and see" (1:35–39). The invitation is an invitation to the readers too; they will discover over the course of the gospel where they themselves should "stay" (6:56, 14:10–11, 14:23, 15:1–9) and how. The readers are encouraged to follow the lead offered by those first disciples who acknowledge Jesus from the start to be the Christ (1:41), the one foretold

---

8. R. Alan Culpepper (*Anatomy of the Fourth Gospel: A Study in Literary Design* [Philadelphia: Fortress, 1983], 232) argues, in contrast, that the reader is simply aligned with the narrator from the Prologue onwards: "The plot of the gospel is so crafted . . . that the narrator's view of Jesus is conclusively established before the reader is exposed to any challenge to it." "Through its irony, the gospel lifts its readers to the vantage point of the narrator. . . . Readers dance with the author, whether they want to or not," 234. Jeffrey Lloyd Staley (*The Print's First Kiss* [SBLDS 82; Atlanta: Scholars Press, 1988], 116) has brought to prominence the shifting relations in which the reader stands to the story's characters: he sees the reader as brought "inside" by the Prologue, and then pushed "outside" by the gospel's "reader victimization strategies." Kelli S. O'Brien ("Written that You May Believe: John 20 and Narrative Rhetoric," *CBQ* 67 [2005]: 284–302) has recently explored a line of thought similar to my own: "The author presents characters who experience confusion, uncertainty, and misunderstanding but who profit from the experience and come to authentic faith—that is, the reader is presented with characters much like him" (296).

by Moses and the prophets (1:45), the son of God and king of Israel (1:49). By the time the readers reach the gospel's first climax, in John 11, they are able to acknowledge Jesus, as Martha does, for themselves: "I have come to believe that you are the Christ, the son of God, the one coming into the world" (11.27). Only kingship is left without open acknowledgment; for the king has not yet come to his enthronement on the cross.

Jesus himself raises the readers' doubts as to whether those first disciples had adequate grounds to declare their trust as they did (1:50). He responds to Nathanael's declaration of faith by a promise that "you [singular: Nathanael] will see greater things than these" (1:50). But he then makes a cryptic promise to the disciples—and so to the readers—when he declares that "you [plural] shall see heaven opened and the angels on the Son of Man" (1:51), just as Israel himself had *seen* the angels on the ladder at Bethel (Gen 28:12).[9] How will this promise be fulfilled in the story of Nathanael and in its reception by the reader? The readers may well ask if they are themselves being promised a heavenly dream and the insights of a seer, or at least a report, within the impending story, of some such visionary privilege. The image evoked of the ladder-like Son of Man is famously strange. The readers have good reason to be enthralled, but at this stage in the story to be uncertain too. They cannot be sure what fulfillment to expect, or even, as they make their way through the gospel and its handling of the Jewish scriptures, whether they will recognize that fulfillment if it comes. John is not clumsily letting his readers sink into confusion; he is, in his early stories, purposefully steering them towards confusion.

The readers will over and again be unsettled. They hear by the end of chapter 2 that many came to trust in Jesus's name, seeing his signs. The readers, reading precisely because they do have some trust in Jesus, feel at home in the setting of such incipient faith. But Jesus did not entrust himself to the newly trusting crowd. Seeing signs, then, does not necessarily promote understanding (2:23–24). Once more the readers are disturbed: are they among the disciples who really *see*? Nicodemus is about to speak for them. His mind too is on the signs of which the readers have just learned, and he concludes that God must be with the person who effects them (3:2). The readers, then, have as much reason as Nicodemus to be unnerved when Jesus insists that nobody can see the Kingdom of God without being born from above (3:3).

---

9. For a valuable account of 1:51, see John Ashton, *Understanding the Fourth Gospel* (Oxford: Oxford University Press, 1991), 342–48. Several scholars have suggested that Jacob's ladder was, in the source text behind Gen 28, a *ziqqurat*; e.g., Frances Flannery-Dailey (*Dreams, Scribes, and Priests: Jewish Dreamers in the Hellenistic and Roman Eras* [JSJSup 90; Leiden: Brill, 2004], 199–200): "If the *Ladder of Jacob* is in fact a Hellenistic Jewish composition, it demonstrates that such an association amongst *ziqqurats*, dream incubation and ascent/descent was preserved in early Judaism." Jesus, the new Temple, is the stairway to heaven on a new *ziqqurat*.

Yet, to be born of the spirit (3:5) is surely an option available only after the spirit has been given. In the gospel's own terms, then, it is an option not open to Nicodemus at the time of his encounter with Jesus.[10] At 3:11–13 Jesus as speaker moves into the first person plural: "We . . . testify to what we have seen," suggesting the witness borne by the later Christian community.[11] He switches back to the first person singular, "I have told you. . .," and then to the third to speak of the Son of Man who "has ascended" already, at the time of speaking, "into heaven." Nicodemus is bemused. So he should be; Jesus's early claims are intended to be baffling—to Nicodemus, and to the readers.[12] Nicodemus asks, "How can it be?" (3:4), and so will the crowd (6:52). They are asking questions that the readers too have good reason to ask. It is no accident that Nicodemus fades from the scene;[13] John's Jesus is addressing the reader. Nicodemus himself grows only slowly in courage and only ambiguously in understanding. Over the course of the gospel he is a foil for John's readers (and in particular, we may suspect, for John's Jewish readers) as their representative at the story's start, and as a warning to them at the end.

The Samaritan woman, by contrast with Nicodemus, shows growth within a single encounter with Jesus. She comes first to "see" Jesus as a prophet (4:19) and then to recognize him tentatively as the Christ. Once more, sight is vital; she urges the people, "Come and see" (4:29). Her townspeople, after Jesus has been with them for two days, will recognize him as the savior of the world (4:42).[14]

---

10. It can be no coincidence that the born-again come and go as mysteriously as Jesus does (3:8). It is natural (but not necessary) to think of the Jesus within the story who "immerses in holy spirit" (1:33) as the Jesus active among the gospel's readers after the death and resurrection-appearance at which he handed the spirit over (19:30, 20:22).

11. Nicodemus speaks for a community: οἴδαμεν, 3:2. So does John's Jesus: *oidamen*, 3:11. "This whole passage would seem more natural on the lips of a Christian catechist long after the foundation of the church, than as a first declaration from Jesus himself," Marie-Joseph Lagrange, *Évangile selon Saint Jean* (Paris: Gabalda, 1925), 72 (author's translation). Robert Kysar ("The Making of Metaphor: Another Reading of John 3:1–15," in *What is John?* [ed. Fernando F. Segovia; Atlanta: Scholars Press, 1996], 1:21–42) is alert to the ambiguous relation in which the reader stands to Nicodemus.

12. Compare the Gospel of Thomas: the opening *logia* help the readers to recognize what they must hope to achieve in their reception of the text, and (by its cryptic style) so to dispose themselves that they can indeed "find the explanation of these words." Thomas is designed to be riddling.

13. When exactly, after 3:10, does Nicodemus leave the conversation? The question is familiar but misses the point of John's technique.

14. Godfrey Carruthers Nicholson (*Death as Departure* [SBLDS, 63; Chico, Calif.: Scholars Press, 1983], 66) asks how we are to rate the Samaritans' confession of 4:41–42, which goes beyond the claim of the woman. He suspects that 4:41–42 stands under correction by 4:31–38. On the contrary, the townspeople have spent two days more with Jesus than the woman had. John is making a point about hearing: from others and for oneself. "Savior" is associated by Luke and Paul with the *risen* Jesus; John 4:42 "is the only instance in the gospels of its being applied

The Gnostic commentator Heracleon, writing on John's gospel ca. 160 C.E., was right: the Samaritan woman is more receptive than the disciples themselves[15] and she has done better, in her one meeting with Jesus, than Nicodemus ever will. From this woman readers learn how to relate to Jesus: with a frisson of attraction and intimacy.[16] As we shall see, the readers shall be encouraged to allow themselves such an experience again.

With the healing of the lame man (5:1–8), the readers witness Jesus's power in action. Nonetheless, they still have good reason to be baffled by his greater promise that "the hour is coming and now is when the dead shall hear the voice of the son of God, and those who hear shall live" (5:25, 28). With the next healing, sight and insight come programmatically to the fore: the man born blind acknowledges Jesus first as a prophet (9:17), and then as one who has come from God (9:33). These first insights have involved little more than common sense, bravely applied. But Jesus then asks the man born blind whether he believes in the Son of Man, of whom the man has no reason ever to have heard. Who, the man asks, is the Son of Man? It is a good question. The readers themselves have been teased by the successive, cryptic allusions to this figure at 1:51, 3:14, in the refinement of 1:51

---

to Jesus during the public ministry" (Brown, *The Gospel according to John (i–xii)*, 1:175). Brown distinguishes clearly between the records of Jesus's earthly ministry and the claims made for his risen life, and so he begs the question. If John too thought of the "Savior" as specifically the risen Jesus, then the Samaritans are presented as coming to see when Jesus was with them what the readers can and must see after Easter.

15. Heracleon, in Origen, *Comm. Jo.* XIII.10.57–11.74, 13.10–35, 15.91–19.118, 25.147–150, 31.187–192, 32.200–202. Cf. Elaine H. Pagels, *The Johannine Gospel in Gnostic Exegesis* (SBLMS, 17; Atlanta: Scholars Press, 1989), 86–93. Modern commentators are less perceptive. The woman of Samaria, wrote Bultmann (*The Gospel of John*, 188), typifies the aberrant life of those who reel from desire to pleasure. Rudolf Schnackenburg (*The Gospel According to John* [3 vols.; New York: Herder and Herder, 1968–82], 432–33) speaks of her sinful way of life and guilt. For Brown (*The Gospel according to John [i–xii]*, 1:175, following Lagrange), she is "mincing and coy, with a certain light grace." None of this is justified by the story John tells. The woman has been married five times. While exegetes infer she was immoral, neither John nor his Jesus says so. Who would have listened to the disreputable woman imagined by these exegetes? See further Luise Schottroff, "The Samaritan Woman and the Notion of Sexuality in the Fourth Gospel," in *What is John?* (vol. 2; ed. Fernando F. Segovia; Atlanta: Scholars Press, 1998), 157–81.

16. Abraham sent his servant to find a wife for Isaac among Abraham's own kin. The servant came to the city of Nahor and waited at a well. Rebekah approached, "Please give me," he said, "a little water to drink from your jar." She did so. By this sign he was assured that Rebekah was the woman he was looking for to be Isaac's wife (Gen 24:1–21). Isaac's own son Jacob first met Rachel, who would be his wife, at a well (Gen 29:1–14). Moses met Zipporah and her sisters at a well in Midian (Exod 2:16). There is more to such encounters than a formulaic story-line. Marriages are made at wells. "A garden locked is my sister, my bride," sings the bridegroom in the Song of Songs, "a fountain sealed; an orchard with trees of myrrh and aloes; a well of living water" (Song 4:12–15). In Nazareth the Greek Orthodox Church of the Archangel Gabriel is built over "Mary's Well."

at 6:62, and at the opaque 8:28.[17] It is *the readers* who are now ready to take up the promise made in 3:15 that everyone trusting in the Son of Man—as they are coming to trust—shall have the life of the new eon. As the healed man finally worships Jesus as the Son of Man (9.35–38), so do the readers. Judgment is under way as the blind see and those with sight become blind (9.39).

Demands and promises have assailed the readers. They must be born again; but how? The dead shall live; but when? In the gospel's climactic miracle the demands are met and the promises fulfilled—within the reader and within their reading of the story. John deploys and enriches his usual technique. Jesus, we hear, "loved Martha and Mary her sister and Lazarus." The three figures form, for John's purposes, a unit. *Together* they represent the readers. Jesus asks Martha, "Haven't I told you (singular) that if you believe you shall see the glory of God?" (11:40). Within the gospel, he has not told Martha, but the readers (who have absorbed 1:14 and 11:4) have good reason to hope they will see this glory. Martha's confession is a reprise of the claims made by Jesus's first disciples in 1:41–49. Now the readers are ready to make the declaration so blandly made by the first disciples at the story's start.

Martha declares her trust in Jesus while Mary admits only what might have been. Here are the voices of the Lazarus who cannot speak for himself. Mary may despair, but the confession of Martha and the devotion of both sisters are enough. They win their brother back from the tomb. John's Jesus acknowledges the tumult of doubt that can accompany trust—trust to which he will, nonetheless, respond. In this way John draws together the threads of his gospel's first half. Jesus has promised that "the hour is coming and now is when the dead shall hear the voice of the son of God, and those who hear shall live" (5:25, cf. v. 28). Now Jesus cries with a loud voice and the dead man emerges from the tomb (11:43–44). Lazarus represents the reader, born again from above in the reception of the gospel itself and so equipped *now* to see the kingdom of God. The last day has dawned, on which Jesus shall raise the readers who in the gospel itself see the Son and trust in him (6:40). Such readers are ready to join the innermost circle of Jesus's disciples for the private discourses of John 13–17 and to "stay" with him. *The reader beloved by Jesus is the beloved disciple.*[18] As Jesus himself is at his father's breast (1:18), so such a disciple will recline on the breast of Jesus. Within the constraints of John's

---

17. The anarthrous phrase at 5:27 has a different function. The crowd will, as we should expect by now, continue to be baffled (12:34).

18. Here is the answer to the familiar question whether Lazarus is the beloved disciple. Three considerations have prompted the idea: 1) Jesus's love for Lazarus; 2) Lazarus's place "among those reclining with him" at the supper of 12:2; and 3) the attention paid to the *soudarion*, 11:44 and 20:7 (Lazarus had good reason to notice the cloth in Jesus's tomb). E.g., Mark W. G. Stibbe, *John as Storyteller* (SNTSMS, 73; Cambridge: Cambridge University Press, 1992), 78–82. But Lazarus should be studied first as a figure within John's gospel, deployed to serve the gospel's ends.

narrative, the confession of Martha triggers the new birth of her brother. However, within John's schema, the readers' new "sight" is not a condition of or preparation for new life; rather, it *constitutes* new life.

The readers were intended to share the opening eagerness of the first disciples, the trust—however frail and untrustworthy—of those who witnessed the first signs, the inquiry and bemusement of the first disciples, Nicodemus, the Samaritan woman, the nobleman, the lame man, the blind man, and Lazarus, Mary and Martha. Different readers, of course, will have found themselves in closer sympathy with different characters, but the text invited all its readers to recognize as their own some part of every positive response to Jesus and to acknowledge how acute and real, as challenges to their own trust, was the distrust that Jesus encounters in the gospel itself. As the lame man is healed, the reader is "healed." As the blind man gains sight the reader gains insight. As Lazarus is summoned to life the reader attains "life."

The second half of the gospel is duly cast as a story to be read by those who have been reborn from above and to this theme we are about to turn. We are ready, meanwhile, to address two pressing questions. First, how much can we say about the circumstances of the readers whom we have been evoking without qualification? Secondly, are there any parallels in ancient literature to John's mystagogic technique?

John's Readers and Their Reading: A Catachetical Setting

Let us follow the widespread view that John's gospel was completed at Ephesus in the 90s c.e. The gospel is steeped in Temple typology although it was written twenty years after the Temple's destruction and several hundred miles from Jerusalem.[19] Large parts of chapters 7–9 would therefore be unintelligible for a majority of readers without assistance from learned guides familiar with the Temple cult. I would claim, then, that this was a gospel designed to be read under instruction, written for authorized use within communities that had instructors who would relay to other readers far more about the Temple and its lore than John records. It was within the context of such instruction and of the community that provided it that John's "life of the new eon" was lived. In the gospel's text we have only a small fragment of the evidence that John's disciples would have hoped to deploy.

Can it be suggested of any other texts of the period that they were written to serve such a mystagogic purpose? We are near the world of Reitzenstein's *Lese-*

---

19. Culpepper (*Anatomy*, 221, 225) argues that John has envisaged Jesus and his disputants as well-informed about the Temple and its rituals, but his own readers (to judge from his comments) as ill-informed. To the contrary, ill-informed and unguided readers would miss the point of large parts of chapters 7–9 and (as we shall see) of chapter 20.

Mysterium, defined by Reitzenstein with reference to the *Corpus Hermeticum*. The author of a hermetic text, according to Reitzenstein, "hopes that, if God wills it and if the reader of the book has turned away from the world, his presentation will exert upon the reader the same effect as an actual mystery. The reader is to experience such a mystery in his imagination."[20] Again, "the sacred action is supposed to be achieved, and can be achieved, within the reader during the reading of the document. . . . The experience of the first divine founder is related, in order to operate upon the reader by the magic of analogy."[21]

Texts in the *Corpus Hermeticum* (and now *The Discourse on the Eighth and Ninth* from Nag Hammadi) are likely to have functioned as preparation for, recollection of, or even substitutes for initiatory rites.[22] Certainly, differences remain between the gospel's use and any such *Lese-Mysterium* inasmuch the gospel and its performance were part of the community's life, not a replacement for it. But we might still frame a fruitful description of John's gospel, as read among readers already baptized, in such terms as Grese has used to describe *CH* XIII:[23]

> The purpose of CH XIII is to bring its readers to an understanding of what their past regeneration has done to them. Yet the regeneration itself also made such self-understanding possible. Thus the purpose of CH XIII is actually equivalent to that of the original regeneration ceremony. In reminding the reader of his former regeneration and explaining to him what that ceremony meant, CH XIII created the understanding that the ceremony should have given. The hymns that conclude CH XIII thus become the joyful response of the reader to his reexpe-

---

20. Richard Reitzenstein, *The Hellenistic Mystery-Religions: Their Basic Ideas and Their Significance* (trans. John E. Steely; Pittsburgh: Pickwick Press, 1978), 52,

21. Reitzenstein, *Mystery-Religions*, 243. For recent analysis of religious reading and its possible effects, see Paul J. Griffiths, *Religious Reading: The Place of Reading in the Practice of Religion* (New York: Oxford University Press, 1999).

22. Reitzenstein's argument has been variously refined and disputed on numerous points. See William C. Grese, *Corpus Hermeticum XIII and Early Christian Literature* (SCHNT 5; Leiden: Brill, 1979), 48. For the development of Reitzenstein's own view, see Brian P. Copenhaver, *Hermetica: The Greek Corpus Hermeticum and the Latin Asclepius* (Cambridge: Cambridge University Press, 1992), li–liii. For differences between *CH* I and *CH* XIII, see André Jean Festugière, *La Révélation d'Hermès Trismégiste* (4 vols.; Paris: Lecoffre, 1949–54), 3:153–54. In particular, *CH* XIII offers in this life an anticipation of what will, for the initiate of *CH* I, be possible only after death. On *The Discourse on the 8th and the 9th*, see Jean-Pierre Mahé, *Hermès en Haute-Egypte* (Quebec: Université Laval, 1978), 47: "The disciple must pass from theory to practice: to come to know and truly to encounter the realities that used to exist for him only by assertion" (author's translation).

23. For a full argument that *CH* XIII illumines John's gospel, see Charles H. Dodd, *The Interpretation of the Fourth Gospel* (Cambridge: Cambridge University Press, 1968), 44–48, 422. For the present argument I draw instead on Grese, who has had the space to delve more deeply and critically into claims that *CH* XIII evokes a process of regeneration. Here, Grese, *Corpus Hermeticum XIII*, 202.

rienced regeneration. When CH XIII is understood in this way, one can even describe it with Reitzenstein's term as a *"Lese-Mysterium."*[24]

We have been considering John 1–11 as first-cousin to a *Lese-Mysterium*. We should not then be surprised to find John's readers introduced in the gospel's second half to the results of their imagined initiation.

JOHN 17–20: ELEVATING THE READER

The readers have been drawn into the inner circle of the reborn, ready to hear Jesus's private instruction to his disciples. This instruction ends at chapter 17. Here Jesus's position is ambiguous: "I am no longer in the world," he says, "and I am coming, father, to you. . . . When I was with them. . . ." And then, by contrast: "Now I am coming to you, and I am saying this in the world" (17:11–13).[25] This Jesus is already on his way to heaven. Those around Jesus listen in on his movement to the Father and their position is ambiguous too. John's Jesus insists that he does not want the disciples taken out of the world (17:15), but he wants them where he is (17:24). The readers are invited, while still in the world, to share

---

24. Further texts likely had comparable functions:

a)   For the Mithras Liturgy, *PGM* 4.478–829, see Hans Deiter Betz, *The "Mithras Liturgy": Text, Translation, and Commentary* (STAC 18; Tübingen: Mohr Siebeck, 2003), 14–38, on the classic interpretations of Dieterich, Cumont, Reitzenstein and Festugière. Betz stresses that the rituals are not purely internalized, by contrast with the rituals of the Hermetic literature. Note that instructions for the proper performance of the ritual are given in the text after the text of the hymns to be recited during the ritual. The Liturgy is a manual of instruction (cf. ibid., 31).

b)   For the apocryphal *Acts of John*, in its present form, as a text designed to be used in or to evoke a two-stage initiation, see Pieter J. Lalleman, *The Acts of John* (SAAA, 4; Leuven: Peeters, 1998), 25–68. For the *Acts of Thomas*, all of whose sections "present the mystery of salvation and the way to become a partaker of it" in encratite life, see Wilhelm Schneemelcher, *New Testament Apocrypha* (2 vols.; Cambridge: James Clarke, 1991–92), 2:327. The ideas underlying the *Acts of Thomas* can be traced to Tatian: "And so am I too reborn in imitation of the Logos and have acquired knowledge of the truth" (*Or.* 5.1). For an identity between resurrection and conversion in the *Acts of John*, Schneemelcher, *New Testament Apocrypha*, 2:165.

25. John 17 is a "heavenly proclamation"; Ernst Käsemann, *The Testament of Jesus* (London: SCM, 1968), 6. "Since at this hour the difference between past and future is almost entirely obliterated and the two interpenetrate each other, it is possible for the evangelist to interchange the two perspectives"; Ernst Haenchen, *The Gospel according to John* (2 vols., Philadelphia: Fortress, 1984), 2:150–51. "John 13:1–17:26 contains a massive prolepsis, which points the reader to examine the love and unity of the members of a Christian community"; Francis J. Moloney, "The Function of John 13–17," in *What is John?* (2 vols.; ed. Fernando F. Segovia; Atlanta: Scholars Press, 1998), 2:64.

something of Christ's ascent even as they read the prayer that represents it.[26] This experience informs their reading of that part of the gospel that still lies ahead.[27] Thus, the readers are (through a device of John's that we know well by now) being introduced to the significance of the Passion story before they read the story itself.

It is notoriously hard to pin down exactly what the crucifixion achieves in John's theology.[28] We can now begin to see why. The readers have already undergone in their imagination their own resurrection at John 11 and ascension at John 17; they have experienced, during their reception of the gospel, the results of Jesus's death. As at John 11, so here at John 17 the readers *experience*, within and through their reading of the narrative, the effect of Jesus's life before reading of the events that completed that life. They are ready to read of his new life only *after* they have been born into their own, and to recognize Jesus's elevation only *after* they themselves have shared it. To understand the narrative of those final events, the readers are to have experienced the benefits that those very events had made possible.

Jesus says, "It is finished" (19.30). To understand John's account of the crucifixion, we must recognize that Passover traditions at the time of Jesus's death did not link the festival with sacrificial atonement but with creation.[29] John's readers

---

26. So, classically, Dodd: "Proclaiming his own eternal unity with the Father, [Jesus] explains to the candidates for initiation how they may become one with him, and so enter into that eternal unity . . . . Having thus prepared them, He offers the prayer in which He brings them with Him into the Father's presence, and accomplishes their union with God" (Dodd, *Interpretation*, 422).

27. In the recently discovered *Gospel of the Savior* (indebted to all four canonical gospels) the discourse between Jesus and the disciples on the evening before his death is followed by a vision of Jesus given to the disciples (1st person plural) "on the mountain:" "We became as spiritual bodies . . . . We saw the heavens, and they [opened] up one after another . . . . We saw our Savior having penetrated all the heavens, [his] feet [placed firmly on] the [mountain with us, his head penetrating the seventh] heaven . . . We became as [those] among the [immortal] aeons, with our [eyes penetrating all] the heavens" (from vv. 28–36). The disciples then overhear a dialogue between the Savior and his father; they are reassured by Jesus himself (with an instruction based on the *Noli me Tangere*, vs 70); and then hear (or are part of) an Amen-responsory. See Stephen Emmel, "The Recently Published *Gospel of the Savior*...Righting the Order of Pages and Events," *HTR* 95 (2002): 45–72, which revises Charles W. Hedrick and Paul A. Mirecki, *Gospel of the Savior: A New Ancient Gospel* (Santa Rose, Calif.: Polebridge, 1999), excerpts from Emmel, 54–55. The privileges given to the leading disciples at the Transfiguration and Gethsemane are conflated in a vision and liturgy that expound, in advance, the significance of the events to follow.

28. Famously Käsemann, *The Testament of Jesus*, 7: "One is tempted to regard [the Passion story] as being a mere postscript that had to be included because John could not ignore this tradition nor yet could he fit it organically into his work."

29. As the Song of the Four Nights reminds us; inserted into *Targum Neofiti* of Exod 12:42, Roger Le Déaut, *La Nuit pascale* (AnBib 22; Rome: Institut Biblique Pontifical, 1963). For hints

are invited to describe and understand themselves as part of the new creation completed by the Word spoken by God. John evokes throughout chapters 18–19 the story of creation, cruelly distorted. The devil enters the garden; Adam, the Man, is displayed in mockery, "Behold, the man" (19:5); and at his death, as the sixth day ends, everything is finished (*tetelestai*). Such completion has been attained once before: "The heaven and the earth . . . were completed (*sunetelesthēsan*); and God completed (*sunetelesen*) his work" (Gen 2:1–2). The parody is grotesque, but the achievement is real. Jesus hands over the spirit at his death, and so imparts life. We notice that we are yet again called to read *well*: to see and accept the interpretations offered by the text.

John's story of Jesus started with a marriage, moved to a call for rebirth (made to Nicodemus), then through such rebirth (in Lazarus), to a final childbirth at its close. For the Beloved Disciple, reborn as Lazarus, is revealed as a child of God begotten from God alone (1:12) and invested with life by the spirit of the father endowed by the son (19:30).[30] The readers can recognize themselves at last as the children of Jesus's mother (19:26–7). They see how the conditions were fulfilled in Jesus's death for themselves, as Jesus's followers, to come to full term.[31] The pain of childbirth (16:20–22) is turning to joy.

John 20: John's Easter Story

"The resurrection," Brown concedes, "does not fit easily into John's theology of the crucifixion."[32] All has been completed at Jesus's death and there is, therefore, nothing left undone. Readers should not expect—and do not get—in the Easter story an account of any further change or achievement. Easter reveals the life of the new eon as the life of those who have risen into Eden. John's neophytes see the sanctuary, Jesus's body, in the sanctuary that is Paradise.

On the first day of the week, as the light rises, Adam and Eve are together again. There is in their Paradise no Judas and so no serpent now. Adam, "the gardener" once more, names one of God's creatures (Gen 2:19–20), and the new

---

of atonement at Passover, see Margaret Barker, *Temple Themes in Christian Worship* (New York: Continuum, 2007), 25–27.

30. To interpret 19:34 as the emergence of the New Eve from the side of Christ (as Eve had been taken from the side of Adam) is implicitly to recognize the blood and water as fluids accompanying birth. Tertullian and Rufinus just hint at this, see Brooke Foss Westcott, *The Gospel of John* (London: John Murray, 1889), 285–86; for the Middle Ages, see Brown, *The Gospel according to John*, 2:949. John himself introduces *koilia* in the (infrequent) sense of "womb" at 3:4, so preparing for such a sense at 7:38.

31. Compare Turid Karlsen Seim, "Descent and Divine Paternity in the Gospel of John: Does the Mother Matter?" *NTS* 51 (2005): 361–75. LSJ (I.5.a) records *telein* for "bringing a child to term."

32. So all commentators acknowledge. See Brown, *The Gospel according to John*, 2:10–13. This is not yet to understand, however, why John tells the story as he does.

creation is complete. The story of creation was cruelly parodied in chapters 18–19, but the events described there did indeed complete a recreation that undoes the Fall. The garden of death has become the garden of love where Solomon's lover has been searching for her beloved: "And when I find him I will cling to him and will not let him go" (Song 3:4).[33] So Jesus forbids Mary Magdalene, the lover who has found her beloved, to go on touching him: "For I have not yet ascended."[34]

Mary Magdalene is the last of the characters to be introduced for an encounter with Jesus. We are inclined to ask what was the quality of faith attained on Easter morning by the Beloved Disciple[35] or by Mary Magdalene,[36] each assessed in isolation from the other. And so we miss the point. John portrays once more a range of responses and expects his readers to recognize in themselves more than one. John allows to the Beloved Disciple, seeing the evidence of the tomb, the first trust, but he amplifies the story of Mary Magdalene into a major scene. For in the story of Jesus and Mary he can generate an atmosphere of sensuous intimacy.[37] He has evoked such a frisson before in the stories of the Samaritan woman and of Mary of Bethany.[38] The study of John calls for particular attention to the forms of insight that could effectively be evoked and encouraged by this sequence of stories in which women and Jesus meet.[39]

---

33. For the Song of Songs, see J. Duncan M. Derrett, *The Victim* (Shipston-on-Stour: Drinkwater, 1992), 30, 88, 93; Ann Roberts Winsor, *A King is Bound in the Tresses* (New York: Peter Lang, 1999), 35–44; and the survey in Jane Schaberg, *The Resurrection of Mary Magdalene* (New York: Continuum, 2002), 330–36.

34. Mary Rose D'Angelo, "A Critical Note: John 20.17 and *Apocalypse of Moses* 31," *JTS* 41 (1990): 529–36, provides an overview and a suggestion with reference to Adam in *Apoc. Mos.* 31:3–4.

35. He comes, says Schnackenburg (*John*, 3:312), to a full faith in the resurrection of Jesus. Schnackenburg can maintain this only by postulating some drastic editorial work in which the Beloved Disciple is a late entry to the story, which once spoke of the confusion of Peter (and Mary). Cf. Hans-Martin Schenke, "The Function and Background of the Beloved Disciple in the Gospel of John," in *Nag Hammadi, Gnosticism and Early Christianity* (ed. Charles W. Hedrick and Robert Hodgson; Peabody, Mass.: Hendrickson, 1986), 111–25.

36. For demeaning interpretations of Mary Magdalene, see the survey in Schaberg, *Resurrection*, 327–30.

37. It is famously disputed how much John knew of the events of Easter Day, how much he had heard from others, and how much in his account he has re-written or composed *de novo*.

38. Within the Gospel only Mary of Bethany and Mary Magdalene touch Jesus. Mary of Bethany does with her oil little less for Jesus than the anonymous sinner of Luke 7:38–50 did with her tears. It is easy to admit that the sinner's action is sexually charged so we should admit the same of Mary's.

39. The Gnostics did not share the phenomenological austerity of Bultmann. Filoramo stresses the physical imagery for the experience of the regenerate in the Gnostic texts and in particular of the "man of light" in *Pistis Sophia*: he is bubbling, restless, standing, willing. See Giovanni Filoramo, "The Transformation of the Inner Self," in *Transformation of the Inner Self in Ancient Religions* (ed. Jan Assmann and Guy G. Stroumsa; SHR 83; Leiden: Brill, 1999), 147.

As Mary Magdalene, so too John's readers find themselves in Paradise. The Temple's sanctuary, decorated with carvings of trees, was designed to recall Eden.[40] Mary sees angels at the head and foot of the place where Jesus had been laid, with an empty space between (20:12) just as angels flanked the throne in the sanctuary of Solomon's Temple.[41] When Mary sees Jesus in this newly created Paradise, she sees him in the sanctuary that he himself is (2:21; chapters 7–9). Paradise is the dwelling of God and the place of visionary disclosure (cf. 2 Cor 12:4). But Jesus insists that he is not yet ascended; this Eden is still *earthly*.

What then is the function of John's Easter story itself? We are ready to formulate our most striking conclusion. For John, the readers could grasp what is being revealed in his Easter story only if they had themselves gone through the rebirth from death that Lazarus has gone through in the story. John did not tell the Easter story to convince his readers of anything, but to give expression to the effects upon them of the conviction they had (as he hoped) already reached. John was describing in the form of a poetic, dream-like story the outcome of the transformation through which the rest of the gospel had already brought the readers. In so doing he gave those readers a rich, allusive language in which to envisage that outcome and the standing it gave them. The world saw the death of Jesus at John 19 while John's readers saw creation completed, and those readers are now shown in the story of a private encounter where they stand in this new-born world.[42]

The Gospel's Reception: Register and Function

Let us assume that liturgy was a prime site for the performance of the gospel. The text is surely too long to have been recited in a single service. It opens with a hymn whose register sets the tone for the narrative to follow. The readers find themselves invited throughout into a strange hinterland between the past of which the story speaks and the present in which Jesus speaks to, challenges, summons, and heals them. Let us imagine a weekly recitation of part of the gospel. Any healing wrought in the readers is not undone by the business of the intervening days. The readers move onwards, week by week, towards new birth, the proleptic ascent of chapter 17 and self-discovery in Eden.

Another text from the time calls for a comparable disposition, sustained over time, in its readers or users—the *Songs of the Sabbath Sacrifice*. Those who took part, through thirteen successive Sabbaths, in the liturgy of the *Songs* moved

---

40. Margaret Barker, *The Older Testament* (London: SPCK, 1987), 239–41, and *The Gate of Heaven* (London: SPCK, 1991), 57–103. Nicolas Wyatt ("Supposing him to be the Gardener (John 20.15): A Study of the Paradise Motif in John," *ZNW* 81 [1990]: 21–38) pursues still further the links between the royal Man, Eden, and burial.

41. Westcott, *The Gospel of John*, 291.

42. The serious implications for exegesis and hermeneutics—and apologetics—are for exploration in a later paper.

each week from the place in the heavenly Temple that they had attained the week before. The business of the community's daily life in between the liturgical performances had not sullied them. John is offering what the *Songs* offered, namely,

> the fullest, most sustained expression of an anthropology which takes the righteous up into the divine life and that of the angels . . . . Like the apocalypses and the Hekhalot texts the *Sabbath Songs* do envisage the possibility of a human ascent from earth to heaven, and it is within this context that a human transformation and a sharing of the life of the angels and that of God himself takes place. However, unlike the stories of ascent in the apocalypses, . . . in the *Sabbath Songs* ascent is a ritualized and communal experience.[43]

To clarify the gospel's role among the readers, John wrote once more, at his story's end, of Jesus's ascent and of the Spirit. The first appearance to the disciples on Easter evening, John 20:19–23, is alive with the echoes of liturgy: the disciples are gathered, the Lord is present and blesses them, "Peace be with you." Jesus breathes upon his disciples (20:22), as God had breathed the breath of life into Adam (Gen 2:7). The power of absolution is pronounced. Allusive as ever, John has evoked the liturgy in which his readers are participating. And in the liturgy Jesus could be imagined as present precisely *as* the Jesus that had ascended to the Father, and so Thomas can be invited, eight days later, to touch the wounds of this Jesus.

For there was, we have seen, at least some liturgy—and we should include the performance of a gospel within it—which was to be experienced as its participants' entrée to heaven. Just such access, as April D. DeConick has shown,[44] seems to have been demanded and offered by the Gospel of Thomas. Where DeConick has discerned conflict between John and Thomas, we seem to be finding convergence. And there is surely still closer convergence to be found: the first person in John's gospel to see the risen Jesus is an individual, Mary Magdalene; so John at first sight seems, in style and function, a natural partner to Thomas (both of them

---

43. Crispin H. T. Fletcher-Louis, *All the Glory of Adam* (STDJ 42; Leiden: Brill, 2002), 392. Fletcher-Louis is heavily revising the interpretation of the *editio princeps*. See Carol A. Newsom, *Songs of the Sabbath Sacrifice* (HSS 27; Atlanta, Ga.: Scholars Press, 1985). Now Christopher R. A. Morray-Jones, "The Temple Within," in *Paradise Now: Essays on Early Jewish and Christian Mysticism* (ed. April D. DeConick; SBLSymS 11; Atlanta: Society of Biblical Literature, 2006), 145–78 (166): a way to understand this liturgy is "to regard it as a process of 'ritual construction.' The performance of these songs, presumably combined with intense visualization of the images described, will have had the effect of 'building' the celestial temple in the personal and collective imagination of the participants." For Paul's encouragement of his congregations to see their life and worship in angelic terms, see Robin Griffith-Jones, *The Gospel according to Paul* (San Francisco, Calif.: Harper, 2004), 287–302.

44. April D. DeConick, *Voices of the Mystics* (JSNTSup 157; Sheffield: Sheffield Academic Press, 2001). I explore the contrasting role of women—and in particular of Mary Magdalene—in the gospels of John and of Thomas in *Beloved Disciple* (San Francisco: HarperOne, 2008).

inspiring and instructing individuals) over against, for instance, the *Songs of the Sabbath Sacrifice* (emphasizing the gathered community).

We have not yet, however, done justice to the *tone* of John's Easter stories. Thomas summons the reader to ascend to the heavenly Holy of Holies that should indeed be linked with a paradise (*Gos. Thom.* 19); John, by contrast, places the reader in an earthly paradise that must be linked with the Holy of Holies. Thomas looks heavenwards; John's Mary Magdalene—in a place of love that has become a place of death and is now revealed and revalued as the place, above all, of life— is ineluctably earthbound.[45] John controls the imaginings (that he himself has stirred) with care. As DeConick has seen, John is *resisting* the Thomasine claims to offer journeys to heaven and a sight of its glories. Such visions were not accessible, nor were they needed. The sight of Jesus on earth had once provided the basis for Thomas' confession, "My Lord and my God." The "sight" of Jesus in the gospel and in any liturgy informed or controlled by the gospel provided that basis for John's readers and so subverted all expectation or hope of mystical journeys to see more. If readers imagined earth aright, according to John, they would discover the truths of heaven; they should not aspire to a sight of heaven to discern the truth about earth.[46]

The gospel's mystagogic devices have brought the readers full circle from the prologue's hymnic account of the Word to the disciples gathered in liturgy. This is the register in which the whole gospel was performed and received. As the readers were to read the beginning and end of the gospel, so they should be disposed to read everything in between: as a disclosure accessible only in the gospel itself, this upside-down apocalypse, where heaven is revealed on earth in the story and role of the gospel itself.[47] Nathanael's successors have been given, in a most surprising form, the dream that Jesus promised them.

How much progress has been made in the readers' apprehension of Jesus between their first encounters with Jesus and their last? Jesus asks Andrew and his

---

45. For the Edenic Temple as the place of *life*, se J. D. Levenson, *Resurrection and the Restoration of Israel* (New Haven, Conn.: Yale University Press, 2006), 82–107.

46. I explore the meaning of "heaven" and of journeys there, among the Gnostics, in *Beloved Disciple*, Part 2. We are likely—however unsure Paul may have been; 2 Cor 12:2—to diagnose such journeys as a function of a highly trained and intently focused imagination among the tradents of a community's exegetical and experiential traditions. We will likely see the journeys as both spurs to and symbols of a lifetime's journey in transformative dedication to prayer, study, discernment, and the community's highest ethical standards. The school of seers evoked in the *Ascension of Isaiah* is discussed by the present author (*The Gospel according to Paul*, 94–98.)

47. "The fourth evangelist conceives his own work as an apocalypse—in reverse, upside down, inside out." Ashton, *Understanding the Fourth Gospel*, 405; and ibid, Part III, *passim*. The present author diagnoses Mark's gospel as a similarly startling apocalypse in "Going back to Galilee to see the Son of Man: Mark's Gospel as an Upside-Down Apocalypse," in *Between Author and Audience: Markan Narration, Characterization, and Interpretation* (ed. E. Struthers Malbon; Sheffield: Sheffield Phoenix, forthcoming).

companion, at the Gospel's start, "What are you looking for?" They address him as Rabbi, "which, translated, is Teacher" (1:38). At its end Jesus will ask Mary, "Who are you looking for?" She will call him Rabbouni, "which means Teacher" (20:16). But the readers who have reached the end of John's Gospel do not simply return to the condition in which they started reading it. Mary represents the recognition that the risen Jesus is the Jesus of whom we have heard throughout the Gospel: a human teacher. Hers is not, however, the only voice heard in this closure. John is as multifocal as ever. The prologue's privileged speaker declares, "No one has seen God, ever; the only-begotten God, . . . *he* has made him known" (1:18). The reader, however Thomasine by inclination, will by the end of the Gospel and *on the basis of the Gospel* and with no privileged journey to heaven be ready to confess Jesus as "My Lord and my God" (20:28).

John: Midwife of Rebirth from Above

I have raised more questions in this paper than I have offered answers. I have no doubt that the questions are integral to the exegesis of John. Until we address them, we can make no claim to "understand" John's gospel on his own terms and we condemn to futility our attempts to understand it on ours. (We cannot gauge the likelihood that John's account at any one point is historically accurate until we have in mind the agenda that drove his historiography.)[48]

At issue throughout the gospel is *knowledge*. But this knowledge is, for John, accessible only in and as rebirth from above, not through the regular apprehension of a regular story. Bultmann was right to investigate the character of the knowledge sought by John.[49] But the required apprehension is dependent for its growth

---

48. This paper is not arguing for an Origenist reading of the gospel, but clearly gives rise to comparable questions. For a classic attack on Origen's supposed indifference to historical accuracy, see Richard P. C. Hanson, *Allegory and Event* (Louisville, Ky.: Westminster John Knox, 2002). David Dawson, *Christian Figural Reading and the Fashioning of Identity* (Berkeley and Los Angeles: University of California Press, 2002) counters such charges. Origen set out to transform his readers by their encounter with the Word.

49. Classically in Bultmann, *The Gospel of John*, 44 on 1:4: "To say that it [the Logos] was the light as the Creator, as the *zōē*, is to say that the possibility of the *illumination* of existence (the salvation that consists in the definitive understanding of existence itself) was inherent in its very origin . . . . The self-understanding that would have been decisive for man, would have been knowledge of his creatureliness . . . . The integral connection between light and life is grounded in the fact that life achieves its authenticity in the proper understanding of itself." Also 5:24: "The life that [the promise of Jesus] promises to the believer must be the object that he longs for in all his desires and hopes, however darkly, misguidedly and mistakenly; it is that authenticity of existence, granted in the illumination that proceeds from man's ultimate understanding of himself" (258). This life is not a condition of the soul. It "is not manifested in the motion of our consciousness or in the effect of our strength" (n. 3; quoting Schlatter). John knows nothing of "the crowning manifestation of Gnosticism, in which the negation of the this-worldly is trans-

on a movement of consciousness and of self-definition to which John devoted all his attention and Bultmann (for good reasons of his own) declined to analyze. It was a movement so drastic that John described its outcome as new birth.

Over all subsequent scholars, writes Ashton, Bultmann "unmatched in learning, breadth and understanding, towers like a colossus. Nevertheless, in spite of his pre-eminence, every answer Bultmann gives to the really important questions he raises—is wrong."[50] If I am right, Bultmann made one fundamentally false move not among those diagnosed by Ashton: Bultmann believed John to be demythologizing, where John was *re-mythologizing*. John defined Jesus by reference to the Temple, its rituals, and its links with Paradise. John was engaging the readers' imagination and the study of John calls for intensive study of the imagination and its possibilities.[51]

The claims made by John for Jesus and so for his own readers and for the world were, on any mainstream Jewish assessment of the world, bizarre. They called for a sustained view of the world that defied the recommendations of reason and any normal assessment of experience. To enable his readers to trust those claims, John wrote a mystagogic text. We will understand very little of it until we have grasped and analyzed John's role as the midwife of his readers' rebirth from above.

---

formed into a positive experience of the other-worldly, in which the other-worldly is reduced to the level of a this-worldly phenomenon." This is true precisely because John is programmatically confounding this distinction.

50. Ashton, *Understanding the Fourth Gospel*, 45.

51. Anthony J. Kelly and Francis J. Moloney (*Experiencing God in the Gospel of John* [New York: Paulist, 2003], especially 76–81) draw on Bernard Lonergan (*Method in Theology* [London: Darton, Longman & Todd, 1971]) for the four dimensions of meaning that they see as applicable to John's Gospel: the cognitive, constitutive, communicative, and effective. They are asking: What meanings does the gospel convey? I am asking the hermeneutical question to which John himself is attending throughout the gospel: How are its many meanings to be conveyed? Neither question can, in the last resort, be answered without reference to the other.

Religious Experience and the Apocalypses

Crispin Fletcher-Louis

In the Jewish texts commonly labeled "apocalypses" there are recounted all sorts of extraordinary religious experiences in which visionaries see what cannot be normally seen and whose encounters with the divine and heavenly worlds entail disturbances to their physical and emotional state: loss of strength, involuntary prostration, catalepsy, trembling, and loss of ordinary consciousness (e.g., *1 En.* 71:11; Dan 10:8–9; 4 Ezra 10:29–30; *Apoc. Ab.* 16:1; 17:1–3). The visionary's religious experience is frequently preceded by the kinds of preparatory practices familiar to any student of mysticism in comparative religion: Enoch recites, mantra-like, the prayers of the watchers before his dream vision (*1 En.* 13); there is fasting (Dan 9:3; 10:2–3; *Apoc. Ab.* 9:7–8; 12:1–2; *2 Bar.* 5:7; 9:2; 12:5; 20:5–6; 21:1; 43:3; 47:2; *Mart. Ascen. Isa.* 2:9–11); there is mourning or weeping for an individual or a community's situation (*T. Levi* 2:3–4; *2 En.* 1:2; *3 Bar.* 1:1–3; 4 Ezra 3:2–36; 5:13; 6:31–37; 9:24–25, 27; *2 Bar.* 9:2; 35:1. Cf. *Mart. Ascen. Isa.* 2:10; Dan 10:2; *1 En.* 90:41); travelers to the world above return transformed (*2 En.* 39).

Are the experiences that these texts describe genuine? Some think so, others do not. My purpose in this paper is to address this question obliquely from the perspective of a more general discussion of the history of the study of apocalyptic. The first part of my argument will be that a properly historical appreciation of the religious experiences to which the ancient Jewish apocalypses witness has been hampered by the intellectual sensitivities and commitments of those who, in the modern period, have studied them. In particular, two modern critical judgments about the nature of mystical experiences have prejudiced historical enquiry. It has often been said, sneeringly, that the problem with mysticism is that it "begins in mist, has an 'I' in the middle and ends in schism." In other words, mysticism suffers two basic problems: it is irrational—it obscures, or clouds, rational discourse—and it threatens social structure since it elevates the individual over against the community and institution, the church in particular. In the second part I will lay out some evidence for a new perspective on "apocalyptic" that provides a solid foundation for a proper appreciation of (the historical actuality, meaning and function of) the experiences they describe.

The History of Apocalyptic Study

Phases One and Two

Roughly speaking, the history of the study of apocalyptic can be divided into three periods.[1] In the first phase—from R. H. Charles and Albert Schweitzer at the end of the nineteenth century to Klaus Koch's seminal book published in 1970—there is broad agreement on the nature of apocalyptic(ism).[2] Koch and at the same time others—notably Michael Stone—drew attention to serious problems in the study of apocalyptic.[3] Consequently, in the 1970s there dawns a second phase of study with two rather different approaches in the work of John Collins and colleagues, on the one hand, and Chris Rowland on the other, each producing major studies in the 1980s. A third phase, that is anticipated by Rowland's work, is perhaps now upon us.

In the first phase, particularly where Schweitzer's vision of the apocalyptic origins of Christianity is most influential, apocalyptic literature is witness to a particular kind of *worldview*, a set of religious *ideas*. The phenomenon that underlies those ideas is dualism: apocalyptic, unlike biblical prophecy, presents a sharp divide between God and his creation such that the future requires dramatic divine intervention to bring about God's purposes; politics and traditional religious practice will not do. There is a sharp dualistic divide also between present quotidian realities and the future, utterly transcendent age to come. This produces the immediate, obvious, defining characteristic of apocalyptic: a particular kind of *transcendent eschatology*. The dualistic nature of apocalyptic can also be seen in the cosmic struggle between God and his angels on the one hand and Satan with his minions on the other. This cosmic dualism parallels a soteriological dualism between the elect and the damned. As a very new theology, apocalyptic is inspired as much by foreign religious ideas—especially Zoroastrianism—as it is by Israel's existing scriptures. The heroes of old—Moses and others—are pitted against new heroes—Enoch and Daniel—who stand apart from Israel's covenantal religious framework. Gone is the national hope of Israel. Apocalyptic brings in a new international and cosmic perspective. Where the biblical prophets looked forward to

---

1. For a more detailed discussion of the first two phases and their relationship to the study of the historical Jesus see Crispin H. T. Fletcher-Louis, "Apocalypticism" and "Jesus and Apocalypticism," in *The Handbook of the Study of the Historical Jesus* (4 vols.; ed. S. E. Porter and T. Holmén; Leiden: Brill, forthcoming).

2. Klaus Koch, *The Rediscovery of Apocalyptic: A Polemical Work on a Neglected Area of Biblical Studies and its Damaging Effects on Theology and Philosophy* (trans. Margaret Kohl; London: SCM Press, 1972).

3. Michael E. Stone, "Lists of Revealed Things in Apocalyptic Literature," in *Magnalia Dei: The Mighty Acts of God. Essays on the Bible and Archeology in Memory of G. Ernest Wright* (ed. F. M. Cross, W. Lemke, and P. D. Miller; New York: Doubleday, 1976), 414–52.

a human, military messiah for the nation of Israel, the apocalypticists announce the imminent arrival of an utterly heavenly, pre-existent Son of Man, who will save the world.

Thus, in this first phase of investigation apocalyptic texts attest to what is primarily an intellectual reality, a system of thought. Scholarship shows little interest in the religious experiences that the apocalypses purport to record. There are *arguments* to justify this disinterest and there are probably also unstated *reasons*. The principal argument against any acceptance of the historical veracity and, therefore, importance of the religious experiences in the apocalypses is the fact that they are pseudepigraphical: they are not genuine accounts of the experiences of ancient visionaries, no more than they are the actual words of an historical Enoch, Daniel, Ezra, or Abraham. And they are best understood as the *literary* product of reflection on and reuse of older tradition.

But in reading the scholarship of this period one may discern other *reasons* for scholarly disinterest in the purported religious experiences in the apocalypses that are not always set out so clearly. Apocalyptic thought is cherished insofar as it acts as a pre-Christian *preparatio evangelica*: apocalypticism anticipates the law- and ritual-free, grace-versus-works theology that is believed to define earliest Christianity. If Christian origins are constructed as a history of *ideas*, then for apocalyptic to function as their forebear its subject matter must also be ideational. Although a certain "charismatic" spirit motivated early Christian thought, the characteristically German aversion to *Enthusiasmus* accommodates the "charismatic" in sociological (i.e., ecclesiological) and not psychological (i.e., mystical or visionary) terms. Mysticism, we recall, is unsystematic, irrational: it begins in "mist."

For this phase of scholarship, if apocalyptic literature has any basis in experience it is a social one. The crisis, real or imagined, of the sect or the oppressed movement is the collective *Sitz im Leben* for apocalyptic.[4] Moreover, that life setting is sometimes viewed as the world of eschatologically enthusiastic circles opposed to, and oppressed by, the cultic and legal theology of the Jerusalem priesthood.[5] On this reading, apocalyptic literature may even seem to anticipate a Protestant critique of Catholic institutionalism.

The first thoroughgoing treatment of apocalyptic in the second phase of scholarship, which responds to the watershed treatments by Koch, Stone, and

---

4. See Otto Plöger, *Theocracy and Eschatology* (trans. S. Rudman; Oxford: Blackwell, 1968 [1959]); Martin Hengel, *Judaism and Hellenism: Studies in their Encounter in Palestine during the Early Hellenistic Period* (2 vols.; trans. John Bowden; London: SCM, 1974 [1969]), 1:194–96.

5. See especially Plöger, *Theocracy and Eschatology*; Paul Vielhauer, "Apocalypses and Related Subjects: Introduction," in *New Testament Apocrypha* (2 vols.; ed. E. Hennecke and W. Schneemelcher; Louisville, Ky.: Westminster, 1965), 2:581–600, 598 and Paul D. Hanson, *The Dawn of Apocalyptic: The Historical and Sociological Roots of Jewish Apocalyptic Eschatology* (Philadelphia: Fortress, 1979 [1975]).

others, is Christopher Rowland's *Open Heaven* (1982).[6] For Rowland, an apocalypse is simply a "revelation of the divine mysteries through visions or some other form of immediate disclosure of the heavenly mysteries, whether as the result of vision, heavenly ascent or verbal revelations."[7] The apocalypses do not have a distinctively new worldview, with a dualistic heart and defining expectation of a transcendent eschatology. Instead, a survey of the interests of the apocalypses is best organized with an eye to its essentially mystical character: following the taxonomy of mystical speculation given in the Mishnah (*Ḥag.* 2.1) it is best to consider the apocalypses' interest in "what is above, what is beneath, what was beforetime and what will be hereafter." This is because the apocalypses offer an experience that transcends the boundaries of ordinary space and time such that all of time is present before God and all space available to those who enter his courts.

For Rowland, the formative setting of the apocalypses is neither an abstract history of ideas nor the sociology of crisis, but what the apocalypses tell us themselves: their revelations are the product of the genuine religious experiences that they in fact describe—visionary encounters with angels and ascents to heaven in the context of scripture study and speculation on God and his creation. The apocalypses have their roots in the visionary texts of the Old Testament (e.g., Isa 6; 1 Kgs 22:19; Ezek 1, 40–48; Zech 1–8). They report the kind of ascetic experiences that comparative study shows accompany ecstasy and altered states of consciousness. Also, there are considerable continuities of literary form and content between the apocalypses and later texts from the rabbinic period, which are best taken as witness to an ongoing stream of mystical practice: there is a direct line of mystical speculation from *1 Enoch's* heavenly ascent text (in the third–fourth centuries B.C.E.) to *merkabah* texts from the fifth century C.E.

Rowland's paradigm of interpretation has won some support, but it has not convinced the majority. For a variety of reasons, the traditional and popular dualistic and eschatological understanding of apocalyptic has maintained a vigorous hold on both the popular and scholarly consciousness. Of course, Rowland's non-eschatological, non-dualistic apocalyptic-as-the-mystical-revelation-of-heavenly-secrets swims upstream against the current of so many western intellectual commitments. In part, however, it has also failed to persuade because it has inherent problems, to which I shall come in a moment.

Continuity with the traditional understanding of apocalyptic that was central to the first phase of apocalyptic studies is maintained in the more widely accepted

---

6. Christopher Rowland, *The Open Heaven: A Study of Apocalyptic in Judaism and Early Christianity* (New York: Crossroad, 1982), cf. idem, "Apocalyptic: the Disclosure of Heavenly Knowledge," in *The Early Roman Period* (vol. 3 of *The Cambridge History of Judaism*; ed. W. Horbury, W. D. Davies, and J. Sturdy; Cambridge: Cambridge University Press, 1999), 776–97.

7. Rowland, *The Open Heaven*, 70–71, cf. generally 9–22, 68–71.

contribution that defines the second phase. This is the work of John J. Collins and those who from the 1970s onwards have followed him in an intensive study of apocalypses and associated texts. In some respects, Collins's understanding of apocalypticism seems to be quite different from that of the first phase. He separates the visionary genre "apocalypse" from "apocalyptic eschatology" and from "apocalypticism"—the worldview born of a particular social context. He attends closely to the particularities of the texts and their historical context and tries to address the criticisms of the traditional eschatological understanding of them raised, in particular, by Michael E. Stone.[8] Collins recognizes the roles of other, speculative concerns, such as astronomy, calendrical measurement, meteorology, cosmic geography, and so forth. At times he also appears to give due recognition to the role of religious experience in the formation of apocalypses. For example, in the second edition of his *Apocalyptic Imagination* (1998), Collins speaks positively of Michael Stone's argument that 4 Ezra's literary structure is best explained if the text records an actual experience of psychological transformation, of conversion, in the seer.[9]

There is not space here for a detailed analysis of Collins's work.[10] Broadly speaking, however, it remains committed to the conceptual parameters of the first phase of apocalyptic study with little room for an approach that seriously engages religious experiences at the defining core of the apocalyptic phenomenon. The theological use made of apocalyptic in the first phase is less obvious in Collins's work and a sociological framework of interpretation has moved to the foreground, but the propositional theology is still there and is determinative. In discussion of the Book of Watchers (*1 En.* 1–36), for example, he says that Enoch's throne vision probably "presupposes" mystical speculation.[11] But while "the possibility that the author [himself] had a mystical experience cannot be discounted," the text is better understood as a piece of literature with a particular social function and setting.[12] Indeed, where Collins and others who work within his paradigm are open to the presence of mystical material in the apocalypses, this is understood within (or subsumed under) a sociological explanation of such experience. Enoch's heavenly ascent offers an individual access to God that

---

8. Stone, "Lists of Revealed Things."

9. John J. Collins, *The Apocalyptic Imagination. An Introduction to Jewish Apocalyptic Literature* (2nd and rev. ed.; Grand Rapids: Eerdmans, 1998), 99–100, 153. See also Michael E. Stone, "On Reading an Apocalypse," in *Mysteries and Revelations: Apocalyptic Studies Since the Uppsala Colloquium* (JSPSup 9; ed. J. J. Collins and J. H. Charlesworth; Sheffield: JSOT Press, 1991), 65–78; idem, *Fourth Ezra: A Commentary on the Book of Fourth Ezra* (Hermeneia; Minneapolis: Fortress, 1990), 31–32; idem, "A Reconsideration of Apocalyptic Visions," *HTR* 96 (2003):167–80.

10. See Fletcher-Louis, "Apocalypticism."

11. Collins, *Apocalyptic Imagination*, 54.

12. Ibid., 57.

bypasses the official temple cult, which is deemed dysfunctional.[13] Enoch represents a new kind of ecstatic mediation over and against that traditionally offered by the priesthood and temple.[14]

For Collins and others it is the texts' ideas that form the core of their message, as a perusal of publications shows. When Collins writes in a recent encyclopedia article on apocalypticism and its roots in biblical prophecy, he does not treat religious experience at all; it is all a matter of the history of ideas and social forces.[15] Given that this approach has dominated scholarship for the last twenty years, it is not surprising that when a New Testament specialist—Luke Timothy Johnson—decides to write a book entitled *Religious Experience in Earliest Christianity: A Missing Dimension in New Testament Studies,* he has nothing at all to say about the contribution that apocalyptic might make to such a subject.[16]

Rowland's case has not carried the day, even though there are now many who agree with him that there is a genuine religious experience dimension to apocalyptic literature and that there is a direct line of continuity between this aspect of Old Testament prophecy through to later *merkabah* mysticism (Ithamar Gruenwald, Michael Stone, Morton Smith, Michael Mach, James Davila, Christopher Morray-Jones, Alan Segal, Moshe Idel, Rachel Elior, Dan Merkur, and Frances Flannery-Dailey have all lent support to this position). Why has Rowland's view not prevailed? It is not that the literary and tradition-historical character of the apocalypses tells against there being records of genuine religious experience. There is now widespread recognition that one can both reuse and develop a literary tradition and, simultaneously, do so in a genuinely visionary mode. All religious experience takes place within a tradition-bound context; all epistemology has a sociological dimension.[17]

The problem is more basic to the defining form and content of the apocalypses. It can always be objected that the pseudonymous authorship of apocalypses

---

13. John J. Collins, *The Apocalyptic Imagination: An Introduction to the Jewish Matrix of Christianity* (New York: Crossroad, 1984), 54; cf. George W.E. Nickelsburg, "Enoch, Levi, and Peter: Recipients of Revelation in Upper Galilee," *JBL* 100 (1981): 575–600.

14. John J. Collins, "Journeys to the World Beyond in Ancient Judaism," in *Apocalyptic and Eschatological Heritage: The Middle East and Celtic Realms* (ed. M. McNamara; Dublin: Four Courts Press, 2003), 20–36, 25.

15. John J. Collins, "From Prophecy to Apocalypticism: The Expectation of the End," in *The Origins of Apocalypticism in Judaism and Christianity* (vol. 1 of *The Encyclopedia of Apocalypticism*; ed. John J. Collins; New York: Continuum, 2000), 129–61. Collins has nothing to say here about the connections between the visionary experiences attributed to the biblical prophets and those attributed to the apocalyptic heroes.

16. Luke Timothy Johnson, *Religious Experience in Earliest Christianity: A Missing Dimension in New Testament Studies* (Minneapolis: Fortress, 1998).

17. See Troels Engberg-Pedersen, "The Construction of Religious Experience in Paul," in this volume.

speaks against their being primarily about dreams and visions.[18] Even though one can detect echoes of a genuine religious experience in so many of the apocalypses, none is plausibly read as a firsthand account of a religious experience, apart perhaps from 4 *Ezra*. As Martha Himmelfarb has shown, the visionary parts of the texts are inextricable from a narrative context that is obviously not that of the actual author: narrative and visionary content are both thoroughly fictional.[19]

Rowland's presentation of the case for religious experience as the defining core of apocalyptic has perhaps failed because in one crucial respect he undercuts the natural course of his own argument. Rowland was the first to make anything of the role of temple symbolism and cosmology in the explanation of apocalyptic texts. Following the observations of J. Maier, Rowland noted that Enoch's ascent to heaven (*1 En.* 14) is patterned after an entry into the Holy of Holies of the Solomonic temple and that this is natural given the notion that the temple is the meeting point of heaven and earth, the gate of heaven.[20] This very non-dualistic function of the temple also explains, he notes, the way in which in some traditions the righteous are transformed in the context of worship in the heavenly world.

However, for Rowland the temple is a bad thing. Christianity and the apocalypses that anticipate Christianity offer *liberation* from the temple and the institutional religion that it represents.[21] Allusions to the cosmology of the temple in *1 En.* 14 are significant for Rowland insofar as *1 En.* 14 exemplifies the apocalypses' interest in an *unmediated, direct* experience of God, one that is essentially anti-temple and anti-institutional in orientation.[22] Rowland works with a particular and limited understanding of the religious experiences that the apocalypses describe. While he posits no necessary intrinsic difference between apocalyptic

---

18. E.g., Martha Himmelfarb, *Ascent to Heaven in Jewish and Christian Apocalypses* (Oxford: Oxford University Press, 1993), 97 in criticism of Rowland.

19. Himmelfarb, *Ascent to Heaven*, 102–4.

20. See Rowland, *The Open Heaven*, 463 n. 16 and n. 18. Cf. Johann Maier, *Vom Kultus zur Gnosis: Studien zur Vor- und Frühgeschichte der "jüdischen Gnosis"* (Salzburg: O. Müller, 1964), 125–28 and J. Maier, "Das Gefährdungsmotiv bei der Himmelreise in der jüdischen Apokalyptik und 'Gnosis,'" *Kairos* 5 (1963): 18–40.

21. For Rowland's view of the temple in biblical theology see C. C. Rowland, "The Book of Revelation: Introduction, Commentary, and Reflections," in *The New Interpreter's Bible: A Commentary in Twelve Volumes* [12 vols.; ed. L. E. Keck; Nashville, Tenn.: Abingdon, 1998], 12:501–736). No doubt there is, in the Old Testament, a serious wrestling with the proper role of sacred space and temple. But Rowland's view that God's approval of Solomon's temple "did not extend to the form, content, and actions in it, as the conditions laid out in the response to Solomon's prayer make clear (1 Kgs 9:3)" is a bold claim that, as far as I can see, has no actual basis in the biblical text (Rowland, "The Book of Revelation," 725).

22. Rowland, *The Open Heaven*, 9–11, 17; Rowland, "Disclosure of Heavenly Knowledge," 780. Here Rowland and Collins are in agreement.

and non-apocalyptic attitudes towards the law,[23] he sees a contrast between indirect modes of discernment, such as the interpretation of scripture, and a direct Spirit-inspired revelation that can be found in the apocalypses.[24]

This approach effectively constrains Rowland from a full appreciation of the function of temple cosmology in the apocalypses. For example, the role of temple and priestly symbolism in the formation of Enoch's ascent suggests, in fact, that the revelation is by no means unmediated and direct; rather, it takes place at a particular time and place, with Enoch's role anticipating that of the priest in mediating divine instruction. The place is the cosmic mountain, Mount Hermon—a mountain with which the Temple in Jerusalem is mystically or ritually identified.[25] The time is the Day of Atonement, the only day of the year when the high priest enters fully into God's presence in the Holy of Holies.[26] Enoch's ascent takes place in a dream that is incubated at the foot of the mountain through the recitation of the prayers of the watchers (*1 En.* 13:7).[27] In short, Rowland's "immediate disclosure of heavenly mysteries" sounds a little too much like a backwards-projection of modern accounts of pure "charismatic" revelation that are defined in contra-distinction to institutional structures.

THE THIRD PHASE: A NEW PERSPECTIVE ON APOCALYPTIC

Since the publication of Rowland's book, there have been two significant advances in our understanding of the apocalypses. These lead to a "new perspective" on apocalyptic with two defining conceptual and *experiential* focal points for what will surely turn out to be a third phase of scholarship.

First, the role of the temple and the priesthood has slowly come to the fore in apocalyptic studies. One study after another has drawn attention to the posi-

---

23. Rowland, *The Open Heaven*, 29–37; Rowland, "Disclosure of Heavenly Knowledge," 783–84.

24. Rowland, *The Open Heaven*, 9–10, 68–69; Rowland, "Disclosure of Heavenly Knowledge," 780.

25. On the identification of Hermon with the Temple Mount see Crispin H. T. Fletcher-Louis, "The Revelation of the Sacral Son of Man: The Genre, History of Religions Context and the Meaning of the Transfiguration," in *Auferstehung—Resurrection. The Fourth Durham-Tübingen-Symposium: Resurrection, Exaltation, and Transformation in Old Testament, Ancient Judaism, and Early Christianity* (WUNT 135; ed. F. Avemarie and H. Lichtenberger; Tübingen: Mohr-Siebeck, 2001), 247–98, see esp. 270–72.

26. For the Yom Kippur connection see Lester L. Grabbe, "The Scapegoat Ritual: A Study in Early Jewish Interpretation," *JSJ* 18 (1987):152–67; Daniel Stökl, "Yom Kippur in the Apocalyptic imaginaire and the Roots of Jesus' High Priesthood," in *Transformations of the Inner Self in Ancient Religions* (SHR 83; ed. J. Assmann and G. G. Stroumsa; Leiden: Brill, 1999), 349–66; Fletcher-Louis, "Sacral Son of Man," 280–91.

27. See now the discussion in Frances Flannery-Dailey, *Dreamers, Scribes, and Priests: Jewish Dreams in the Hellenistic and Roman Eras* (JSJSup 90; Leiden: Brill, 2004), 158.

tive function of Israel's cult in the formation of this or that apocalyptic text or tradition.[28] There is no evidence that the apocalypses were written from an anti-temple perspective. On the contrary, recent scholarship leads to the conclusion that the particular religious experiences attested in the apocalypses are not so much a reflection of individual para-institutional mysticism, *but an expression of the divine encounter believed to take place in and through Israel's temple worship, especially priestly offices. In all this, temple cosmology—the belief that cultic space and time is a sacramental model of the universe—facilitates the experiences of transcendence, especially ascent to heaven, that so define apocalyptic literature.*

Secondly, and following some of Rowland's own suggestions, we now know that the pre-Christian apocalypses are particularly interested in the experience of human transformation.[29] It is not just, as is now widely recognized, that ascent to heaven for the privileged and heroic few climaxes in transformation to an angelic or divine identity. It is that transformation is an experience of the recovery of a true Adamic identity. This points to the fundamental theological proposition that undergirds the apocalypses and which they are written to promulgate, namely, that the apocalypses are distinctive in their proclamation that as the image of God, it is the true humanity—Israel and her representatives—that rightfully receives and communicates divine revelation. In contrast to the idolatrous (mantic) alternatives adopted by her neighbors, Israel alone (as the true humanity) has genuine access to the ecstatic experiences by which the creator god communicates his reality, wisdom, and perspective on history.[30] Here the apocalypses rely on the theological anthropology that lies at the heart of the Hebrew Bible's priestly (and much in the prophetic) critique of idolatry: idolatry with all its associated cultic and "magical" techniques is foolish because humanity is to the one true living and creator god what the statues and images of the nations

---

28. In addition to the literature cited in Fletcher-Louis, "Apocalypticism," see Michael Mach, "From Apocalypticism to Early Jewish Mysticism?" in *The Origins of Apocalypticism in Judaism and Christianity* (vol. 1 of *The Encyclopedia of Apocalypticism*; ed. J. J. Collins; New York: Continuum, 2000), 229–64; also see Flannery-Dailey, *Dreamers, Scribes, and Priests*.

29. See Martha Himmelfarb, "Revelation and Rapture: The Transformation of the Visionary in the Ascent Apocalypses," in Collins and Charlesworth, *Mysteries and Revelations*, 79–90; Christopher R. A. Morray-Jones, "Transformational Mysticism in the Apocalyptic-Merkabah Tradition," *JJS* 43 (1992):1–31; Crispin H.T. Fletcher-Louis, *Luke-Acts: Angels, Christology and Soteriology* (WUNT 2.94; Tübingen: Mohr-Siebeck, 1997), esp. 109–215; idem, *All the Glory of Adam: Liturgical Anthropology in the Dead Sea Scrolls* (STDJ 42; Leiden: Brill, 2002), 1–55; Margaret Barker, "The High Priest and the Worship of Jesus," in *The Jewish Roots of Christological Monotheism: Papers from the St. Andrews Conference on the Historical Origins of the Worship of Jesus* (JSJSup 63; ed. C. C. Newman, J. R. Davila and G .S. Lewis; Leiden: Brill, 1999), 93–111.

30. For the sharp differences between the revelatory experiences in the apocalypses and the techniques of mantic wisdom employed in non-Israelite societies see Andreas Bedenbender, "Jewish Apocalypticism: A Child of Mantic Wisdom?" *Henoch* 24 (2002): 189–96.

are to their gods.[31] Idolatry means a tragic emptying of human transcendence into that which cannot bear divine immanence.[32] And the apocalypses carry this theological battle cry out to the dark heart of the everyday ancient pagan world: they proclaim that it is not the diviners, magicians, and priests of the idols that receive divine revelation—supposedly communicated through those idols—but the truly human ones—Israel and her righteous (especially her priestly) representatives.

THREE TEXTS ILLUSTRATING THE NEW PERSPECTIVE

The current, third phase of the understanding of apocalyptic can be illustrated in a brief discussion of three texts that illustrate the literary genre and its content. All agree that Daniel and *1 Enoch* are apocalypses. A minority have recognized that *Joseph and Aseneth* is also generically apocalyptic (or that it contains an apocalypse).[33] The first two and almost certainly *Joseph and Aseneth* are pre-Christian.[34] The three texts are thus close relations generically, theologically, and in their views of religious experience. All that they have in common is obvious only when what each says individually is clarified.

---

31. On this see Crispin H. T. Fletcher-Louis, "God's Image, His Cosmic Temple and the High Priest: Towards an Historical and Theological Account of the Incarnation," in *Heaven on Earth: The Temple in Biblical Theology* (ed. T. D. Alexander and S. Gathercole; Carlisle: Paternoster, 2004), 81–99; idem, "The Image of God and the Biblical Roots of Christian Sacramentality," in *The Gestures of God: Explorations in Sacramentality* (ed. C. Hall and G. Rowell; London: Continuum, 2004), 73–89.

32. On this tragedy, see especially the discussion of Ezek 16 in Fletcher-Louis, "God's Image, His Cosmic Temple and the High Priest."

33. See Edith M. Humphrey, *The Ladies and the Cities: Transformation and Apocalyptic Identity in Joseph and Aseneth, 4 Ezra, and the Apocalypse and the Shepherd of Hermas* (JSPSup 17; Sheffield: Sheffield Academic Press, 1995), 35–39; idem, "On Bees and Best Guesses: The Problem of *Sitz im Leben* from Internal Evidence, as Illustrated by Joseph and Aseneth," *Currents in Research: Biblical Studies* 7 (1999): 223–36, 229–30 and cf. Gideon Bohak, *Joseph and Aseneth and the Jewish Temple in Heliopolis* (Atlanta: Scholars, 1996), 17; Rowland, "Disclosure of Heavenly Knowledge," 776–77.

34. I incline to the view of Bohak, *Joseph and Aseneth and the Jewish Temple*, that the text comes from the second century B.C.E. world of Oniad-led Judaism based at Leontopolis in Ptolemaic Egypt. In this case it is close in time to Daniel and the developing Enochic tradition. Against the view of Ross S. Kraemer, *When Aseneth Met Joseph: A Late Antique Tale of the Biblical Patriarch and His Egyptian Wife, Reconsidered* (Oxford: Oxford University Press, 1998) that the text is post-Christian see now John J. Collins, "Joseph and Aseneth: Jewish or Christian?" *JSP* 14 (2005): 97–112 and George J. Brooke, "Men and Women as Angels in Joseph and Aseneth Tradition," *JSP* 14 (2005): 159–77.

Daniel and the New Perspective

In Dan 1–6, Israel's hero is set over against the Chaldean diviners, much like Moses and Joseph in the court of Pharaoh and his magicians.[35] Daniel, not the Chaldean diviners, is privy to the secrets of a man's dream-life and the future course of history. Daniel 1–6 focus on the man Daniel—his plight, challenges, privileges, and authority: they expound a particular kind of theological anthropology. Chapters 7–12 of Daniel focus on the content of his revelatory experiences—both what and how it is revealed. The exposition has a particular interest in the temple cult: its cosmology, its plight, promised privileges, and its home to divine presence and authority.

In the first part, Daniel and his friends represent the true humanity. Daniel is possessed of God's spirit, like Adam (Dan 4:5, 6, 15; 5:11, 14; cf. Gen 2:7).[36] In so many respects Daniel is like his Chaldean counterparts,[37] but he is also not like them. It is not just that the God he worships is superior to theirs, or that their idols are dead and dumb, while his God is living. It is also that he is truly human and, like his God, is alive. He is able to speak what God reveals, while the servants of the lifeless idols are not. Their idolatry leads to human degradation—the life of the animals and a loss of sanity (chapter 4).[38]

Throughout Dan 1–6, Daniel's superiority of access to divine revelation accompanies a mockery of pagan idolatry. At the end of chapter 2, Daniel is the

---

35. Compare the humanity-as-God's-true-idol theology of the early chapters of Exodus where Moses plays Daniel to the foreign cult and its diviners, discussed by Gregory Y. Glazov, *The Bridling of the Tongue and the Opening of the Mouth in Biblical Prophecy* (JSOTSup 311; Sheffield: Sheffield Academic Press, 2001), 54–110.

36. For Gen 1 and the language of creation throughout Daniel see Jacques B. Doukhan, "Allusions à la Création dans le Livre de Daniel," in *The Book of Daniel in the Light of New Findings* (BETL 106; ed. A. S. van der Woude; Leuven: Leuven University Press, 1993), 285–92 and André Lacocque, "Allusions to Creation in Daniel 7," in *The Book of Daniel: Composition and Reception* (2 vols.; ed. J. J. Collins and P. W. Flint; Leiden: Brill, 2001), 114–31.

37. See Jack Newton Lawson, "'The God who Reveals Secrets': the Mesopotamian Background to Daniel 2.47," *JSOT* 74 (1997): 61–76 and Karel van der Toorn, "Scholars at the Oriental Court: The Figure of Daniel against Its Mesopotamian Background," in *The Book of Daniel: Composition and Reception* (2 vols.; ed. J. J. Collins and P. W. Flint; Leiden: Brill, 2001), 37–54.

38. The story of Nebuchadnezzar's fall recalls Gen 1–3. See Alexander A. DiLella, "Daniel 4:7-14: Poetic Analysis and Biblical Background," in *Mélanges bibliques et orientaux en l'honneur de M. Henri Cazelles* (AOAT 212; ed. A. Caquot and M. Delcor; Neukirchen-Vluyn: Neukirchener Verlag, 1981), 247–58. His position as cosmic tree sheltering the "beasts of the field" and "the birds of the air" gave him the position of humanity in Gen 1:26–30. His position after his "fall" echoes Gen 3:18 where the cursed Adam and Eve eat "the plants of the field" (see Doukhan, "Allusions à la Création," 211–14 and compare Gary A. Anderson, "The Penitence Narrative in The Life of Adam and Eve," *HUCA* 63 (1992): 1–38.

recipient of Nebuchadnezzar's worship. Daniel does not object and we are invited to ponder the contrast between the proper veneration of Daniel and the improper worship of the cult statue at the start of chapter 3. The former is no contravention of the biblical prohibition against idolatry, since Daniel's critique of idolatry is grounded in the conviction that the true humanity is God's living image that therefore has no need of an idol. This is certainly the way Dan 2:46–3:11 was read in Jewish antiquity,[39] and, I suggest, the point is developed in subsequent chapters.

In what follows, Daniel's friends, who trust in their God who sends them angelic assistance, are inviolable against the destructive power of the fiery furnace. As a late-biblical story, the fiery furnace evokes a complex biblical intertextuality that includes a common motif in the critique of idols. The wooden core of an idol is flammable, laughs Deutero-Isaiah (Isa 44:15–17); by way of proof that they are not what they are claimed to be, the idols that would seduce Israel are to be destroyed by fire (Deut 7:5, 22; 12:3). Those who were seduced to idolatry believed that the idol "came out of the fire" in which its metal was smelted, as if the idol had a life of its own (Exod 32:24). But any smelted metal could easily be melted down again and ground to powder (Exod 32:20). Only the living God speaks from the midst of fire and is not destroyed by it (Exod 3:2; Deut 4:12, 15, 33; 5:4, 24, 26; 9:10; 10:4). And his image-idol[40] is Israel, the nation "brought forth from the furnace of iron" (Deut 4:20, cf. Isa 43:2), which cannot be destroyed by any fire (cf. Isa 48:10; Jer 11:4).[41]

The same point is probably reiterated in Dan 6. Again in humble dependence upon his god, who sends angelic assistance, Daniel is unharmed by the ravenous lions. So he finds himself in the position given to humanity before its fall in Gen 1:28 (cf. Ps 8). When he puts him in his leonine pit, Belshazzar seals it with his seal "that nothing might be changed concerning Daniel" (Dan 6:17). Once again, the pagan king's pretensions to divine authority are lampooned: he and his seal

---

39. See the discussion of this passage in Fletcher-Louis, *All the Glory of Adam*, 102–3. For its *Receptionsgeschichte*, see Crispin H. T. Fletcher-Louis, "The Worship of the Jewish High Priest by Alexander the Great," in *Early Christian and Jewish Monotheism* (JSNTSup 63; ed. L. T. Stuckenbruck and W. S. North; Edinburgh: T&T Clark, 2004), 71–102, see p. 79.

40. The phrase "image-idol" as a translation for *tselem* makes the point that the image of God in these texts functions as the true idol of God. The translation "image" for *tselem* misses the force of the word, which normally refers to a cult statue—something that a deity needs to manifest itself in the world.

41. For Israel as the true human image of God in Deutero-Isaiah's critique of idolatry see Richard J. Clifford, "The Function of Idol Passages in Second Isaiah," *CBQ* 42 (1980): 450–64. For the post-biblical theme of humanity as God's idol inviolable against destructive fire, see Crispin H. T. Fletcher-Louis, "Humanity and the Idols of the Gods in Pseudo-Philo's Biblical Antiquities," in *Idolatry: False Worship in the Bible, Early Judaism, and Christianity* (ed. S. C. Barton; Edinburgh: T&T Clark, 2007), 58–72. For the notion that the truly divine humanity is somehow able to inhabit the realm of fire without destruction see Ezek 28:14, 16.

(that bears his image and perhaps that of his god) are about to be overruled.[42] The living god and one who bears his image—Daniel—are about to be vindicated in defiance of a bankrupt pagan authority.

In the second half of Daniel (chapters 7–11), the focus shifts from the place of exile to the homeland and to the defiled temple in Jerusalem: the cosmic center against which the chaotic nations rage and the point at which decisive judgment will be declared and authority handed over to the truly human high priest on his ascent to meet the Ancient of Days at an eschatological Day of Atonement (Dan 7).[43] Daniel himself does not ascend to heaven—he is not a priest—but his experiences take place at times of intense ritual significance (9:21). Only the priest is able to effect the cosmic purgation of sin and chaos that will cleanse the temple of its defilement and desolation (cf. 8:9–14; 9:24–27). While the angle of vision has changed, Daniel's visionary claim rests on the same theological anthropology laid out in chapters 1–6. Like Daniel himself, the future priest will receive supreme dominion and human service (or "worship," cf. Dan 7:14). The truly righteous are the truly human. The pagan idolaters, like the grass-eating Nebuchadnezzar, are subhuman; they are freaks even of the animal kingdom (7:3–8).

1 ENOCH AND THE NEW PERSPECTIVE

We have already noted the presence of cultic material in the Book of Watchers (1 En. 1–36). In this, and the other earliest part of the Enochic corpus, the Astronomical Book (1 En. 72–82), the temple and its concerns are all pervasive, as is now widely acknowledged.[44] Temple time and space—anchored in ancient West Semitic traditions of sacred cosmography centered on Hermon—provide one of the two prime conceptual drivers for this early Enochic material.

The other driver—which has curiously escaped the notice of modern commentators—is the belief that it is the image of God, i.e. humanity, for whom and through whom God's revelatory experience is to take place. The narrative is motivated in the first place by the plea for a right ordering of human and cosmic relations (chapters 2–5) and then by the crisis caused by a demonic attack on the human vocation to increase and fill the earth with blessing (chapters 6–9, cf. Gen

---

42. For images in Mesopotamian royal glyptic art of the king boasting of his authority over lions, see, e.g., figs. 15i, 556 and 558 (Daruis I) in Dominique Collon, *First Impressions: Cylinder Seals in the Ancient Near East* (London: British Museum, 1987), 128–30.

43. For this reading of Dan 7 see Crispin H. T. Fletcher-Louis, "The High Priest as Divine Mediator in the Hebrew Bible: Dan 7:13 as a Test Case," in *SBL Seminar Papers 1997* (SBLSP 36: Atlanta: Scholars, 1997), 161–93.

44. See, e.g., George W. E. Nickelsburg, *1 Enoch 1: A Commentary on 1 Enoch, Chapters 1–36; 81–108* (Hermeneia; Minneapolis: Fortress, 2001), 54, 231–32, 239–47.

1:28; 12:1–3, 17:2, 6, 8; 22:17–18; 26:3–4) that is resolved through the righteous remnant in Noah (*1 En.* 10:16–22).[45]

Enoch, like Noah, is the true human being—the seventh from Adam—who walked with (the) elohim, the angels/gods (*1 En.* 12–36, cf. Gen 3:8; 5:22, 24; 6:9). Enoch is set over against the fallen watchers who are confined to the world below, unable to gain direct access to God. Enoch—the human being—does have direct visual and aural access to God's throne room. Enoch enters where even the faithful angels cannot (14:21–15:1) and receives the word of judgment on the angels (elohim, gods) who threaten the life of humanity. In the introduction to the recounting of his visions, Enoch says his vision is "what I now speak with my tongue of flesh and the breath of the mouth which the Great One has given to man (so that) he might speak with it—and so that he might have understanding with his heart as he (the Great One) has created and given it to man. Accordingly he has created me and given me the word of understanding. . . . " (14.2). This recalls the anthropology of Gen 2 as a whole, which stresses humanity's fleshly nature (2.21–24) and the breath of God given to Adam (2.7),[46] as well as the widespread view in the literature of the period that at their creation Adam and Eve were peculiarly endowed with wisdom and understanding (Sir 17:7; 4Q417 1 I, 17–18; 4Q504 8 [recto] 5).

Enoch is the Jewish counterpart to the Mesopotamian antediluvian king Enmeduranki, who is the patron and founder of a guild of diviners.[47] Like Daniel, he is both like and unlike those engaged in the pursuit of mantic wisdom in the Mesopotamian world. He does receive revelation in a dream, but he is not engaged in the kinds of divination that define the pagan (and idolatrous) pursuit of divine revelation: he does not practice haruspicy, oneiromancy, libanomancy, or leconomancy. To Enoch there is revealed, in the Astronomical Book, the movement of the heavenly bodies, but this is not the source of prognostications about the future.[48] Enoch receives his revelation without the usual idolatrous apparatus of mantic wisdom and it is a revelation that judges the source of pagan forms of magic and divination (*1 En.* 7–8).[49] It is not, as Randall Argall has suggested, that

---

45. For this theme in the Book of Watchers see Crispin H. T. Fletcher-Louis, "The Aqedah and the Book of Watchers (*1 Enoch* 1–36)," in *Studies in Jewish Prayer* (JSSSup 17; ed. R. Hayward and B. Embry; Oxford: Oxford University Press, 2005), 1–33.

46. Genesis 2:7 is interpreted in terms of the breath of God issuing in human ability to speak in the targums (*Tg. Onq., Tg. Neof.,* and *Tg. Yer.*).

47. See especially James C. VanderKam, *Enoch and the Growth of an Apocalyptic Tradition* (CBQMS 16; Washington, D.C.: The Catholic Biblical Association of America, 1984).

48. Ibid., 103.

49. It is for this reason that the label "mantic wisdom" for the Enochic tradition is rightly questioned by Randall A. Argall, *1 Enoch and Sirach: A Comparative Literary and Conceptual Analysis of the Themes of Revelation, Creation and Judgment* (SBLEJL 8; Atlanta: Scholars Press, 1995), 251.

Enoch receives "revealed wisdom" as opposed to a "mantic wisdom," since the latter was also believed to be revealed.[50] It is that Enochic wisdom is revealed to the human being without the divinatory techniques that characterise the world of ancient Near Eastern idolatry. This is so because the early Enoch literature assumes the same theological anthropology present in Daniel: (the true) humanity is the living image-idol of the one God to whom, through whom and for whom revelation takes place in concrete and "ecstatic" experiences of divine encounter. The depiction of Enoch exalted to divine Glory in the Similitudes (*1 En.* 37–71, cf. Gen 5.22–24) and dressed in Aaron's garments of Glory in subsequent Enochic material (e.g., *2 En.* 22) simply spells out what is central to the tradition from its inception.

JOSEPH AND ASENETH AND THE NEW PERSPECTIVE

Joseph and Aseneth is the only certainly pre-Christian text to use the verb ἀποκαλύπτω to describe any of its content and it does so, in two instances, in language that is redolent of the whole "apocalyptic" tradition (16:14 and 22:13). The central portion of the book—from the revelation brought by the angel in chapter 14 onwards—is full of apocalyptic features, as anyone familiar with Daniel, *1 Enoch* and similar works will perceive. Generically, the text is regularly labeled a romance, but as several recent voices have pointed out, this is not a satisfactory summation of its genre.[51] Because the text conveys the two defining features of other, near contemporary, apocalypses it should be treated along with them.

It is difficult to miss the high theological anthropology in the text. Joseph is a divine son of God, whose first appearance evokes a solar theophany (chapters 5–6). On her conversion to the Jewish faith, Aseneth joins a heavenly community of both angels and divine humans, of whom Jacob, Joseph's father, is the pre-eminent representative (22:3–8).[52] As in Daniel and *1 Enoch*, the theological anthropology is grounded in a pre-lapsarian vision; the life of Eden is restored in the community of faith (16:14–16).

---

50. The comments of Jack N. Lawson on Daniel apply equally to Enoch (Lawson, "The God who Reveals Secrets").

51. See Kraemer, *When Aseneth Met Joseph*, 10–11; Eric S. Gruen, *Heritage and Hellenism: the Reinvention of Jewish Tradition* (Berkeley: University of California Press, 1998), 93–94 and notice the differences as well as the similarities between *Joseph and Aseneth* and the genre "Romance" discussed in Catherine Hezser, "'Joseph and Aseneth' in the Context of Ancient Greek Erotic Novels," *Frankfurter Judaistische Beiträge* 24 (1997):1–40.

52. This aspect of the text is discussed in Fletcher-Louis, *Luke-Acts*, 161–62, 165–68; Kraemer, *When Aseneth Met Joseph*, 110–54 and Brooke, "Joseph and Aseneth." Like Daniel, *Joseph and Aseneth* has a particular interest in the depiction of Joseph in the court of the Pharaoh in Gen 41.

Coupled with this theological anthropology and at the heart of the tale there is a critique of pagan idolatry. Although scholars have missed the point, the critique of idolatry is grounded in the text's theological anthropology. Aseneth must surrender her dead and dumb idols (2:2; 3:6; 8:5; 10:12–13; 11:7–9; 12:5, 9, 12; 13:11) before God sends his angel to receive her into his household. Ross Kraemer has seen how loudly the language in 12:5 echoes the statements in Ps 115:4–8 and Ps 135:15–18 that the idols of the nations "have mouths, but do not speak; . . . have eyes, but do not see."[53] She fails however, to consider the significance of the fact that both psalms say of the idols that "those who make them become like them" (115:8; 135:18), which is the inverse of the biblical principle that the true humanity that worships and trusts in the living God becomes like him and is restored to its originally intended identity as his living image-idol. There are five considerations which indicate that this is the restoration that Aseneth experiences during her transformation.

(1) There is the dramatic power of the encounter with Joseph that sets in motion her repentance. The narrative seems to say that it is her meeting with the divine man Joseph that provokes the rejection of her idols. The point is never made explicitly, but it is implicit. Joseph is a living embodiment of divinity that brings to consciousness the lifelessness of Aseneth's idols. The images of the gods can be destroyed (10:12; 11:4; 12:12); the righteous partake of incorruptibility (8:5; 15:5; 16:16).

(2) In her paganism, Aseneth is adorned with fine clothing and precious stones engraved with the names and the faces of her idols (3:6, cf. 2:4). Indeed, her home is designed as a temple for these idols (chapter 2). In 18:5–6, "after her repentance and transformation, Aseneth again adorns herself in clothing and jewelry that are described almost identically to her initial garments, except that, unsurprisingly, they contain no images or names of Egyptian gods."[54] Kramer sees this anti-parallelism as an aspect of Aseneth's transformation from strange woman to the epitome of Wisdom. But it is just as, if not more, likely to reflect the conviction that the true human being is an image-idol of the one God. Once her finery is stripped of its idols, Aseneth is presented as one who wears the kind of golden and jewel-studded garments that adorn the statues of the gods; only there is one God here and it is the (true Israelite) human being who represents him.[55]

---

53. Kraemer, *When Aseneth Met Joseph*, 41, 45.

54. Ibid., 23.

55. For the garments of the gods that adorn ancient statues see A. Leo Oppenheim, "The Golden Garments of the Gods," *JNES* 8 (1949):172–93. For Israel's high priest dressed in these garments see Fletcher-Louis, "Alexander the Great"; "God's Image, His Cosmic Temple and the High Priest"; "The Image of God and the Biblical Roots"; "Humanity and the Idols." The way this glorious clothing adorns the female half of the divine humanity in *Joseph and Aseneth* has a close parallel in the Qumran War Scroll (1QM 12:10–16). See Fletcher-Louis, *All the Glory of Adam*, 432–42.

(3) That this clothing functions in this way is supported by the reference to the allegory of abandoned and rescued Israel in Ezek 16. Again, Kraemer has spotted a number of parallels between Ezek 16:1–14 and the account of Aseneth's conversion.[56] These are important because, in its own way, Ezek 16 is a classic and profound meditation of the conviction that the true humanity—in this case Israel depicted as God's bride and queen—is to the one true God what the idols of the nations are to their gods.[57] There is every reason to suppose that the author of *Joseph and Aseneth* was echoing this meaning of Ezek 16 in his description of Aseneth.

(4) At the center of the revelation given to Aseneth by God's principal angel (chapters 14–16), there is the strange allegory of the honeycomb (16:1–17:4), the interpretation of which has frustrated modern scholars. One suggestion now deserves our fuller attention: that the honeycomb has some connection with the Egyptian form of the ancient Near East's Opening of the Mouth ritual by which the idols of the gods were activated with the divine life.[58] In an appendix to a wide-ranging study of biblical passages in which the mouth is restrained and then opened, Gregory Glazov has now re-examined this possibility.[59] In view of the way in which the Opening of the Mouth ritual is evoked in the call of Moses (Exod 3:1–4:17) and at the purification of Isaiah's lips (Isa 6) as part of an old, pre-exilic critique of idolatry, and given the role of bees and honey in the Egyptian cult of the idols, Glazov makes a plausible case that *Joseph and Aseneth* alludes to contemporary Egyptian practices. Through this allusion to well-known Egyptian rituals, *Joseph and Aseneth* claims that that through the Jewish sacrificial system that is symbolised by the honeycomb Aseneth receives the identity that is otherwise given, through the Opening of the Mouth ritual, to the cult statue.

All these observations point to the same conclusion for which we have argued in our discussion of Daniel and the early parts of *1 Enoch*: these texts articulate the view that the right and proper experience of the divine world is possible only for the true humanity which, in its worship of the living God, bears the life and identity of that God and so is open to his revelation. This humanity, so the apocalypses claim, is quite unlike that which gives itself to lifeless idols.

(5) Finally, we should consider a brief comment in the longer text of *Joseph and Aseneth* that probably reflects the same kind of polemic against the mantic prophecy and divination of the pagan world that we have encountered in Daniel and *1 Enoch*. At *Jos. Asen.* 12:9, during her confession and disavowal of the gods

---

56. Kraemer, *When Aseneth Met Joseph*, 29–30.

57. See the discussion of the passage in Fletcher-Louis, "God's Image, His Cosmic Temple and the High Priest"

58. Noted, but dismissed, by C. Burchard , "Joseph and Aseneth," in *The Old Testament Pseudepigrapha* (ed. James H. Charlesworth; 2 vols.; Garden City, N.Y.: Doubleday, 1983–85), 2:230 n. 2.

59. Glazov, *Bridling of the Tongue*, 379–380.

and their idols, Aseneth cries out: "the ancient savage lion pursues me, because he is the father of the gods of the Egyptians and his children are the gods of the idol maniacs (εἰδωλομανῶν)." The word εἰδωλομανής is rare and not otherwise attested before the second century C.E. But its meaning is not in dispute: it refers to the devotees to the idols who believe that the gods communicate to them through visions, "as if coming from the idols and the statutes" themselves (Athenagoras, *Leg.* 27.1). Although this word is not otherwise attested in Jewish Greek literature, only in patristic texts, its meaning belongs to a Jewish as much as a Christian vocabulary and it nicely sums up the implicit attitude to idolatry in all three of our texts.[60]

If *Joseph and Aseneth* satisfies one of our two conceptual and experiential apocalyptic concerns, a high theological anthropology coupled with a critique of idolatry, then what about the other? Most scholarship has had little to say about the text's relationship to the Jewish temple and its cosmology. Recently, two detailed studies by Gideon Bohak and Ross Kraemer, though reaching very different conclusions, have agreed that an interest is Israel's temple space is present in this work.[61] This is clear in the depiction of Aseneth's house in chapter 2 and Bohak has made a persuasive case that the whole text looks, allegorically, to the Oniad temple at Leontopolis. Even though, in the nature of the case, Bohak's thesis cannot be established with certainty, the central "apocalyptic" section that deals with the allegory of the honeycomb created by the bees from the garden of delights (ch. 16) assumes the identification of the Jewish temple with Eden, which is a fundamental component of the temple cosmology complex.

THE SIMILARITIES BETWEEN DANIEL, 1 ENOCH AND JOSEPH AND ASENETH

These three texts share both a theology and a generic identity. They are all concerned to ascribe genuine religious experience of God and his revelation to individuals who exemplify a particular anthropology. This anthropology entails a critique of non-Israelite patterns of idolatry and provides the rationale for thinking that God communicates to and through those who live as God's image-idol. The revelatory experiences are "direct" and "immediate" insofar as they do not come through the statues of the gods, by means of magical arts or prescribed techniques of ecstasy.[62] In this sense, Rowland's estimation of apocalyptic experiences was on the mark. However, as texts faithful to the biblical worldview, the

---

60. So, Burchard's view that the word is "wohl christlich" is over hasty, *Joseph und Aseneth kritisch herausgegeben* (PVTG 5; ed. C. Burchard, C. Burfeind and U. B. Fink; Leiden: Brill, 2003), 161.

61. Kraemer, *When Aseneth Met Joseph*, 119–20; Bohak, *Joseph and Aseneth and the Jewish Temple*.

62. This explains the absence of genuine techniques of ecstasy from Second Temple texts that has been noted by Martha Himmelfarb, "The Practice of Ascent in the Ancient Mediter-

apocalypses assume that the true image-idol restored in Israel and represented by her leaders is constituted by and mediated through a particular cultic time and space: that of the temple in Jerusalem (and its "heterodox" rivals).

Lining up our three texts against one another we see how their shared theological content is expressed in a shared literary form and structure. A substantial opening portion of all three texts is taken up with a narrative that introduces the visionary and, in so doing, articulates the texts' particular theological anthropology (*1 En.* 1–13 parallels Dan 1–6 which parallels *Jos. Asen.* 1–13).[63] The encounter with the heavenly world, with a propagandist orientation towards (a particular form of) Israel's cultic cosmology then follows (*1 En.* 14–36; Dan 7–12, *Jos. Asen.* 14–17).

Religious Experience and the New Perspective on Apocalyptic

In none of these texts is there a *direct* account of a religious experience: they are fictional and in the case of Daniel and *1 Enoch* they are pseudepigraphic. There is no direct and simple correlation between what they describe and something that happened. On this point, as we have already noted, Martha Himmelfarb is right. But that does not mean that there is no correlation between what they describe and ancient Jewish religious experiences at all.

On the contrary, this New Perspective on Apocalyptic means that religious experience lies at the very heart of the literary phenomenon. *The apocalypses espouse a particular kind of religious experience because they have a particular theology (and theological anthropology) worked out in the context of a particular cultic context and cosmology.* They are not—as scholarship held earlier—obsessed with a particular set of eschatological and dualistic *ideas* (and hence "theology" in the purely intellectual or propositional sense). Neither are they—as has become fashionable to assert in recent decades—the product of a particular *sociology* (and "experience" in the narrowly materialist and functional sense). Nor are they to be explained as the product of a somewhat paranoid, psychological experience of dissonance (as if they are a simple anticipation of distasteful forms of late modern western Christianity). Rather, judging by these three texts—an admittedly incomplete set of witnesses—*the apocalypses are the "classic" texts that attest the popular piety of temple-centered Jewish practice and belief in the late Persian, Hellenistic, and Roman eras.* There is every reason to believe their authors and readers expected themselves or some of their contemporaries to experience the

---

ranean World," in *Death, Ecstasy, and Otherworldly Journeys* (ed. J. J. Collins and M. Fishbane; Albany, N.Y.: SUNY Press, 1995), 123–37.

63. The additional narrative (chapters 18) after the angelophany in *Jos. Asen.* 14–17 has a parallel in both the form and the content of *T. Levi* 2–8 where vision and narrative are interspersed.

kind of encounters with the heavenly world described in these texts. An experience of something of what the Ur-Priest Enoch witnessed on his ascent to heaven could reasonably be expected for the priests and would-be priests who followed him. What the royal hero and lay leader Daniel achieved provided a model for Jewish prophets who were denied direct access to the mysteries reserved for the priesthood. And Aseneth's journey from the world of dead and dumb idols attests the kind of revelatory encounter with the heavenly mysteries for which any Jew, Jewess or proselyte might hope.

PART 3
PAUL AND RELIGIOUS EXPERIENCE

THE CONSTRUCTION OF RELIGIOUS EXPERIENCE IN PAUL

Troels Engberg-Pedersen

My aim in this essay is two-fold: to argue that, against our current habits, we need to bring the notion of religious experience into the analysis of Paul and to suggest a sufficiently philosophically sophisticated way of doing this. I begin by sketching the current situation within Pauline studies with regard to the idea of religious experience. This will remind us that throughout the twentieth century there has been a marked reluctance to use this idea in enlightened, scholarly analysis of Paul. We shall also note the general background to that reluctance in recent philosophy of religion and acknowledge that the reluctance is both understandable and to some extent well founded. Next, I will turn to my plea for reinstalling the notion of religious experience in the analysis of Paul. Here we will consider the character of Pauline religious experience, as indicated by his letters, and I will end up suggesting both why we need the notion for a proper analysis of Paul and how we may accommodate the insights that lie behind the reluctance to use it. So, "religious experience" in Paul? Yes, but in an appropriately refined way.

AGAINST "RELIGIOUS EXPERIENCE" IN PAUL

A number of ideas and perspectives have flowed together over the last few decades to suggest that a reference to religious experience in the analysis of Paul is more problematic than it is useful.

First, while so-called liberal theology at the turn of the twentieth century was quite happy to speak of Paul's individual religious experience, neo-orthodoxy (alias dialectical theology) was decidedly against such discussion.[1] For instance, in Werner Georg Kümmel's famous analysis of the "I" in Rom 7, which dates as far back as 1929,[2] the emphasis was very strongly—and in many ways rightly—on

---

1. For liberal theology compare, e.g., Paul Wernle, *Der Christ und die Sünde bei Paulus* (Freiburg/Leipzig: Mohr Siebeck, 1897).

2. See Werner Georg Kümmel "Römer 7 und die Bekehrung des Paulus," in *Römer 7 und das Bild des Menschen im Neuen Testament. Zwei Studien* (ed. W. G. Kümmel; Munich: Kaiser, 1974).

moving away from seeing Paul's uses of "I" in that passage as standing for his individual religious experience.[3]

Second, while the scholarly reaction to neo-orthodoxy, which started about forty years ago, for example with Krister Stendahl, has in many ways meant a return to issues and perspectives addressed by liberal theology, the move away from neo-orthodoxy did not involve a return to an interest in Paul's individual religious experience. On the contrary, Stendahl himself famously rejected the reading of Paul that found him to be speaking of his own troubled conscience vis-à-vis God, a prime example of an individual religious experience.[4] Instead, Paul was seen—and in itself quite rightly—to be speaking paradigmatically in those passages, and of something quite different, namely, the relationship between Jews and Gentiles vis-à-vis God.[5] The emphasis on this latter theme as the focus of Paul's thought was taken up and placed at the heart of what became the "new" perspective on Paul in the wake of E. P. Sanders' ground-breaking book, *Paul and Palestinian Judaism*.[6] The focus on ethnicity as a main category for understanding Paul has meant that there has been just as little room for interest in individual religious experience in post-neo-orthodox analysis of Paul as there was, for entirely different reasons, in neo-orthodoxy itself.[7]

Third, the literary turn in New Testament studies in general has discouraged interest in individual religious experience supposedly lying behind the text. Instead, scholarly interest has been focused—and again in itself quite rightly—on the rhetoric of the text, either in purely literary terms or as part of the text's communicative functions.[8] The text itself has been the center of interest.

Fourth, and finally, while there has also been a very important social historical and social anthropological interest in the Pauline letters, this interest has been

---

3. Similarly, in the work of Rudolf Bultmann one has the pervasive sense that even speaking of a "religious experience" in Paul is a betrayal. Paul's "existential" claims, as interpreted by Bultmann, were anything but claims about "experience." They were theological claims.

4. Krister Stendahl, "The Apostle Paul and the Introspective Conscience of the West," *HTR* 56 (1963): 199–215. Also in idem, *Paul among Jews and Gentiles* (Philadelphia: Fortress, 1976).

5. This is the theme of Stendahl, *Paul among Jews and Gentiles*.

6. E. P. Sanders, *Paul and Palestinian Judaism* (London: SCM, 1977).

7. It is curious that Sanders shared the general reluctance about invoking a Pauline "religious experience" in explanation of the radical importance that Paul attached to the Christ event in Sanders' own picture. Heikki Räisänen did invoke some form of psychological explanation for Paul's various statements about the Mosaic law, but in a theoretically undeveloped form. See in particular chapter 8 of Heikki Räisänen, *Paul and the Law* (WUNT 29; 2nd ed.; Tübingen: Mohr Siebeck, 1987).

8. Here belongs, of course, the huge amount of rhetorical analysis of Paul that has taken place within the last twenty-five years, starting from Hans Dieter Betz, *Galatians: A Commentary on Paul's Letter to the Churches in Galatia* (Hermeneia; Philadelphia: Fortress, 1979).

emphatically socially oriented—and again in itself rightly so.[9] To a large extent, an interest in individual religious experience in the case of Paul has been seen as anachronistic and out of tune with the fundamentally non-individualistic ancient Mediterranean culture.[10]

In short, attempts at addressing topics verging on something "psychic" in relation to Paul have been few and far between. Gerd Theissen made a carefully pondered attempt in 1983, but with few repercussions.[11] More recently, Luke Timothy Johnson pleaded strongly in 1998 that we need to place the phenomenon of religious experience squarely on the map of our analysis of early Christianity.[12] In spite of these attempts, however, the general reluctance remains in place.[13]

Nor is it difficult to understand why this is the case, if one considers the concomitant developments in reflections on religious experience within philosophy of religion. From George Lindbeck to Jonathan Smith,[14] philosophers of religion have argued against (in Lindbeck's terms) an "experiential-expressive" model of religion (in vogue from Schleiermacher to Eliade) and for a "cultural-linguistic" model: "We have no experience without interpretation" since "there is no uninterpreted experience."[15] And since " . . . experience . . . is always mediated," we cannot "experience a world independently of the conventional ways in which

---

9. The classic accounts of Paul in his socio-historical and intellectual contexts by Wayne Meeks and Abraham Malherbe spend very little time, if any, on his "religious experience." See Wayne A. Meeks, *The First Urban Christians: The Social World of the Apostle Paul* (2d ed; New Haven, Conn.: Yale University Press, 2003) and Abraham J. Malherbe, *Paul and the Thessalonians: The Philosophical Tradition of Pastoral Care* (Philadelphia: Fortress, 1987).

10. This is the hard line taken by writers identifying themselves as being engaged in "social scientific" analysis of Paul. See, e.g., Bruce J. Malina, *The New Testament World: Insights from Cultural Anthropology* (London: SCM, 1981), especially chapter 3 on "The First-Century Personality," and Bruce J. Malina and Jerome H. Neyrey, *Portraits of Paul: An Archaeology of Ancient Personality* (Louisville, Ky.: Westminster John Knox, 1996).

11. Gerd Theissen, *Psychologische Aspekte paulinischer Theologie* (FRLANT 131; Göttingen: Vandenhoeck & Ruprecht, 1983).

12. Luke Timothy Johnson, *Religious Experience in Earliest Christianity: A Missing Dimension in New Testament Studies* (Minneapolis: Fortress, 1998).

13. In relation to Johnson, this reluctance is wholly in place. As Christopher Mount has shown, Johnson's basic conception contains a tacit move from speaking (rightly) of the early Christians' claims to have had religious experiences instigated by God to claiming (wrongly) that these experiences were in fact instigated by God. Christopher Mount, "'Jesus Is Lord': Religious Experience and the Religion of Paul" (paper presented at the annual meeting of the SBL, Washington, D.C., November 18, 2006).

14. George A. Lindbeck, *The Nature of Doctrine: Religion and Theology in a Postliberal Age* (London: SPCK, 1984); Wayne Proudfoot, *Religious Experience* (Berkeley and Los Angeles: University of California Press, 1985); Jonathan Z. Smith, "Bible and Religion" and "A Twice-Told Tale: The History of the History of Religions' History," in *Relating Religion: Essays in the Study of Religion* (Chicago: University of Chicago Press, 2004).

15. Proudfoot, *Religious Experience*, 70.

it is socially represented," and "the re- in re-presentation [always] remains . . . at the level of representation. . . ."[16] Against such a background, there is little wonder that Pauline studies, too, have focused on the representations of religious experience in Paul, on the rhetoric of religious experience as part of the argument of the letters, and on the communicative functions of whatever references to Paul's own religious experience may be found in them.

We should accept nearly all of this without further ado.[17] We should accept that Paul was not concerned about his personal experiences per se, but rather about using them for rhetorical purposes in an argument about ethnicity. We should certainly also accept that Paul's experiences always came in interpreted form. Still, I will argue that we also need to find room for attending to Paul's religious experience, as expressed in his letters, on its own. Paul did have certain experiences to which he is referring in his letters and which he went on to use for his various letter-writing purposes. Just because his reference to his own religious experiences serves certain functions and that the experiences themselves always came in interpreted form, we should not conclude that there was nothing to be interpreted and to serve those functions. That would be a fallacy of philosophical "idealism," against which Proudfoot rightly warns.[18] On the contrary, we should precisely insist on the "realist" claim that there was something (or other): that something happened (in Paul's brain, mind, psyche, or body), which he then interprets and uses in the ways he does in the letters.

Note, however, that the argument may also be turned round. If an interpreter of Paul already agrees that there is religious experience on its own in Paul and that we should attend to this too as part of any attempt to make overall sense of the Pauline project, then the point of the sketch just given of the current thinking on religious experience—both in general and in Paul—is to insist that we should retain almost all of those insights. Paul's religious experiences did in fact come in interpreted form. He did focus on issues of ethnicity in relation to his understanding of the Christ event. He did use the reference to his own religious experience for the various rhetorical purposes suggested. And, in particular, he was not concerned to relate his own religious experiences for their own sake, but always as part of a relationship with others. Still, he did have them.

---

16. Smith, *Relating Religion*, 207, 366.

17. I do not, however, accept the claim sometimes made in the Malina school that the ancient world had no real notion of "the self."

18. See Proudfoot, *Religious Experience*, 70. For present purposes philosophical "idealism" may be defined as a metaphysical position according to which what is real is fundamentally confined to the contents of human minds. In the present case the "idealist" position will take it that what is real about a religious experience is just the interpretation with which any example of a religious experience necessarily comes.

For "Religious Experience" in Paul

Let us remind ourselves of three texts in which Paul appears to be speaking of his own religious experience. There is one in Galatians, one in 2 Corinthians, and one in Philippians.

In Gal 1:12 and 1:15–16 Paul famously describes how he was torn out of his previous kind of life by having Jesus Christ "revealed" to him by God. No matter whether we understand Paul to be describing a "conversion" or a "calling,"[19] should we say that he is here giving an account of a religious experience in the sense of a single, datable psychological event that occurred at or just before the moment when Paul would say to himself, (as German poet Rainer Maria Rilke did later on seeing the Belvedere Apollo in the Vatican), "Du musst dein Leben ändern" ("You must change your life")? Is Paul here referring to a singular event like the one immortalized to us by Luke in Acts 9, or by Michelangelo Caravaggio in his famous painting of Paul's conversion in the church of Santa Maria del Popolo in Rome? Not necessarily. Paula Frederiksen has taught us that such an autobiographical account may well reflect a long period of development that is then for rhetorical purposes described in a manner that contracts it into a single moment.[20] That is not an objection, however, to the claim that Paul is describing here a religious experience in the sense in which I intend to use the term. What makes it an experience (and in this case clearly a religious one) does not depend on its being either datable or momentary. Instead, it depends on two features: that the account of it, the "interpretation," invokes (1) an "I" (or at least an individual) and (2) the "interior" of that "I" (or individual). That is in fact the case here, since Paul's expression ἐν ἐμοί (in "God . . . decided . . . to reveal His son ἐν ἐμοί") is best taken to mean "in me."[21]

---

19. Stendahl famously insisted that Paul is describing a call, not a conversion. That was due to Stendahl's cognitive interests that had to do with Paul's relation to Judaism, (namely, that Paul did not "convert" from Judaism). The notion of Paul's "conversion" as a prime example of a "religious experience" will not go away, however, even though it has not played any very important role within recent Pauline scholarship. For a modern discussion of "conversion" see Lewis R. Rambo, *Understanding Religious Conversion* (New Haven, Conn.: Yale University Press, 1993). The most substantial discussion of Paul's "conversion" along similar lines is the one to be found in Alan F. Segal, *Paul the Convert: The Apostolate and Apostasy of Saul the Pharisee* (New Haven, Conn.: Yale University Press, 1990).

20. Paula Frederiksen, "Paul and Augustine: Conversion Narratives, Orthodox Traditions, and the Retrospective Self," *JTS* 37 (1986): 3–34.

21. Compare Gal 2:19–20, in which Paul unmistakably claims that Christ lives "in me." Even if we decided to translate ἐν ἐμοί of 1:16 as "to me," Paul would probably have had in mind some internal experience. I proceed to claim that he is in fact talking of a vision, compare also his statement in 1 Cor 15:8: ἔσχατον δὲ πάντων ... ὤφθη κἀμοί. Second Corinthians 4:6 shows that Paul took a vision to be very much also something interior.

Exactly how, then, did God reveal his son, Jesus Christ, in Paul? Second Corinthians 4:6 suggests one possible answer: Paul says that God, who in the first creation said, "Let light shine forth from darkness," himself "shone forth in our hearts to illuminate knowledge of God's glory on the face of Jesus Christ," as it were in the kind of "new creation" that Paul goes on to speak of in 2 Cor 5:17.[22] In other words, Paul has had a vision; he has seen the glory of God on the face of Christ—in the sense of "has seen" with which I am constantly working: that he takes himself to have seen it. Here, too, we have the two features that define the phenomenon described as that of an "experience": an individual and his or her interior. And here this phenomenon is distinctly described as that of a vision. Whether Paul in fact thought of the "revelation" in Gal 1:12 and 15–16 as a vision as well cannot be completely settled. It is noteworthy, however, that when he moves on in Gal 3:1–5 to apply what he has said about his own "experience" of Christ to his addressees, he starts out from referring explicitly to something they have seen (namely, Jesus Christ drawn before their eyes as crucified), and only then refers to what they had also heard (namely, from Paul himself).[23]

Taking ἐν ἐμοί in Gal 1:16 to mean "in me" points to one more feature of the "experience" Paul is describing that is brought out more explicitly in Gal 2:19–20, namely, that of a particularly intimate relationship between the "I" and Christ: "I have been crucified together with Christ. As for living, I no longer live, but Christ lives in me." I understand this in a literal, physical, bodily sense. Paul has the (physical) πνεῦμα ('spirit') living within himself.[24] Thus understood—and by all means, as reconstructed (and indeed, constructed) after the event—Paul's account is very much an account of a psychological "experience" (and of course, a "religious" one).

So far, then, we have two defining features of what makes a given phenomenon a psychological experience: it occurs (1) to an individual (2) in his or her interior.[25] Further, we have noted two forms of such an experience, which may or

---

22. See also Gal 6:15.

23. My own guess is that Paul intends his addressees to understand that they have seen Christ in Paul, namely, when he came to them the first time in bodily weakness, compare his description of that in Gal 4:13–15, a passage which in the light of the renewed reference to the Galatians' eyes (4:15 with 3:1) constitutes an inclusio with the earlier passage.

24. This is a very large claim, for which I cannot argue here. Nothing in my argument hangs on whether it is true. The point here is only that if it is, then Paul's understanding of "what has happened to him" is of such a kind that it becomes immediately natural to understand it, categorically, as something that did happen to him. (After all, physical events do occur.) Please note here that it is a very far cry from this to claim that what happened to him had the exact form that Paul himself understood it to have—of the πνεῦμα actually entering him or whatever. To move from "something happened to him" to "it happened to him the way he took it to happen" is of course wholly fallacious.

25. It should be noted here that the reference to the "interior" is only meant to help identify a way of speaking as referring to what we understand under an "experience." Since talk of

may not go together: an inner vision in an individual and a sense on the part of an individual of an intimate, bodily relationship with Christ.

The two features and the last form are also found in our third passage, Phil 3:7–10. Here Paul is at one level talking of the kind of knowledge he has acquired. That is important since it shows that there is absolutely no contradiction between describing Paul's experience in cognitive terms and in those other terms we are trying to track down. However, Paul also uses a far more experiential terminology when he describes himself as moving from having an intimate, almost bodily relationship with all those features of his former self that served to identify that self—towards having the same kind of intimate, and indeed bodily, relationship with Christ, dead and alive.

Let us take note of these expressions in somewhat more detail. As it happens, the passage is shot through with expressions of a bodily kind that are used to make the experience to which Paul is alluding come alive corporeally. It is not always easy to gauge the extent to which the language used is just ordinary Greek and devoid of any live metaphoricity, or alternatively has kept those bodily overtones that either point to a genuinely bodily understanding or at least to a genuinely live metaphoricity.[26] Still, there is enough to go on.

(1) Certain advantages "were for me" (ἦν μοι, Phil 3:7), says Paul. That is, "I had them, they were mine." Did he, as it were, keep them close to his body? The expression at least seems to indicate that they were in some intimate way his, as he then looked at them from the inside. (2) Then, however, he came to think of them as "because of Christ—a loss" (διὰ τὸν Χριστὸν ζημίαν, Phil 3:7). What an oxymoron! Moreover, he continues to think of everything in that way "because of the [literally?] overwhelming character (τὸ ὑπερέχον) of the knowledge (γνῶσις) of Christ Jesus, my Lord (τοῦ κυρίου μου, Phil 3:8)." Here it is not just the knowledge (γνῶσις) of Christ that is overwhelming. Rather, as is indicated by "my Lord," it is Christ himself who overwhelms. Apparently, the "I" stands in a particularly close and direct relationship with Christ. (3) In fact, as a result of this direct relationship with Christ, Paul has now "lost" his own former advantages (τὰ πάντα ἐζημιώθην) in the sense that he thinks of them as "dirt" (σκύβαλα)—clearly something one would want to leave behind and move away from—in order that he may "gain" Christ (Χριστὸν κερδήσω, 3.8). (4) The latter

---

the "interior" is only a metaphor that should probably itself be spelled out in terms that would include the notion of "experience," the reference to the "interior" does not tell us anything about what an experience is.

26. As will become clear throughout the ensuing discussion, the issue under discussion is to a large degree to what extent one should understand Paul's various locutions metaphorically or literally. I accept much of the understanding of metaphors set forth by G. Lakoff and M. Johnson, *Metaphors We Live By* (Chicago: University of Chicago Press, 1980), which stresses the "live" character of spatial connotations in metaphors. However, I believe that Paul's thought was generally more directly literal than "just" metaphorical.

expression probably indicates that Christ constitutes an "advantage" Paul wants to obtain in the sense of getting something for himself (compare on ἦν μοι in Phil 3:7), so that he can truthfully claim that he (Christ) is his (Paul's). The Greek term κερδαίνειν means "obtain for oneself" in such a way that one has or possesses the valued object. This is also the way the term is used in Phil 3:7—and already in Phil 1:21. In the present context, however, there also seems to be an idea of moving towards the valued object, or perhaps being drawn towards it. (5) At least, Paul goes on immediately to indicate the state he will be in when he has "obtained" Christ: that of being "found in him" (Phil 3:9). This suggests the idea of Paul leaving behind or throwing away those advantages that were previously dear to him in order to "obtain" Christ as the single new advantage that now counts in the very specific sense of being found in him. This also connotes the idea of some bodily movement on Paul's part in the direction of a Christ who is also understood in bodily terms.[27]

All through this passage Paul is striving hard, so it seems to me, to bring to expression in bodily terms an experience that he claims to have had. We should not in the least deny the constructed character of his account. On the contrary, we should insist on it. The account is clearly a construction "after the event." It need not even presuppose any distinct, datable, and momentary event at all. *A fortiori*, the experience also presents itself very much as interpreted. Furthermore, it is quite obvious that Paul's account serves a range of rhetorical purposes in the letter, most importantly that of inviting the readers to share in Paul's own sense of where they are going (Phil 3:12–16, culminating in 3:17, Συμμιμηταί μου γίνεσθε). Still, I want to insist that the way in which this text, like the two others we have considered from Galatians and 2 Corinthians, attempts to bring out the bodily character of something that has happened to Paul suggests an account of a genuine Pauline religious experience.

Since Paul's theme in the Philippians text is also knowledge, we may support the claim just made by comparing that text with a modern distinction between two types of knowledge. In 1911, Bertrand Russell famously distinguished between "knowledge by acquaintance" and "knowledge by description" (or "propositional knowledge"). To know something by acquaintance is to have it come before the mind without its being mediated by a description of what the thing is. Knowing by acquaintance is in fact experiencing the thing.[28] In Phil 3:7–10 Paul

---

27. This notion of a movement towards Christ is taken up in Phil 3:11 and the whole of 3:12–16.

28. See Mark Sainsbury, "Acquaintance and Description," in *The Oxford Companion to Philosophy* (ed. T. Honderich; Oxford: Oxford University Press, 1995), 4. Sainsbury uses the distinction between *connaître* and *savoir* as a comparison for the distinction between knowledge that we acquire by acquaintance on the one hand and that which is acquired by description on the other: "We are not acquainted with Sir Walter Scott, so we know him only by description, for example as *the author of Waverley*. By contrast, we can know *one of our experiences* 'by acquain-

is relying on a similar idea of knowledge when he speaks of "the overwhelming (character) of the knowledge of Christ Jesus, my Lord." This is knowledge "by acquaintance," knowledge derived from the immediate experience of the thing. It is true that Paul brings in the intimate and bodily character of his "experience"— which is what I have been after here—in order to make clear the unmediated and direct character of his knowledge. But the fact that he does proceed in this way shows that he had in fact had—and put emphasis on having had—a religious experience.

The Importance of Religious Experience in Paul

Why should the claim that Paul invokes a genuine religious experience be that important? Is it not, after all, rather obvious that he does, even though enlightened scholars have in general not been happy to see those texts in that way? I can only sketch an answer here.[29]

In a famous passage (1 Cor 9:16), Paul claims that "a necessity lies upon me: woe is onto me if I do not preach the gospel," and, moreover, if he does not preach it the way he goes on to describe: as a Jew to Jews and a Greek to Greeks. In its context Paul's claim about a "necessity" lying upon him may be spelled out in a number of ways. But the intensity of the passages we have been considering suggests that the necessity is also, as we would say, a psychological one, one that is grounded in a religious experience. This observation yields two connected answers to the question why it should be important to insist on the existence of the phenomenon of "religious experience" in Paul.

The first answer points to the importance of insisting on philosophical and historical realism even where one agrees on the constructed character of any experience of the world. Far too often, philosophers and others have fallen into the trap of concluding from the in itself quite correct observation that there is

---

tance,' that is, without the intermediary of any definite description. More generally, to know a thing by description is to know *that* there is something uniquely thus and so; to know a thing by acquaintance is for it *to come before the mind* without the intermediary of any description. Knowledge by description involves knowledge of *truths*, whereas knowledge by acquaintance does not: it is knowledge of *things*." (My italics apart from those of "the author of Waverley"). See Bertrand Russell, "Knowledge by Acquaintance and Knowledge by Description," *Proceedings of the Aristotelian Society* 11 (1910–1911): 108–28. Also see idem, *The Collected Papers of Bertrand Russell* (London: Routledge, 1992), vi. Please note that even when something is known by acquaintance, it does come before the mind in some interpreted form or other, only it is not explicitly "described," that is, taken or stated to *be* this or that, as in "Scott is the author of Waverley."

29. For a more developed answer see my essay "Paul's Necessity: A Bourdieuesque Reading of the Pauline Project," in *Beyond Reception: Mutual Influences between Antique Religion, Judaism, and Early Christianity* (ed. D. Brakke, A. C. Jacobsen, and J. Ulrich, Frankfurt: Peter Lang, 2006), 69–88.

no uninterpreted experience to the idealist claim that reality just "consists of mind."[30] That will not do. No matter how much construction goes into scholarly "reconstructions" of Paul and Paul's own "reconstruction" of his religious experience, both we and he are and were talking about the real world, about certain things happening and then being interpreted. They need not have happened in precisely the way they were interpreted. In fact, they may well have happened in quite different ways. But they did happen, in some form or other (whether in the brain, mind, psyche, body, or whatever).

The second answer points to the necessity of adopting this particular perspective if one fully wants both to understand and to explain the specific shape of Paul's construction of "Christ within" as part of and in response to its broader cultural context. To put the point most succinctly, what we see in Paul is (1) a person who had been brought up with and into a certain *habitus* (as defined by French sociologist Pierre Bourdieu) of a reasonably well-defined Hellenistic Jewish kind—where a *habitus* stands for a socially inculcated, bodily way of seeing things; and (2) a person who then strives in a struggle for power with his fellow Jews to develop and articulate a religious "field" (again from Bourdieu) that was not intended by himself to be new, but was in fact new.[31] As part of that struggle he came very close to articulating a notion of "self" that probably was not available to him beforehand in quite that way.[32] In articulating that notion, he also developed the idea of a religious experience in the way we have seen: of an individual, "inner" type of event with a strongly bodily dimension to it. Thus there is absolutely no conflict between emphasizing the role of ethnicity in Paul and speaking of his religious experience. It is the fact that we can see Paul's "theology" (if one so wishes), or his construction of the Christ event, as invoking and articulating a religious experience—the idea of which was developed out of a quite concrete, historical struggle for power—that does make it terribly important to recognize the existence of a real religious experience in Paul (though by all means as reconstructed, and indeed constructed, "after the event"). Paul was a real person who was trying to use and develop all available cognitive means to support his case in direct confrontation with others. As part of that struggle, which was in fact an ethnic one, Paul developed the idea of an individual, bodily religious experience—with enormous consequences.

Note the precise content of the claim I am making here. I am speaking of Paul's interpretation of his religious experience and also of his having had such

---

30. The quotation is from Proudfoot, *Religious Experience*, 70.

31. For present purposes the central idea in Bourdieu is that of a socially defined, bodily *habitus* that may be changed by an individual in a process that consists in breaking through, by an effort of articulation, to a new *habitus* that remains a socially defined and bodily one.

32. This happens most clearly in Gal 2:19–20 and Phil 3:7–10 (and indeed, in Rom 7). I have studied this whole issue in "Philosophy of the Self in the Apostle Paul," forthcoming.

an experience on its own as something to be interpreted by him. In both cases I am putting emphasis on the bodily character, partly because it appears to be there in the first place (fitting particularly well into a Bourdieuesque reading of Paul) and partly because if it is there, then my "realist" claim about the existence of a religious experience to be interpreted follows immediately. In his interpretation, Paul strove to articulate his experience in bodily terms. A partial reason for this is presumably that the experience itself was a bodily one. Paul felt it like that, and he attempted to articulate it in accordance with its immediately sensed character.

If this general picture is correct, then we as scholars should recognize and accept that even in their reconstructed and constructed form, Paul's references to a religious experience point to something that was genuinely there, though definitely not necessarily in the specific way it was interpreted by him. In this refined form—but only in that—we should reinstall the concept of religious experience in the analysis of Paul.

Paul's Rapture: 2 Corinthians 12:2–4 and the Language of the Mystics

Bert Jan Lietaert Peerbolte

Mystics are not crazy, or at least, not necessarily so.[1]

In 1974, in a lecture at Ormon College, Melbourne, Michael Stone argued that the literary descriptions of visions in apocalyptic writings may originate in the actual practice of ecstacy. Stone argued: ". . . my view is, that while in many cases the extant books may preserve mere literary formulations about these matters, behind them there probably does live a genuine practice of ecstasis."[2] Stone's suspicion is most likely correct. The genre of apocalyptic must have originated in circles of ecstatic mystics who developed a literary corpus that at the same time enabled them to communicate their experiences to a broader audience while also focusing on the literary—i.e., fictional—settings and characters they chose for their writings.[3]

Many publications on apocalyptic literature choose to overlook the practice of ecstasy that must have formed the socio-religious context out of which the genre itself sprang.[4] In itself this neglect can be pardoned because apocalyptic writings should be understood on internal literary grounds as descriptions of

---

1. Eugene d'Aquili, Andrew B. Newberg, *The Mystical Mind: Probing the Biology of Religious Experience* (Minneapolis: Fortress, 1999), 206.

2. Michael E. Stone, "Apocalyptic—Vision or Hallucination?" in *Selected Studies in Pseudepigrapha & Apocrypha: With Special Reference to the Armenian Tradition* (SVTP 9; Leiden: Brill, 1991), 428.

3. See especially Christopher Rowland, *The Open Heaven: A Study of Apocalyptic in Judaism and Early Christianity* (London: SPCK, 1992), 240–47.

4. See, e.g., John J. Collins, *The Apocalyptic Imagination: An Introduction to Jewish Apocalyptic Literature* (2nd ed.; Grand Rapids: Eerdmans, 1998), which does not discuss the possible practice of *ecstasis*, but interprets the sources entirely from a literary point of view. For a highly critical approach to any visionary practice as context of apocalyptic texts, see Marta Himmelfarb, *Ascent to Heaven in Jewish and Christian Apocalypses* (New York: Oxford University Press, 1993).

intricate heavenly realities that are mediated through a literary device. Usually, the content of the things revealed is communicated to the reader in a setting in which a sage from the past uses *vaticinia ex eventu* to prove himself trustworthy. To these *vaticinia* certain esoteric knowledge is added, the implication being that it is, of course, just as trustworthy.[5] This literary genre can be understood, to a high degree, without asking whether or not it sprang from a context in which visions were practiced. Yet it is important to take seriously at least the possibility that this literary genre may have originated in a social setting in which people actually experienced visions. This consideration is even more important for the study of Paul, since he was thoroughly influenced by apocalyptic ideas. Thus, any attempt to deal with Paul and his religious experience has to pay attention to the mystical world of apocalypticism to which Paul was greatly indebted.

The practice of visions and the world of religious experience itself seem to be banished from the great works on Paul. The reasons are clear, of course: Paul is reluctant in communicating his personal experience, he appears to downplay its relevance, and Paul's letters focus on his theological ideas and ideals rather than on his own person. Ever since Albert Schweitzer's *Die Mystik des Apostels Paulus* (1930), interpreters of Paul apparently take heed not to spend too much time on Paul's *experience*.[6] The noteworthy exception here is, of course, Paul's conversion experience. As a result, this specific experience receives so much attention that it has been deemed the origin of the whole of Paul's gospel.[7] It furthermore appears that Paul's ἐν χριστῷ language warrants the conclusion that a mystical bond between Christ and the believers was crucial to his understanding of the gospel.[8] This bond, however, is to be distinguished from the *unio mystica* that is described in mystical literature when referring to the experience of a mystic who becomes one with the deity he "sees" and experiences. Traces of experiences of the deity are found in Paul too. Paul sometimes refers to "revelations" as the origin of his

---

5. This literary technique is especially employed in, for example, the dream visions of Enoch (*1 En.* 83–90).

6. Albert Schweitzer, *Die Mystik des Apostels Paulus* (Tübingen: Mohr, 1930). Recently the importance of mysticism for Paul was argued by Hans-Christoph Meier, *Mystik bei Paulus: Zur Phänomenologie religiöser Erfahrung im Neuen Testament* (TANZ 26; Tübingen: Francke, 1998).

7. The most notable expression of this view is given by Seyoon Kim, *The Origin of Paul's Gospel* (2nd rev. ed.; WUNT 2.4; Tübingen: Mohr Siebeck, 1984); see also his *Paul and the New Perspective: Second Thoughts on the Origin of Paul's Gospel* (WUNT 2.140; Tübingen: Mohr Siebeck, 2002).

8. *Pace* Meier, *Mystik bei Paulus*, 27–39, who argues that ἐν χριστῷ means "oriented toward Christ." Meier denies any mystical meaning of the phrase.

actions,[9] and describes how Christ lives "in him" and he "in Christ."[10] For Paul this terminology expresses the fundamental form of his religious experience.

Two exceptions in which Paul is presented exactly in this context as a visionary are James D. Tabor's *Things Unutterable* (1986) and Bernhard Heininger's *Paulus als Visionär* (1995).[11] James Tabor places Paul's description of his heavenly ascent in 2 Cor 12:2–4 in the context of Hellenistic ascent narratives and concludes that "broadly speaking, he (i.e., Paul) presents a Hellenistic way of salvation."[12] Tabor treats Paul's apocalyptic context as part of a larger, Hellenistic context in which ascent narratives functioned. Interesting and important as the parallels that Tabor mentions may be, it would seem wise to focus more on the immediate context in which Paul should be positioned and approach the rapture experience Paul describes as part of that specific, Jewish apocalyptic context.

In his excellent study mentioned above, Bernhard Heininger situates Paul in his religious context as a visionary who not only experienced visions, but also regarded these visions as important for his self-understanding. In his conclusion Heininger puts it sharply: "Paulus ist Visionär im engeren Sinn (1 Kor 9,1), Empfänger einer Erscheinung (1 Kor 15,8), er verfügt über das Charisma der Enthüllung (1 Kor 14,6) und ist erleuchtet (2 Kor 4,6), reist schließlich in den Himmel (2 Kor 12,2–4) und hat Ekstasen (2 Kor 5,13)."[13] Heininger rightly considers Paul's visionary experiences as originating in his apocalyptic context and especially connects this line with traditions on Enoch and Daniel.

The description Paul gives in 2 Cor 12:1–11 inevitably leads to the conclusion that the experience described here was indeed fundamental to Paul.[14] For this reason, three questions should be asked in the present contribution. First, how does Paul describe this experience and what can we learn from the language he uses? Second, should Paul's rapture be understood in terms of Jewish mysticism, and if so how should we label the experience he describes? Finally, the

---

9. See, e.g., 1 Cor 14:6; 2 Cor 12:1, 7; Gal 1:12; 2:2.

10. Cf., e.g., Rom 6:11, 23; 8:1, 2, 39; 12:5. In 1 Cor 1:2 Paul addresses the believers in Corinth as those who are "sanctified in Christ Jesus" (ἡγιασμένοι ἐν Χριστῷ Ἰησοῦ). See also 1 Cor 1:30.

11. James D. Tabor, *Things Unutterable: Paul's Ascent to Paradise in its Greco-Roman, Judaic, and Early Christian Contexts* (Studies in Judaism; Lanham, Md.: University Press of America, 1986); Bernhard Heininger, *Paulus als Visionär: Eine religionsgeschichtliche Studie* (Herder's Biblical Studies 9; Freiburg: Herder, 1995).

12. Tabor, *Things Unutterable*, 124.

13. Heininger, *Paulus als Visionär*, 301–2.

14. Tabor is correct in stating the importance of 2 Cor 12:2–4 as follows: "Here we have a precious bit of evidence of an actual *experience* of ascent to heaven from the early Roman imperial period. I emphasize the element of experience, because Paul's text is the only *firsthand* account of such a journey to heaven surviving from this period." Tabor, *Things Unutterable*, 1 (italics Tabor).

relevance of the pericope under discussion here for our understanding of Paul's views in general will be addressed.

PAUL'S RAPTURE AS DESCRIBED IN 2 COR 12:2–4

In his article on "mysticism" in the *Anchor Bible Dictionary*, Helmer Ring-gren is quite reluctant to draw any firm conclusions from Paul's description in 2 Cor 12:2–4. In his words:

> In the NT Paul reports that he knows a man who had been caught up to paradise in the third heaven and heard unspeakable words that a man is not allowed to utter (2 Cor 12:2, 4). It is likely that this refers to some kind of mystical experi-ence and possible that the unspeakable words allude to the ineffability of that experience (however, it could refer to the name of Yahweh, which should not be pronounced). Since Paul is markedly reticent about the details of his experience, even to the point of speaking about himself in the third person, it is impossible to draw any further conclusions.[15]

Indeed Paul's reticence is an important feature of the pericope under discussion. Why does Paul apparently talk about himself in the third person? Why does he not give an explicit description of his own experience? Related to this issue are questions regarding the content of what Paul describes. Where should we locate "paradise" and the "third heaven?" What is the meaning of the reference to the "ineffable things" that Paul heard? And how does his description relate his rap-ture to Christ? An attempt to situate Paul in the socio-religious context of his day and ask for the relevance and impact of religious experience in Paul should start with these exegetical questions concerning 2 Cor 12:2–4.

In regard to Paul's enigmatic third-person speech, although other options have been defended,[16] the majority view is that Paul describes an experience of

---

15. Helmer Ringgren, "Mysticism," *ABD* 4: 945–46.

16. Most notably Hans-Dieter Betz has maintained that the whole pericope under discus-sion is actually a parody by Paul of an event of rapture and healing miracles (vv. 2–4, 7–10). See Betz, *Der Apostel Paulus und die sokratische Tradition: Eine exegetische Untersuchung zu seiner "Apologie" 2 Korinther 10–13* (Tübingen: Mohr Siebeck, 1972), 72–74; 84–100; and idem, "Eine Christus-Aretalogie bei Paulus (2Kor 12,7–10)," *ZTK* 66 (1969), 288–305. Michael Goul-der argues that not only the "man in Christ" Paul speaks of is not a reference to Paul himself, but also that Paul was highly critical of visionary experiences and their meaning. Cf. Goulder, "The Visionaries of Laodicea," *JSNT* 43 (1991), 15–39; and Goulder, "Vision and Knowledge," *JSNT* 56 (1994), 53–71. A critique is given by C. R. A. Morray-Jones, "Paradise Revisited (2 Cor 12:1–12): The Jewish Mystical Background of Paul's Apostolate. Part 1: The Jewish Sources," *HTR* 86 (1993): 177–218, and "Paradise Revisited (2 Cor 12:1–12): The Jewish Mystical Back-ground of Paul's Apostolate. Part 2: Paul's Heavenly Ascent and Its Significance," *HTR* 86 (1993):

his own in the pericope under discussion.[17] Already John Chrysostom pointed out that the whole passage would lose its rhetorical point if Paul were speaking of someone else.[18] The reason that Paul describes his own experience in the third person can be none other than rhetorical: by referring to himself in the third person Paul points out that he is not "boasting," while at the same time it enables Paul to make his point as clearly as possible.[19] Paul's remarks in this pericope are part of the final section of the so-called "Fool's speech" of 2 Cor 11:1–12:10,[20] and Paul obviously uses a rhetorical device here to convey a double message to his readers: firstly, that he had actually had a visionary experience of the kind about which his opponents were boasting; and secondly, that he distances himself from the "boasting" of his opponents.

If the description indeed refers to Paul's own personal experience, another question arises: Does Paul speak of one rapture-experience, of which he gives two different descriptions? Or does he talk of two separate events? Theoretically, it is possible to regard Paul's description of the rapture to the third heaven as a different event than his visit to paradise. Here too the majority of interpreters consider vv. 2–4 as a description of one rapture-experience, and it would seem that this view is correct: a number of contemporary texts locate paradise in the third heaven and for that reason the two descriptions in vv. 2–4 refer to one event (cf. below).

For our understanding of the nature of this particular experience, it is important to distinguish between the language used to describe this experience retrospectively and the event itself. Our analysis begins with the language that Paul uses and then will return to the nature of his experience and the way in which it relates him to Christ.

The terms with which Paul describes his experience are ὀπτασίας καὶ ἀποκαλύψεις κυρίου (v. 1). The plural indicates that the experience described in vv. 2–4 is only one out of a series of similar events. Paul repeatedly asserts that he

---

272–73. According to Morton Smith, the "man in Christ" was Jesus himself; Smith, "Ascent to the Heavens and the Beginning of Christianity," *ErJb* 50 (1981): 403–29.

17. See the discussion by Margaret E. Thrall, *A Critical and Exegetical Commentary on the Second Epistle to the Corinthians*, (2 vols.; ICC; Edinburgh: T&T Clark, 2000), 2:776–78, and Ralph P. Martin, *2 Corinthians* (WBC; Waco, Tex.: Word Books, 1986), 390–91.

18. Chrysostom, *PG* 61, 576; see Thrall, *Second Epistle to the Corinthians*, 778.

19. J. Zmijewski, *Der Stil der paulinischen "Narrenrede": Analyse der Sprachgestaltung in 2 Kor 11,1–12,10 als Beitrag zur Methodik von Stiluntersuchungen neutestamentlicher Texte* (Bonner biblische Beiträge 52; Köln, Bonn: Peter Hanstein, 1978), 336: "vielmehr hängt die distanzierende Form wohl mit seiner Absicht zusammen, sich seiner selbst nicht zu rühmen, es sei denn seiner Schwachheiten (vgl. 12,5; 11,30), weil er nur diese zum Erweis seiner Apostolizität als maßgebend erachtet."

20. For an analysis of 2 Cor 12:1–10, see Zmijewski, *Der Stil der paulinischen "Narrenrede"*, 324–411.

does not know whether the experience occurred "inside the body or outside of it" (v. 2: εἴτε ἐν σώματι οὐκ οἶδα, εἴτε ἐκτὸς τοῦ σώματος οὐκ οἶδα, ὁ θεὸς οἶδεν; v. 3: εἴτε ἐν σώματι εἴτε χωρὶς τοῦ σώματος οὐκ οἶδα, ὁ θεὸς οἶδεν). The emphasis on this point is frequently understood as an indication that Paul is fully aware of the fact that in the Jewish tradition a rapture experience was usually considered as something that happened to the entire person, soul *and* body, whereas the pagan Greek tradition described such events as spiritual in nature, concerning only the soul.[21] Paul describes the content of his experience in two ways: as being "caught up into the third heaven" (ἁρπαγέντα τὸν τοιοῦτον ἕως τρίτου οὐρανου; v. 3), and "into paradise," where he heard unutterable words (ἡρπάγη εἰς τὸν παράδεισον καὶ ἤκουσεν ἄρρητα ῥήματα ἃ οὐκ ἐξὸν ἀνθρώπῳ λαλῆσαι; v. 4).[22]

Paul indicates that he was taken up in heavenly glory by circumscribing this state of exaltation with the combined images of "third heaven" and "paradise." As said, the two descriptions given here refer to one and the same event.[23] Some descriptions of the heavens in Jewish sources roughly contemporary to Paul speak of three, others of seven levels of the heavenly realm.[24] A number of these texts locate paradise in the third heaven,[25] and for this reason we may conclude that Paul had one event in mind.

This brings us to the meaning of what Paul mentions as ἄρρητα ῥήματα (v. 4). Since Paul introduces ῥήματα with the verb ἤκουσεν, he clearly speaks of "words" he "heard."[26] Given the visionary character of the experience Paul describes, this "hearing" should be interpreted as part of his "altered state of consciousness" (see below) rather than an ordinary act of physical hearing. But what does he mean by the adjective ἄρρητα?

It can hardly be by accident that Paul used this specific word, for it denotes the divine and therefore ineffable character of the things he heard. The use of this

---

21. On the language used, see Martin, *2 Corinthians*, 401.

22. The verb ἁρπάζω is used in Rev. 12:5 for the child that is "taken away" to the throne of God, and in 1 Thess 4:17 it describes the fate of the believers who will be "taken up" to Christ. See also Acts 8:39, where it describes how Philip is "taken away."

23. Thrall, *Second Epistle to the Corinthians*, 790–93, discusses the alternative interpretations. Clement of Alexandria, e.g., argues that Paul was taken to the third heaven and *from there* onward to paradise. Cf. Thrall, *Second Epistle to the Corinthians*, 791, n. 143. For the reception of 2 Cor 12:1–10 in Clement and other church fathers, see Riemer Roukema, "Paul's Rapture to Paradise in Early Christian Literature," in *The Wisdom of Egypt: Jewish, Early Christian, and Gnostic Essays in Honour of Gerard P. Luttikhuizen* (ed. Anthony Hilhorst, George H. van Kooten; Ancient Judaism and Early Christianity 59; Leiden: Brill, 2005), 267–83.

24. A brief survey of the evidence is given by Martin, *2 Corinthians*, 401–2.

25. "Paradise" is located in the third, i.e., highest, heaven in *Life of Adam and Eve* 37:5. In *2 En.* 8 the same combination is found, though the description there continues to the full number of seven heavens—cf. Thrall, *Second Epistle to the Corinthians*, 792.

26. Paul consistently uses the word ῥήμα as "word": cf. Rom 10:8, 17–18. Only in 2 Cor 13:1 the noun may be translated as "case," but this is a particular quotation from the Law.

adjective in many texts contemporary to Paul proves this. Thus, in the opening lines of the Greek Apocalypse of Baruch (*3 Baruch*), it is used in order to characterize the content of the revelation Baruch received: Διήγησις καὶ ἀποκάλυψις Βαροὺχ περὶ ὧν κελεύματι θεοῦ ἀρρήτων εἶδεν ("Narration and apocalypse of Baruch concerning the secret things he saw by the command of God.").[27] Harry Gaylord chooses to translate ἄρρητα as "secret things," perhaps to portray the nearness of the expression to the language of the mystery cults. Undoubtedly, the term indicates that the object characterized by this epithet is of a heavenly nature,[28] the clearest example of which appears in *Jos. Asen.* 15:12b. In this text, Aseneth asks the heavenly messenger who announces God's acceptance of her for his name. His reply reveals that this name is a heavenly secret:

ἵνα τι τοῦτο ζητεῖς τὸ ὄνομα μου Ἀσενέθ; τὸ ἐμὸν ὄνομα ἐν τοῖς οὐρανοῖς ἐστίν ἐν τῇ βίλῳ τοῦ ὑψίστου γεγραμμένον τῷ δακτύλῳ τοῦ θεοῦ ἐν ἀρχῇ τῆς βίβλου πρὸ πάντων ὅτι ἐγω ἄρχων εἰμί τοῦ οἴκου τοῦ ὑψίστου. καὶ πάντα τὰ ὀνόματα τὰ γεγραμμένα ἐν τῷ βιβλῷ τοῦ ὑψίστου ἄρρητα ἐστι καὶ ἀνθρώπῳ οὔτε εἰπεῖν οὔτε ἀκοῦσαι ἐν τῷ κόσμῳ τούτῳ ἐγκεχώρηται ὅτι μεγάλα ἐστι τὰ ὀνόματα ἐκεῖνα καὶ θαυμαστὰ καὶ ἐπαινετὰ σφόδρα.

"Why do you seek this, my name, Aseneth? My name is in the heavens in the book of the Most High, written by the finger of God in the beginning of the book before all (the others), because I am chief of the house of the Most High. And all names written in the book of the Most High are unspeakable, and man is not allowed to pronounce nor hear them in this world, because those names are exceedingly great and wonderful and laudable."[29]

In this same writing, the mystical character of Joseph's brother Judah is pointed out by referring to his ability "to see letters written in heaven by the finger of God" and the fact that "he knew the unspeakable (mysteries) of the Most High God" (*Jos. Asen.* 22:13).[30]

The opening line of the Apocalypse of Zephaniah, preserved in Clement's *Stromata* (5.11.77), describes the angelic liturgy in heaven and mentions God as the "unspeakable one," in Wintermute's translation "the ineffable most high God":

καὶ ἀνελαβέν με πνεῦμα καὶ ἀνήνεγκέν με εἰς οὐρανὸν πέμπτον καὶ ἐθεώρουν ἀγγέλους καλουμένους κυρίους, καὶ τὸ διάδημα αὐτῶν ἐπικείμενον ἐν πνεύματι

---

27. Translation of H. E. Gaylord, Jr., in *The Old Testament Pseudepigrapha* (2 vols.; ed. J. H. Charlesworth; New York: Doubleday, 1983), 1:663.

28. *Jos. Asen.* 12:4 shows that it was also used to characterize things too awful to describe.

29. Translation by C. Burchard, in: Charlesworth, *OTP.* 2:227.

30. *Jos. Asen.* 27:1 uses the adjective ἄρρητος to describe Benjamin's "unspeakable" beauty. Nothing mystical here.

ἁγίῳ καὶ ἦν ἑκάστου αὐτῶν ὁ θρόνος ἑπταπλασίων φωτὸς ἡλίου ἀνατέλλοντος, οἰκοῦντας ἐν ναοῖς σωτηρίας καὶ ὑμνοῦντας θεὸν ἄρρητον ὕψιστον.

And a spirit took me and brought me up into the fifth heaven. And I saw angels who are called "lords," and the diadem was set upon them in the Holy Spirit, and the throne of each of them was sevenfold more (brilliant) than the light of the rising sun. (And they were) dwelling in the temples of salvation and singing hymns to the ineffable most high God.[31]

These parallels suggest that the adjective ἄρρητος was used in apocalyptic and other early Jewish literature as a characterization of heavenly glory. This use of the word coincides with what we find in pagan Greek texts.[32] For example, in his description of the Greek mysteries, Iamblichus also uses this particular adjective in order to refer to the heavenly character of the thing defined by it. In his *On the Mysteries*, he explains that the "ineffable beauty" is a characteristic of the gods (II.5.73.9–10), not of their messengers.[33] Iamblichus gives perhaps the clearest expression of the idea that the sphere of the gods, the heavenly sphere, cannot be described in human terms, in II.11.97.4–7:

καὶ γὰρ μὴ νοούντων ἡμῶν αὐτὰ τὰ συνθήματα ἀφ' ἑαυτῶν δρᾷ τὸ οἰκεῖον ἔργον, καὶ ἡ τῶν θεῶν, πρὸς οὓς ἀνήκει ταῦτα, ἄρρητος δύναμις αὐτὴ ἀφ' ἑαυτῆς ἐπιγινώσκει τὰς οἰκείας εἰκόνας, ἀλλ' οὐ τῷ διεγείρεσθαι ὑπὸ τῆς ἡμετέρας νοήσεως

For even when we are not engaged in intellection, the symbols themselves, by themselves, perform their appropriate work, and the ineffable power of the gods, to whom these symbols relate, itself recognises the proper images of itself, not through being aroused by our thought.[34]

Later in the text, Iamblichus pictures the experience of a mystical union with a spirit that descends and enters into a person. One of the elements that accompanies such a religious experience is the presence of fire (III.6.113.6–8):

εἰ γὰρ παρουσία τοῦ τῶν θεῶν πυρὸς καὶ φωτός τι εἶδος ἄρρητον ἔξωθεν ἐπιβαίνει τῷ κατεχομένῳ, πληροῖ τε αὐτὸν ὅλον ἐπὶ κράτει κτλ.

---

31. Translation by C. Burchard, in Charlesworth, *OTPseud* 2: 508.

32. For ἄρρητος as a technical term in the mystery cults, see Meier, *Mystik bei Paulus*, 107, n. 23.

33. See also *De Mysteriis* II.11.96.14.

34. Text and translation: Iamblichus, *On the Mysteries* (trans. E. C. Clarke, J. M. Dillon, and J. P. Hershbell; SBLWGRW 4; Atlanta: Society of Biblical Literature, 2003), 114–15.

For if the presence of the gods' fire and an ineffable form of light from without invades the person possessed, these fill him completely with their power (etc.).[35]

Iamblichus even speaks of what we would probably call the *unio mystica*, the mystical union, as the highest stage of prayer (V.26.237.13–238.4):

φημὶ δὴ οὖν ὡς τὸ μὲν πρῶτον τῆς εὐχῆς εἶδός ἐστι συναγωγόν (. . .), τὸ δ' ἐπὶ τούτῳ κοινωνίας ὁμονοητικῆς συνδετικόν (. . .), τὸ δὲ τελεώτατον αὐτῆς ἡ ἄρρητος ἕνωσις ἐπισφραγίζεται, τὸ πᾶν κῦρος ἐνιδρύουσα τοῖς θεοῖς, καὶ τελέως ἐν αὐτοῖς κεῖσθαι τὴν ψυχὴν παρέχουσα.

I declare then, that the first degree of prayer is the introductory (. . .), the second is conjunctive (. . .), the most perfect, finally, has as its mark ineffable unification, which establishes all authority in the gods, and provides that our souls rest completely in them.[36]

Especially these last two examples point out that with the epithet ἄρρητος Paul uses standard vocabulary to describe a heavenly state of being, a mystical experience.

At the same time, his description of this experience as a "rapture," as a heavenly ascent, is related to the language of Jewish apocalypticism rather than to that of Iamblichus and the mysteries. There, a "spirit" or a deity takes possession of the believer, whereas in Paul's description he experienced a heavenly ascent.

In sum, it is no accident that Paul uses the word ἄρρητος to describe the content of his experience. It is a term found in both Jewish and pagan sources to express the ineffable character of heaven or the gods. Paul furthermore describes his experience as having entailed a visual and an auditory component. The combination of these two senses is found throughout apocalyptic literature in descriptions of visions and dreams.[37] If the practice of visionary *ecstasis* should indeed be postulated as the *Sitz im Leben* of apocalyptic literature in general, this is also the socio-religious context of Paul's interpretation of his experience as a heavenly rapture. Since the structure of Paul's thought, the vocabulary he uses, and the eschatological expectations that permeate his letters all indicate that Paul was, to say the least, profoundly influenced by apocalyptic ideas,[38] his remark on the "abundance of revelations" he experienced (2 Cor 12:7) and his interpreta-

---

35. Ibid., 132–33.

36. Ibid., 274–75.

37. See the discussion of Daniel and other apocalyptic texts by Heininger, *Paulus als Visionär*, 66–72 and 111–35; also Meier, *Mystik bei Paulus*, 123–52.

38. This was convincingly argued by J. Christiaan Beker, *Paul the Apostle: The Triumph of God in Life and Thought* (Philadelphia: Fortress, 1980); see also M. C. de Boer, "Paul and Apocalyptic Eschatology," in *The Origins of Apocalypticism in Judaism and Christianity* (vol. 1 of *Encyclopedia of Apocalypticism*; ed. John J. Collins; New York: Continuum, 1998), 345–83.

tion of the rapture experience he offers in 2 Cor 12:2–4 suggest that Paul not only shared the language of apocalyptic Judaism, but also its practice of *ecstasis*. This practice of *ecstasis* was of course not limited to Judaism—it was part and parcel of the ancient world.

As we saw, Paul refers to his rapture experience as one of a series of events he characterizes as "visions and revelations of the Lord" (12:1). It is likely that the two categories mentioned—visions and revelations—differ from each other,[39] but in both cases the genitive κυρίου raises the questions: Who is this κύριος—God or Christ? And what is the status of the genitive? Since Paul frequently speaks of Jesus as the κύριος and also applies LXX quotations focusing on the κύριος to Jesus,[40] it is very likely that here, too, he has Jesus in mind as the one who is central to the visions and revelations. This means, however, that if we take the description of Paul's rapture experience as formulated against the background of apocalyptic language of heavenly journeys, and consider Paul's visit to the third heaven, to paradise, as a visit to God's glory, Paul rhetorically positions this visit as an ascent to Christ. What exactly was Christ's role in the rapture experience, according to Paul, depends on the interpretation of the genitive κυρίου. The most likely options here would be a *genitivus auctoris* ("revelations stemming from the Lord") or an objective genitive ("revelations concerning the Lord").[41] The latter would draw 2 Cor 12:2–4 in the proximity of Gal 1:12, where Paul speaks of a "revelation of the Lord," clearly intending that the Lord, Christ, has been revealed within (!) Paul. The words τὸν υἱὸν αὐτοῦ in Gal 1:16 unmistakably identify Christ as the *object* of the revelation Paul mentions there. The context in 2 Cor 12:2–4 renders it likely that here, too, Christ is intended as the object of visions and revelations rather than as the originator of the revelation.[42] This means that for Paul the heavenly glory he had witnessed in his rapture experience is closely connected to Christ in his exalted state. This christology presupposes that the risen Christ has been exalted to a heavenly state, which is consistent with Paul's reference in his letters to Christ as a heavenly figure.[43] The description here corresponds to the situation presupposed, for example, in Rom 1:4 (Christ declared Son of God

---

39. Thrall, *Second Epistle to the Corinthians*, 774, points at the fact that an ὀπτασία must refer to a vision, whereas the rest of the passage 12:1–10 only describes an auditory experience.

40. See esp. David D. Capes, *Old Testament Yahweh Texts in Paul's Christology* (WUNT 2.47; Tübingen: Mohr Siebeck, 1992). On Paul's use of the title κύριος as a christological title, Capes concludes: "[Paul] employed the title as a christological designation more than any other title, with the exception of Χριστός (184).

41. Thrall, *Second Epistle to the Corinthians*, 774–775; Martin, *2 Corinthians*, 396 simply notes "κυρίου is *gen. auctoris*."

42. Meier, *Mystik bei Paulus*, 81, decides otherwise: "Christus sei nicht Inhalt der Visionen sondern ihr Urheber."

43. On Jesus's heavenly status in Paul see James D. G. Dunn, *The Theology of Paul the Apostle* (Edinburgh: T&T Clark, 1998), 234–65; Larry W. Hurtado, *Lord Jesus Christ: Devotion to Jesus in Earliest Christianity* (Grand Rapids: Eerdmans, 2003), 79–153.

in power by his heavenly exaltation after his resurrection) and the "high" christology of the Song of Christ in Phil 2:6–11 (God "abundantly exalted Christ" in
heaven).[44] A link of Paul's rapture experience to the glory of Christ also explains
why Paul mentions this specific experience in his argument against those whom
he addresses as the "super-apostles" in his fool's speech of 2 Cor 11:1–12:10.[45]
If one of the criteria for apostleship was that one had "seen the Lord," this rapture experience gave Paul every reason to "boast."[46] The fact that he mentions the
whole episode in the third person makes his point as strong as it can: Paul does
not boast, he does not picture himself as one whose ministry is based on these
kinds of visionary experiences, but at the same time the intended readers of the
letter know very well that he is talking about himself here.

Paul's Experience and Jewish Mysticism

In the same year that Michael Stone lectured in Melbourne, a Dutch psychiatrist, Maarten Lietaert Peerbolte, published a "transpersonal psychological
analysis" of *Poimandres*, the first treatise of the *Corpus Hermeticum*.[47] In this
analysis he argued that the nature of the experience described in *Poimandres*
is that of an altered state of consciousness evoked by extreme concentration in
the act of meditation.[48] It seems that the experience Paul describes here should
also be understood in exactly these terms. The three most important constitu-
ents mentioned for an "altered state of consciousness" are: a) the experienced loss
of personal boundaries; b) the experience of wholeness, i.e., of coinciding with
oneself and the world; and c) an experienced loss of temporality.[49] At least two
of these three elements are indeed included in the description given here: Paul
stresses the fact that he doesn't know whether the event happened inside or outside the body, thereby implying that his personal boundaries were set aside.[50]

---

44. On Jesus as the κύριος in that passage, see L. J. Lietaert Peerbolte "The Name above
all Names (Philippians 2:9)," in *The Revelation of the Name YHWH to Moses: Perspectives from
Judaism, the Pagan Graeco-Roman World, and Early Christianity* (ed. George H. van Kooten;
TBN 9; Leiden: Brill, 2006), 187–206.

45. Zmijewski, *Narrenrede*, 345, on Paul's experience: "Es stellt einen von Christus, dem
Kyrios, *verursachten*, aus der *personalen Gemeinschaft* mit ihm erwachsenden Vorgang dar. . . ."

46. This point was important in the discussion on apostolic status (1 Cor 9:1); cf. L. J.
Lietaert Peerbolte, *Paul the Missionary* (CBET 34; Leuven: Peeters, 2003), 177–84.

47. M. Lietaert Peerbolte, *Poimandres: Grieks-hermetisch geschrift in het Nederlands vertaald
met eeen transpersonalistische beschouwing* (Occident-serie; Deventer: Ankh-Hermes, 1974).

48. Lietaert Peerbolte, *Poimandres*, 18. The stress Lietaert Peerbolte lays on the sexual
meaning of the imagery used in *Poimandres* is probably somewhat overdone.

49. Lietaert Peerbolte, *Poimandres*, 88.

50. See Thrall, *Second Epistle to the Corinthians*, 782: "It may be that the third person
narration derives originally from the nature of the experience itself, that is, from the ecstatic
phenomenon of the displacement of the ego."

And he interprets his rapture as an ascent into heaven, into paradise even, which clearly implies an experience of wholeness or healing. Paul doesn't say anything on the loss of temporality, but the stress on his being "taken away" indicates a rupture in Paul's life, and suggests a proximity to the third characteristic of an altered state of consciousness. Apparently, Paul experienced this mental state and interpreted it in apocalyptic terms.[51]

One of the major insights of psychology is that it is impossible to separate images and words used to interpret an experience from that experience itself.[52] The one is closely connected to the other, and any attempt to reconstruct the "experience *an sich*" by removing the interpreting words is doomed to fail. In light of this, the discourse Paul uses to describe his experience should be analyzed by situating it in its social context. This means we have to compare Paul with the Jewish mystical movement in which he was rooted.

Paul's use of the terms ὀπτασία and ἀποκάλυψις indicates that he considers what happened to him as originating outside of himself. He was "taken up" into the third heaven and into paradise: the verb ἁρπάζω betrays that Paul regarded this experience as an entry into a sacred realm. Here, Paul uses traditional discourse to describe his "altered state of consciousness." Unfortunately, we are not informed about the origin of Paul's experience. Did he practice the rituals and ascetic rules known from later mystics that were probably also known to the mystics we usually label as "apocalypticists"? Paul mentions an "abundance of revelations" (2 Cor 10:7), so it could be that he lived according to the rules set for mystics. The apocryphal *Acts of Paul* present us a picture of Paul who fasts and preaches an ascetic life.[53] This second-century narrative portrayal of Paul may actually contain a historical kernel here. The specific description of the rapture experience and the dating of the event as fourteen years earlier do imply that also for Paul this particular experience was unusual. Still, it is clear that this rapture experience was not the only event in Paul's life that he could characterize as a "revelation."

In his work on Jewish mysticism, Gershom Scholem has explicitly treated 2 Cor 12:2–4 as originating from a mystical tradition. In his view, Paul's description of his visionary experience places Paul among apocalypticists who practiced ecstasy in a manner that later became very popular in circles of *merkabah mysti-*

---

51. The apocalyptic character of Paul's interpretation of what happened to him is given in the fact that he describes the event as a rapture into the third heaven. This point forms a notable difference with the description of the visions of, e.g., Hermas (see *Visio* I 1,3; II 1,1) or the mantics described by Iamblichus (*De mysteriis* III,9–17).

52. This point is well made by Heininger, *Paulus als Visionär*, 36–43.

53. See, e.g., *Acts of Paul and Thecla* 5 ("the word of God about abstinence and the resurrection") and 23 (where Paul fasts in a new tomb with Onesiphoros and his wife and children). Translation taken from J. K. Elliott, *The Apocryphal New Testament: A Collection of Apocryphal Christian Literature in an English Translation* (Oxford: Clarendon, 1993).

cism.[54] The crucial experience in apocalyptic texts, and which is developed more strongly in the *merkabah* tradition, is the visionary experience of God seated on his throne.[55] Scholem considered Paul's vision to stand in line with this tradition of visionary ecstasy.

However, Scholem's views on *merkabah* mysticism have not gone unquestioned. Peter Schäfer takes issue with Scholem's early dating of *merkabah* texts, his supposition that these texts once had one original form and the centrality of the throne-vision for these mystics.[56] Schäfer's critique of Scholem's views makes us aware that that one cannot easily assume an early date for *merkabah* literature. For this reason it is risky to explain 2 Cor 12:1–12 entirely from the perspective of this type of mysticism.[57]

Even though there is obvious reason to be careful in assuming a direct connection between Paul and *merkabah* mysticism—especially because of the much later date of the *hekhalot* writings—two influential publications on Paul do relate Paul's mysticism and the experience he describes in the passage under discussion to a line of Jewish mysticism that ultimately developed into *merkabah* mysticism. These are the works of Alan F. Segal, who discusses Paul's ecstasy in his 1990 monograph *Paul the Convert*, and C. R. A. Morray-Jones, who devoted two important articles to 2 Cor 12:1–12 in *Harvard Theological Review* (1993). Both publications deserve our attention.

In his *Paul the Convert*, Alan F. Segal offers a thorough analysis of "Paul's ecstasy" and discusses the text under consideration here as a major example of it.[58] Segal treats 2 Cor 12 as standing in a long tradition of apocalyptic, prophetic, and also pagan texts describing religious experiences.[59] In Segal's view not only has the vision of Ezek 1 literarily influenced Paul, but also the actual visions from the pre-Christian era. In particular, the christological concept of heavenly

---

54. G. Scholem, *Jewish Gnosticism, Merkabah Mysticism, and Talmudic Tradition* (New York: KTAV, 1960), 14–19.

55. The prime sources of this genre are Ezek 1 and Isa 6. Influence of these texts is felt in, e.g., *1 En.* 14 and Rev 4. I have discussed this in a Dutch article: "De theologie van het boek Openbaring" ("The Theology of the Book of Revelation"), *Gereformeerd Theologisch Tijdschrift* 99 (1999): 3–12.

56. See, e.g., P. Schäfer, "Merkavah Mysticism and Magic," in *Gershom Scholem's Major Trends in Jewish Mysticism 50 Years After: Proceedings of the Sixth International Conference on the History of Jewish Mysticism* (ed. P. Schäfer and J. Dan; Tübingen: Mohr Siebeck, 1993), 59–78.

57. For a careful discussion of the problem, see Ithamar Gruenwald, "Reflections on the Nature and Origins of Jewish Mysticism," in Schäfer and Dan, *50 Years After*, 25–48.

58. A. F. Segal, *Paul the Convert: The Apostolate and Apostasy of Saul the Pharisee* (New Haven, Conn.: Yale University Press, 1990), 34–71.

59. Segal mentions, for example, the visions of Ezek 1, Isa 6, and Dan 7, but also *merkabah* mysticism, and pagan examples such as *Poimandres*, the Paris Magical Papyrus (PGM IV), and Apuleius' *Golden Ass*. See Segal, *Paul the Convert*, 53–56.

man, i.e., the Son of Man, has been an important catalyst for Paul's view of Jesus Christ as heavenly Lord. Segal argues that the concept of heavenly man is found in writings that reflect a mystical tradition in early Judaism: Philo's writings, the "Parables of Enoch," *2 Enoch, Ascension of Isaiah, 2 Baruch, 3 Enoch*. Similar views are found in *Poimandres* and the great Paris magical codex (PGM IV). According to Segal, "Paul's conversion experience and his mystical ascension form the basis of his theology."[60] Paul actually spoke the language of the mystics, developed an open attitude with regard to theophanies, and subsequently became the recipient of such a theophany. The result of Paul's use of this mystical language is clear in four aspects of Paul's work: 1) he developed the concept of the divinity of Jesus Christ as heavenly Lord; 2) he used this language to express the transformation that the believers experienced upon being initiated into the group of worshippers of Christ; 3) Paul came to regard immortality as the main goal of the believers' reception of apocalypses; 4) he developed a language in which bodily vs. spiritual existence became the criterion for judging true vs. untrue faith.

It is evident that Segal regards Paul's use of the language of the mystics as crucial for understanding Paul. Even though the third and fourth point mentioned above may not have been brought about solely by Paul's use of mystical language, Segal is right in stressing the importance of this particular discourse for Paul. One of the remaining points of discussion is whether or not this language is directly linked to the discourse of *merkabah* mysticism found in later *hekhalot* sources.

Three years after Segal stressed the importance of the language of the mystics for understanding Paul, C. R. A. Morray-Jones presented an extended discussion of rabbinic material on the visit to *pardes* by Rabbi Aqiba and three others to reach a conclusion similar to that of Segal.[61] After presenting a reconstruction of the *pardes* episode on the basis of a number of rabbinic texts,[62] Morray-Jones discusses Paul's ascent in 2 Cor 12. The conclusion of the discussion is worth quoting at full length:

> We may conclude, then, that Paul is describing an ascent to the heavenly temple and a merkabah vision of the enthroned and "glorified" Christ. The context in which this account occurs suggests that he bases his claim to apostolic authority on this vision. "Merkabah mysticism" was, therefore, a central feature of Paul's experience and self-understanding. Since this is so, there are no grounds for the assumption that his visions were purely spontaneous, involuntary events. It is quite probable that they were induced by the use of a mystical technique,

---

60. Segal, *Paul the Convert*, 69.
61. C. R. A. Morray-Jones, "Paradise Revisited."
62. The texts discussed are: *t. Ḥag.* 2.1; *y. Ḥag.* 77b; *b. Ḥag.* 14b–15b; *Cant. R.* 1.28; *Hekhalot Zuṭarti* and *Merkabah Rabbah*.

which may have been less elaborate than some of those described in the *hekhalot* sources but cannot have been markedly different in its essentials.[63]

Morray-Jones identifies the vision Paul refers to in 2 Cor 12:2–4 as the one described in Acts 22:17–22 and thus considers this vision to be the crucial step in the development of Paul's self-understanding as the apostle for the nations.[64]

The case for reading 2 Cor 12:1–12 as part of a tradition of Jewish mysticism is more than convincing even though questions with regard to the date of *merkabah* traditions remain. But given the fact that Paul apparently saw Christ, and not YHWH, as the main character of his vision,[65] the content of what he communicates through his description of the vision differs strongly from comparable descriptions in other Jewish sources. This point will be discussed in the final section of this contribution.

PAUL, CHRIST, AND VISIONARY EXPERIENCES

According to Morray-Jones's discussion of 2 Cor 12, the vision Paul describes here was crucial to his self-understanding as apostle to the nations. The whole argument hinges upon Morray-Jones's identification of this particular vision with the one described in Acts 22:17–22. Unfortunately, this identification is far from certain.[66] Morray-Jones bases his reconstruction on the fact that *merkabah* visions have the heavenly temple as their *locus* and on the agreement between the narrative contexts of 2 Cor 12:1–12 and Acts 22:17–22. This proposed identification may be correct, but the evidence is far from conclusive. Nevertheless, if these two descriptions of visions cannot be traced back to one event in Paul's life, the question remains: what is the importance of this vision for Paul's views?

The first distinction to make here is between the importance of visionary experiences in general for Paul and the importance of this particular vision. Let us begin with the latter. The description Paul gives of this vision in 2 Cor 12:2–4 is part of the defense of his apostolic status. As in 1 Cor 9:1 ("Have I not seen Jesus our Lord?"), Paul bases his status on the fact that he has *seen* Jesus Christ. Apparently, the experience of seeing Christ was fundamental to his status as apostle, and in this respect Morray-Jones's reconstruction is at least plausible. Another option would be to identify this vision as the event that took place near Damascus that

---

63. Morray-Jones, "Paradise Revisited, Part 2," 283.

64. Ibid., 292.

65. The centrality of Christ in this vision is also stressed by ibid., 269–74. See also Segal, *Paul the Convert*, 36: ". . . Paul reveals modestly that he has had several ecstatic meetings with Christ over the previous fourteen years."

66. See, e.g., Meier, *Mystik bei Paulus*, 121: " . . . die Konstruktion verdankt sich offensichtlich dem Wunsch, die spärlichen Informationen in 2Kor12 durch den lukanischen Visionsbericht aufzufüllen. . . ."

made Paul change his way. Nothing however in 2 Cor 12 points at this, and the fact that Paul doesn't interpret his rapture in any way as the call he received from Christ is a counter-indication.[67] After describing his visionary experience in the third person, an instrument Paul uses to create a rhetorical distance between himself and his experience, Paul hastens to add a remark on the angel of Satan (vv. 6–9). Paul's remarks on this angel and the thorn in the flesh have resulted in many speculations.[68] On the one end of the spectrum are explanations of those who regard Paul as having had some kind of disease, while on the other end of the same spectrum Morray-Jones, in line with Scholemm understands this remark as referring to the guardian angels who try to prevent Paul from entering into ever higher vaults of heaven.[69] Be this as it may, it is clear that Paul stresses his weakness rather than the fact that he receives an "abundance of revelations" (verse 7). Yet these words specifically indicate that the rapture experience Paul describes in verses 1–5 was not a single phenomenon in his life. The two things that we can learn from this are that Paul regularly had experiences he labeled as "revelations"—probably similar to the altered state of consciousness experience he refers to in verses 2–4—and that for Paul this "abundance of revelations" was proof of the fact that Christ was active in and through him. In that sense Paul considered these revelations proof of his own status.

The interpretation Paul gives in 1 Cor 12:1–10 of his own rapture experience indicates that it is the closeness to Christ that for Paul defined the relevance of this experience. This brings us to the meaning of visionary experiences for Paul in general. One important element of the passage discussed in this contribution is that Paul is passive throughout this rapture experience: he describes the event not as something he himself did, but as something that happened to him. So the actual *subject* of the event is not Paul, but Christ. This interpretation of Paul's rapture is coherent, for example, with the view he expresses in Gal 2:20 ("it is no longer I who live, but it is Christ who lives in me") or Phil 1:21 ("For me, living is Christ . . . "). Segal emphasizes the mystical discourse Paul uses when speaking about baptism.[70] Indeed, in Rom 6:1–11 Paul claims that through baptism believers not only share in the death of Christ, but they also do so in the expectation of sharing in his resurrection. It is not by accident that Paul refers to the state of the baptized in 2 Cor 4:4–6 in terms of "enlightenment" (φωτισμός) and "knowledge" (γνῶσις). Combine this with the fact that Paul can speak of his gospel as a "secret" (μυστήριον; cf. 1 Cor 2:1; also Rom 11:25; 1 Cor 15:51), and it is clear that mystical language is crucial for understanding Paul and his view of Christ.

---

67. In Gal 1:16 Paul speaks of his call as of the moment that God made his Son known "in" Paul (cf. my *Paul the Missionary*, 167–170). This is hardly a description of a visionary experience of the kind Paul describes in 2 Cor 12:2–4.

68. For a survey, see Martin, *2 Corinthians*, 412–17.

69. Morray-Jones, "Paradise Revisited, Part 2," 281–84.

70. Segal, *Paul the Convert*, 58–71.

The mystical experience Paul describes in 2 Cor 12 may have something to do with the "hidden wisdom in a mystery" (σοφία ἐν μυστηρίῳ ἡ ἀποκεκρυμμένη) that Paul mentions in 1 Cor 2:7 as the object of the initiates' talk.[71] By mentioning the words he heard as "unspeakable," Paul refers to the status of what he heard as hidden knowledge, as the mysteries of Christ.[72] This picture does come close to Paul as a teacher of esoteric, apocalyptic mysteries. The openness with which he writes about the "secrets of Christ" may actually be misguiding: Paul's letters were never intended for a general public, but only for those who had already been initiated into the mysteries of Christ. What becomes clear from 2 Cor 12:1–10 is that Paul's use of mystical language is not a marginal phenomenon in Paul. It shows that this discourse was crucial to Paul and to his understanding of the gospel.[73] Further study of Paul's use of baptismal language is necessary because it may clarify the way in which Paul adapts mystical language to a newly formed Christ-context, but this would exceed the scope of this article. For now it is enough to state that, for Paul, the experience of the divine was the touchstone of his gospel: in Paul's own eyes it was this repeated experience that made him into what he was, "an apostle—sent neither by human commission nor from human authorities, but through Jesus Christ and God the Father, who raised him from the dead" (Gal 1:1).

CONCLUSION

In the above I have argued that Paul's description of his rapture experience in 2 Cor 12 opens up our understanding of Paul because it reveals to us how strongly Paul was indebted to the discourse of apocalyticism and its visionary practices. Even though Paul downplays his experience and only refers to it as part of his "fool's speech," between the lines he points out that the direct experience of the divine was fundamental to his understanding of his ministry. Paul describes

---

71. The same combination of the senses as found here is referred to by Paul in the passage immediately following 1 Cor 2:7—in vv. 9–10 Paul speaks of "what no eye has seen, nor ear heard, nor the human heart conceived, what God has prepared for those who love him." Apart from the same combination of senses, Paul also interprets the transmission of this knowledge as a "revelation."

72. Edwin D. Freed (*The Morality of Paul's Converts* [BibleWorld; London: Equinox, 2005], 19–49) rightly stresses the point that Paul pictures the believers in Christ as consisting of two groups: those who have already been baptized (i.e., initiated), and those who have not and are still preparing themselves for baptism. The baptized ones can be compared to people who had been initiated in a mystery cult.

73. This point is well made by Meier, *Mystik bei Paulus*, 156: "An der Erfahrung des Raptus wird schließlich deutlich, was eingangs über Zusammenhang von Mystik und Weltbild gesagt wurde. Hier ist klar zu erkennen, daß im neutestamentlichen Zeitalter das antike Weltbild keine reine Theorie und daß die transzendente Topographie für Paulus keine gelehrte Spekulation war."

his rapture in 2 Cor 12:2–4 in terms he shared with his apocalyptic context. He indicates that the practice of (visionary) religious experiences was an important characteristic of this context as well as of his own ministry, that these experiences could take the shape of an "altered state of consciousness," and that they were interpreted as secret, hidden knowledge that was revealed to him as visionary. For this reason any attempt to focus on Paul as a theologian is bound to fail if the experiential character of Paul's faith is not taken into account.

Dreams/Visions and the Experience of God in Luke-Acts

John B. F. Miller

Introduction, Method, and Purpose

As the title suggests, the purpose of this discussion is to explore dreams and visions as a facet of religious experience in the New Testament text of Luke-Acts.[1] Before beginning such a discussion, however, we must consider a couple of important of questions. How does Luke's portrayal of dreams/visions[2] as religious experience fit within the spectrum of attitudes towards dreams/visions in antiquity?[3] How may one understand the relationship between dreams/visions

---

1. The roots of this study lie in a more comprehensive treatment of dreams/visions in Luke-Acts. See John B. F. Miller, "'Convinced that God Had Called Us': Visions and the Perception of God's Will in Luke-Acts" (Ph.D. diss., Princeton Theological Seminary, 2004); also idem, *Convinced that God Had Called Us: Dreams, Visions, and the Perception of God's Will in Luke-Acts* (Leiden: Brill, 2007). Unless otherwise noted, all translations in this study are my own.

2. Use of the combinative term dream/vision in this study requires some explanation. In contemporary English usage, one is used to distinguishing between dreams and visions as sleeping and waking experiences (respectively). Hanson notes "the difficulty, if not impossibility, of distinguishing between a dream and a vision" based solely on terminology; see John Hanson, "Dreams and Visions in the Graeco-Roman World and Early Christianity," *ANRW* 23.2:1395–1427, quote on 1408. For exceptions to this generalization see Frances Flannery-Dailey, *Dreamers, Scribes, and Priests: Jewish Dreams in the Hellenistic and Roman Eras* (JSJSup 90; Leiden: Brill, 2004), 60. The ambiguity suggested by Hanson does obtain, however, in Luke-Acts. In Acts 10:3, Cornelius sees a vision (ὅραμα) while praying (cf. Acts 10:30). In 16:9, a vision (ὅραμα) appears to Paul during the night (διὰ νυκτός)—presumably indicating a dream Paul had while sleeping. This ambiguity led Hanson to use the hyphenated term "dream-vision" ("Dreams and Visions," 1408), a variation of which ("dream/vision") is used in the present study.

3. Identifying dreams/visions in ancient literature is slightly more complicated than it may appear. For a general discussion of the terminology used to identify dreams/visions in antiquity and of dreams/visions reports in Graeco-Roman literature, see Hanson, "Dreams and Visions." For a discussion of specific parameters used to identify dreams/visions in Luke-Acts,

and religious experience? A full and adequate answer to either of these questions is beyond the scope of the present study. Nevertheless, an understanding of dreams/visions as part of religious experience in antiquity is essential for the treatment of Luke-Acts that follows. Therefore, I would like to offer abbreviated answers to these questions, outline briefly the methodology employed in this study, and then move on to a discussion of two passages that highlight Luke's use of dreams/visions in his depiction of Paul: the conversion (Acts 9, 22, and 26) and the dream/vision at Troas (Acts 16). I will then conclude with some thoughts on the significance of dreams/visions for understanding the experience of God in early Christianity based on the evidence in Luke-Acts.

ATTITUDES TOWARD DREAMS/VISIONS IN ANTIQUITY

Much of the recent scholarship on dreams/visions, especially in biblical literature, has been form-critical in nature, or has focused on comparisons between biblical dream/vision reports and those from surrounding cultures.[4] Although my work is informed by these important studies, I am interested in a more specific question: To what extent were dreams/visions regarded as a reliable medium of revelation in antiquity? In scholarly discussions of dreams/visions, one frequently encounters the misleading conclusion that dreams/visions were accepted universally as a significant form of communication from an otherworldly source.[5] In turn, this conclusion has led to rather perfunctory readings of dream/vision reports that assume that instructions received in a dream/vision would be accepted and followed automatically, on the assumption that it contained reliable information. Such generalizations, however, flounder after a careful sifting of

---

see Miller, *Convinced that God had Called Us*, 11–20. Acts employs explicit visionary terminology to describe both of the events considered below: Paul refers to his experience on the road to Damascus as an ὀπτασία in his second retelling of the event (Acts 26:19), and the narrator uses the term ὅραμα to describe the dream/vision Paul has at Troas (Acts 16:9).

4. Questions of form criticism are discussed in Ernst Ludwig Ehrlich, *Der Traum im Alten Testament* (BZAW 73; Berlin: Alfred Töpelmann, 1953), and refined further by Wolfgang Richter, "Traum und Traumdeutung im AT: Ihre Form und Verwendung," *BZ* 7 (1963): 202–20. For a form-critical treatment of the Graeco-Roman material, see Hanson, "Dreams and Visions." For excellent discussions on the related subject of theophany in Jewish Scripture, see the work of James Muilenburg, "The Speech of Theophany," *Harvard Divinity Bulletin* 28 (1964): 35, 47, and his student Kenneth Kuntz, *The Self-Revelation of God* (Philadelphia: Westminster, 1967). For a discussion of theophany emphasizing comparisons with non-biblical ancient Near Eastern material, see Frank M. Cross, *Canaanite Myth and Hebrew Epic: Essays in the History of the Religion of Israel* (Cambridge, Mass.: Harvard University Press, 1973). See also Patrick D. Miller, *The Divine Warrior in Early Israel* (Cambridge, Mass.: Harvard University Press, 1973), and Thomas W. Mann, *Divine Presence and Guidance in Israelite Traditions* (Baltimore: Johns Hopkins University Press, 1977).

5. See, e.g., the otherwise excellent study of Hanson, "Dreams and Visions," 1396.

the available evidence. Instead, one finds a spectrum of attitudes toward dreams/ visions in antiquity.

In Greco-Roman literature, for example, one finds a number of exceptions to the belief in the reliability of dreams/visions. These range from the Homeric conceptions of "destructive dreams"[6] and the "Gates of Horn/Ivory"[7] to the more philosophical/physiological understanding of dreams—the belief that dreams are generated physiologically and have no revelatory significance—found in the works of Heraclitus, Herodotus, Aristotle, Cicero, and others.[8] Disparate positive and negative views meld somewhat in the later oneirocritical traditions, in which one finds a distinction between the ἐνύπνιον (an insignificant dream) and the ὄναρ/ὄνειρος (a dream worthy of interpretation).[9]

For the most part, Jewish sources present dreams/visions in a more consistently positive manner, but again there are exceptions. Examples of revelatory dreams/visions abound in Jewish Scripture.[10] In some passages, however, dreams/ visions appear to be viewed negatively in connection with false prophecy.[11] In a handful of texts, one also finds Jewish parallels to the philosophical/physiological view of dreams.[12] In later Jewish material negative evaluations can be found in Sirach,[13] and even in Philo's De somniis. Although Philo focuses primarily on a

---

6. "Destructive dreams" are dreams sent by gods or goddesses who wish to deceive a person, e.g., the οὖλος ὄνειρος sent by Zeus to Agamemnon that leads Agamemnon to believe that he will capture Troy immediately (Il. 2.6).

7. In Od. 19.560–69, Penelope explains to her elderly visitor (actually, Odysseus in disguise) that dreams come to humans through one of two gates: those passing through the gate of horn presage events that will come to pass; those passing through the gate of ivory are deceptive.

8. Against the revelatory power of dreams, see Heraclitus, Frag. 89 D; Herodotus, Hist. 7.16. For the psychobiological power of dreams see Aristotle, Somn. 459a and Div. somn. 462b; also E. R. Dodds, The Greeks and the Irrational (Berkeley and Los Angeles: University of California Press, 1963), 118, 131. For a scathing critique of dreams, see Cicero, Div. Over the course of time, language was developed to describe dreams that were deceptive in nature. In the work of Chariton, one find the first use of the Greek term ψευδόνειρος or "false dream" (Chaer. 3.7).

9. E.g., Artemidorus, Onir. 1.1. Charles Allison Behr suggests that this two-fold classification may be traced back to Plato, whose own view of dreams is somewhat mixed. Charles A. Behr, Aelius Aristides and the Sacred Tales (Amsterdam: Adolf M. Hakkert, 1968), 173; cf. Resp. 571–72 and the spurious Epin. 985.

10. E.g., Gen 40:8; Num 12:6; 1 Kgs 3:4–14; Job 33:15–16; see also the חזה language found in most of the prophetic material.

11. E.g., Jer 14:14 and 23:25–28.

12. E.g., Isa 29:8 and Eccl 5:2.

13. This text offers what is possibly the most scathing critique of dreams/visions as a vehicle of revelation in all of early Jewish literature: "Empty and false hopes are for the senseless man, and dreams excite fools. The one who pays attention to dreams is like someone trying to catch shadows or chase the wind" (Sir 34.1–2). The critique then becomes even more pointed: "Thus, a vision of dreams is the likeness of a face seeing itself. Can anything coming from some-

positive evaluation of dream experiences, there are some dreams that Philo suggests occur when "the soul puts itself in motion and gives itself over to frenzy."[14]

Since there are a variety of attitudes toward dreams/visions in antiquity, one does well to avoid generalizations and presumptions, and to evaluate each piece of evidence individually. In relation to the spectrum of attitudes noted above, Luke presents dreams/visions in a largely positive way. With one exception, these dreams/visions involve some sort of divine intermediary (e.g., an angel, voice from heaven, the risen Jesus, the Holy Spirit, etc.). The one exception is Paul's rather anomalous dream/vision at Troas, which will be taken up below. Also important for this discussion is the degree to which Luke employs subtlety in his presentation of dreams/visions. Of particular interest for the present study are the nuanced variations between the narrator's description of each dream/vision and the way that characters in Luke's story sometimes interpret these visionary encounters. These differences relate to what may be the most complicated question in the present investigation: What is the relationship between dreams/visions and religious experience?

DREAMS/VISIONS AND THE QUESTION OF RELIGIOUS EXPERIENCE

Thus, with some significant exceptions, already discussed, dreams/visions in the literature of early Judaism and early Christianity typically represent a claim to divine revelation. That is, they are presented as straightforward (theorematic) messages from a divine source, or as enigmatic (allegorical) messages that are *interpreted* as divine communication.[15] All dreams/visions presented as a message from a divine source or interpreted as divine communication would seem to qualify necessarily as a form of "religious experience," since texts featuring such dream/vision reports represent them as *interactions with the divine*. At least two significant problems, however, surface immediately.

First, such dreams/visions represent an appeal to divine authority. This appeal is all the more problematic when one considers the prevailing individual nature of the dream/vision experience. Although one finds some examples of group visionary experience in ancient sources,[16] most dreams/visions are experienced by an individual. It is hardly uncommon for critics—both ancient and

---

thing unclean be clean? Can anything true come from falsehood? Divination and augury and dreams are worthless, and they appear as in the mind of someone suffering birth pains" (Sir 34.3–5).

14. Philo, *Somn.* 2.1.1.

15. On these distinctions, see Artemidorus, *Onir.* 1.2.

16. In Luke-Acts, for example, one may consider the Pentecost episode (Acts 2) a group dream/vision experience.

modern—to question the veracity of such reports, along with their concomitant appeals to divine authority.[17]

A second problem, and one of greater concern for the present study, has to do with descriptions of dreams/visions in ancient texts. Even in texts that present dreams/visions as communication from the divine, this "religious experience" often seems ironically flat: a message is given that subsequently comes to fruition, or a command is given that is subsequently carried out. Descriptions of this sort of dream/vision focus almost exclusively on divine irruption into the human realm, offering little explanation of the visionary's understanding of his or her experience. Lukan examples of this sort can be found in Luke 2:15 (in which the shepherds immediately assume that the angel's pronouncement has come to pass[18]) and Acts 8:26–27 (in which an angel tells Philip to arise and go, and the next verse indicates that he "arose and went").

As Bovon has observed, this emphasis on divine irruption is an unquestionable and important part of Lukan theology.[19] It is precisely this element of Lukan theology, however, that has drawn severe criticism from some scholars. Such assessments focus on the irruptive nature of dreams/visions as divine experiences of God in Luke-Acts that obviate an engaged response on the part of the recipient. Haenchen's argument is illustrative:

> in endeavoring to make the hand of God visible in the history of the Church, Luke virtually excludes all human decision. Instead of the realization of the divine will *in* human decisions, *through* human decisions, he shows us a series of supernatural interventions in the dealings of men. . . . As Luke presents them, these divine incursions have such compelling force that all doubt in the face of them *must* be stilled. . . . But here faith loses its true character of decision, and

---

17. For an ancient dispute over the veracity of a report of dream incubation, see Hyperides, *In Defense of Euxenippus*. Similarly, Seneca says of Junius Otho: "Wherever he lacked a pretext, he described a dream" (Seneca, *Controversiae* 7.7.15); also, Quintilian, *Inst.* 4.2.94.

18. In Luke 2:15, the shepherds say to one another, "Let us go to Bethlehem and see this thing that has happened." The use of the perfect participle in the latter half of the phrase (ἴδωμεν τὸ ῥῆμα τοῦτο τὸ γεγονός) is telling; they regard the event proclaimed by the angel as something that has already taken place.

19. As Bovon says, "A la différence de plusieurs auteurs juifs contemporains et des apologètes du second siècle, Luc ne s'intéresse guère au côté insondable et ineffable de Dieu." François Bovon, "L'Importance des Médiations dans le Projet Théologique de Luc," *NTS* 21 (1975): 31. On the importance of providence and the "plan of God" as a theme in Luke-Acts, see Schulz, "Gottes Vorsehung bei Lukas," *ZNW* 54 (1963): 104–16; John Squires, *The Plan of God in Luke-Acts* (SNTSMS 76; Cambridge: Cambridge University Press, 1993). On the related subject of divine necessity in Luke-Acts, see Charles Cosgrove, "The Divine ΔΕΙ in Luke-Acts: Investigations into the Lukan Understanding of God's Providence," *NovT* 26 (1984): 168–90.

the obedience from faith which Luke would have liked to portray turns into something utterly different: very nearly the twitching of human puppets.[20]

Thus, for Haenchen and others, the irruptive nature of dreams/visions in Luke-Acts is problematic because it emphasizes God's action to the exclusion of human action.

To put it differently, one might suggest that Haenchen's discomfiture had partly to do with the *exterior* nature of the dream/vision experiences of Cornelius, Peter, and Paul in Luke's narrative: he regarded these dreams/visions as external and overpowering—"all doubt in the face of them *must* be stilled."[21] As a result, these dreams/visions obviate faith and the human decisions it necessitates. Others scholars, however, contend that Haenchen and those following his line of reasoning have missed something, namely, a more nuanced understanding of Luke's dreams/visions as multidimensional experiences of God.[22] That is, when one focuses exclusively on the irruptive, exterior facet of dreams/visions, one ignores the more *interior* facet of interpretation.

Although there are a few "flat" dream/vision reports in Luke-Acts, there are also a number that feature characters interpreting their dreams/visions—interpreting their experience of God in these encounters. These scenes offer striking examples of characters attempting to understand their experience of God, despite the fact that they seem to perceive these experiences as the reception of divine instruction or commands. In the remaining discussion, I would like to examine two portions of Acts in which one finds the Lukan Paul interpreting his own dreams/visions.

---

20. Haenchen compares Paul's dream/vision at Troas to the Cornelius-Peter episode. Ernst Haenchen, *The Acts of the Apostles: A Commentary* (trans. B. Noble, G. Shinn, H. Anderson, and R. McL. Wilson; Philadelphia: Westminster, 1971), 362, 485; see also Richard Pervo, *Profit with Delight: The Literary Genre of the Acts of the Apostles* (Philadelphia: Fortress, 1987), 74.

21. This is not to suggest that one should overlook what one may assume were Haenchen's larger philosophical and theological problems with the irruptive focus of Lukan theology. Instead, I note these comments because they emphasize what many critics—both ancient and modern—have addressed, namely, that many dream/vision reports focus on the external aspect of this experience, to the exclusion of the internal aspect.

22. See especially Robert C. Tannehill, *The Narrative Unity of Luke-Acts: A Literary Interpretation* (2 vols.; Minneapolis: Fortress, 1990–1994), 2:131. Similarly, on Peter's focus on the role of God in Acts 11:1–18 see Ronald Witherup, "Cornelius Over and Over and Over Again: 'Functional Redundancy' in the Acts of the Apostles," *JSNT* 49 (1993): 45–66; also Edith Humphrey, "Collision of Modes?—Vision and Determining Argument in Acts 10:1–11:18," *Semeia* 71 (1995): 65–84.

METHOD AND PURPOSE

The method I will use to evaluate this material is narrative criticism, with emphasis on what Seymour Chatman calls "character filters'" within the narrative.[23] This term refers to places at which the point-of-view shifts from the narrator to another character within the story. These "filtered" accounts foreground something I wish to highlight, namely, the ways in which Lukan characters interpret their dreams/visions in their attempt to understand these experiences of God. This method of reading illumines the contrast suggested above between the *exterior* and *interior* facets of the dream/vision experience. The narrator's account will typically focus on the exterior elements of a dream/vision, for example, the circumstances surrounding a visionary experience, what sort of intermediary delivers the visionary message, and the visionary's initial response.[24] When the point of view shifts to the character, the reader is given a glimpse into the interior aspect of the visionary experience, namely, how that character interprets his or her dream/vision in light of other circumstances within the narrative and how the character understands his or her dream/vision as an experience of God.

This focus on character filtration and the exterior/interior aspects of dreams/visions is helpful for understanding both of the texts that occupy the remainder of this study. The dream/vision leading to Saul's conversion is narrated in Acts 9, providing the exterior description of the event. Paul then describes the event twice (Acts 22 and 26), permitting the reader a glimpse of his interior perspective of this dream/vision. The narrative describing Paul's dream/vision at Troas unites these exterior and interior elements much more closely. The exterior experience in which Paul sees a Macedonian man asking for help (Acts 16:9) is followed immediately by the interior experience in which the characters interpret Paul's dream/vision as a call to carry the good news to Macedonia (Acts 16:10). The shift between narrator and character filter in both stories is rather subtle. What is important for the present discussion is that these stories feature both dream/vision *and* interpretation, inextricably bound in the Lukan Paul's experience of God.

It may also be prudent to clarify what this paper does not pursue. I am not particularly concerned about the historicity of Acts, nor am I concerned about the historicity of what some scholars presume are Luke's sources. I am not attempting to uncover or draw conclusions about the visionary experience of

---

23. Seymour Chatman, *Coming to Terms: The Rhetoric of Narrative in Fiction and Film* (Ithaca, N.Y.: Cornell University Press, 1990), 144.

24. This is not to suggest, however, that the narrator's version of a dream/vision is always devoid of interior description. Each scene must be evaluated individually.

the historical Paul.[25] Rather, I am interested in Luke's narrative as a narrative. This does *not* mean that I am uninterested in what this narrative offers by way of historical evidence for the relationship between dreams/visions and religious experience in early Christianity. Even if one presumes a high degree of error in Luke's presentation of events, the narrative itself describes the way dreams/visions were understood by some early Christians.[26] The underlying premise of this discussion, therefore, is that the depiction of dreams/visions in Luke-Acts offers significant historical insight into the complex manner in which dreams/visions could be understood as experiences of God within some segments of early Christianity.

TEXTUAL DISCUSSION: SAUL'S/PAUL'S CONVERSION (ACTS 9, 22, AND 26)

In Acts 9, one finds the narrator's brief account of Saul's visionary encounter on the road to Damascus. Saul is surrounded by a bright light from heaven (9:3). A voice asks Saul why Saul persecutes him and commands him to go into the city, where Saul will be told what he is to do (9:4–6). Saul's actions are minimal. He remains helpless until Ananias comes to lay hands upon him. Aside from falling to the ground and inquiring about the identity of his interlocutor, Saul contributes nothing in this description of the visionary encounter; the experience is almost entirely exterior. What is so striking about the statement in 9:6, of course, is that Saul/Paul never is told what he must do—at least not in so many words. Nevertheless, this asseveration is important for Paul's own retelling of the event. It is in Paul's character-filtered versions of this visionary encounter in Acts 22 and 26 that the reader finds Paul's own understanding of what he would need to do. It is in these retellings that one finds Paul's interior experience of this dream/vision as an experience of God.

How the event changes in Paul's interpretation of his experience becomes clear in his retelling of his encounter with Ananias.[27] In 9:17, Ananias says,

---

25. A related issue I shall not address is the matter of "altered states of consciousness" (ASC). For a treatment of Lukan dreams/visions as they relate to ASC aimed at a popular audience, see John Pilch, *Visions and Healing in the Acts of the Apostles: How Early Believers Experienced God* (Collegeville, Minn.: Liturgical Press, 2004).

26. Christopher Rowland draws a similar conclusion in his treatment of Stephen's dream/vision in Acts 7. Christopher Rowland, *The Open Heaven: A Study of Apocalyptic in Judaism and Early Christianity* (New York: Crossroad, 1982), 370.

27. There are a number of minor variations between the narrator's account in Acts 9 and Paul's character-filtered account in Acts 22 and 26. I will focus only on the variations that are most significant for the present discussion.

The differences between the three accounts of Saul's call/conversion in Acts 9, 22, and 26 have been assessed in remarkably different ways in the history of scholarship. In the late nineteenth and early twentieth centuries, scholars solved the problem of these differences by arguing

"Brother Saul, the Lord sent me—Jesus, who appeared to you on the road on which you were traveling—in order that you might regain your sight and be filled with the Holy Spirit." Paul's character-filtered version in Acts 22 contains a significant addition, placing on Ananias' lips a call statement: "The God of our ancestors has chosen you to know his will, and to see the Righteous One and hear the voice from his mouth, for you will be a witness for him to all people of the things that you have seen and heard" (22:14–15). In the original narration, Saul learns only that he will be told what is necessary for him to do (9:6), and that the Lord has sent Ananias in order that he might regain sight and be filled with the Holy Spirit (9:17). At this later point in the story, Paul interprets that visionary experience much more extensively: he reflects back onto his initial conversion the call to witness that has dominated his subsequent actions in the narrative.

Paul's most dramatic departure from the original narration of events occurs in 22:17–21. Here, Paul describes an ecstatic vision he had while praying in the Temple: "I saw [the Lord] saying to me, 'Hurry! Get out of Jerusalem quickly, because they will not accept your testimony concerning me.'" This divine warning to leave the city is remarkably different from the narrated version in 9:29–30. In the original account, the ἀδελφοί hear of a plot to kill Paul, so they escort him to Caesarea and send him off to Tarsus. In Paul's interpretation of the event, he attributes this act of human deliverance to the Lord. After reporting his brief protest in 22:19–20, Paul then claims that the Lord told him, "Go, for I will send you far away to the Gentiles" (22:21). In Paul's filtered version of his earlier experience, Jesus—now identified with the "God of [his] ancestors" (22:14)—has thus not only called him to be a witness, but has rescued Paul, initiated his mission to the Gentiles, and has done so in the Temple.

If Paul's filtered account of his conversion in Acts 22 only loosely resembles the narrator's version of events, the retelling in chapter 26 represents an even greater interpretive departure. Following a few syntactic embellishments in verses 12–13, the first important difference is found in the addition of the enigmatic

---

for the use of different source material, e.g., E. Hirsch, "Die drei Berichte der Apostelgeschichte, über die Bekehrung des Paulus," *ZNW* 28 (1929): 305–12. More recently, a number of scholars have abandoned source hypotheses in favor of examining Luke's narrative as a coherent whole, e.g., Beverly Gaventa, "The Overthrown Enemy: Luke's Portrait of Paul" *SBLSP* 24 (1985): 439–49; idem, *From Darkness to Light: Aspects of Conversion in the New Testament* (Philadelphia: Fortress, 1986), 52–95; Ronald Witherup, "Functional Redundancy in the Acts of the Apostles: A Case Study," *JSNT* 48 (1992): 67–86; William Kurz, *Reading Luke-Acts: Dynamics of Biblical Narrative* (Louisville, Ky.: Westminster John Knox, 1993), 125–31; and Daniel Marguerat, "Saul's Conversion (Acts 9, 22, 26) and the Multiplication of Narrative in Acts," in *Luke's Literary Achievement: Collected Essays* (ed. Christopher M. Tuckett; JSNTSup 116; Sheffield: Sheffield Academic Press, 1995), 127–55.

phrase: "it is hard for you to kick at the goads" (26:14).[28] The last recognizable words from the original narration are "I am Jesus, whom you are persecuting" (26:15). What follows builds on the creative interpretation in Paul's first retelling. In 22:14, Paul says he was told by Ananias that the "God of our ancestors" had "chosen" (προχειρίζομαι) Paul to be a "witness" (μάρτυς) of "all that [he had] seen and heard." In 26:16, it is the Lord who tells Paul directly that he has "hand picked" (προχειρίζομαι) him to be both a "servant" and "witness" (μάρτυς) of "the things which [he] has seen and of the ways in which [the Lord] will appear to [him]." In both accounts, Paul's interpretive recollection ascribes the initiation of the Gentile mission to visions in which the Lord is speaking (22:21 and 26:17). In the interpretive recollection found in chapter 26, however, the Lord commissions Paul directly in the first appearance on the road to Damascus, and imbues this mission with its explicit purpose: "to open their eyes, in order that they may turn from darkness to light and from the power of Satan to God, in order that they may receive forgiveness of sins and a portion among those sanctified by faith in me" (26:18).[29]

The way that Paul filters this second retelling reflects the broader development of his role in the narrative.[30] The narrator causes the reader to linger over this development by allowing the character who experienced the events of Acts 9 to interpret and reinterpret them (Acts 22 and 26, respectively). Paul, once the zealous persecutor "breathing threats and murder," now sees the futility of his struggle against those following Jesus: "it is hard for you to kick at the goads" (26.14). Similarly, Paul now interprets the visionary encounter leading to his conversion as a call in light of his experiences proclaiming the message of Jesus to both Jews and Gentiles.[31] In the initial narration of Saul's dream/vision one finds the exterior description of the event: this experience leaves Saul rebuked, blind, and powerless. In the interior descriptions of the event, found in Paul's interpretive retellings, he becomes the chosen, protected, and empowered witness of God.

---

28. For a brief discussion of the use of this phrase in antiquity, see Gaventa, *From Darkness to Light*, 83.

29. So also Alan Segal, *Paul the Convert: The Apostolate and Apostasy of Saul the Pharisee* (New Haven, Conn.: Yale University Press, 1990), 7.

30. Luke Timothy Johnson offers the following: "more significant than the incidental details distinguishing this version [Acts 26] from the others . . . is the evidence in this retelling of Paul's growing awareness of the meaning of the event"; Luke Timothy Johnson, *The Acts of the Apostles* (SP 5; Collegeville, Minn.: Liturgical Press, 1992), 441; cf. Charles K. Barrett, *A Critical and Exegetical Commentary on The Acts of the Apostles* (ICC; 2 vols.; Edinburgh: T&T Clark, 1994–1998), 2:1159.

31. As Segal (*Paul the Convert*, 7) has observed, "Paul's vocation, the command to proselytize the gentiles, is a fundamental theme of Luke's narrative." I contend that Luke develops this theme through the interior description of Paul's interpretation of his visionary encounter.

Paul's experience of God on the road to Damascus is now understood in light of his subsequent experience as God's witness.

PAUL'S DREAM/VISION AT TROAS

Acts 15:36–16:5 describes the beginning of Paul's so-called "second missionary journey," and its initial success. Churches are strengthened (15:40); Timothy, a new disciple/assistant, is acquired (16:1–3); more churches are strengthened and their numbers grow (16:5). These summary successes are followed in 16:6–8 by even more abbreviated frustrations. Paul and his companions travel through Phrygia and Galatia, prevented by the Holy Spirit from speaking the word in Asia (16:6). Their frustration is heightened in 16:7 when they "attempt" to enter Bithynia, but the "Spirit of Jesus" will not permit them. Thus prevented from entering Bithynia, they pass Mysia and come down to Troas. There, a dream/vision appears to Paul "during the night," in which "a certain Macedonian man" asks Paul to "come to Macedonia and help us."

Following the narrator's exterior account of the vision in verse 9, one finds a striking transition to interior description in verse 10. The text simply states, "when *he* saw the vision, *we* immediately sought to go to Macedonia."[32] The participial phrase that follows in verse 10 is perhaps the most significant aspect of this vision for the topic at hand: συμβιβάζοντες ὅτι προσκέκληται ἡμᾶς ὁ θεὸς εὐαγγελίσασθαι αὐτούς, "*convinced* that God had called us to proclaim the good news to them." The characters interpret Paul's experience as a call from God.[33]

---

32. The ongoing debate over the nature and significance of the "we" passages in Acts is beyond the scope of this discussion. For summaries of the various opinions on this issue, see Haenchen, *Acts of the Apostles*, 489–91 and Barrett, *The Acts of the Apostles*, 772–73. See also William S. Campbell, *The "We" Passages in the Acts of the Apostles: The Narrator as Narrative Character* (SBLSBL 14; Atlanta: Society of Biblical Literature, 2000). My interest here is not in the introduction of the first person, but in the way the characters represented as "we" interpret Paul's dream/vision.

33. Most, if not all, commentaries and scholarly discussions of this passage also share the characters' interpretation that Paul's dream/vision is a directive from God. See, e.g., the following studies, ranging from the sixteenth century to the present: Jean Calvin, *The Acts of the Apostles, 14–28* (trans. J. W. Fraser; London: Oliver and Boyd, 1966), 70; Alfred Wikenhauser, "Religionsgeschichtliche Parallelen zu Apg 16,9," *BZ* 23 (1935–36): 180–86; Martin Dibelius, *Studies in the Acts of the Apostles* (trans. M. Ling and P. Schubert; London: SCM Press, 1956; repr. Mifflintown, Pa.: Sigler Press, 1999), 76; Henry Cadbury, *The Making of Luke-Acts* (2nd ed.; London: Macmillan, 1958; repr. Peabody, Mass.: Hendrickson, 1999), 305; Haenchen, *Acts of the Apostles*, 485; Pervo, *Profit with Delight*, 74; Edmund Farahian, "Paul's Vision at Troas (Acts 16:9–10)" in *Luke and Acts* (ed. Gerald O'Collins and Gilberto Marconi; trans. Matthew O'Connell; New York: Paulist Press, 1993), 197–207; Tannehill, *Narrative Unity*, 2:195; F. Scott Spencer, *Acts* (Readings: A New Biblical Commentary; Sheffield: Sheffield Academic Press, 1997), 161–64; Charles Talbert, *Reading Acts: A Literary and Theological Commentary on the*

Nevertheless, for the present discussion it is important to linger over what the narrative does, and does not, say: it is only in the characters' own interpretation of the dream/vision that God is mentioned at all. Considering both the frequency of dreams/visions in Luke-Acts, and the element of divine agency that pervades all of these *except* the Troas vision,[34] puzzling questions arise: Why the change? Why here? These questions invite an examination of the Troas episode within the broader context of Paul's missionary activity in Acts.

Since a number of commentators have described Paul's dream/vision at Troas as a second commissioning scene,[35] paralleling the original commission of Barnabas and Saul in Acts 13:1–3, it is interesting to begin the present contextual survey with this first commission. In 13:2, the Holy Spirit addresses the believers in Antioch, saying "Set apart for me Barnabas and Saul for the work that I have called them to do."[36] Chapters 13–14 then describe a series of encounters in which Paul and Barnabas find themselves and their message sometimes received warmly and sometimes opposed. Although this opposition is often extreme, it is overshadowed by the success of their mission. A Roman proconsul is converted in 13:12. Paul and Barnabas speak on three successive Sabbaths in Psidian Antioch, by the end of which time "nearly the whole city" has turned out to hear their message (13:44). Even the Jewish opposition they face (13:45) is balanced by the receptivity of the Gentiles (13:48–49). In Iconium, a great crowd of Jews and Gentiles become believers (14:1). Again, the apostles face opposition in Iconium, but the narrative highlights instead the spread of the "good news" (14:7). When Paul heals an impaired man in Lystra, the response of the Gentiles is to receive him and Barnabas as gods, attempting to offer them sacrifice as incarnations of Hermes and Zeus (14:11–12). Paul is even stoned and left for dead in 14:19, but in 14:20 he simply gets up and goes into the city. On the very next day, he and Barnabas go to Derbe, where they make a large number of disciples (14:21). In each case, significant opposition is overshadowed by more significant success.

Following the scene of the Jerusalem council in Acts 15, Paul suggests a return tour to Barnabas: "Let us visit the brothers in every city in which we proclaimed the word of the Lord [to see] how they are doing" (15:36).[37] This is an

---

Acts of the Apostles (New York: Crossroad, 1997), 148; Joseph Fitzmyer, *Acts of the Apostles: A New Translation with Introduction and Commentary* (AB 31; New York: Doubleday, 1998), 577–79; and Beverly Gaventa, *The Acts of the Apostles* (ANTC; Nashville, Tenn.: Abingdon, 2003), 234–35.

34. A different reading, arguing that this Macedonian figure is a "dream angel," is found in Flannery-Dailey, *Dreamers, Scribes, and Priests*, 203.

35. E.g., Talbert, *Reading Acts*, 147; Spencer, *Acts*, 161.

36. On including strictly auditory experiences of the Holy Spirit within the parameters of dreams/visions scenes in Luke-Acts, see Miller, *Convinced that God had Called Us*, 18–20.

37. For those who might question the idea that this account somehow parallels the commissioning found in 13:2, Luke's use of the particle δή is rather overwhelming. In Acts, this

interesting and peculiar transition point in the text. The commission for the first journey comes directly from the Holy Spirit (13:2). Luke gives no indication of divine guidance for this second journey to parallel that found in 13:2–4. Paul's initial course in chapter 15 is also problematic, since he begins this "return" in Syria and Cilicia—regions never mentioned as part of his initial travels. After being joined by Timothy in Lystra (16:1–3), Paul's journey takes another turn, this time to the north and west. Again, the narrative provides no reason for this redirection. In this context, however, the "spiritual" hindrance Paul and his companions encounter in chapter 16 is quite striking.

After running into several "spiritual" roadblocks in 16:6–7, the characters[38] treat Paul's ὅραμα as a breakthrough: they interpret this event as divine guidance for the course of their mission. They seek "immediately" (εὐθέως) to go to Macedonia, because they have concluded (συμβιβάζω) that God has called them to do so. Thus, the reader might expect breakthrough results. Despite their speedy arrival in the "prominent" city of Philippi, however, such expectations are not fulfilled.[39]

Their initial work in Philippi results in only one convert: Lydia. Paul's subsequent encounter with the slave possessed by a Pythian spirit (16:16–18) contrasts markedly with his encounter with Bar Jesus (13:6–12). In the earlier story, the false prophet is defeated and the Roman proconsul is converted. In Acts 16, Paul's ability to cast out the Pythian spirit only lands him in jail. In contrast to the angelic prison rescues in Acts 5:19–20 and 12:6–10, it is interesting to note that this passage features neither an angel, nor an escape. After an earthquake shakes the foundations of the prison, leaving the prisoners free of their bonds, the jailer finds that no one has left (16:26–29). Indeed, given the characters' assumptions of divine agency in Paul's dream/vision at Troas, it is interesting to notice the *continuing absence* of divine agency in this part of Acts.[40] A hopeful beginning to

---

particle is found only at 13:2 and 15:36; so also Haenchen, *Acts of the Apostles*, 473.

38. The reference to "characters" here is a reflection of the first-person plural in the narrative. I am not using this term as a way of siding with any particular interpretation in the ongoing discussions of the "we" passages (see above). In any case, the narrator has made clear that Paul is not alone, but is accompanied, at the very least, by Silas and Timothy.

39. Conzelmann argued that the speed of the journey from Troas to Philippi confirms the divine origin of Paul's ὅραμα. Hans Conzelmann, *Acts of the Apostles* (trans. J. Limburg, A. Thomas Kraabel, and D. H. Juel; Hermeneia; Philadelphia: Fortress, 1987), 129.

40. "God," "Jesus," and "Lord" are mentioned frequently in Acts 16:11–17:15 ("God" [16:14, 17, 25, 34; 17:13], "Jesus" [16:18, 31; 17:3, 7], "Lord" [16:31–32]). (I am not including here the uses of κύριος in 16:14, 15, 16, 19, and 30, since these refer neither to God or Jesus). With the singular exception of 16:14, however, God, Jesus, and Lord are always the object of action rather than the subject of action.

For the suggestion that language for lightning, thunder, and earthquake both in Acts and in Euripides' *Bacchae* relates to rituals of initiation for so-called "mystery" cults like that of Dionysius, see Richard Seaford, "Thunder, Lightning and Earthquake in the Bacchae and the Acts

the mission in Philippi ends with only Lydia and the Philippian jailer responding positively to Paul's message.

In Acts 17, one finds something approaching the more familiar pattern of Acts 13–14. Paul and Silas spend several Sabbaths in the synagogue of Thessalonica, and "some of the Jews, a significant number of worshiping Greeks, and not a few of the leading women" are persuaded by Paul's message (17:4). Although this marks the greatest success since "we" left Troas, it still does not compare to descriptions like "nearly the whole city" of Psidian Antioch turning out to hear Paul in 13:44. Paul and Silas find greater receptivity among the Jews in Beroea (17:11). As in 14:19, however, the opponents of Paul's message will travel to other towns to stop the spread of the word; because of this opposition, Paul is whisked away to the coast in 17:14, from which he will depart Macedonia and sail to Achaia. This departure from Macedonia is not telegraphed in the narrative. There is no deliberation about where to go next, nor is there any hint of divine guidance. Luke does not even tell the reader that Paul has left Macedonia and entered Achaia, which Luke elsewhere recognizes as two distinct territories (Acts 18:12, 18:27, 19:21). Like the initial interpretation of Paul's vision in 16:10, the transfer is immediate (εὐθέως). It is also quiet, however: a rather odd ending to the story that began in the tension described in 16:6–8 and the dream/vision interpreted as a resolution of that tension in 16:9–10.

Given the way in which the narrative transitions immediately from the exterior description of Paul's dream/vision to the characters' interior interpretation of this event, it is interesting to note just how "human" this part of Acts is. Paul's so-called second journey begins with a human decision (Acts 15:36), describes a transition based on human interpretation (16:10), and continues in a rather anticlimactic way until Paul quietly leaves Macedonia (17:15). Rather than becoming entangled in the unanswerable question of whether the author *intends* us to agree with the characters' interpretation, I am suggesting that it is more helpful to see that their interpretation is . . . well, if not wrong, then perhaps not exactly right. However one views their interpretation, this discussion has sought to underscore the importance of it being *their interpretation*. I am arguing, therefore, that Luke's depiction of this event is crucial for our understanding of his presentation of dreams/visions as experiences of God precisely because the characters' understanding of this experience finds its basis solely in their interpretation of Paul's dream/vision *as* an experience of God.

---

of the Apostles," *What is a God? Studies in the Nature of Greek Divinity* (ed. Alan B. Lloyd; London: Duckworth, 1997), 139–52.

Concluding Comments on Dreams/Visions, Interpretation, and Religious Experience

The sheer frequency of dreams/visions in Luke-Acts suggests they are important for Luke. The question is, why? What is the advantage of presenting the story of God, Jesus, the Spirit, and the early followers of Jesus in this particular way? Could Luke have told the story without these visionary encounters? Looking more broadly at the New Testament and early Christian literature, one could argue that dreams/visions need not be an integral part of such a story. What, then, do dreams/visions add to Luke-Acts?

A number of scholars have highlighted the importance of dreams/visions for Luke's depiction of God in the narrative, and they are correct in doing so. This narrative is about God and the active role of God in human events. Luke's use of dreams/visions further highlights this element of the story by underscoring the irruptive nature of God's actions, vividly depicting God at work *within* the scenes of human history, and suggesting an even broader understanding of God at work *behind* the scenes of human history. One could stop there. The way that dreams/visions facilitate Luke's depiction of God's involvement in human events provides sufficient reason for their inclusion in the story. Stopping at this point, however, only provides half of the answer—the exterior half of the answer.

As noted above, there is a spectrum of character responses to the dreams/visions in Luke-Acts. In some cases, the irruptive, exterior aspect of the dream/vision seems to overpower everything else. In others, however, human characters play a much more important interpretive role, highlighting an interior facet of the dream/vision experience. On two separate occasions, Paul interprets his initial vision of the risen Jesus in light of his *subsequent* experience proclaiming Jesus as the Christ. In these passages, the reader encounters a character who—despite divine intervention—is portrayed as working out the meaning of his visionary experiences. Following his encounter with the risen Lord, Saul is left blind and helpless. It is only after devoting himself to proclaiming Jesus as the Christ that Saul, now Paul, describes his "Damascus road" experience as a call to bear witness to the Gentiles. The interior aspect of his experience of God is found in his continually evolving understanding of what this dream/vision means—a point that is emphasized by the fact that the dream/vision itself changes in each of his interpretive recollections of the event. Paul and his companions interpret his dream/vision at Troas as a call from God to proclaim the gospel in Macedonia. This interpretation, however, does not resonate with the subsequent narrative. If it is important to notice that Luke-Acts is about God and the plan of God it is equally important to notice that the story is also about God's people and their attempt, sometimes even their struggle, to understand their experience of God.

The consultation yielding the essays in this volume met with the express purpose of defining the rather amorphous concept of "religious experience" in early Judaism and early Christianity. Texts provide crucial primary evidence in this quest, and Luke-Acts is unquestionably important for our understanding of early Christianity. The present study has focused on dreams/visions because they emphasize two significant facets of religious experience: the exterior element of divine irruption and the interior element of individual interpretation. Although the exterior portion of this experience is fairly obvious and mentioned frequently, the interior facet of interpreting dreams/visions is often ignored—especially when such interpretation is a subtle part of the textual evidence.[41] Rather, both must be taken together, if one wishes to understand the import of dreams/visions as part of the experience of God in Luke-Acts. Indeed, the text of Luke-Acts itself compels the reader to consider both the exterior and interior features of these dream/vision experiences. In a number of significant dreams/visions in the Lukan narrative, God's irruptive exterior action is inextricably bound with the interior interpretive action of the recipients. Interpretation is, therefore, integral for understanding these scenes as evidence of the experience of God in Luke-Acts, and integral to the definition of at least some experiences of God in early Christianity.

---

41. As opposed, for instance, to the *angelus interpres* so commonplace in the texts of Hellenistic Judaism (e.g., Dan 7:16; see Flannery-Dailey, *Dreamers, Scribes, and Priests*, 124).

THE CONFLUENCE OF TRAUMA AND TRANSCENDENCE IN THE PAULINE CORPUS

Colleen Shantz

As Troels Engberg-Pedersen has argued, there are many valid reasons that religious experience has been set aside in Pauline studies.[1] In some cases the neglect was a secondary and unintended effect of a primary effort to correct anachronistic interpretations of a particular set of troublesome texts (e.g., to rectify the early "psychological" readings of Augustine or Luther). In others it was the result of responsible concerns for the limits of what one can claim about *experience* on the basis of a surviving *textual* remnant. To this list, one might also add the bad track record of most academic study of religious experience, especially religious ecstasy or altered states of consciousness (ASCs) that are undertaken and interpreted in religious contexts. Outside of the fascination with conversion events, Western observers have not been particularly generous in assessments of religious experience. In fact, the exotic depictions of religious experience have been especially fruitful generators of a sense of the inferior otherness of the cultures in which they are practiced.[2]

The philosopher Bernhard Waldenfels has pithily categorized the strategies with which Western thinkers control encounters with the exoticized Other. He names our biases as egocentricism, logocentricism, and ethnocentricism.[3]

---

1. "The Construction of Religious Experience in Paul," in this volume. Recently, there have been attempts to redress the neglect. See, for example: Luke Timothy Johnson, *Religious Experience in Earliest Christianity: A Missing Dimension in New Testament Studies* (Minneapolis: Fortress, 1998); John Ashton, *The Religion of Paul the Apostle* (New Haven, Conn.: Yale University Press, 2000); and Gilbert I. Bond, *Paul and the Religious Experience of Reconciliation: Diasporic Community and Creole Consciousness* (Louisville, Ky.: Westminster John Knox, 2005).

2. Vincent Crapanzano makes this point at greater length in the introduction to *Case Studies in Spirit Possession Contemporary Religious Movements* (ed. Vincent Crapanzano and Vivian Garrison; New York: Wiley, 1977), 1–40.

3. Bernhard Waldenfels, *Der Stachel des Fremden* (1 aufl.; Frankfurt: Suhrkamp, 1990), 60–64.

Though the three reductions are interrelated, each describes a specific nuance of Western bias. Within an egocentric perspective the individual is constructed as a self-contained, self-sufficient agent in control of their engagement of the external world and behavior. For example, in the case of spirit possession, "western models usually consider [it] in psychoanalytic perspective as a 'projection' of repressed inner emotions or conflicts onto another person—in this case, onto a spiritual being as an alter ego."[4] Logocentrism compels observers to rationalize all behavior, to seek "reasonable"—typically instrumental—explanations for practices such as spirit possession, speaking in tongues, or religious trance. Frequently, ecstatic religious behavior is interpreted as a means to manipulate the larger social group within which it is practiced—it is decoded as a means to gain power, resources, or other privilege.[5] For Waldenfels, logocentrism and egocentrism culminate together in ethnocentricism, which claims not merely that Western ideologies of ideal humanness are preferable in particular circumstances, but that they may be "defended boundlessly as the vanguard of a universal reason."[6] Thus, in anthropological literature, ethnocentrism drives the historically persistent prejudice that casts religious experience as illness or moral weakness, both deviations from human wholeness and soundness. While practices of spirit possession bear the brunt of such bias, visionary practices, soul journey, and mediumship have all likewise been misrepresented.

In contrast to such depictions by *observers*, those who *practice* religious ecstasy describe it not as projection, but introjection; not only as strategic, but often as pleasurable or even beautiful or comic; and not as a sign of the unfitness of the "victims," but frequently with great respect for those who undertake it or are undertaken by it. These academic biases have not resulted in universally inaccurate or misconstrued pictures of particular cases.[7] For example, some shamans (as perhaps some biblical scholars) may have been mentally unsound. Likewise, no doubt some have manipulated their circumstances through use of their

4. Christian Strecker, "Jesus and the Demoniacs," in *The Social Setting of Jesus and the Gospels* (ed. Wolfgang Stegemann, Bruce J. Malina, and Gerd Theissen; Minneapolis: Fortress, 2002), 117–33, 120.

5. Such arguments frequently draw on the legacy of I. M. Lewis's landmark study of spirit possession and its instrumental arguments. I. M. Lewis, *Ecstatic Religion: A Study of Shamanism and Spirit Possession* (3d ed.; London: Routledge, 2003).

6. Waldenfels, *Der Stachel*, 62. The full quotation reads: "Egozentirk und Logozentrik begegnen sich auf besondere Weise in einer Ethnozentrik, die im Falle der abendländischen Tradition dazu führt, daß die eigene Lebensform nicht nue verteidigt (wogegen nichts zu sagen wäre), sondern schrankenlos verteidigt wird als Vorhut einer universalen Vernunft."

7. In fact, logocentric interpretations, in particular, have sometimes been part of a general effort to humanize ecstatic practice in its "attempt to render familiar what had seemed to be so strange" (Janice Boddy, "Spirit Possession Revisited: Beyond Instrumentality," *Annual Review of Anthropology* 23 [1994]: 407–34, 427).

ecstatic practice. But, at the very least, such attitudes have created blind spots in our views of early Christianity; and, at worst, they have contributed to reductionist and misrepresentative readings of ecstatic phenomena.

Fortunately, recognition of the gap between ethnographers' interpretations and practitioners' self-descriptions has led to more recent descriptions of religious experience with the deepest possible contextualization.[8] At the same time that ethnography has been changing, medical studies have been amassing a growing body of research exploring ecstatic religious states as a universal bodily/ neurological phenomenon. This essay is an exercise in attending to both developments. In it I attempt to read Paul's ecstatic experience with as much particularity as the evidence allows. That particularity can now include the recognition that the human body and its neurology are fundamental components of the context of religious experience.

IDENTIFYING RELIGIOUS EXPERIENCE IN THE TEXT.

Twice Paul speaks directly and unequivocally of his ecstatic experience. In 1 Cor 14:18 he expresses his gratitude to God that he speaks in tongues more than all of the Corinthians, and in 2 Cor 12:1–4 he describes, in such tantalizing brevity, his apprehension of the third heaven. The latter phenomenon he places in the category of "visions and revelations." In addition to these two explicit references, the trio of Gal 1:11–17, 1 Cor 9:1, 1 Cor 15:(3–)8 are frequently identified as allusions to an initiatory vision of Christ. Even if all of the latter three statements refer to the same event, this brief list already suggests a more robust ecstatic practice than is typically recognized for Paul.

But there is also another set of texts that, although they do not directly describe a single ecstatic event, are colored by and filled with the phenomena of religious ecstasy; they are Rom 8 and 2 Cor 3–5. Among the ecstatic residue in both of these passages are the many references to the spirit and its indwelling— references that would, in another context, be identified as signs of possession. The passages refer to δόξα (glory) not as reputation, but as physical radiance or light (2 Cor 3:7–11), and both include language about the image or likeness of the risen Christ (2 Cor 3:18; Rom 8:29). Notably, they each describe the members of the assemblies groaning and moaning, sublinguistically, in prayer (Rom 8:23,

---

8. Boddy's detailed review of ethnographic literature ("Spirit Possession") outlines both the continuing biases and the turn to thicker contextualization.

26).[9] Finally, they are characterized by allusions to bodily transformation[10] and keen emphasis on experience shared with the risen figure of Jesus (Rom 8:10–11, 29; 2 Cor 3:18, 5:1–5).

Each in its own way, the two sections also show signs that Paul is straining at the limits of language in order to say something of what he knows as bodily experience. In the case of Rom 8, he expresses experiences of union through repeated use of συν- compound words.[11] The occurrences include spirits witnessing together (συμμαρτυρέω, Rom 8:16), suffering with and being glorified with Christ (συμπάσξω and συνδοχάζω 8:17), groaning with and laboring with creation (συστενάζω and συνωδίνω 8:22), taking hold of our weakness with us (συναντιλαμβάνομαι, 8:26), and being conformed to the image of the risen Christ (8:29).[12] In the case of 2 Corinthians, Paul labors with mismatched sets of images as he attempts to describe bodily transformation. He begins with the comparison of temporary (σκηνή) and permanent dwellings to describe contrasting bodily states (5:1) but then adopts verbs of dressing and undressing (5:4) to describe the transformation from one to another. Paul follows this clumsy construction with talk of his longing and groaning for such transformation (5:2–4) and the possibility of being out of or away from the body (5:8). Finally, he crowns the whole section with the admission that these words might make him appear mad, ἐξίστημι in contrast to σωφρονέω.[13] "The love of Christ has hold (συνέχει) of us,"

---

9. Although attempts have been made to render στενάζω with the sense of "sighing" they cannot be supported either by the use of the word in other contexts or by its use in these texts. The entry for στενάζω in the TDNT ("στενάζω, στεναγμός, συστενάζω" [ed. Gerhard Friedrich; trans. & ed. Geoffrey W. Bromiley; Grand Rapids: Eerdmans, 1971] vol. VII: 600–603) is paradigmatic of the effort to avoid ecstatic implications of the word. Johannes Schneider suggests that the Greek tragic poets employ the word to describe characters who sigh "at destiny or individual blows of fate" (600). Schneider further suggests that: "Sighing takes place by reason of a condition of oppression under which man suffers and from which he longs to be free because it is not in accord with his nature, expectations, or hopes" (601). The translation of Ezek 21 that he produces based on those assumptions is almost absurd: "But thou, son of man, sigh! With broken thighs and in bitter grief, sigh! When they ask thee why thou sighest, then answer them: Because of a message of terror" (21:14). The scriptural examples suggest something more primal in στενάζω than groaning in resignation with one's lot in life.

10. In the Romans passage the material transformation extends beyond humans to a metamorphosis for all of creation.

11. In his comprehensive study (*The Theology of Paul the Apostle* [Grand Rapids: Eerdmans, 1998], 390–412), James Dunn has tallied forty or so of these compound constructions and deals with them under the category of "participation in Christ." As he puts it, "to focus solely on the actual 'with Christ/him' references would be a mistake. For the real force of the 'with Christ' motif is carried by" Paul's distinctive compounds (402).

12. All but one of these words is distinctive to Paul in the New Testament and several of them appear in this chapter only.

13. The suggestion that ἐξίστημι refers to ecstatic behavior has been made before: Wilhelm Bousset, *Kyrios Christos: Geschichte des Christusglaubens von den Anfängen des Christentums*

Paul claims (5:14). He is not in control of this experience and his extraordinary and inventive attempts to describe it betray the fact that it owes more to ecstatic and bodily knowing than to systematic reflection on a tradition. As John Ashton puts it, "These are all, surely, characteristically fumbling attempts of the genuine mystic to give expression to the ineffable."[14]

THE PAIRING OF SUFFERING AND ECSTASY

Another set of Paul's experiences recounted in his letters—sometimes, again, in quite specific detail and sometimes in generalities—pertains to his physical suffering. Events such as public judicial beatings and stonings, shipwrecks, and deprivation are thus also part of Paul's contextual particularity. However, even more intriguing is the regularity with which he pairs his reflections of religious ecstasy with statements about suffering and pain. For example, in 2 Cor 3 and 4, Paul is discussing Moses' glorious transformation on Sinai (3:7–18, an idea on which he seems to have reflected at greater length) as an analogy for the anticipated transformation of the faithful in Christ (4:16–18). Yet, at the transition point in this extended comparison he interjects a statement about suffering (4:7–12), including the arresting image of carrying the death of Jesus in the body. Furthermore, the entire section is followed by a full-blown catalogue of hardships in 6:3–10. Likewise, Rom 8 contains the list of occasions of suffering endured through hardship, distress, famine, and nakedness, etc. (8:35–36), as well as the image of the suffering of all creation in decay (8:19–22). In the case of Paul's account in 2 Cor 12 of the heavenly journey, we find that this report of an ecstatic event is also bracketed by reflections on suffering. The passage preceding the vision—the so-called "fool's speech"—contains the most extensive and detailed of his *peristasis* catalogues (2 Cor 11:21b–33); likewise, immediately following the account of the ascent, Paul declares that his abundance of revelations occasioned his suffering from the much-assessed "thorn in the flesh" (12:7).

Given the repeated and close connection of the two ideas—suffering and ecstasy—this pattern warrants further attention. Paul's lists of hardships have been assessed quite thoroughly for their rhetorical function in the letters. As a discursive phenomenon, they are not difficult to justify and they have been con-

---

bis Irenaeus. (6th ed.; Göttingen: Vandenhoeck & Ruprecht, 1967), 187; Hans Windisch, *Der Zweite Korintherbrief* (Göttingen: Vandenhoeck & Ruprecht, 1924), 179; F. F. Bruce, *1 and 2 Corinthians* (New Century Bible; London: Oliphants, 1971), 207; and many authors since. See Moyer Hubbard ("Was Paul out of his Mind? Re-Reading 2 Corinthians 5.13," *JSNT* 70 [1998]: 40–42) for an overview of the history of the discussion. Hubbard himself presents a contrary thesis, arguing that the contrast between ἐξίστημι and σωφρονέω addresses the shortcomings of Paul's rhetorical style.

14. Ashton, *Religion of Paul,* 149. In this quotation Ashton is not referring specifically to 2 Cor 3–5, but rather to the breadth of Paul's language of participation in Christ.

vincingly described as one of his strategies for self-commendation. Parallels in Greco-Roman rhetoric have convinced most people that Paul was simply using a ready-made rhetorical form. Certainly the context of the fool's speech, (2 Cor 11:1–33) in the midst of his refutation of the *über*-apostles, provides compelling evidence for the argument. So, that Paul should adopt a common pattern of self-commendation is not unexpected, and yet nothing in rhetorical analysis predicts that he should routinely couple it with statements of ecstatic knowledge.

Furthermore, identification of the rhetorical form hardly exhausts the nature of these passages; in fact, to a certain extent it may distort their nature. The focus on rhetorical convention can easily blunt the force of the severity and sheer quantity of abuse that Paul endured. Jennifer Glancy has recently demonstrated that, while the form may be recognizable, Paul's use of it is not without peculiarity since some of the items in Paul's lists do not fit at all comfortably in the paradigm of self-praise.[15] In particular, the details of his whippings, beatings, and stonings at the hands of Roman and Jewish authorities are not occasions for admiration. While it is true that some military figures displayed their battle scars as signs of their valor, such wounds are in no way comparable to the welts of corporal punishment. As Glancy has shown, authors who point to parallels in some rhetorical self-defense fail to distinguish between the contexts in which wounds are received. The *habitus* of Paul's Greco-Roman audiences is far too firmly invested in another view of beatings—one that did not allow just any body to be whipped, but only a debased body. In Glancy's words, a "back welted by a whip" is not "a breast pierced in battle."[16] Paul's scars do not tell the story of victory, but of humiliation; they brand him as a slave or some other devalued body.

This is not to say that Paul was soliciting a negative appraisal of his sufferings. He may, as some suggest, be attempting deliberately to reverse prevailing masculine values of domination, strength, and victory through presentation of this alternate view of success,[17] but, either way, these details cannot function as straightforward self-commendation. Something new is afoot here that requires more than the use of a rhetorical form to carry it. And something other than cultural convention has led Paul to raise his physical debasement to so prominent a place in the conversation. Given these contingencies, the question about Paul's combination of these sets of sufferings with ecstatic experience takes greater depth.

Trauma and transcendence have also long been combined in descriptions of shamanism and at least one author has argued that such is also the explanation

---

15. Jennifer A. Glancy, "Boasting of Beatings (2 Corinthians 11:23-25)," *JBL* 123 (2004): 99–135.

16. Ibid., 134.

17. J. Louis Martyn, *Galatians: A New Translation with Introduction and Commentary* (AB 33A; New York: Doubleday, 1997), 568.

for Paul.[18] The early and influential ethnography of arctic shamanism, in particular, has contributed to the notion of a standard shamanic "career" that begins in suffering. As the construction would have it, the key elements in the career are the shaman's initiation crisis, which is preceded by illness or trauma that triggers, in turn, a trance experience. Some of those who successfully enter trance reemerge cured. Furthermore, the cycle of those events is typically interpreted as an experience of death and rebirth. Some of those who undergo it then enter training to become shamans and hence to act as healers themselves.

While this pattern of transition to shamanism is common enough, it is far from the only one. Other transitions to shamanic status are inaugurated by circumstantial signs or natural portents, dreams and/or visions, even a slow change in personality or a period of erratic behavior, inheritance of the status, and the purchase or theft of shamanic power.[19] Likewise, among those who do experience pain, it is not always attributable to the same causes. Sometimes pain is a side-effect of the ecstatic state itself, in which case more experienced shamans or mediums intervene in a variety of ways to teach novices the means to temper their states. More commonly, other forms of pain serve as a trigger for ASC: accident (as documented in near-death experiences); intentional use of prolonged fasting, or sensory deprivation; intense persistent activity like Sufi dancing; or even voluntary ingestion of toxins to induce religiously significant trance.[20] In all of these cases, the shamanic "career" shows many signs of cultural (and even individual) specificity that preclude such broad claims of universality. Furthermore, the category of shamanism is also culturally specific. Without such a role established in a given society, it is both irresponsible and not particularly helpful to label someone's experience as "shamanic." At best it oversimplifies, universalizes,

---

18. Ashton, *Religion of Paul*, 29–61.

19. Peggy Ann Wright, "The Nature of the Shamanic State of Consciousness: A Review," *Journal of Psychoactive Drugs* 21 (1989): 25–33.

20. Felicitas D. Goodman (*Speaking in Tongues; a Cross-Cultural Study of Glossolalia* [Chicago: University of Chicago Press, 1972]) and William Wedenoja ("Ritual Trance and Catharsis: A Psychological and Evolutionary Perspective," in *Personality and the Cultural Construction of Society: Papers in Honor of Melford E. Spiro* [ed. David K. Jordan, Marc J. Swartz and Melford E. Spiro: Tuscaloosa, Ala.: University of Alabama Press, 1990], 275-307) both document such interventions. Furthermore, a number of societies that have established traditions of mediums or other ecstatic practitioners use austerities and even near-toxic levels of botanical extracts to induce and teach control of ASC. For examples see Jeremy Narby and Francis Huxley, *Shamans through Time: 500 Years on the Path to Knowledge* (London: Thames & Hudson, 2001), 67–68, 170–74, 253–54. Rhawn Joseph (*Neuropsychiatry, Neuropsychology, and Clinical Neurology: Emotion, Evolution, Cognition, Language, Memory, Brain Damage, and Abnormal Behavior* [2nd ed.; Baltimore: Williams & Wilkins, 1996] 280–82) reports the personal accounts of a number of documented out-of-body experiences that occurred spontaneously during traumatic and life-threatening events.

and domesticates behaviors and interpretations, stripping them of both particularity and power.

In Paul's case there are other, more particular, potential links between suffering and ecstasy. For one, his several circumstances of severe pain through
injury and accident provide a probable occasion for alterations in consciousness
that frequently accompany religious experience. Any of the punishments that
Paul mentions in his list of hardships was capable of inflicting the sort of bodily
response that triggers the ascendancy of the autonomic nervous system and a
more focused tuning of brain and neural activity. Cicero's disturbing account
of Gaius Servilius's death due to injuries inflicted during his beating with rods
bears graphic witness to the severity of this Roman punishment (*Against Verres*
II.5.140–42). Richard Cassidy's study of the range of conditions under which a
prisoner might be incarcerated in the Roman Empire provides the concrete details
of various sorts of deprivation.[21] The significance of the link between trauma and
ecstasy is deepened by the fact that Paul seems to have practiced voluntary austerities as well (1 Cor 9:24–27).

Whether Paul's experiences of pain and altered states of consciousness actually coincided in time remains beyond the evidence of the text. What is certain is
the fact that they coincided in Paul's body.[22] Thanks to the pain and humiliation
of his hardships, Paul knew what it was to carry around the death of Jesus in his
body (2 Cor 4:10). But thanks to his religious experience, he knew what it was to
be bodily transformed into his "glorious likeness" as well (3:18).

PAUL'S BODY OF KNOWLEDGE

Over the past two decades studies of the functioning of the brain and central nervous system have begun to document the neurological characteristics of
altered states of consciousness. While clinicians have begun to measure brain
activity during ASCs, understanding of the phenomena relies largely on extrapolation from documentation of brain functioning in other circumstances. When
that catalogue of information is compared to ecstatics' descriptions of their experiences, a set of suggestive patterns emerges. On that basis, one neuropsychologist
in particular—Eugene G. d'Aquili—created a model of brain and nervous system
activity during religious ecstasy.[23]

---

21. See Richard J. Cassidy, *Paul in Chains: Roman Imprisonment and the Letters of St. Paul*
(New York: Crossroad, 2001).

22. Paul never says that the experience of suffering was the direct cause of his ecstasy—in
fact in his interpretation of events (2 Cor 12:7–10) he suggests the opposite dynamic—but still
he holds them together.

23. See Eugene G. d'Aquili and Andrew B. Newberg in *The Mystical Mind: Probing the Biology of Religious Experience* (Minneapolis: Fortress, 1999). Since d'Aquili's recent death, Newberg
has continued this work. The details in this section are based on their work.

Although ASCs are "abnormal" with regard to their relative frequency, many of them are quite normal with regard to human capacity and adaptive benefit; nonetheless, in the ensuing description I will use the designation "normal conscious" as the alternative to ASC. Altered states rely on ordinary neurocognitive processes functioning in extraordinary ways. During normal consciousness, the autonomic nervous system—which includes specific neocortical centers, the limbic system,[24] and associated glands—fluctuates between states of arousal and those of quiescence as it responds to stimuli in the body and immediate environment.[25] At times the body tunes more intensively to one or the other system, effectively "ignoring" stimuli that would otherwise interrupt and rebalance the interplay between the two. That tuning can be generated by extraordinary environmental conditions, or it can be controlled by a person's behavior, either as their primary objective or as an unintended side effect. The former is perhaps best known in the quiescent practices of meditation; the latter as the occasional consequence of participation in extreme physical activity or mental processing.[26] So it is that a rather limited set of neural functions dominates experience. If such tuning intensifies sufficiently, it results in the extraordinary emotional, chemical, and cognitive phenomena of religious ASCs.

During intense phases of religious ecstasy the combined effects of changes in brain activity provide an odd set of phenomena to be interpreted. In normal consciousness, information about the body is available from two sources: first, from the body itself via the nervous system, and second from the "map" of somatic memories registered on the surface of the cerebral cortex (particularly in the right hemisphere). Specific areas of our brains also function as secondary and "executive" areas of specialization that coordinate somatic information from these sources in ways that allow us to act, choose, and move through space. According to the modeling, during ASC, these features interact in distinctive ways. On the one hand, normal sensation, from both the cortical map of somatic features and directly from the body, is neurologically blocked from the brain regions that bring it to consciousness. On the other hand, the executive region of the brain that is

---

24. The limbic system is a set of quite primitive (viz., having developed early in the evolution of the human brain) brain structures. They play a fundamental role in the survival functions of mating, memory, mood, motivation, fighting, feeding, and fear. The limbic system is also essential to generating and moderating the emotional meaning of thought and is indispensable to attention as well as the creation and retrieval of memories. Although we are not typically conscious of the workings of the limbic system, nonetheless, consciousness is impossible without it.

25. In biology, these functions of the autonomic nervous system are subdivided into the sympathetic (controlling arousal) and parasympathetic (controlling quiescence) systems.

26. This includes the well known example of long-distance runners and the more uneasy news that even air-traffic controllers have been documented as experiencing ASCs during their work.

responsible for our overall awareness of our bodies is far more active than usual. The human subject is left to interpret this strange combination of neurological silence and noise in an intelligible way. Thus, the body is perceived as present, but its sensations—its weight, boundaries, pain, voluntary motion—are all absent from consciousness. The body, as it has been known, is stripped away and yet subjects continue to know themselves as embodied. In an attempt to interpret these phenomena as coherently as possible, ecstatics frequently report the sensation of floating or flying without physical boundaries between themselves and the people and objects in their awareness. Not surprisingly, descriptions of ascent are also common in interpretations of ecstatic experiences. Paul's ascent is among them: "whether in the body or apart from the body I do not know" (2 Cor 12:2).

Another effect of intense ecstatic experience is the release of a number of body chemicals that have analgesic and euphoric effects.[27] These somatic, chemical phenomena amplify the efforts of the ecstatic to interpret her experience. The combined effect of these endogenous chemicals is to reduce not only the experience of bodily pain, but to temper the emotional states that accompany it as well.[28] Together they leave the practitioner with a profound sense of wellness and pleasure lasting for as long as days or even weeks.[29] Moreover, these very powerful neurological experiences appear to reconfigure the map of the body that is burned into the cerebral cortex so that the ecstatic is quite literally—bodily—permanently changed by her experience.

What has taken conceptual and rhetorical form in parts of Paul's letters is what Paul has experienced in religious ecstasy. These comments are some of the epistemological correlates of Paul's ecstasy; this is Paul's body of knowledge. Through it we begin to see some of the other ways of knowing to which logocentric approaches, in particular, have been insensitive. As discussed above, some

---

27. Within the brain, neurotransmitters both enable impulses to cross some nerve synapses (excitatory transmitters) and block passage at others (inhibitory transmitters), thus managing which parts of the brain and nervous system communicate with one another at any given moment. Still others are modulatory; that is, they act more slowly on synapses and set "tone" of network. Thus, they "enable it to function in many different ways according to the general state or conditions under which it operates." Trevor Robbins, "The Pharmacology of Thought and Emotion," in *From Brains to Consciousness* (ed. Steven Rose; New York: Allen Lane, 1998), 37. In this way neurotransmitters change our perceived experience by facilitating which parts of the system are active and which are inhibited and the degree of change. Neuromodulators frequently affect the body more directly by synchronizing the activity of the peripheral nervous system with the prevailing brain state. For example, they trigger an increase in heart rates to correspond with the stimulation of arousal states in the brain.

28. Joseph, *Neuropsychiatry*, 369. Initial studies in which endorphins are injected into spinal fluid (i.e., away from the targeted brain centers where they are naturally released) and thereby dispersed more rapidly throughout the body suggest that pain is relieved without some of the usual accompanying emotional effects.

29. Wedenoja, "Ritual Trance," 288.

shamanic traditions, especially those that include severe illness as an aspect of initiation, interpret these bodily changes as an experience of death and rebirth as they pass through an otherworldly route. For Paul, whose context includes reflection on the death and resurrection of Jesus, ecstatic transformation can also be interpreted as a type of death and rebirth. In his case, however, his body contains the knowledge of transformation into a nearly divine state—"a resurrection like his" (Rom 6:5). In addition, Paul's sense of his body is also more permeable than egocentricism would allow. This point is best seen in one final example of suffering and ecstasy in Paul's letters.

Unlike the previous examples, Paul's letter to the Philippians is not primarily a recollection of pain and transformation, but an anticipation of them. Although the conditions of imprisonment already likely entail significant discomfort, it is clear that Paul is expecting something still worse. As he weighs his possible fates, he prefers the release of death (Phil 1:23). In this context Paul speaks of his hopes in bodily terms: "It is my eager anticipation and hope that I will be put to shame in nothing, but in all boldness—as always even now—Christ will be magnified/greatly manifested (μεγαλυνθήσεται) in my body whether through life or through death" (1:20). The concreteness of the statement is inescapable; Paul's body is the site within which Christ is presented. His ecstatic experience has made him permeable, even to the presence of another within him.

Thus, in Phil 1, Paul expresses some of the adaptive value of ecstatic experience. As he anticipates a possible death sentence and his own execution, he draws on his ecstatic experience of union with Christ. The neurocognitive experience of temporarily sharing the identity of the exalted Christ is now "written" on Paul's person. As anthropologist Janice Boddy suggests, this is a way of knowing that is "quite different from the infinitely differentiating, rationalizing, and reifying thrust" of most of our thinking.[30] In ecstatic experience "the body is the ground for legitimating objective knowledge, internalizing it, and making it experientially real."[31] Thus, through religious experience Paul's very body came to contain the perception that he was not alone and that the strength of others—in particular the strength of Christ to whom he was joined in trance—was available to him. It is one thing for Paul to assent to the idea that he has divine protection and quite another for him to have experienced the nearness and tangibility of that idea through the transformation of his own body. Paul has, quite literally within himself, the resources on which he can draw if the time comes to face execution. As he contemplates that possibility from prison the fear that accompanies that future is a natural stimulus to (and sign of) the neurological activity that would help to activate the somatic memory of union. At the same time, the knowledge is not only instrumental; it is not simply a device to enhance survival. Paul also

---

30. Boddy, "Spirit Possession," 407.
31. Ibid., 425.

speaks of pleasure and desire that no longer stop at the boundary between life and death (1:21).

Paul may be drawing on similar resources at the end of his letter to the Galatians. The whole of the letter is a series of pleas to adhere to the account of Christ's significance that Paul originally presented to them.[32] He appeals to the Galatians through honor, experience, analogy, affection, midrash, and threats. At the end, frustrated with the limits of his words, he takes up the pen in his own unskilled hand to physically demonstrate his conviction (Gal 6:11). Having spent his passion he seems still to despair of convincing them and so he concludes with the declaration that he bears the στίγματα of Jesus in his body (17b). That last declaration has the tone of self-consolation about it. Paul's own resources may have failed, but he is reassured in the face of such strong opposition (and failure in his task) by his bodily knowledge of communion with Jesus.

CONCLUSION

Paul's thick ecstatic context includes the correlation of at least the following: first, a particular bodily neurological state in ecstasy; second, additional bodily experience of pain and suffering that required an account and consolation; third, a social context within which they are interpreted and reciprocally molded; fourth, acquaintance with the story of one who likewise suffered pain and humiliation; and, fifth, an intense interest in reflecting on glorification of that same person. The result of this distinctive combination of factors is a shift in theology that is thoroughly embedded in a new somatic reality, in other words, a change in *habitus*.[33] Paul's own body was the epistemological engine for that change and religious ecstasy was especially effective in fuelling it because it feels far more real than ordinary experience.[34]

One of the most distinctive, pronounced, and yet marginalized, aspects of Paul's theological constructions is the notion of participation in Christ, conveyed especially through his habitual in-Christ idioms. Albert Schweitzer was perhaps the first to identify its importance in Paul's letters. He memorably contrasted it

---

32. In this context, it is noteworthy that Paul's highest expression of that message in the letter, Gal 3:28, is also a vision of the dissolution of boundaries and a version of *unio mystica*: "for all are one in Christ Jesus."

33. The term habitus as Pierre Bourdieu has defined it consists of "systems of durable, transposable *dispositions*" that function dialectically both to generate and to structure our actions, attitudes, and assumptions. So engrained is habitus in the very person that its dispositions "can be objectively 'regulated' and 'regular' without in any way being the product of obedience to rules" (see Bourdieu, *Outline of a Theory of Practice* [trans. Richard Nice; Cambridge: Cambridge University Press, 1977], 72).

34. Many people who experience religious ecstasy find the event to be "more real" and certainly more intense than normal experience. D'Aquili and Newberg, *Mystical Mind*, 113

with justification by faith, which, in comparison, amounted to no more than "a subsidiary crater" that formed on the side of the greater theme of participation in Christ.[35] Yet the theme of participation has not been successfully integrated into most efforts to construct a coherent theological stance for Paul. Most students of the letters are content merely to flag its significance,[36] possibly name it as idiomatic, and move on to more systematic matters. I would suggest that this neglect is due at least in part to our inability to account for religious experience as formative of thought. As long as scholarship remains so thoroughly logocentric in its orientation, other sorts of knowing will be relegated to the margins of the Pauline corpus. What else might we see, and how else might we see it, if we found ways to begin with experience?

---

35. Albert Schweitzer, *The Mysticism of Paul the Apostle* (trans. William Montgomery; New York: H. Holt, 1931), 3.

36. Even James Dunn, as respectful as he of the significance of the concept for Paul (and as massive as his study is), simply suggests the need for more work in relating participation in Christ to other ideas in Paul's letters, like baptism and the body of Christ (*The Theology of Paul the Apostle*, 395).

Response to Papers by Troels Engberg-Pedersen, Colleen Shantz, Bert Peerbolte, and John B. Miller

Rollin A. Ramsaran

Troels Engberg-Pedersen begins his paper with "a sketch of the current situation within Pauline studies with regard to the notion of 'religious experience.'" He provides an interesting and accurate hesitation or "against" position of scholars in engaging Paul's religious experience (as something "psychic"). This occurs theologically, beginning at the turn of the twentieth century, through neo-orthodoxy and the lingering effects of post-neo-orthodoxy and methodologically through (a) literary approaches that weight the text itself over elements "behind the text" and (b) historical and sociological approaches that work only with a "non-individualistic ancient Mediterranean cultur[al]" perspective. His survey limits inquiry to "in Paul" as in Paul's person, so to speak, rather than religious experience of Paul, his converts, those in opposition or disagreement with him, and so forth. Such is true of all four papers in the group. An underlying burden of the paper is to demonstrate on philosophical grounds that religious experience in Paul, while certainly interpreted, is still a quite real event—something indeed did happen.

At one point, namely, in his discussion of Gal 3:1–5, Troels moves briefly to the experience of the believers in Galatia—in the realm of *imitatio* of Paul's own religious experience, to be sure. If the perspective of religious experience were broadened somewhat beyond Paul, then one might reference a decidedly current shift to engage the "for" position towards religious experience in Pauline studies. Here I am thinking about Luke T. Johnson's *Religious Experience in Earliest Christianity*; Klaus Berger, *Identity and Experience in the New Testament*; Michael Gorman, *Cruciformity: Paul's Narrative Spirituality of the Cross*; and Gilbert I. Bond, *Paul and the Religious Experience of Reconciliation*.[1]

---

1. Luke T. Johnson, *Religious Experience in Earliest Christianity: A Missing Dimension in New Testament Studies* (Minneapolis: Fortress, 1998); Klaus Berger, *Identity and Experience in*

Troels presents a "for" case to the question of religious experience in Paul through an examination of texts from Galatians, 2 Corinthians, and Philippians. The result is helpful, especially in offering identifying criteria and definitional boundaries that may be tested or applied to other similar texts. Troels states: "We have two defining features of what makes a given phenomenon a psychological 'experience': it occurs to an individual in his or her interior. And we have noted two forms of such an 'experience', which may or may not go together: an inner vision in an individual and a sense on the part of an individual of an intimate, bodily relationship with Christ." One is left wondering whether, in Troel's estimation, Paul was prone to visions on an ongoing basis or whether they were occasional (e.g., Paul's call/conversion and texts such as 2 Cor 12:2–4). Was the ongoing "intimate, bodily relationship" based on Paul's initial vision remembered and reactivated or was it based on confirmatory visions (e.g., "of the knowledge of the glory of God in the face of Jesus Christ"; 2 Cor 4:6)? A further question comes to mind: Is not Christ's presence at least sometimes (much of the time?) spoken of in Paul as a *mediated* experience? Here I am thinking of *mediation by the Spirit*. Of the major texts discussed, in my estimation, two appear to be visionary and two speak of religious experience strongly in the context of a *mediating* Spirit:[2]

Galatians 1:16	"pleased to reveal his Son to me" (in a vision)
Galatians 2:19–20	"crucified with Christ" (cf. 6:14) and "Christ lives in me"

In the context of the letter might not Paul mean: "Christ lives in me by/through the Spirit"? Note particularly the Spirit as the marker of the believer's life (3:1–5) and life *lived by the Spirit* (esp. 5:25 with chaps 5–6 inclusive).

2 Cor 4:6	"the knowledge of the glory of God in the face of Jesus Christ" (in a vision)
Phil 1:19–26; 3:7–11	("loss & gain" and "death & life")

The Philippian passages form "bookends" to the whole discussion in between— a discussion started in 1:19, where the context is set with the striking phrase: "through … the help *of the Spirit* of Jesus Christ."

Colleen Shantz presents an intriguing paper that sets religious experience in a context of suffering and ecstasy. Building on key texts in Rom 8 and 2 Cor

---

the New Testament (trans. Charles Muenchow; Minneapolis: Fortress, 2003 [German ed. 1991]); Michael J. Gorman, *Cruciformity: Paul's Narrative Spirituality of the Cross* (Grand Rapids: Eerdmans, 2001); and Gilbert I. Bond, *Paul and the Religious Experience of Reconciliation: Diasporic Community and Creole Consciousness* (Louisville, Ky.: Westminster John Knox, 2005).

2. What follows is further elaborated in Rollin A. Ramsaran, "Religious Experience 'In Christ': A Modest Pauline Appraisal" (paper presented at the annual meeting of the Society of Biblical Literature, San Diego, Calif., November 21, 2007).

3–5, she presents her main case from Phil 1:20. Along the way, she points out a spectrum of texts such as Gal 1:11–17 (Paul's "initiatory vision of Christ"), 2 Cor 12:1–4 (a visionary experience), and 1 Cor 14:18 (Paul's individual expression of speaking in tongues). She quickly leaves aside 1 Cor 14:18, but nevertheless categorizes it as "spirit possession." Another text that comes to my mind is 1 Cor 2:6–16—the apprehension of the "divine mind" by the Spirit (although this text does not express a moment in Paul's own peculiar religious experience but rather it expresses the possibility of all believers). One question occurs concerning the terminology regarding, at least, the Greco-Roman period in which Paul is found. In examining or mining for religious experience is it important or necessary to distinguish between (1) *ex stasis* (out of/from being/body—characteristic of shaman activity) = ecstatic expression and (2) *en theos* (god/divine spirit within/ possession—characteristic of prophetic activity) = enthusiastic expression? Troels's paper very much stressed "interiority" and Colleen's paper, as I read it, fixates visionary experience in the body via biological/neurological phenomena. Paul, in 2 Cor 12:4, seems to know both expressions ("whether in the body or out of the body") although he seems unconcerned to distinguish between the two.

If I understand Colleen rightly (as a complete novice with regard to biological and neurological research!), there is a correlating pattern of suffering and ecstasy (religious experience) expressed in some of Paul's letters. I think this is a significant observation and contribution. The suffering may trigger ASC/ ecstasy that acts to (1) produce an intensive awareness without bodily sensation (*ex stasis*—out of normal being/body perception) and (2) temper the pain and even flatten emotive response (a cognitive/ spiritual defense mechanism?). Paul's body reorganizes through neurological reconfiguration/remapping to produce the ASC/ecstasy and this "map" lingers on to provide a routing function for later "episodes" of ecstasy triggered by troubling/suffering stimuli. With regard to Phil 1:20, Paul has an anticipation of suffering and can "channel" trance in preparation for it. Paul is aware of bodily transformation through ecstatic trance-like union with the exalted Christ. At this point, reference and explication of a text such as 2 Cor 4:16–17 would, in my estimation, strengthen the argument: "Though our outer nature is wasting away, our inner nature is being renewed every day. For this slight momentary affliction is preparing for us an eternal weight of glory beyond all comparison." I do wonder if a similar analysis could be pointed toward anticipated suffering from a neurological standpoint. Do bodies reconfigure/remap neurologically in response to pain/suffering stimuli—even in anticipatory stages? (For instance, anticipation of regular abuse by a spouse that correlates to a partner's end of the week drinking/rage pattern.) Such might strengthen the Phil 1 argument and the inherent claim to frequent ecstatic activity on Paul's part.

Finally, I agree with Colleen's suggestion that Paul's "habitual in-Christ idioms" need further investigation. I think that many, if not most, of Paul's "in Christ" statements refer to community identification and interaction under a per-

ceived Lordship to Christ that is actuated by the Spirit's presence—less likely is
that most believers follow Paul's revelatory and visionary route.

Bert Jan Peerbolte presents a fine paper on 2 Cor 12:1–4—Paul's ascent or
"rapture" to the third heaven. He is interested in the nature of the experience
and how this ascent/visionary experience connects to Paul's Christology. Bert
Jan deals skillfully with the exegetical/rhetorical issues of (1) is Paul speaking of
himself or someone else, (2) that Paul's third heaven is paradise (there are no
further heavens upward), and (3) Paul's use of ἄρρητα describes audible heavenly
matters that represent the untranslatable perspective open to mystics. Key for his
textual argument is an identification of "Lord" with Christ in 12:1 and his decision for κυρίου as an objective genitive ("revelations concerning the Lord") over
a genitive of possession ("revelations stemming from the Lord"). This decision
is based on analogy with Gal 1:12—"revelation of the Lord" = "Lord, Christ has
been revealed to Paul." Suffice it to say, I think the argument could be strengthened by (1) attempting to see the source/possession of revelations in/by the Spirit
as the more familiar pattern (cf. 1 Cor 12–14) and (2) making appeal to 2 Cor
4:10 as an analogous vision of the exalted Christ (see both Engberg-Pedersen and
Shantz). Other things come to mind, such as the predominant early-Christian use
of Ps 110 as throne imagery (Jesus at "the right hand of God") and the mystical
throne vision tradition in Israel's scriptures, which is handled through an examination of issues around *merkabah* mysticism.

On the nature of Paul's religious experience in 2 Cor 12:1–4, Bert Jan sides
with a description similar to Colleen: an altered state of consciousness (ASC)
based on markers of "(a) the experienced loss of personal boundaries, (b) the
experience of wholeness, and (c) a special loss of temporality" (a somewhat more
difficult fit). Altered states of consciousness are the provenance of "mystics" and,
I think, Bert Jan wants to assert that what we have termed "apocalyptists" in
streams of early Judaism are really "mystics." But, which stream of the variety
of apocalyptic worldviews—Enochian, Judean, or other? And which stream of
apocalyptic worldview best fits Paul? Paul ends up being a "mystic" with multiple
revelatory experiences. Granted I stand in a long line of New Testament scholars
who, since Schweitzer, shy away from labeling Paul as "mystic" and "ecstatic"—
certainly because in our *hubris* we do not think that Paul would have liked the
labels much either. If by "ecstatic" we mean something like outside normal course
of being or "beside oneself, then it seems like Paul would have had limited interest. Consider: "For if I pray in a tongue, my spirit prays but my mind is unfruitful"
(1 Cor 14:14). Also, in 1 Cor 2:6–16, Paul acknowledges that the Spirit of God
is able to know the depths of God, and mature believers have this Spirit which
grants to them "the mind of Christ." I am not sure reading this conclusion in 1
Cor 2:16 in a "mystical tenor" is warranted or even helpful in the larger context of
1 Corinthians. Paul certainly had visionary and ecstatic religious experiences. But
I would venture to say he had other types of religious experiences as well. What
was most important to Paul at what times and for what purposes?

John Miller's paper enters, of course, in a different key. He chooses to engage Paul's religious experience through the eyes of Luke's Acts of the Apostles. All those critical issues, of course, come rushing to the surface: can we really get to the religious experience of another person (their "interiority" as Troels might label it)? Do we have a better shot at it from primary sources (Paul's own letters—his own words—about his experience) than from secondary sources (Luke's interpreted, rhetorical, tendentious recounting of Paul's experience)? We know the issues based on the vast amount of work done on the "speeches" in Luke-Acts, of which Paul's retelling of his call/conversion in Acts 22 and 26 are a part.

I am very glad for this paper because it does highlight the interpretive issue—certainly recognized by Bert Jan ("we don't have access to Paul's experience. . . . What we do have is access to Paul's description of his experience") and Troels (Paul's "constructed and reconstructed 'after the event'" interpretations of religious experience). John's paper explicates Troels's position from a point beyond Paul's direct testimony (Luke's interpreted ["interpreting"] stance). John's narrative criticism approach pushes me (us) to read Paul's conversion/call narratives (Acts 9, 22, 26) and the Troas incident as an informed implied reader.[3] Hence, there are a number of interpretive levels stretching back to whatever was Paul's religious experience!

So what are we after and why? All four papers seem to indicate that religious experience was real (scientific, psychological, theoretical, philosophical, and historical warrants are offered) and this experience had profound and powerful lasting influences on the shaping/reorienting of Paul's worldview (or shall we say Paul's and Luke's?).

John's is a fine, well-thought-out presentation. He pushes to understand Paul's (via Luke) religious experience in light of what might be assumed about religious experience of the time. I think some key points are made: Most people in antiquity thought of life as being engaged by divine forces (most experience was religious for them at that time—what is our modern frame of mind?). Acts connects encounter with the divine (for believers in Christ) as taking place through the Spirit (as I indicated above, I think that is true with Paul as well). John examines "dream-visions" as a important component of religious experience as *perceived divine guidance (or lack there of)*. The driving force of his paper is to indicate that "interpretation [is] a vital component *of that experience*"[4] (i.e., an encounter with the divine, a revelation).

Moving along those lines, maybe we might be able to put forward at least one framework that gives some defining scope: One experiences the divine through encounter (vision, dream, "Spirit") and religious experience continues in trying

---

3. John wants us to be well informed about dream/visions and their capacity to be either believed or questioned. His work in this area is insightful.

4. Italics are mine.

to work out the import of that revelation in terms of what? Shall it be divine guidance (John); "call" and place (Troels, John); "historical struggle for power" (Troels); consolation (Colleen)? But here I go being "functional" again instead of "experiential." Bert Jan seemed to avoid that trap. How do we escape our training, reading lenses, assumptions, vested interests, and commitments when it comes to speaking of something like "religious experience"?

Bibliographyy

Anderson, Gary A. "The Penitence Narrative in *The Life of Adam and Eve.*" *HUCA* 63 (1992): 1–38.

Arbel, Vita Daphna. *Beholders of Divine Secrets: Mysticism and Myth in the Hekhalot and Merkavah Literature* Albany, N.Y.: State University of New York Press, 2003.

Argall, Randall A. *1 Enoch and Sirach: A Comparative Literary and Conceptual Analysis of the Themes of Revelation, Creation and Judgment.* SBLEJL 8. Atlanta: Scholars Press, 1995.

Aristotle. *On the Soul, Parva Naturalia, On Breath.* Translated by W. S. Hett. LCL. Cambridge, Mass.: Harvard University Press, 1957.

Artemidorus. *The Interpretation of Dreams—Oneirocritica.* Trans. Robert J. White; Torrance, Calif.: Original Books, 1990.

Ashton, John. *The Religion of Paul the Apostle.* New Haven, Conn.: Yale University Press, 2000.

———. *Understanding the Fourth Gospel.* Oxford: Oxford University Press, 1991.

Aune, David. "Mastery of Passions: Philo, 4 Maccabees and Earliest Christianity," Pages 125–58 in *Hellenization Revisited: Shaping a Christian Response within the Graeco-Roman World.* Edited by Wendy E. Helleman. Lantham, Md.: University Press of America, 1994.

Baert, Edward. "Le thème de la vision de Dieu chez s. Justin, Clément d'Alexandrie et s. Grégoire de Nysse." *FZPhTh* 12 (1965): 439–97.

Baird, William. "Visions, Revelation, and Ministry: Reflections on 2 Cor 12:1–5 and Gal 1:11–17." *JBL* 104 (1985): 651–62.

Barclay, John M. G., *Jews in the Mediterranean Diaspora: From Alexander to Trajan (323 BCE – 117 CE).* Berkeley and Los Angeles: University of California Press, 1996.

Barker, Margaret. *The Gate of Heaven: The History and Symbolism of the Temple in Jerusalem.* London: SPCK, 1991.

———. "The High Priest and the Worship of Jesus." Pages 93–111 in *The Jewish Roots of Christological Monotheism: Papers from the St. Andrews Conference on the Historical Origins of the Worship of Jesus.* Edited by C. C. Newman, J. R. Davila and G. S. Lewis. JSJSup 63. Leiden: Brill, 1999.

———. *The Older Testament.* London: SPCK, 1987.

Barrett, C. K. *A Critical and Exegetical Commentary on The Acts of the Apostles.* 2 vols. ICC. Edinburgh: T&T Clark, 1994–1998.

Beckford, James A. "Accounting for Conversion." *BJS* 29 (1978): 249–62.

Bedenbender, Andreas. "Jewish Apocalypticism: A Child of Mantic Wisdom?" *Henoch* 24 (2002): 189–96.

Behr, C. A. *Aelius Aristides and the Sacred Tales.* Amsterdam: Adolf M. Hakkert, 1968.

Beker, J. Christiaan. *Paul the Apostle: The Triumph of God in Life and Thought.* Philadelphia: Fortress, 1980.

Bell, Catherine. *Ritual Theory, Ritual Practice.* New York: Oxford University Press, 1992.

Betz, Hans-Dieter. *Der Apostel Paulus und die sokratische Tradition. Eine exegetische Untersuchung zu seiner "Apologie" 2 Korinther 10–13.* Tübingen: Mohr Siebeck, 1972.

———. "Eine Christus-Aretalogie bei Paulus (2Kor 12,7–10)." *ZTK* 66 (1969): 288–305.

———. *Galatians: A Commentary on Paul's Letter to the Churches in Galatia.* Hermeneia. Philadelphia: Fortress, 1979.

———. *The Mithras Liturgy.* Studien und Texte zu Antike und Christentum 18. Tübingen: Mohr Siebeck, 2003.

Biale, David. *Gershom Scholem: Kabbalah and Counter-History.* 2nd ed. Cambridge, Mass.: Harvard University Press, 1982.

Birnbaum, Ellen. *The Place of Judaism in Philo's Thought; Israel, Jews and Proselytes.* Brown Judaic Studies 290. Atlanta: Scholars Press, 1996.

Bockmuehl, Marcus. *Revelation and Mystery in Ancient Judaism and Pauline Christianity.* WUNT 36. Tübingen: Mohr Siebeck, 1990. Repr., Grand Rapids: Eerdmans, 1997.

Boddy, Janice. "Spirit Possession Revisited: Beyond Instrumentality." *Annual Review of Anthropology* 23 (1994): 407–34.

———. *Wombs and Alien Spirits: Women, Men, and the Zar Cult in Northern Sudan.* Madison, Wisc.: University of Wisconsin Press, 1989.

Bohak, Gideon. *Joseph and Aseneth and the Jewish Temple in Heliopolis.* Atlanta: Scholars Press, 1996.

Bond, Gilbert I. *Paul and the Religious Experience of Reconciliation: Diasporic Community and Creole Consciousness.* Louisville, Ky.: Westminster John Knox, 2005.

Borgen, Peder. "Heavenly Ascent in Philo: an Examination of Selected Passages." Pages 246–68 in *Pseudepigrapha and Early Biblical Interpretation.* Edited by James H. Charlesworth and Craig A. Evans. Sheffield: JSOT, 1993.

———. "Philo of Alexandria: Reviewing and Rewriting Biblical Material." *Studia Philonica Annual* 9 (1997): 37–53.

Boring, M. E. *Sayings of the Risen Jesus.* SNTSMS 46. Cambridge: Cambridge University Press, 1982.

Bourdieu, Pierre. *Language and Symbolic Power.* Cambridge: Cambridge University Press, 1991.

———. *The Logic of Practice.* Translated by Richard Nice. Stanford: Stanford University Press, 1990.

———. *Outline of a Theory of Practice.* Translated by Richard Nice. Cambridge: Cambridge University Press, 1977.

Bousset, D. W. *Kyrios Christos: A History of Belief in Christ from the Beginnings of Christianity to Irenaeus.* Translated by J. E. Steely. Nashville: Abingdon Press, 1970.

———. *Kurios Christos: Geschichte des Christusglaubens von den Anfängen des Christentums bis Irenaeus.* 6th ed. Göttingen: Vandenhoeck & Ruprecht, 1967.

Bovon, François. "L'Importance des Médiations dans le Projet Théologique de Luc." *NTS* 21 (1975): 23–39.

Boyarin, Jonathan, ed. "Introduction." Pages 1–9 in *The Ethnography of Reading.* Berkeley and Los Angeles: University of California Press, 1993.

Brooke, George J. "Men and Women as Angels in *Joseph and Aseneth* Tradition." *JSP* 14 (2005): 159–77.

Brown, Peter. "The Rise and Function of the Holy Man in Late Antiquity." *JRS* 61 (1971): 80–101.

Brown, Raymond Edward. *The Community of the Beloved Disciple*. New York: Paulist Press, 1979.

——. *The Gospel According to John*. 2 vols. Garden City, N.Y.: Doubleday, 1966–70.

Bruce, F. F. *1 and 2 Corinthians*. London: Oliphants, 1971.

Buell, Denise K. "Rethinking the Relevance of Race for Early Christian Self-Destruction." *HTR* 94 (2001): 449–76.

——. *Why This New Race? Ethnic Reasoning in Early Christianity*. New York: Columbia University, 2005.

Bultmann, R. *The Gospel of John*. Oxford: Blackwell, 1971.

Burchard, Christoph. "Joseph and Aseneth." Pages 177–247 in vol. 2 of *The Old Testament Pseudepigrapha*. Edited by J. H. Charlesworth. 2 vols. New York: Doubleday, 1985.

——, Carsten Burfeind, and Uta Barbara Fink, eds. *Joseph und Aseneth kritisch herausgegeben*. PVTG 5. Leiden: Brill, 2003.

Burkert, Walter. *Ancient Mystery Cults*. Cambridge: Harvard University Press, 1987.

——. *Greek Religion: Archaic and Classical*. Translated by John Raffan. Oxford: Blackwell, 1985.

Cadbury, Henry J. *The Making of Luke-Acts*. 2nd ed. London: Macmillan, 1958. Repr., Peabody, Mass.: Hendrickson, 1999.

Calabi, Francesca. "La luce che abbaglia: una metafora sulla inconscibilità di Dio in Filone di Alessandria." Pages 223–32 in *Origeniana octava, I: Origen and the Alexandrian Tradition: Origene e la tradizione alessandrina (Papers of the 8th International Origen Congress, Pisa, 27–31 August 2001)*. Edited by L. Perrone, P. Bernardino, and D. Marchini. Leuven: Leuven University Press and Uitgeverij, 2003.

Calvin, Jean. *The Acts of the Apostles, 14–28*. Translated John W. Fraser. London: Oliver & Boyd, 1966.

Campbell, William S. "Who are We in Acts? The First-Person Plural Character in the Acts of the Apostles." PhD diss., Princeton Theological Seminary, 2000.

Capes, David D. *Old Testament Yahweh Texts in Paul's Christology*. WUNT 2.47. Tübingen: Mohr Siebeck, 1992.

Carabine, Deirdre. "A Dark Cloud: Hellenistic Influences on the Scriptural Exegesis of Clement of Alexandria and the Pseudo-Dionysius." Pages 61–74 *in Scriptural Interpretation in the Fathers*. Edited by Thomas Finan and Vincent Twomey. Dublin: Four Court Press, 1995.

Carsen, D. A. "The Purpose of the Fourth Gospel: John 20.21 Reconsidered." *JBL* 106 (1987): 439–51.

Cassidy, Richard J. *Paul in Chains: Roman Imprisonment and the Letters of St. Paul*. New York: Crossroad, 2001.

Chadwick, Henry. "Clement of Alexandria." Pages 168–81 in *The Cambridge History of Later Greek and Early Medieval Philosophy*. Edited by A. H. Armstrong. Cambridge: Cambridge University Press, 1967.

——. "Philo." Pages 133–57 in *The Cambridge History of Later Greek and Early Medieval Philosophy*. Edited by A.H. Armstrong. Cambridge: Cambridge University Press, 1967.

Chariton, *Callirhoe*. Translated by G. P. Goold. LCL. Cambridge, Mass.: Harvard University Press, 1995.

Charlesworth, James H., ed. *Old Testament Pseudepigrapha*. 2 vols. New York: Doubleday, 1983, 1985.

Chatman, Seymour. *Coming to Terms: The Rhetoric of Narrative in Fiction and Film*. Ithaca, N.Y.: Cornell University Press, 1990.

Chrysostom, *Patrologia graeca*. Edited by J.-P. Migne. 162 vols. Paris, 1857–1886.

Cicero. *De Senectute, De Amicitia, De Divinatione*. Translated by William Armistead Falconer. LCL. New York: Putnam's Sons, 1923.

Clifford, Richard J. "The Function of Idol Passages in Second Isaiah." *CBQ* 42 (1980): 450–64.

Clinton, Kevin. "Stages of Initiation in the Eleusinian and Samothracian Mysteries." Pages 50–78 in *Greek Mysteries: The Archaeology and Ritual of Ancient Greek Secret Cults*. Edited By Michael B. Cosmopoulos. London: Routledge, 2003.

Collins, Adela Yarbro. *Mark: A Commentary*. Hermeneia. Minneapolis: Fortress, 2007.

Collins, John E. *Mysticism and New Paradigm Psychology*. Savage, Md.: Rowman & Littlefield, 1991.

Collins, John J. *The Apocalyptic Imagination: An Introduction to Jewish Apocalyptic Literature*. 2nd Rev. ed. Grand Rapids: Eerdmans, 1998.

————. *A Commentary on the Book of Daniel*. Hermeneia. Minneapolis: Fortress, 1993.

————. "From Prophecy to Apocalypticism: The Expectation of the End." Pages 129–61 in *The Encyclopedia of Apocalypticism. Volume 1. The Origins of Apocalypticism in Judaism and Christianity*. Edited by J. J. Collins. New York: Continuum, 2000.

————. "*Joseph and Aseneth*: Jewish or Christian?" *JSP* 14 (2005): 97–112.

————. "Journeys to the World Beyond in Ancient Judaism." Pages 20–36 in *Apocalyptic and Eschatological Heritage: The Middle East and Celtic Realms*. Edited by M. McNamara. Dublin: Four Courts Press, 2003.

Collon, Dominique. *First Impressions: Cylinder Seals in the Ancient Near East*. London: British Museum, 1987.

Conzelmann, Hans. *Acts of the Apostles*. Translated by James Limburg, A. Thomas Kraabel, and Donald H. Juel. Hermeneia; Philadelphia: Fortress, 1987.

Copenhaver, B. P. *Hermetica: The Greek Corpus Hermeticum and the Latin Asclepius*. Cambridge: Cambridge University Press, 1992.

Coppola, Francis Ford. *Youth without Youth*. Sony Pictures, 2007.

Corbin, Henry. "Shi'i Hermeneutics." Pages 109–202 in *Shi'ism: Doctrines, Thought and Spirituality*. Edited by S. H. Nasr, H. Dabashi, and S. V. R. Nasr. Albany, N.Y.: State University of New York Press, 1988.

Cosgrove, Charles. "The Divine ΔEI in Luke-Acts: Investigations into the Lukan Understanding of God's Providence." *NovT* 26 (1984): 168–90.

Crapanzano, Vincent. *Case Studies in Spirit Possession: Contemporary Religious Movements*. Edited by Vincent Crapanzano and Vivian Garrison. New York: Wiley, 1977.

Cross, Frank M. *Canaanite Myth and Hebrew Epic: Essays in the History of the Religion of Israel*. Cambridge, Mass.: Harvard University Press, 1973.

Crossan, John Dominic. *Jesus: A Revolutionary Biography*. San Francisco: HarperSanFrancisco, 1994.

Culianu, Ioan P. *Expériences de l'Extase: Extase, ascension et récit visionnaire de l'hellénisme au moyen âge*. Paris: Payot, 1984.

Culianu, Ioan P. *Psychanodia I: A Survey of the Evidence of the Ascension of the Soul and its Relevance*. Leiden: Brill, 1983.

Culpepper, R. A. *Anatomy of the Fourth Gospel: A Study in Literary Design*. Philadelphia: Fortress, 1983.

D'Angelo, M. R. "A Critical Note: John 20.17 and Apocalypse of Moses 31." *JTS* 41 (1990): 529–36.

D'Aquili, Eugene G. and Andrew B. Newberg. *The Mystical Mind: Probing the Biology of Religious Experience*. Theology and the Sciences. Minneapolis: Fortress, 1999.

Dahl, Nils A. *The Crucified Messiah*. Minneapolis: Augsburg, 1974.

Dan, Joseph. "In Quest of a Historical Definition of Mysticism." *Studies in Spirituality* 3 (1993): 58–90.

Davies, M. *Rhetoric and Reference in the Fourth Gospel*. JSNTSup 69. Sheffield: JSOT Press, 1992.

Davies, Stephan L. *Jesus the Healer: Possession, Trance, and the Origins of Christianity*. New York: Continuum, 1995.

Dawson, David. *Allegorical Readers: Cultural Revision in Ancient Alexandria*. Berkeley and Los Angeles: University of California Press, 1992.

————. "Plato's Soul and the Body of the Text in Philo and Origen." Pages 89–107 in *Allegory: Antiquity to the Modern Period*. Edited by Jon Whitman. Leiden: Brill, 2000.

Dawson, J. D. *Christian Figural Reading and the Fashioning of Identity*. Berkeley and Los Angeles: University of California Press, 2002.

De Boer, Martinus. *The Defeat of Death: Apocalyptic Eschatology in 1 Corinthians 15 and Romans 5*. JSNTSup 22. Sheffield, England: JSOT Press, 1988.

————. "Paul and Apocalyptic Eschatology." Pages 345–83 in *The Origins of Apocalypticism in Judaism and Christianity*. Vol. 1 of *Encyclopedia of Apocalypticism*. Edited by John J. Collins. New York: Continuum, 1998.

De Montaigne, Michel. *The Complete Essays*. Translated by M. A. Screech. Harmondsworth: Penguin, 1995.

Dean-Otting, Mary. *Heavenly Journeys: A Study of the Motif in Hellenistic Jewish Literature*. Frankfurt: Peter Lang, 1984.

DeConick, April D. *Voices of the Mystics*. JSNTSup 157. Sheffield: Sheffield Academic Press, 2001.

————. "What is Early Jewish and Christian Mysticism?" Pages 1–24 in *Paradise Now: Essays on Early Jewish and Christian Mysticism*. Edited by April D. DeConick. SBLSymS 11. Atlanta: Society of Biblical Literature, 2006.

Delling, Gerhard. "The 'One Who Sees God' in Philo." Pages 28–42 in *Nourished with Peace: Studies in Hellenistic Judaism in Memory of Samuel Sandmel*. Edited by F. E. Greenspahn, E. Hilgert, B. L. Mack. Chico, CA: Scholars Press, 1984.

Derrett, J. D. M. *The Victim*. Shipston-on-Stour: Drinkwater, 1992.

Derridas, Jacques. *On Grammatology*. Translated by G. C. Spivak. Corrected edition. Baltimore: Johns Hopkins University Press, 1998.

Deutsch, Celia M. *Lady Wisdom, Jesus, and the Sages; Metaphor and Social Context in Matthew's Gospel*. Valley Forge, Pa.: Trinity Press International, 1996.

————. "Text Work, Ritual and Mystical Experience: Philo's De Vita Contemplativa." Pages 287–311 in *Paradise Now: Essays on Early Jewish and Christian Mysticism*. Edited by April DeConick. SBLSymS 11. Atlanta: Society of Biblical Literature, 2006.

Dibelius, Martin. *Studies in the Acts of the Apostles*. Translated by Mary Ling and Paul Schubert. London: SCM, 1956. Repr., Mifflintown, Pa.: Sigler Press, 1999.

DiLella, Alexander A. "Daniel 4:7–14: Poetic Analysis and Biblical Background." Pages

247–58 in *Mélanges bibliques et orientaux en l'honneur de M. Henri Cazelles*. AOAT 212. Edited by A. Caquot and M. Delcor. Neukirchen-Vluyn: Neukirchener Verlag, 1981.

Dillon, John. *The Middle Platonists; 80 B.C. to A.D. 220*. Rev. ed. Ithaca, N.Y.: Cornell University Press, 1996.

———. "Reclaiming the Heritage of Moses: Philo's Confrontation with Greek Philosophy." *Studia Philonica Annual* 7 (1995): 108–23.

Dodd, C. H. *The Interpretation of the Fourth Gospel*. Cambridge: Cambridge University Press, 1968.

Dodds, E. R. *The Greeks and the Irrational*. Berkeley and Los Angeles: University of California Press, 1951.

Douglas, Mary. *Purity and Danger*. London: Routledge, 2002.

Doukhan, Jacques B. "Allusions à la Création dans le Livre de Daniel." Pages 285–92 in *The Book of Daniel in the Light of New Findings*. Edited by A. S. van der Woude. BETL 106. Leuven: Leuven University Press, 1993.

Driver, Tom F. "Ritualizing: The Animals Do It and So Do We." Pages 12–31. *Liberating Rites: Understanding the Transformative Power of Ritual*. Boulder, Colo.: Westview, 1998.

Dunn, James D. G. *Baptism in the Holy Spirit: A Re-Examination of The New Testament Teaching on the Gift of the Spirit in Relation to Pentecostalism Today*. Philadelphia: Westminster, 1977.

———. *Jesus and the Spirit: A Study of the Religious and Charismatic Experience of Jesus and the First Christians as Reflected in the New Testament*. Philadelphia: Westminster, 1975.

———. *The Theology of Paul the Apostle*. Grand Rapids: Eerdmans, 1998.

Edwards, Mark J. "Clement of Alexandria and His Doctrine of the Logos." *VC* 54 (2000): 159–77.

Ehrlich, Ernst Ludwig. *Traum im Alten Testament*. BZAW 73. Berlin: Alfred Töpelmann, 1953.

Eliade, Mircea. *Images and Symbols: Studies in Religious Symbolism*. New York: Sheed & Ward, 1961.

———. *Patterns in Comparative Religion*. New York: Sheed & Ward, 1958.

———. *The Sacred and the Profane: the Nature of Religion*. Translated by W. R. Trask. San Diego: Harcourt Brace, 1959.

———. *Two and the One*. New York: Harper & Row, 1969. Reprint of *Two and the One*. Translated by J. M. Cohen. London: Harvill, 1965.

———. *Youth without Youth*. Edited by M. Calinescu. Translated by M. L. Ricketts. Chicago: University of Chicago Press, 2007.

Elliott, J. K., trans. *The Apocryphal New Testament. A Collection of Apocryphal Christian Literature in an English Translation based on M.R. James*. Oxford: Clarendon Press, 1993.

Emerson, Ralph W. *Essays & Lectures*. Edited by Joel Porte. New York: Library of America, 1983.

Emmel, S. "The Recently Published Gospel of the Savior ('Unbekanntes Berliner Evangelium'): Righting the Order of Pages and Events." *HTR* 95 (2002): 45–72.

Engberg-Pedersen, Troels. *Paul and the Stoics*. Edinburgh: T&T Clark, 2000.

———. Engberg-Pedersen, Troels. "Paul's Necessity: A Bourdieuesque Reading of the

Pauline Project." Pages 69–88 in *Beyond Reception: Mutual Influences between Antique Religion, Judaism, and Early Christianity*. Edited by David Brakke, Anders-Christian Jacobsen, and Jörge Ulrich. Frankfurt: Peter Lang, 2006.

Eshel, Esther. "Apotropaic Prayers in the Second Temple Period." Pages 69–88 in *Liturgical Perspectives: Prayer and Poetry in Light of the Dead Sea Scrolls, Proceeding of the Fifth International Symposium of the Orion Center for the Study of the Dead Sea Scrolls and Associated Literature, 19–23 January, 2000*. Edited by Esther G. Chazon. STDJ 48. Leiden: Brill, 2003.

Evans, Nancy. "Sanctuaries, Sacrifices and the Eleusinian Mysteries." *Numen* 49 (2002): 227–54.

Fanon, Frantz. *The Wretched of the Earth*. New York: Grove Press, 1968.

Farahian, Edmond. "Paul's Vision at Troas (Acts 16:9–10)." Pages 197–207 in *Luke and Acts*. Edited by G. O'Collins and G. Marconi. Translated by Matthew O'Connell. New York: Paulist, 1993.

Festugière, André Jean. *Personal Religion among the Greeks*. 2nd ed. Berkeley and Los Angeles: University California Press, 1960.

———. *La Révélation d'Hermès Trismégiste*. 4 vols. Paris: Lecoffre, 1949–54.

Filoramo, G. "The Transformation of the Inner Self." Pages 137–50 in *Transformation of the Inner Self in Ancient Religions*. Edited by J. Assmann and G. G. Stroumsa. SHR 83. Leiden: Brill, 1999.

Fitzmyer, Joseph A. *Acts of the Apostles: A New Translation with Introduction and Commentary*. AB 31. New York: Doubleday, 1998.

Flannery-Dailey, Frances. *Dreamers, Scribes, and Priests: Jewish Dreams in the Hellenistic and Roman Eras*. JSJSup 90. Leiden: Brill, 2004.

Flasche, Rainer. *Die Religionswissenschaft Joachim Wachs*. Berlin: de Gruyter, 1978.

Fletcher-Louis, Crispin H. T. *All the Glory of Adam: Liturgical Anthropology in the Dead Sea Scrolls*. STDJ 42. Leiden: Brill, 2002.

———. "Apocalypticism." *The Handbook of the Study of the Historical Jesus*. Edited by S. E. Porter and T. Holmén. 4 vols. Leiden: Brill, *forthcoming*.

———. "The Aqedah and the Book of Watchers (*1 Enoch* 1–36)." Pages 1–33 in *Studies in Jewish Prayer*. Edited by R. Hayward and B. Embry. JSSSup 17. Oxford: Oxford University Press, 2005.

———. "God's Image, His Cosmic Temple and the High Priest: Towards an Historical and Theological Account of the Incarnation." Pages 81–99 in *Heaven on Earth: The Temple in Biblical Theology*. Edited by T. D. Alexander and S. Gathercole. Carlisle: Paternoster, 2004.

———. "The High Priest as Divine Mediator in the Hebrew Bible: Dan 7:13 as a Test Case." *SBLSP* 36 (1997): 161–93.

———. "Humanity and the Idols of the Gods in Pseudo-Philo's *Biblical Antiquities*." Pages 58–72 in *Idolatry: False Worship in the Bible, Early Judaism, and Christianity*. Edited by S. C. Barton. Edinburgh: T&T Clark, 2007.

———. "The Image of God and the Biblical Roots of Christian Sacramentality." Pages 73–89 in *The Gestures of God: Explorations in Sacramentality*. Edited by C. Hall and G. Rowell. London: Continuum, 2004.

———. "Jesus and Apocalypticism." *The Handbook of the Study of the Historical Jesus*. Edited by. S. E. Porter and T. Holmén. 4 vols. Leiden: Brill, forthcoming.

———. *Luke-Acts: Angels, Christology and Soteriology*. WUNT 2.94. Tübingen: Mohr Siebeck, 1997.

————. "The Revelation of the Sacral Son of Man: The Genre, History of Religions Context and the Meaning of the Transfiguration." Pages 247–98 in *Auferstehung - Resurrection. The Fourth Durham-Tübingen-Symposium: Resurrection, Exaltation, and Transformation in Old Testament, Ancient Judaism, and Early Christianity*. Edited by F. Avemarie and H. Lichtenberger. WUNT 135. Tübingen: Mohr Siebeck, 2001.

————. "The Worship of the Jewish High Priest by Alexander the Great." Pages 71–102 in *Early Christian and Jewish Monotheism*. Edited by L. T. Stuckenbruck and W. S. North. JSNTSup 63. Edinburgh: T&T Clark, 2004.

Flusser, David. "Psalms, Hymns, and Prayers," Pages 551–77 in *Jewish Writings of the Second Temple Period*. Edited by Michael Stone. CRINT 2.2. Philadelphia: Fortress, 1984.

Forbes, Christopher. "Comparison, Self Praise, and Irony: Paul's Boasting and the Conventions of Hellenistic Rhetoric." *NTS* 32 (1986): 1–30.

Fossum, Jarl. *The Name of God and the Angel of the Lord: Samaritan and Jewish Concepts of Intermediation and the Origin of Gnosticism*. WUNT 36. Tübingen: Mohr Siebeck, 1985.

Foucault, Michel. *Archeology of Knowledge and the Discourse on Language*. New York: Pantheon Books, 1979.

Frankfurter, David. *Religion in Roman Egypt: Assimilation and Resistance*. Princeton, N.J.: Princeton University Press, 1998.

Frederiksen, Paula. "Paul and Augustine: Conversion Narratives, Orthodox Traditions, and the Retrospective Self." *JTS* 37 (1986): 3–34.

Freed, Edwin D. *The Morality of Paul's Converts*. London: Equinox, 2005.

Freud, Sigmund. *The Future of an Illusion*. Vol. 21 of *The Standard Edition of the Complete Psychological Works of Sigmund Freud*. Edited by J. Strachey with A. Freud. London: Hogarth, 1961.

Gaster, Theodor. *Myth, Legend, and Custom in the Old Testament*. New York: Harper and Row, 1969.

————. "Myth, Mythology." Pages 481–87 in vol. 3 of *The Interpreter's Dictionary of the Bible*. Edited by G. A. Buttrick. 4 vols. New York: Abingdon, 1962.

————. "Myth and Story." *Numen* 1 (1954): 184–212.

Gaventa, Beverly R. *From Darkness to Light: Aspects of Conversion in the New Testament*. OBT. Philadelphia: Fortress, 1986.

————. *Acts of the Apostles*. ANTC. Nashville, TN: Abingdon, 2003.

————. "The Overthrown Enemy: Luke's Portrait of Paul." *SBLSP* (1985): 439–49.

Gaylord, H. E., trans., *Greek Apocalypse of Baruch*. Pages 651–79 in vol. 1 of *The Old Testament Pseudepigrapha*. Edited by J. H. Charlesworth. 2 vols. New York: Doubleday, 1983.

Geertz, Clifford. *The Interpretation of Cultures*. New York: Basic Books, 1973.

Glancy, Jennifer A. "Boasting of Beatings (2 Corinthians 11:23–25)." *JBL* 123 (2004): 99–135.

Glazov, Gregory Y. *The Bridling of the Tongue and the Opening of the Mouth in Biblical Prophecy*. JSOTSup 311. Sheffield: Sheffield Academic Press, 2001.

Good, Byron. *Medicine, Rationality, and Experience: An Anthropological Perspective*. Cambridge: Cambridge University Press, 1994.

Goodenough, Erwin. *By Light, Light; the Mystic Gospel of Hellenistic Judaism*. New Haven, Conn.: Yale University Press, 1935.

Goodman, Felicitas D. *How About Demons? Possession and Exorcism in the Modern World.* Bloomington, Ind.: Indiana University Press, 1988.

———. *Speaking in Tongues: A Cross-Cultural Study of Glossolalia.* Chicago: University of Chicago Press, 1972.

———. "Vision and Knowledge." *JSNT* 56 (1994): 53–71.

———. "The Visionaries of Laodicea." *JSNT* 43 (1991): 15–39.

Grabbe, Lester L. "The Scapegoat Ritual: A Study in Early Jewish Interpretation." *JSJ* 18 (1987):152–67.

Grese, W. G. *Corpus Hermeticum XIII and Early Christian Literature.* SCHNT 5. Leiden: Brill, 1979.

Griffith-Jones, R. *The Four Witnesses: The Rebel, the Rabbi, the Chronicler, and the Mystic.* San Francisco: Harper, 2000.

———. "Going back to Galilee to see the Son of Man: Mark's Gospel as an Upside-Down Apocalypse." In *Between Author and Audience: Markan Narration, Characterization, and Interpretation.* Edited by E. Struthers Malbon. Sheffield: Sheffield Phoenix, forthcoming.

———. *The Gospel according to Paul: The Creative Genius Who Brought Jesus to the World.* San Francisco: Harper, 2004.

Griffiths, Paul J. *Religious Reading: The Place of Reading in the Practice of Religion.* New York: Oxford University Press, 1999.

Grimes, Ronald L. *Deeply into the Bone: Re-Inventing Rites of Passage.* Berkeley and Los Angeles: University of California Press, 2000.

Gruen, Eric S. *Heritage and Hellenism: The Reinvention of Jewish Tradition.* Berkeley and Los Angeles: University of California Press, 1998.

Gruenwald, Ithamar. *Apocalyptic and Merkabah Mysticism.* Leiden: Brill, 1979.

———. "Reflections on the Nature and Origins of Jewish Mysticism." Pages 25–48 in *Gershom Scholem's Major Trends in Jewish Mysticism 50 Years After: Proceedings of the Sixth International Conference on the History of Jewish Mysticism.* Edited by P. Schäfer and J. Dan. Tübingen: Mohr Siebeck, 1993.

Haas, Christopher. *Alexandria in Late Antiquity; Topography and Social Conflict.* Baltimore: Johns Hopkins University Press, 1997.

Hadot, Pierre. *Philosophy as a Way of Life; Spiritual Exercises from Socrates to Foucault.* Edited by Arnold I. Davidson. Translated by Michael Case. Oxford: Blackwell, 1995.

Haenchen, Ernst. *The Acts of the Apostles: A Commentary.* Translated by Bernard Noble, Gerald Shinn, Hugh Anderson, and R. McL. Wilson. Philadelphia: Westminster, 1971.

———. *The Gospel according to John.* 2 vols. Philadelphia: Fortress, 1984.

Hanson, John S. "Dreams and Visions in the Graeco-Roman World and Early Christianity." *ANRW* 23.2:1395–1427. Part 2, *Principat,* 23.2. Edited by H. Temporini and W. Haase. New York: de Gruyter, 1980.

Hanson, Paul D. *The Dawn of Apocalyptic: The Historical and Sociological Roots of Jewish Apocalyptic Eschatology.* Philadelphia: Fortress, 1979.

Hanson, R. P. C. *Allegory and Event: A Study of the Sources and Significance of Origen's Interpretation of Scripture.* New ed. Louisville: Westminster John Knox, 2002.

Harrington, Daniel. *The Gospel of Matthew.* Collegeville, Minn: Liturgical, 1991.

Harvey, A. E. *Jesus on Trial: A Study in the Fourth Gospel.* London: SPCK, 1976.

Hayward, C. T. R. "Philo, the Septuagint of Genesis 32:24–32 and the Name 'Israel': Fighting the Passions, Inspiration and the Vision of God." *JJS* 51 (2000): 209–26.

Heininger, Bernhard. *Paulus als Visionär: Eine religionsgeschichtliche Studie*. Herder's Biblical Studies 9. Freiburg: Herder, 1995.

Hengel, Martin. *Judaism and Hellenism: Studies in their Encounter in Palestine during the Early Hellenistic Period*. 2 vols. London: SCM Press, 1974.

——. *The Pre-Christian Paul*. Philadelphia: Trinity Press International, 1991.

Herodotus. *Histories*. Translated A. D. Godley. LCL. Cambridge, Mass.: Harvard University Press, 1971.

Hezser, Catherine. "'Joseph and Aseneth' in the Context of Ancient Greek Erotic Novels." *Frankfurter Judaistische Beiträge* 24 (1997): 1–40.

Himmelfarb, Martha. *Ascent to Heaven in Jewish and Christian Apocalypses*. New York, Oxford: Oxford University Press, 1993.

——. "The Practice of Ascent in the Ancient Mediterranean World." Pages 123–37 in *Death, Ecstasy, and Otherworldly Journeys*. Edited by J. J. Collins and M. Fisbhane. Albany: SUNY Press, 1995.

——. "Revelation and Rapture: The Transformation of the Visionary in the Ascent Apocalypses." Pages 79–90 in *Mysteries and Revelations: Apocalyptic Studies Since the Uppsala Colloquium*. JSPSup 9. Edited by J. J. Collins and J. H. Charlesworth. Sheffield: Sheffield Academic Press, 1991.

——. *Tours of Hell: The Development and Transmission of an Apocalyptic Form in Jewish and Christian Literature*. Philadelphia: University of Pennsylvania Press, 1984.

Hirsh, E. "Die drei Berichte der Apostelgeschichte über die Bekehrung des Paulus." *ZNW* 28 (1929): 305–12.

Hollenbach, Paul. "Jesus, Demoniacs, and Public Authorities: A Socio-Historical Study." *JAAR* 99 (1981): 567–88.

Homer. *Iliad*. Translated by A. T. Murray and Rev. William F. Wyatt. 2 vols. LCL. Cambridge, Mass.: Harvard University Press, 1999.

——. *Odyssey*. Translated by A. T. Murray. 2 vols. Rev. ed. LCL. Cambridge, Mass.: Harvard University Press, 1995.

Horsley, Richard A. *Archaeology, History, and Society in Galilee: The Social Context of Jesus and the Rabbis*. Valley Forge, Pa.: Trinity Press International, 1996.

——. "Further Reflections on Witchcraft and European Folk Religion." *HR* 19 (1979): 71–95.

——. A. *Galilee: History, Politics, People*. Valley Forge, Pa.: Trinity Press International, 1995.

——. *Hearing the Whole Story: The Politics of Plot in Mark's Gospel*. Louisville, Ky.: Westminster John Knox, 2001.

——. *Paul and Empire: Religion and Power in Roman Imperial Society*. Harrisburg, Pa.: Trinity Press International, 1997.

——. "Pneumatikos vs. Psychikos: Distinctions of Spiritual Status among the Corinthians." *HTR* 69 (1976): 269–88.

——. "Who Were the Witches? The Social Role of the Accused in the European Witch Trials." *Journal of Interdisciplinary History* 9 (1979): 689–715.

Hubbard, Moyer. "Was Paul out of his Mind? Re-Reading 2 Corinthians 5.13." *JSNT* 70 (1998): 40–42.

Humphrey, Edith M. "Collision of Modes? Vision and Determining Argument in Acts 10:1–11:18." *Semeia* 71 (1995): 65–84.

————. *The Ladies and the Cities: Transformation and Apocalyptic Identity in Joseph and Aseneth, 4 Ezra, and the Apocalypse and the Shepherd of Hermas.* JSPSup 17. Sheffield: Sheffield Academic Press, 1995.

————. "On Bees and Best Guesses: The Problem of *Sitz im Leben* from Internal Evidence, as Illustrated by *Joseph and Aseneth.*" *Currents in Research: Biblical Studies* 7 (1999): 223–36.

Hurtado, Larry W. *Lord Jesus Christ: Devotion to Jesus in Earliest Christianity.* Grand Rapids: Eerdmans, 2003.

Husser, Jean-Marie. *Dreams and Dream Narratives in the Biblical World.* Translated by Jill M. Munro. The Biblical Seminar 63. Sheffield: Sheffield Academic Press, 1999.

Hyperides. *Minor Attic Orators: Lycurgus, Dinarchus, Demades, Hyperides.* Translated by J. O. Burtt. LCL. Cambridge, Mass.: Harvard University Press, 1954.

Iamblichus. *On the Mysteries.* Translated with Introduction and Notes by Emma C. Clarke, John M. Dillon, and Jackson P. Hershbell. SBLWGRW 4. Atlanta: SBL, 2003.

Iser, W. "The Reading Process: A Phenomenological Approach." Pages 50–69 in *Reader-Response Criticism: From Formalism to Post-structuralism.* Edited by J. P. Tompkins. Baltimore: Johns Hopkins University Press, 1980.

James, William. *The Varieties of Religious Experience: A Study in Human Nature.* New York: The Modern Library, 1994.

Jensen, Jeppe Sinding. *The Study of Religion in a New Key: Theoretical and Philosophical Soundings in the Comparative and General Study of Religion.* Aarhus: Aarhus University Press, 2003.

Johnson, Luke T. *The Acts of the Apostles.* SP 5. Collegeville, Minn.: Liturgical Press, 1992.

————. *Religious Experience in Earliest Christianity: A Missing Dimension in New Testament Studies.* Minneapolis: Fortress, 1998.

Joseph, Rhawn. *Neuropsychiatry, Neuropsychology, and Clinical Neurology: Emotion, Evolution, Cognition, Language, Memory, Brain Damage, and Abnormal Behavior.* 2nd ed. Baltimore: Williams & Wilkins, 1996.

Jung, Carl. *Memories, Dreams, Reflections.* Edited by A. Jaffé. Translated by R. and C. Winston. New York: Vintage, 1963.

————. "Response to Job." Pages 519–650 in *The Portable Jung.* Edited by J. Campbell. New York: Viking, 1975.

Kant, Immanuel. *Foundations of the Metaphysics of Morals.* Translated by L. W. Beck. 2nd ed. Upper Saddle River, N. J.: Prentice Hall 1989.

————. *Critique of Practical Reason.* Translated by H. W. Cassirer. Milwaukee, Wisc.: Marquette University Press, 1998.

————. *Critique of Pure Reason.* Translated by N. K. Smith. New York: Palgrave Macmillan, 2003.

Käsemann, E. *The Testament of Jesus: Study of the Gospel of John in the Light of Chapter 17.* London: SCM, 1968.

Katz, Steven. "Language, Epistemology, and Mysticism." Pages 22–74 in *Mysticism and Philosophical Analysis.* Edited by S. Katz. New York: Oxford University Press, 1978.

Kee, Howard Clark. "The Terminology of Mark's Exorcism Stories." *NTS* 14 (1968): 232–46.

Keesing, Roger M. "Models, 'Folk' and 'Cultural.'" Pages 369–95 in *Cultural Models in Language and Thought.* Edited by Dorothy Holland and Naomi Quinn. Cambridge: Cambridge University Press, 1987.

Kelly, A. J., and F. J. Moloney. *Experiencing God in the Gospel of John*. New York: Paulist Press, 2003.

Kenyon, Susan M. "The Case of the Butcher's Wife: Illness, Possession and Power in Central Sudan." Pages 89–108 in *Spirit Possession: Modernity and Power in Africa*. Edited by H. Behrend and U. Luig. Madison, Wisc.: University of Wisconsin Press, 1999.

Kim, Seyoon. *The Origin of Paul's Gospel*. 2nd rev. ed. WUNT II.4. Tübingen: Mohr Siebeck, 1984.

──────. *Paul and the New Perspective: Second Thoughts on the Origin of Paul's Gospel* WUNT II.140. Tübingen: Mohr Siebeck, 2002.

Kittel, G., and G. Friedrich, eds. *Theological Dictionary of the New Testament*. Translated by G. W. Bromiley. 10 vols. Grand Rapids: Eerdmans, 1964–1976.

Kitzberger, I. R. "Mary of Bethany and Mary of Magdala: Two Female Characters in the Johannine Passion Narrative." *NTS* 41 (1995): 564–86.

Kleinman, Arthur. *Patients and Healers in the Context of Culture*. Berkeley and Los Angeles: University of California Press, 1980.

Koch, Klaus. *The Rediscovery of Apocalyptic*. London: SCM Press, 1972.

Kovacs, Judith L. "Concealment and Gnostic Exegesis: Clement of Alexandria's Interpretation of the Tabernacle." *StPatr* 31 (1997): 414–37.

──────. "Divine Pedagogy and the Gnostic Teacher." *JECS* 9 (2001): 3–25.

Kraemer, Ross S. *When Aseneth Met Joseph: A Late Antique Tale of the Biblical Patriarch and His Egyptian Wife, Reconsidered*. Oxford: Oxford University Press, 1998.

Kramer, Fritz W. *The Red Fez: Art and Spirit Possession in Africa*. Translated by Malcolm R. Green. New York: Verso, 1993.

Kümmel, W. G. *Römer 7 und das Bild des Menschen im Neuen Testament: Zwei Studien*. Munich: Kaiser, 1974.

Kuntz, J. Kenneth. *The Self-Revelation of God*. Philadelphia: Westminster, 1967.

Kurz, William S. *Reading Luke-Acts: Dynamics of Biblical Narrative*. Louisville: Westminster John Knox, 1993.

Kysar, R. "The Making of Metaphor: Another Reading of John 3.1–15." Pages 21–42 in *What is John?* Edited by F. F. Segovia. Vol. 1. Atlanta: Scholars Press, 1996.

Lacocque, André. "Allusions to Creation in Daniel 7." Pages 114–31 in *The Book of Daniel: Composition and Reception*. Edited by J. J. Collins and P. W. Flint. 2 vols. Leiden: Brill, 2001.

Lagrange, M. J. *Évangile selon Saint Jean*. Paris: Gabalda, 1925.

Lakoff, G., and M. Johnson. *Metaphors We Live By*. Chicago: University of Chicago Press, 1980.

Lalleman, P. J. *The Acts of John: A Two-Stage Initiation into Johannine Gnosticism*. Studies on the Apocryphal Acts of the Apostles 4. Leuven: Peeters, 1998.

Lampe, Peter. "Paul's Concept of a Spiritual Body." Pages 103–114 in *Resurrection: Theological and Scientific Assessments*. Edited by T. Peters, R. J. Russell, and M. Welker. Grand Rapids: Eerdmans, 2002.

Lawson, Jack N. "'The God who Reveals Secrets': the Mesopotamian Background to Daniel 2.47." *JSOT* 74 (1997): 61–76.

Le Déaut, R. *La Nuit pascale: Essai sur la Signification de la Pâque Juive à Partir du Targum d'Exode XII 42*. AB 22. Rome: Institut Biblique Pontifical, 1963.

Lem, Stanislaw. *Peace on Earth*. San Diego: Harcourt, 1994.

Levison, John R. "Inspiration and the Divine Spirit in the Writings of Philo Judaeus." *JJS* 26 (1995): 271–323.

Levenson, J. D. *Resurrection and the Restoration of Israel*. New Haven, Conn.: Yale University Press, 2006.

Lewis, I. M. *Ecstatic Religion: An Anthropological Study of Spirit Possession and Shamanism*. Baltimore: Penguin, 1971.

———. *Ecstatic Religion: A Study of Shamanism and Spirit Possession*. 3rd ed. London: Routledge, 2003.

Lieu, Judith M. *Christian Identity in the Jewish and Graeco-Roman World*. Oxford: Oxford University Press, 2004.

Lilla, Salvatore R.C. *Clement of Alexandria; a Study in Christian Platonism and Gnosticism*. Oxford: Oxford University Press, 1971.

Lincoln, A. T. *Truth on Trial: The Lawsuit Motif in the Fourth Gospel*. Peabody: Hendrickson, 2000.

Lindars, B. *The Gospel of John*. London: Oliphants, 1972.

Lindbeck, G. A. *The Nature of Doctrine: Religion and Theology in a Postliberal Age*. London: Society for Promoting Christian Knowledge, 1984.

Lonergan, B. *Method in Theology*. London: Darton, Longman & Todd, 1971.

Lorenzen, Thorwald. *Resurrection and Discipleship: Interpretive Models, Biblical Reflections, Theological Consequences*. Maryknoll, New York: Orbis Books, 1995.

Mach, Michael. "From Apocalypticism to Early Jewish Mysticism?" Pages 229–64 in *The Encyclopedia of Apocalypticism. Volume 1: The Origins of Apocalypticism in Judaism and Christianity*. Edited by J. J. Collins. New York: Continuum, 2000.

Mack, Burton. *Logos und Sophia; Untersuchungen zur Weisheitstheologie im hellenistischen Judentum*. SUNT 10. Göttingen: Vandenhoeck & Ruprecht, 1973.

Mahé, J.-P. *Hermès en Haute-Egypte: Les Textes Hermeìtiques de Nag Hammadi et Leurs Paralleĺles Grecs et Latins*. Quebec: Université Laval, 1978.

Maier, Johann. "Das Gefährdungsmotiv bei der Himmelreise in der jüdischen Apokalyptik und 'Gnosis.'" *Kairos* 5 (1963): 18–40.

———. *Vom Kultus zur Gnosis: Studien zur Vor- und Frühgeschichte der "jüdischen Gnosis."* Salzburg: O. Müller, 1964.

Malherbe, Abraham J. *The Cynic Epistles*. Atlanta: Scholars Press, 1977.

———. *Moral Exhortation: A Greco-Roman Sourcebook*. Philadelphia: Westminster, 1986.

———. *Paul and the Thessalonians: The Philosophical Tradition of Pastoral Care*. Philadelphia: Fortress, 1987.

Malina, Bruce J. *The New Testament World: Insights from Cultural Anthropology*. London: SCM, 1981.

———, and J. H. Neyrey. *Portraits of Paul: An Archaeology of Ancient Personality*. Louisville, Ky.: Westminster John Knox, 1996.

Mann, Thomas W. *Divine Presence and Guidance in Israelite Traditions*. Baltimore: Johns Hopkins University Press, 1977.

Marguerat, Daniel. "Saul's Conversion (Acts 9, 22, 26) and the Multiplication of Narrative in Acts." Pages 127–55 in *Luke's Literary Achievement: Collected Essays*. Edited by C. M. Tuckett. JSNTSup 116. Sheffield: Sheffield Academic Press, 1995.

Martin, Ralph P. *2 Corinthians*. WBC 40. Waco, Tex.: Word Books, 1986.

Martyn, J. Louis. *Galatians: A New Translation with Introduction and Commentary*. New York: Doubleday, 1997.

Mason, Steve. "PHILOSOPHIAI: Graeco-Roman, Judean and Christian." Pages 31–58 in *Voluntary Associations in the Graeco-Roman World*. Edited by John S. Kloppenborg and Stephen G. Wilson. London: Routledge, 1996.

Masquelier, Adeline "The Invention of Anti-Tradition: Dodo Spirits in Southern Niger." Pages 34–50 in *Spirit Possession: Modernity and Power in Africa*. Edited by H. Behrend and U. Luig. Madison, Wisc.: University of Wisconsin Press, 1999.

Mattern, Susan P. *Rome and the Enemy: Imperial Strategy in the Principate*. Berkeley and Los Angeles: University of California Press, 1999.

McGinn, Bernard. *The Presence of God: A History of Western Christian Mysticism*. Vol. 1 of *The Foundations of Mysticism*. New York: Crossroad, 1991.

Mealand, David. "Philo of Alexandria's Attitude to Riches." *ZNW* 69 (1978): 258–64.

Meeks, Wayne. *The First Urban Christians: The Social World of the Apostle Paul*. 2nd ed. New Haven, Conn.: Yale University Press, 2003.

———. "The Stranger from Heaven in Johannine Sectarianism." Pages 141–73 in *The Interpretation of John*. Edited by J. Ashton. Edinburgh: T&T Clark, 1986.

Méhat, André. *Étude sur les 'Stromates' de Clément d'Alexandrie*. Patristica Sorbonensia 7. Paris: Édition du Seuil, 1966.

Meier, Hans-Christoph. *Mystik bei Paulus: Zur Phänomenologie religiöser Erfahrung im Neuen Testament*. TANZ 26. Tübingen, Basel: Francke, 1998.

Meier, Heinrich. *Leo Strauss and the Theological-Political Problem*. Translated by M. Brainard. Cambridge: Cambridge University Press, 2006.

Merkelbach, Reinhold. *Abrasax: Ausgewählte Papyri religiösen und magischen Inhalts. Band 3: Zwei griechisch-ägyptische Weihezeremonien (die Leidener Weltschöpfung; die Pschaei-Aion-Liturgie)*. Papyrologica Coloniensia 18.3. Opladen: Westdeutscher Verlag, 1992.

Merkur, Dan. *Gnosis: An Esoteric Tradition of Mystical Visions and Unions*. Albany, N.Y.: State University of New York Press, 1993.

———. "The Visionary Practices of Jewish Apocalypticists." Pages 119–48 in *The Psychoanalytic Study of Society 14: Essays in Honor of Paul Parin*. Edited by L. B. Boyer and S. A. Grolnick. Hillsdale, Mass.: Analytic, 1989.

Meyer, Marvin, ed. *The Ancient Mysteries, a Sourcebook: Sacred Texts of the Mystery Religions of the Ancient Mediterranean World*. San Francisco: Harper, 1987.

Miller, John B. F. *Convinced that God Had Called Us: Dreams, Visions, and the Perception of God's Will in Luke-Acts*. Biblical Interpretation Series. Leiden: Brill, 2007.

———. "'Convinced that God had Called Us': Visions and the Perception of God's Will in Luke-Acts." PhD diss., Princeton Theological Seminary, 2004.

Miller, Patrick D. *The Divine Warrior in Early Israel*. Cambridge, Mass.: Harvard University Press, 1973.

Moloney, F. J. "Can Everyone be Wrong? John 11.1–12.8." *NTS* 49 (2003): 505–27.

———. "The Function of John 13–17." Pages 43–66 in *What is John?* Edited by F. F. Segovia. Vol. 2. Atlanta: Scholars Press, 1998.

Momigliano, Arnaldo. "The Moving Finger Writes: Mughira ibn Sa'id's Islamic Gnosis and the Myths of its Rejection." *HR* 25 (1985): 1–29.

Mondésert, Claude. *Clément d'Alexandrie; introduction à sa pensée religieuse à partir de l'Écriture*. Paris: Aubier, 1944.

Morray-Jones, Christopher R. A. "Paradise Revisited (2 Cor 12:1–12): The Jewish Mystical Background of Paul's Apostolate. Part 1: The Jewish Sources." *HTR* 86 (1993): 177–218.

———. "Paradise Revisited (2 Cor 12:1–12): The Jewish Mystical Background of Paul's Apostolate. Part 2: Paul's Heavenly Ascent and its Significance." *HTR* 86 (1993): 265–92.

————. "The Temple Within." Pages 145–78 in *Paradise Now: Essays on Early Jewish and Christian Mysticism*. Edited by A. D. DeConick. SBLSymS 11. Atlanta: Society of Biblical Literature, 2006.

————. "Transformational Mysticism in the Apocalyptic-Merkabah Tradition." *JJS* 43 (1992):1–31.

————. *A Transparent Illusion: The Dangerous Vision of Water in Hekhalot Mysticism: A Source-Critical and Tradition-Historical Inquiry*. JSJSup 59. Leiden: Brill, 2002.

Mount, Christopher. "'Jesus Is Lord': Religious Experience and the Religion of Paul." Paper presented at the annual meeting of the Society of Biblical Literature. Washington DC, November 2006.

Muilenburg, James. "The Speech of Theophany." *HDB* 28 (1964): 35–47.

Myers, Ched. *Binding the Strong Man: A Political Reading of Mark's Story of Jesus*. Maryknoll, N.Y.: Orbis, 1988.

Narby, Jeremy and Francis Huxley. *Shamans through Time: 500 Years on the Path to Knowledge*. London: Thames & Hudson, 2001.

Newsom, C. A. *Songs of the Sabbath Sacrifice*. HSS 27. Atlanta: Scholars Press, 1985.

Nicholson, G. C. *Death as Departure*. SBLDS 63. Chico, CA: Scholars Press, 1983.

Nickelsburg, George W. E. "Enoch, Levi, and Peter: Recipients of Revelation in Upper Galilee." *JBL* 100 (1981): 575–600.

————. *1 Enoch 1: A Commentary on 1 Enoch, Chapters 1–36; 81–108*. Hermeneia. Minneapolis: Fortress, 2001.

————. "Tobit and Enoch: Distant Cousins with Recognizable Resemblance." *SBLSP* 27 (1988): 54–68.

Nikiprowetzky, V. *Le commentaire de l'Écriture chez Philon d'Alexandrie*. ALGHJ 11. Leiden: Brill, 1977.

Nock, A. D. *Conversion: The Old and the New in Religion from Alexander the Great in Augustine of Hippo*. Oxford: Oxford University Press, 1933.

O'Brien, K. S. "Written That You May Believe: John 20 and Narrative Rhetoric." *CBQ* 67 (2005): 284–302.

Obeyesekere, Gananath. *Medusa's Hair: An Essay on Personal Symbols and Religious Experience*. Chicago: University of Chicago Press, 1981.

Oppenheim, A. Leo. "The Golden Garments of the Gods." *JNES* 8 (1949): 172–93.

Osborn, Eric F. *Clement of Alexandria*. Cambridge: Cambridge University Press, 2005.

Otto, Rudolf. *The Idea of the Holy: An Inquiry into the Non-Rational Factor in the Idea of the Divine and Its Relation to the Rational*. Translated by John W. Harvey. London: Oxford University Press, 1980.

Pagels, E. H. *The Johannine Gospel in Gnostic Exegesis*. SBLMS 17. Atlanta: Scholars Press, 1989.

Pearson, Birger. *The Pneumatikos-Psychikos Terminology in 1 Corinthians*. SBLDS 12. Missoula, MT: Scholars Press, 1973.

Peerbolte, L. J. Lietaert. "The Name above all Names (Philippians 2:9)." Pages 187–206 in *The Revelation of the Name YHWH to Moses: Perspectives from Judaism, the Pagan Graeco-Roman World, and Early Christianity*. Edited by George H. van Kooten. Themes in Biblical Narrative 9. Leiden, Boston: Brill, 2006.

————. *Paul the Missionary*. Contributions to Biblical Exegesis and Theology 34. Leuven: Peeters 2003.

————. *Poimandres: Grieks-hermetisch geschrift in het Nederlands vertaald met eeen trans-*

personalistische beschouwing. Occident-serie. Deventer: Ankh-Hermes, 1974.

————. "De theologie van het boek Openbaring. *Gereformeerd Theologisch Tijdschrift* 99 (1999): 3–12.

Pépin, Jean. *Mythe et allégorie: les origins grecques et les contestations judéo-chrétiennes.* 2nd ed. Paris: Études Augustiniennes, 1976.

Pervo, Richard I. *Profit with Delight: The Literary Genre of the Acts of the Apostles.* Philadelphia: Fortress, 1987.

Phillips, Thomas E. "Revisiting Philo: Discussions of Wealth and Poverty in Philo's Ethical Discourse." *JSNT* 83 (2001): 111–21.

Philo. *Philo.* Translated by F. H. Colson, G. H. Whitaker, and Ralph Marcus. 10 vols. LCL. Cambridge, Mass.: Harvard University Press, 1929–1962.

Pilch, John J. "Altered States of Consciousness: A 'Kitbashed' Model." *BTB* 26 (1996): 33–38.

————. *Visions and Healing in the Acts of the Apostles: How the Early Believers Experienced God.* Collegeville, Minn.: Liturgical Press, 2004.

Plöger, Otto. *Theocracy and Eschatology.* Oxford: Blackwell, 1968.

Proudfoot, Wayne. *Religious Experience.* Berkeley and Los Angeles: University of California Press, 1985.

Quintilian. *The Institutio Oratoria of Quintilian.* Translated by H. E. Butler. LCL. Cambridge, Mass.: Harvard University Press, 1939.

Quispel, Gilles. "Hermetism and the New Testament, Especially Paul." *Aufsteig und Niedergang der römischen Welt* II.22. Edited by H. Temporini and W. Haase. New York: de Gruyter, 1998.

Räisänen, Heikki. *Paul and the Law.* Wissenschaftliche Untersuchungen zum Neuen Testament 29. 2nd ed. Tübingen: Mohr Siebeck, 1987.

Rambo, Lewis R. *Understanding Religious Conversion.* New Haven, Conn.: Yale University Press, 1993.

Rappaport, Roy A. *Ritual and Religion in the Making of Humanity.* Cambridge: Cambridge University Press, 1999.

Reese, James, M. *Hellenistic Influence on the Book of Wisdom and Its Consequences.* AnBib 41. Rome: Pontifical Biblical Institute, 1970.

Reitzenstein, R. *The Hellenistic Mystery-Religions: Their Basic Ideas and Significance.* Pittsburgh: Pickwick, 1978.

————. *Poimandres: Studien zur griechischägyptischen und frühchristlichen Literatur.* Leipzig: Teubner, 1904.

René Girard, *Violence and the Sacred.* Translated P. Gregory. Baltimore: Johns Hopkins University Press, 1977.

Richter, Wolfgang. "Traum und Traumdeutung im AT: Ihre Form und Verwendung." *BZ* 7 (1963): 202–20.

Ridings, Daniel. "Clement of Alexandria and the Intended Audience of the *Stromateis.*" *StPatr* 31 (1997): 517–21.

Ringgren, Helmer. "Mysticism." Pages 945–46 in vol. 4 of *Anchor Bible Dictionary.* Edited by D. N. Freedman. 6 vols. New York: Doubleday, 1992.

Robbins, Trevor. "The Pharmacology of Thought and Emotion." Pages 33–52 in *From Brains to Consciousness.* Edited by Steven Rose. New York: Allen Lane, 1998.

Robinson, James M. "On the Gattung of Mark (and John)." Pages 99–129 in *Jesus and Man's Hope.* 2 vols. Pittsburgh: Theological Seminary, 1970–71.

Rosenthal, Franz. "I Am You: Individual Piety and Society in Islam." Pages 33–60 in *Individualism and Conformity in Classical Islam*. Edited by A. Banani and S. Vryonis, Jr. Malibu, Calif.: Undena, 1977.

Rouhemer, Riemer. "La transcendence et la proximité de Dieu dans le christianisme ancient." *RHPR* 82 (2002): 15–31.

Roukema, Riemer. "Paul's Rapture to Paradise in Early Christian Literature." Pages 267–83 in *"The Wisdom of Egypt: Jewish, Early Christian, and Gnostic Essays in Honour of Gerard P. Luttikhuizen*. Edited by Anthony Hilhorst and George H. van Kooten. Ancient Judaism and Early Christianity 59. Leiden: Brill, 2005.

Rowland, Christopher C. "Apocalyptic: the Disclosure of Heavenly Knowledge." Pages 776–97 in *The Early Roman Period*. Vol. 3 of *The Cambridge History of Judaism*. Edited by W. Horbury, W. D. Davies and J. Sturdy. Cambridge: Cambridge University Press, 1999.

——. "The Book of Revelation: Introduction, Commentary, and Reflections." Pages 501–736 in *The New Interpreter's Bible: A Commentary in Twelve Volumes*. Edited by L. E. Keck. 12 vols. Nashville: Abingdon, 1998.

——. *The Open Heaven: A Study in Apocalypticism in Judaism and Early Christianity*. New York/London: Crossroad/SPCK, 1982/1992.

——. "Visionary Experience in Ancient Judaism and Christianity." Pages 41–56 in *Paradise Now: Essays on Early Jewish and Christian Mysticism*. Edited by A. D. DeConick. SBLSymS 11. Atlanta: Society of Biblical Literature, 2006.

Runia, David T. *Philo in Early Christian Tradition*. CRINT 3. Assen: Van Gorcum and Fortress, 1993.

Sainsbury, Mark. "Achilles Paradox." Page 4 in *The Oxford Companion to Philosophy*. Edited by Ted Honderich. Oxford: Oxford University Press, 1995.

Sanders, E. P. *Paul and Palestinian Judaism*. London: SCM, 1977.

Schaberg, J. *The Resurrection of Mary Magdalene: Legends, Apocrypha, and the Christian Testament*. New York: Continuum, 2002.

Schäfer, P. "Merkavah Mysticism and Magic." Pages 59–78 in *Gershom Scholem's Major Trends in Jewish Mysticism 50 Years After: Proceedings of the Sixth International Conference on the History of Jewish Mysticism*. Edited by P. Schäfer and J. Dan. Tübingen: Mohr Siebeck, 1993.

——, ed. *Geniza-Fragmente zur Hekhalot-Literatur*. TSAJ 6. Tübingen: Mohr Siebeck, 1984.

—— and Shaul Shaked, eds. *Magische Texte aus der Kairoer Geniza*. 3 vols. TSAJ 42: Tübingen: Mohr Siebeck, 1994–1999.

Schäfer, Peter, ed. Zusammenarbeit mit Margarete Schlüter und Hans Georg von Mutius, *Synopse zur Hekhalot-Literatur*. TSAJ 2. Tübingen: Mohr Siebeck, 1981.

Schenke, H.-M. "The Function and Background of the Beloved Disciple in the Gospel of John." Pages 111–25 in *Nag Hammadi, Gnosticism and Early Christianity*. Edited by C. W. Hedrick and R. Hodgson. Peabody: Hendrickson, 1986.

Schleiermacher, Friedrich. *On Religion: Speeches to Its Cultured Despisers*. Translated by R. Crouter. Cambridge: Cambridge University Press, 1996.

Schmidt, T. Ewald. "Hostility to Wealth in Philo of Alexandria." *JSNT* 19 (1983): 85–97.

Schnackenburg, R. *The Gospel According to St. John*. 3 vols. New York: Herder and Herder, 1968–1982.

Schneemelcher, W. *New Testament Apocrypha*. 2 vols. Cambridge: James Clarke, 1991–1992.

Scholem, Gershom. *Jewish Gnosticism, Merkabah Mysticism, and Talmudic Tradition.* New York: The Jewish Theological Seminary of America, 1960.

Schottroff, L. "The Samaritan Woman and the Notion of Sexuality in the Fourth Gospel." Pages 157–81 in vol. 2 of *What is John?* Edited by F. F. Segovia. Atlanta: Scholars Press, 1998.

Schulz, S. "Gottes Vorsehung bei Lukas." *ZNW* 54 (1963): 104–16.

Schüssler Fiorenza, E. "A Feminist Interpretation for Liberation: Martha and Mary: Lk. 10.38–42." *Religion and Intellectual Life* 3 (1986): 21–36.

Schweitzer, Albert. *The Mysticism of Paul the Apostle.* Translated by William Montgomery. New York: H. Holt, 1931.

———. *Die Mystik des Apostels Paulus.* Tübingen: Mohr, 1930.

Scott, James C. *Domination and the Arts of Resistance.* New Haven, Conn.: Yale University Press, 1990.

Scroggs, Robin. *The Last Adam: A Study in Pauline Anthropology.* Philadelphia: Fortress, 1966.

Seaford, Richard. "Thunder, Lightning and Earthquake in the *Bacchae* and the Acts of the Apostles." Pages 139–52 in *What is a God? Studies in the Nature of Greek Divinity.* Edited by Alan Lloyd. London: Duckworth, 1997.

Segal, Alan F. "Heavenly Ascent in Hellenistic Judaism, Early Christianity and their Environment." *ANRW* 23.2:1334–94. Part 2, 23.2. Edited by H. Temporini and W. Haase. Berlin: de Gruyter, 1980.

———. *Paul the Convert: The Apostolate and Apostasy of Saul the Pharisee.* New Haven, Conn.: Yale University Press, 1990.

———. *Life After Death: a History of the Afterlife in Western Religion.* New York: Doubleday, 2004.

———. *Rebecca's Children: Judaism and Christianity in the Roman World.* Cambridge, Mass.: Harvard University Press, 1986.

———. "Religious Experience and the Construction of the Transcendent Self." Pages 27–40 in *Paradise Now: Essays on Early Jewish and Christian Mysticism.* Edited by A. D. DeConick. SBLSymS 11. Atlanta: Society of Biblical Literature, 2006.

———. *Two Powers in Heaven: Early Rabbinic Reports about Christianity and Gnosticism.* Leiden: Brill, 1977.

Seim, T. K. "Descent and Divine Paternity in the Gospel of John: Does the Mother Matter?" *NTS* 51 (2005): 361–75.

Seneca the Elder. *The Elder Seneca: Declamations in Two Volumes.* Translated by M. Winterbottom. LCL. Cambridge, Mass.: Harvard University Press, 1974.

Shantz, Colleen. *Paul in Ecstasy.* New York: Cambridge University Press, forthcoming.

Shumaker, Wayne. *Renaissance Curiosa.* Binghamton, N.Y.: Center for Medieval and Early Renaissance Studies, 1982.

Simonetti, Manlio. "Teologia e cristologia nell'Egitto cristiano." Pages 11–38 in *Egitto cristiano: aspetti e problemi in età tardo-antica.* Edited by Alberto Camplani. Roma: Institutum Patristicum Augustinianum, 1997.

Smith, J. Z. "Bible and Religion." Pages 197–214 in *Relating Religion: Essays in the Study of Religion.* Chicago: University of Chicago Press, 2004.

———. "A Twice-told Tale: The History of the History of Religions' History." Pages 362–74 in *Relating Religion: Essays in the Study of Religion.* Chicago: University of Chicago Press, 2004.

Smith, Morton. "Ascent to the Heavens and the Beginning of Christianity." *ErJb* 50 (1981): 403–29.

———. *Clement of Alexandria and a Secret Gospel of Mark*. Cambridge, Mass.: Harvard University Press, 1975.

———. *Jesus the Magician*. New York: Harper and Row, 1978.

Snow, David and Richard Machalek. "The Sociology of Conversion." *Annual Review of Sociology* 10 (1984): 167–90.

Sourvinou-Inwood, Christiane. "Festival and Mysteries: Asepcts of the Eleusinian Cult." Pages 25–49 *Greek Mysteries*. Edited by M. Cosmopoulos. London: Routledge, 2003.

Spencer, F. Scott. *Acts*. Readings: A New Biblical Commentary. Sheffield: Sheffield Academic Press, 1997.

Spicq, Ceslas. *Theological Lexicon of the New Testament*. Translated and edited by James D. Ernest. 3 vols. Peabody, Mass.: Hendrickson, 1994.

Spivak, Gayatri Chakravorty. "Can the Subaltern Speak?" Pages 271–313 in *Marxism and the Interpretation of Culture*. Edited by C. Nelson and L. Grossberg. Chicago: University of Illinois Press, 1988.

———. "Subaltern Studies: Deconstructing Historiography." Pages 3–34 in *Selected Subaltern Studies*. Edited by Ranajit Guha and Gayatri Spivak. Oxford: Oxford University Press, 1988.

Squires, John. *The Plan of God in Luke-Acts*. SNTSMS 76. Cambridge: Cambridge University Press, 1993.

Staley, J. L. *The Print's First Kiss*. SBLDS 82. Atlanta: Scholars Press, 1988.

Stendahl, K. "The Apostle Paul and the Introspective Conscience of the West." *HTR* 56 (1963): 199–215.

Stibbe, M. W. G. "The Elusive Christ." *JSNT* 44 (1991): 20–39.

———. *John as Storyteller: Narrative Criticism and the Fourth Gospel*. SNTSMS 73. Cambridge: Cambridge University Press, 1992.

Stökl, Daniel. "Yom Kippur in the Apocalyptic *imaginaire* and the Roots of Jesus' High Priesthood." Pages 349–66 in *Transformations of the Inner Self in Ancient Religions*. Edited by J. Assmann and G. G. Stroumsa. SHR 83. Leiden: Brill, 1999.

Stone, Michael E. "Apocalyptic: Vision or Hallucaination?" *Milla wa-Milla* 14 (1974): 47–56.

———. "Apocalyptic: Vision or Hallucination?" Pages 419–28 in *Selected Studies in Pseudepigrapha Apocrypha With Special Reference to the Armenian Tradition*. SVTP 9. Leiden: Brill, 1991.

———. *Fourth Ezra: A Commentary on the Book of Fourth Ezra*. Minneapolis: Fortress, 1990.

———. "Lists of Revealed Things in Apocalyptic Literature." Pages 414–52 in *Magnalia Dei: The Mighty Acts of God. Essays on the Bible and Archeology in Memory of G. Ernest Wright*. Edited by F. M. Cross, W. Lemke, and P. D. Miller. New York: Doubleday, 1976.

———. "On Reading an Apocalypse." Pages 65–78 in *Mysteries and Revelations: Apocalyptic Studies Since the Uppsala Colloquium*. Edited by J. J. Collins and J. H. Charlesworth. JSPSup 9. Sheffield: JSOT Press, 1991.

———. "A Reconsideration of Apocalyptic Visions." *HTR* 96 (2003): 167–80.

Strecker, Christian. "Jesus and the Demoniacs." Pages 117–133 in *The Social Setting of Jesus and the Gospels.* Edited by Wolfgang Stegemann, Bruce J. Malina, and Gerd Theissen. Minneapolis: Fortress, 2002.

Stroumsa, G. "Clement, Origen, and Jewish Esoteric Traditions." Pages 53–70 in *Origeniana sexta.* Edited by Giles Dorval, Alain Le Boulluec and Monique Alexandre. Leuven: Leuven University Press and Peeters, 1995.

Sundkler, Bengdt G. M. *Bantu Prophets in South Africa.* 2nd ed. London: Oxford University Press, 1961.

Tabor, James D. *Things Unutterable: Paul's Ascent to Paradise in its Greco-Roman, Judaic, and Early Christian Contexts.* Studies in Judaism. Lanham, Md.: University Press of America, 1986.

Talbert, Charles H. *Reading Acts: A Literary and Theological Commentary on the Acts of the Apostles.* New York: Crossroad, 1997.

Tannehill, Robert. *The Narrative Unity of Luke-Acts: A Literary Interpretation.* 2 vols. Minneapolis: Fortress, 1990–1994.

Taylor, Brian "Recollection and Membership: Converts Talk and the Ratiocination of Commonality." *Sociology* 12 (1978): 316–23.

Temporini, Hildegard, and Wolfgang Haase, eds. *Aufstieg und Niedergang der römischen Welt: Geschichte und Kultur Roms im Spiegel der neueren Forschung.* Part 2, *Principat,* 23.2. New York: de Gruyter, 1980.

―――. *Aufstieg und Niedergang der römischen Welt: Geschichte und Kultur Roms im Spiegel der neueren Forschung.* Part 2, *Principat,* 33.1. New York: de Gruyter, 1989.

Theissen, Gerd. *Psychologische Aspekte paulinischer Theologie.* FRLANT 131, Göttingen: Vandenhoeck & Ruprecht, 1983.

Thrall, Margaret E. *A Critical and Exegetical Commentary on the Second Epistle to the Corinthians, vol. 2: VIII–XIII.* ICC. Edinburgh: T&T Clark, 2000.

Torjesen, Karen Jo. "The Alexandrian Tradition of the Inspired Interpreter." Pages 287–99 in *Origeniana Octava.* Edited by L. Perrone, P. Bernardino and D. Marchini. Leuven: Leuven University Press and Peeters, 2003.

Turner, Victor. *The Ritual Process: Structure and Anti-Structure.* Chicago: Aldine, 1969. Repr., Baltimore: Penguin, 1974.

Van den Hoek, Annewies. *Clement of Alexandria and His Use of Philo in the Stromateis: An Early Christian Reshaping of a Jewish Model.* VCSup 3. Leiden: Brill, 1988.

Van der Horst, Willem. *Chaeremon, Egyptian Priest and Stoic Philosopher: The Fragments Collected and Translated with Explanatory Notes.* Études préliminaries aux religions orientales dans l'empire romain. Leiden: Brill, 1984.

Van der Leeuw, Gerardus. *Religion as Essence and Manifestation: A Study in Phenomenology.* Princeton, N.J.: Princeton University Press, 1986.

Van der Toorn, Karel. "Scholars at the Oriental Court: The Figure of Daniel against Its Mesopotamian Background." Pages 37–54 in *The Book of Daniel: Composition and Reception.* Edited by J. J. Collins and P. W. Flint. 2 vols. Leiden: Brill, 2001.

Van Gennep, Arnold. *The Rites of Passage.* Translated by M. B. Vizedom and G. L. Caffee. Chicago: University of Chicago Press, 1960.

VanderKam, James C. *Enoch and the Growth of an Apocalyptic Tradition.* CBQMS 16. Washington, D. C.: The Catholic Biblical Association of America, 1984.

Vielhauer, Paul. "Apocalypses and Related Subjects: Introduction." Pages 581–600 in *New Testament Apocrypha.* Edited by E. Hennecke and W. Schneemelcher. 2 vols. Louisville, Ky.: Westminster, 1965.

Waldenfels, Bernhard. *Der Stachel des Fremden*. Frankfurt: Suhrkamp, 1990.

Wan, Sze-Kar. "Charismatic Exegesis: Philo and Paul Compared." *Studia Philonica Annual* 6 (1994): 54–82.

Wasserstrom, Steven M. "The Master-Interpreter: Notes on the German Career of Joachim Wach (1922–1935)." *Hermeneutics in History: Joachim Wach, Mircea Eliade, and the Science of Religions*. Edited by Christian Wedemayer and Wendy Doniger. Oxford: Oxford University Press, forthcoming.

----------. *Religion after Religion: Gershom Scholem, Mircea Eliade, and Henry Corbin at Eranos*. Princeton: Princeton University Press, 1999.

Weber, Samuel and Hent de Vries, eds. *Religion and Media*. Palo Alto, Calif.: Stanford University Press, 2001.

Wedderburn, A. J. M. "The Problem of the Denial of the Resurrection in 1 Corinthians XV." *NovT* 23 (1981): 229–41.

Wedenoja, William. "Ritual Trance and Catharsis: A Psychological and Evolutionary Perspective." Pages 275–307 in *"Personality and the Cultural Construction of Society: Papers in Honor of Melford E. Spiro."* Edited by David K. Jordan, Marc J. Swartz and Melford E. Spiro. Tuscaloosa, Ala.: University of Alabama Press, 1990.

Werline, Rodney A. *Pray Like This: Understanding Prayer in the Bible*. London: T&T Clark, 2007.

Wernle, Paul. *Der Christ und die Sünde bei Paulus*. Freiburg: Mohr, 1897.

Westcott, B. F. *The Gospel of John*. London: John Murray, 1889.

Wikenhauser, Alfred. "Religionsgeschichtliche Parallelen zu Apg 16, 9." *BZ* 23 (1935–36), 180–86.

Williams, C. H. *I Am He: The Interpretation of "Ani Hu" in Jewish and Early Christian Literature*. WUNT 2.113. Tübingen: Mohr Siebeck, 2000.

Williams, R. *The Wound of Knowledge*. London: Darton, Longman, and Todd, 1979.

Wind, Edgar. *Pagan Mysteries in the Renaissance*. New York: W. W. Norton, 1968.

Windisch, Hans. *Der Zweite Korintherbrief*. Göttingen: Vandenhoeck & Ruprecht, 1924.

Wink, Walter. *The Human Being: Jesus and the Enigma of the Son of Man*. Minneapolis: Fortress, 2002.

Winsor, A. R. *A King is Bound in the Tresses: Allusions to the Song of Songs in the Fourth Gospel*. New York: P. Lang, 1999.

Winston, David. "Philo and the Contemplative Life." Pages 198–231 in *Jewish Spirituality*. Vol. 1 of *From the Bible Through the Middle Ages*. Edited by Arthur Green. New York: Crossroad, 1986.

----------. "Philo's Nachleben in Judaism." *Studia Philonica Annual* 6 (1994): 103–10.

----------. "Sage and Super-Sage in Philo of Alexandria." Pages 172–80 in *The Ancestral Philosophy: Hellenistic Philosophy in Second Temple Judaism*. Edited by Gregory E. Sterling. Providence: Brown Judaic Studies, 2001.

----------. "Was Philo a Mystic?" Pages 151–70 in *The Ancestral Philosophy: Hellenistic Philosophy in Second Temple Judaism*. Edited by Gregory E. Sterling. Providence: Brown Judaic Studies, 2001.

Winter, Bruce W. *Philo and Paul among the Sophists: Alexandrian and Corinthian Responses to a Julio-Claudian Movement*. 2nd ed. Grand Rapids: Eerdmans, 2002.

Witherington III, B. *Women in the Ministry of Jesus: A Study of Jesus' Attitudes to Women and Their Roles as Reflected in His Earthly Life*. Society for New Testament Studies Monograph Series 51. Cambridge: Cambridge University Press, 1984.

Witherup, Ronald. "Cornelius Over and Over and Over Again: 'Functional Redundancy' in the Acts of the Apostles." *JSNT* 49 (1993): 45–66.

———. "Functional Redundancy in the Acts of the Apostles: A Case Study." *JSNT* 48 (1992): 67–86.

Wright, N. T. *The Resurrection of the Son of God.* Minneapolis: Fortress, 2003.

Wright, Peggy Ann. "The Nature of the Shamanic State of Consciousness: A Review." *Journal of Psychoactive Drugs* 21 (1989): 25–33.

Wyatt, N. "Supposing him to be the Gardener (John 20.15): a Study of the Paradise Motif in John." *ZNW* 81 (1990): 21–38.

Zaehner, R. C. *Hinduism and Muslim Mysticism.* New York: Schocken, 1969.

Zmijewski, J. *Der Stil der paulinischen "Narrenrede": Analyse der Sprachgestaltung in 2 Kor 11,1–12,10 als Beitrag zur Methodik von Stiluntersuchungen neutestamentlicher Texte.* Bonner biblische Beiträge 52. Köln: Peter Hanstein, 1978.

Zuntz, G. "On the hymns in CH XIII." *Hermes* 83 (1955): 68–92.

CONTRIBUTORS

Celia Deutsch
Adjunct Associate Professor
Barnard College, Columbia University
New York City, New York, USA
Author of *Lady Wisdom, Jesus, and the Sages; Metaphor and Social Context in Matthew's Gospel* (Trinity Press International, 1996)

Troels Engberg-Pedersen
Professor
University of Copenhagen, Denmark
Author of *Paul and the Stoic Self* (Oxford University Press, forthcoming 2009)

Frances Flannery
Associate Professor of Religion
James Madison University
Harrisonburg, Virginia, USA
Author of *Dreamers, Scribes and Priests: Jewish Dreams in the Hellenistic and Roman Eras* (Brill, 2004).

Crispin Fletcher-Louis
Principal
Westminster Theological Centre
London, England
Author of *All the Glory of Adam: Liturgical Anthropology in the Dead Sea Scrolls* (Brill, 2002)

Robin Griffith-Jones
Master of the Temple
Temple Church
London, England
Author of *The Gospel According to Paul* (Harper San Francisco, 2004)

Richard A. Horsley
Distinguished Professor of Liberal Arts and the Study of Religion
University of Massachusetts–Boston
Boston, Massachusetts, USA
Author of *Jesus in Context: People Power and Performance* (Fortress, 2008), and *Scribes, Visionaries and the Politics of Second Temple Judaea* (Westminster John Knox, 2007)

Bert Jan Lietaert Peerbolte
Professor
Vrije Universiteit-Amsterdam
Amsterdam, Netherlands
Author of *Paul the Missionary* (Peeters, 2003)

John B. F. Miller
Assistant Professor of Religion
McMurry University
Abilene, Texas, USA
Author of *Convinced that God had Called Us: Dreams, Visions, and the Perception of God's Will in Luke-Acts* (Brill, 2007)

Rollin A. Ramsaran
Emmanuel School of Religion
Johnson City, Tennessee, USA
Author of *Liberating Words: Paul's Use of Rhetorical Maxims in 1 Corinthians 1–10* (Trinity Press International, 1996)

Nicolae Roddy
Associate Professor, Hebrew Bible
Creighton University
Omaha, Nebraska, USA
Author of *The Romanian Version of the Testament of Abraham: Text, Translation, and Cultural Context* (Society of Biblical Literature, 2001)

Alan F. Segal
Professor of Religion and Ingeborg Rennert Professor of Jewish Studies
Barnard College, Columbia University
New York City, New York, USA
Author of *Life After Death: A History of the Afterlife in Western Religion* (Doubleday, 2004)

Colleen Shantz
Assistant Professor of New Testament
St. Michael's College, Toronto School of Theology
Toronto, Ontario, Canada
Author of *Paul in Ecstasy: The Neurobiology of the Apostle's Life and Thought* (Cambridge, forthcoming)

Steven M. Wasserstrom
Moe and Izetta Tonkon Professor of Judaic Studies and Humanities
Reed College
Portland, Oregon, USA
Editor of *The Fullness of Time: Poems by Gershom Scholem,* selected, edited and introduced by Steven M. Wasserstrom, translated by Richard Sieburth (Ibis Editions: Jerusalem, 2003)

Rodney A. Werline
Associate Professor and the Marie and Leman Barnhill Endowed Chair of Religious Studies
Barton College
Wilson, North Carolina, USA
Author of *Pray Like This: Understanding Prayer in the Bible* (T & T Clark, 2007)

Subject Index

Adam 28, 36, 38, 38 n. 35, 39, 117, 117 n. 30, 118, 118 n. 34, 120, 120 n. 43, 133, 133 n. 29, 135, 135 n. 38, 136 n. 39, 138, 140 n. 55, 164 n. 25

altered states of consciousness (ASC) 9, 23, 42, 42 n. 4, 79 n. 16, 128, 164, 169, 170, 174, 176, 184 n. 25, 193, 199, 199 n. 20, 200, 201, 201 n. 26, 209, 210

American Academy of Religion (AAR) 8, 75, 75 n. 1, 75 n. 4, 77, 83 n. 1

angel, angelic, angelic transformation, angelomorphism 8, 17–19, 20 n. 2, 24–29, 33–35, 39, 40, 49–51, 62, 62 n. 12, 63, 63 n. 12, 109, 111 n. 16, 119, 120, 120 n. 43, 126, 128, 133, 133 n. 29, 134 n. 34, 136, 138, 139, 140, 141, 143 n. 63, 165, 166, 174, 180, 181, 181 n. 18, 188 n. 34, 189, 192 n. 41

anthropological, anthropology 1, 9, 18, 23, 28 n. 15, 38 n. 35, 42, 43, 43 n. 7, 44, 51, 59 n. 1, 60 n. 4, 61, 69, 70 n. 33, 120, 133, 133 n. 29, 135, 137, 138, 140, 142, 143, 148, 149 n. 10, 194, 194 n. 7

apocalypse, apocalyptic, apocalypticism, apocalypticist 6, 6 n. 25, 9, 9 n. 35, 15 n. 14, 16, 16 nn. 14–15, 19, 20, 20 nn. 1–2, 22–24, 24 n. 10, 25, 26, 27 n. 13, 29, 30, 32, 34, 34 n. 27, 36, 37, 37 n. 34, 39, 40, 49, 62, 76 n. 9, 80, 106, 118, 120, 121, 121 n. 47, 125, 126, 126 nn. 1–3, 127, 127 n. 5, 128, 128 n. 6, 129, 129 nn. 9–11, 130, 130 nn. 13–15, 131, 131 n. 18, 132, 132 n. 26, 133, 133 nn. 28–30, 134, 134 n. 33, 138 n. 47, 139, 141–43, 159, 159 nn. 2–4, 160, 161, 165–67, 167 nn. 37–38, 168, 170, 170 n. 51, 171, 172, 175, 184 n. 26, 210

ascend, ascension, ascent 9, 15, 17, 20, 20 n. 3, 21, 21 n. 3, 22, 23, 24 n. 10, 26, 27, 35, 59, 65, 76, 89, 89 n. 24, 89 n. 26, 90, 90 n. 27, 90 n. 29, 92–94, 96 n. 65, 97, 102, 103, 106, 107, 109 n. 9, 110, 116, 118–21, 121 n. 46, 128, 129, 131, 131 nn. 18–19, 132, 133, 133 n. 29, 137, 142 n. 62, 144, 159 n. 4, 161, 161 n. 11, 161 n. 14, 162 n. 16, 163 n. 16, 167–69, 172, 197, 200, 202, 210

ascetic, asceticism 93, 99, 101, 102, 128, 170

Asmodeus 68

astronomy 90, 91, 102, 129, 137, 138

audience 8, 9, 18, 36, 95, 95 n. 57, 122 n. 47, 159, 184 n. 25, 198

beast(s) 62–64, 67, 135 n. 38

beatings 197, 198, 198 n. 15, 200

Beelzebul 51, 54, 55, 61

Belial 50, 53

blindness 25, 66, 85, 91, 106, 108, 111–13, 186, 191, 195

body, bodily 8, 8 n. 34, 9, 13, 14, 14 n. 4, 15, 15 n. 12, 16–20, 22–24, 24 n. 9, 28–32, 32 n. 23, 33–34, 34 n. 27, 35–37, 37 n. 34, 38–40, 46, 47, 68–70, 77, 84, 87, 89, 89 n. 26, 92, 92 n. 46, 93, 99, 101, 116 n. 27, 117, 150, 152, 152 n. 23, 153–56, 156 n. 31, 157, 163, 164, 169, 172, 195–97, 199–202, 202 nn. 27–28, 203, 204, 205 n. 36, 208, 209

brain 79, 150, 156, 199 n. 20, 200, 201, 201 n. 24, 202 nn. 27–28

eye(s) 15, 30, 37, 84, 91, 96, 116 n. 27, 140, 152, 152 n. 23, 175, 175 n. 71, 186

Index of Ancient Texts

Index of Modern Authors

INDEX OF MODERN AUTHORS

CPSIA information can be obtained at www.ICGtesting.com
Printed in the USA
BVOW070159041211

277502BV00002B/113/P